MW01253161

Idolizing the Idea

Political Theory for Today

Series Editor: Richard Avramenko, University of Wisconsin

Political Theory for Today seeks to bring the history of political thought out of the jargon-filled world of the academy into the everyday world of social and political life. The series brings the wisdom of texts and the tradition of political philosophy to bear on salient issues of our time, especially issues pertaining to human freedom and responsibility, the relationship between individuals and the state, the moral implications of public policy, health and human flourishing, public and private virtues, and more. Great thinkers of the past have thought deeply about the human condition and their situations—books in Political Theory for Today build on that insight.

Recent titles in the series:

Idolizing the Idea: A Critical History of Modern Philosophy, by Wayne Cristaudo
Eric Voegelin Today: Voegelin's Political Thought in the 21st Century, edited by Scott Robinson, Lee Trepanier, and David Whitney
Walk Away: When the Political Left Turns Right, edited by Lee Trepanier and Grant Havers
Democracy and Its Enemies: The American Struggle for the Enlightenment, by Paul N. Goldstene
Plato's Mythoi: The Political Soul's Drama Beyond, by Donald H. Roy
Tradition v. Rationalism: Voegelin, Oakeshott, Hayek, and Others, edited by Lee Trepanier and Eugene Callahan
Aristocratic Souls in Democratic Times, edited by Richard Avramenko and Ethan Alexander-Davey

Idolizing the Idea

A Critical History of Modern Philosophy

Wayne Cristaudo

LEXINGTON BOOKS
Lanham • Boulder • New York • London

Published by Lexington Books
An imprint of The Rowman & Littlefield Publishing Group, Inc.
4501 Forbes Boulevard, Suite 200, Lanham, Maryland 20706
www.rowman.com

6 Tinworth Street, London SE11 5AL

British Library Cataloguing in Publication Information Available

Library of Congress Cataloging-in-Publication Data Names: Cristaudo, Wayne, 1954- author. Title:
Idolizing the idea : a critical history of modern philosophy / Wayne Cristaudo. Description: Lanham :
Lexington Books, 2019. | Series: Political theory for today | Includes bibliographical references. |
Summary: "Ever since Plato made the case for the primacy of ideas over names, philosophy has
tended to elevate the primacy of its ideas over the more common understanding and insights that are
circulated in the names drawn upon by the community. Commencing with a critique of Plato's
original philosophical decision, Cristaudo takes up the argument put forward by Thomas Reid that
modern philosophy has generally continued along the 'way of ideas' to its own detriment. His argument identifies the major paradigmatic developments in modern philosophy commencing from the
new metaphysics pioneered by Descartes up until the analytic tradition and the anti-domination
philosophies which now dominate social and political thought. Along the way he argues that the
paradigmatic shifts and break-downs that have occurred in modern philosophy are due to being
beholden to an inadequate sovereign idea, or small cluster of ideas, which contribute to the occlusion
of important philosophical questions. In addition to chapters on Descartes, and the analytic tradition
and anti-domination philosophies, his critical history of modern philosophy explores the core ideas of
Locke, Berkeley, Malebranche, Locke, Hume, Reid, Kant, Fichte, Hegel, Schelling, Marx, Kierkegaard, Schopenhauer, Nietzsche, Husserl and Heidegger. The common thread uniting these disparate
philosophies is what Cristaudo calls 'idea-ism.' Rather than expanding our reasoning capacity, 'idea-
ism' contributes to philosophers imposing dictatorial principles or models that ultimately occlude and
distort our understanding of our participative role within reality. Drawing upon thinkers such as
Pascal, Vico, Hamann, Herder, Franz Rosenzweig, Martin Buber and Eugen Rosensock-Huessy
Cristaudo advances his argument by drawing upon the importance of encounter, dialogue, and a more
philosophical anthropological and open approach to philosophy"-- Provided by publisher. Identifiers:
LCCN 2019039864 (print) | LCCN 2019039865 (ebook) | ISBN 9781793602350 (cloth : alk. paper) |
ISBN 9781793602367 (electronic) Subjects: LCSH: Idea (Philosophy) | Philosophy, Modern. | Phi-
losophy--History. | Plato. Classification: LCC B105.I28 C75 2019 (print) | LCC B105.I28 (ebook) |
DDC 190--dc23 LC record available at https://lccn.loc.gov/2019039864 LC ebook record available at
https://lccn.loc.gov/2019039865

To the memory of my teacher Eugen Rosenstock-Huessy
and in friendship to Michael Gormann-Thelen

der Gegenstand eurer Betracthungen und Andacht ist nicht Gott, sondern ein bloßes Bildwort, wie eure allgemeine Menschenvernunft, die ihr durch ein mehr als poetische Licenz zu einer wirklichen Person vergöttert, und dergleichen Götter und Personen macht ihr durch die Transubstantiation eure Bildwörter so viel, daß das größte Heidenthum und blindeste Papstthum in Vergleichung eurer philosophischen Idolatrie am jüngsten Gerichte gerechtfertigt und vielleicht losgesprochen seyn wird.
(*New Apology of the Letter h by Itself*)

(The object of your deliberation and worship is not God, but a mere verbal image, as is your universal human reason, which you have divinized into a real person by an exaggerated poetic license; and through the transubstantiation of your verbal images, you make so many of these sort of gods and persons, so that on judgment day the coarsest paganism and blindest Papacy in comparison with your philosophical idolatry will be justified, and perhaps will be excused.)

"Neue Apologie des Buchstabens h von ihm selbst" in *Hamann's Schriften*, Herausgegeben von Friedrich Roth, Vierter Theil (Berlin: C. Reimer, 1823), 145.

Contents

Preface

This book started its life as an attempt to reconsider the role of philosophy within the social and human sciences, something along the lines of Peter Winch's *The Idea of a Social Science and its Relation to Philosophy*. It evolved into a more chronological treatment of the nature and role of the "idea" in modern philosophy, and critical reflection upon paradigmatic occlusion due to what I call modern philosophical idea-ism, and its counter tendencies. What remained constant was the idea that the human sciences are what we may loosely call attempts at "answers" to questions, and that philosophy can assist in the closer scrutiny of the value of the questions. At the same time, philosophy is misguided when it thinks it can isolate itself from, and hence preside, unencumbered by nothing more than (those) reason(s) that satisfy) itself, over anthropological, sociological, historical, psychological and other insights that are disclosed through the human sciences. Our knowledge is all of a piece. But not as Hegel believed because reason itself is a developing "all-in-one." None of us can know life in its all-ness, only in its pieces. Even though the pieces have to be organized into totalities, our totalities have to be open to change. They must be porous in order to conform to an inescapable feature of life, viz. that it involves transformation.

What remained constant throughout the writing of this book was opposition to the idea that philosophical inquiry should be dedicated either to identifying and robustly demonstrating *implacable* and *unassailable* sources of appeal and illumination, or defending values or norms such as "rights," or "freedom," or "equality," which, on account of their venerable stature, and/or the consensuses that have gathered around them, are beyond further philosophical scrutiny. Our ideas—and hence the principles which are stitched together from them—are answers to questions, and hence they are only as good as the questions that have helped in their "excavation" and formation. A poor idea is simply a poor answer, and the most common way to recognize a poor answer is to see it wither when pressed by more difficult and relevant questions: better questions are better precisely because they expose weaknesses that inhere to other questions. The better question forces us to reconsider that what we thought we could safely assume or take for granted, no longer holds. The better question, once taken up by enough people, inaugurates a paradigm shift within philosophy. But there is no guarantee that the new paradigm has not succumbed to the same underlying tendency which is recurrent in philosophy: viz., being satisfied with an overarching (cluster of) idea(s) and principle, which then serve to dictate (and hence occlude) our focus. Unfortunately, modern philosophy, as this book demonstrates in its treatment of the history of modern philosophy, has tended to make tyrants and false "gods" of ideas. Idea-ism is the most common form of modern idolatry, something we can readily grasp, if we open ourselves to an insight that emerged from the pre-philosophical orientation central to the world-making of the hermeneutical people of the Book.

For the people of the Book a false god is any god other than the real creator of all living things. From this perspective, if ideas are not the *original* creator of living things, and if the highest power is not reason then philosophy's "original sin" is idolatry. Further insofar as the Jews and Christians took the contingent event of creation as the basis of a narrative path that proceeds by way of contingencies, the Bible is not idea-ist. Yet, I think one need not be either Jewish or Christian, to be open to the psychological and anthropological insights of this book that is so polychronic and polyvocal that it played a decisive role in the narrative formation of what would eventually become Western civilization. The Bible provided the basis for the development of hermeneutics—and thus helps us appreciate that a collective and its narratives make a world. Concomitantly, as Herder's works demonstrated, it was only a short step to recognizing that all peoples are shaped by their narrative appeals and sacred names, and more broadly their thought and culture. In common parlance we can use the word "idea" in a manner that makes "sense" and "matters" without requiring that the term be defined philosophically. To an important extent, then, the critique of idea-ism in this book is also a defense of the everyday use of what we mean by an "idea." And this is pitted against transforming the idea and hence a set of ideas into ultimate appeals—and thereby becoming idols.

The ideological prisons of the twentieth and our century are very much the product of our idolizing of ideas, and the act of forgetting that ideas come from people and are originally attempts to help us as we seek to preserve and flourish within the world by forming bonds of solidarity and creating institutions that help carry us and what we value across the times.

If this book proceeds largely by way of a critique of modern philosophy, and some aspects of the Platonic legacy from antiquity, it is also an attempt to draw out what is best from philosophy, and use that against the recurrent entrapment of its own making.

Acknowledgments

This book, unwittingly, began with a life-changing chance encounter in a library, when I randomly picked up Harold Berman's *Law and Revolution: The Formation of the Western Legal Tradition*. The book immediately grabbed my attention, but my attention was even more aroused by a number of intriguing references to the work *Out of Revolution* by Eugen Rosenstock-Huessy, which provided much of the theoretical framework of Berman's work. Rosenstock-Huessy would change my entire intellectual life, making me reconsider all that I thought I knew. Almost three decades later he would remain the most important teacher of my life. This book is devoted to his memory, and I hope something of his spirit is present in its pages. It is also dedicated to another one of Rosenstock-Huessy's "students," my friend Michael Gormann-Thelen. Our quests have intersected in the thickets for some twenty years. Every so often we hail each other and then disappear again. He will wish I had spent less time on the highway and explored more obscure thickets.

For proofreading and comments on the work, my deepest gratitude to my philosopher friends Brian Mooney, and Jürgen Lawrenz. Jürgen is also the translator of *In the Cross of Reality: Volume 1 The Hegemony of Spaces*. He too is part of the trail of encounters I embarked upon through my interest in Rosenstock-Huessy.

I am grateful to Charles Darwin University, and my present home the College of Indigenous Futures, Art and Society, for giving me the chance to write this book. Many thanks to Giselle Byrnes for having supported my initial move from Hong Kong, and Dennis Shoesmith, Martin Jarvis, and Christian Bök for making our Friday afternoon "meetings" so enjoyable. Many thanks also to Richard Avramenko for providing a home for this book in the series Political Theory Today. I am also grateful to all the editorial staff at Lexington Books for their fantastic support. Finally, a special thank you to Edna Rosenthal, for our weekly Skype conversations which have been so vitalizing in my relative isolation, and Lelani Paras, and Jennifer Buckley, who have helped me in so many ways since before this book was even conceived.

AUTHOR PERMISSIONS

I wish to thank:

- © Salvador Dali, Fundació Gala-Salvador Dali/VEGAP. Copyright Agency, 2019, for granting the license (28677) to reproduce painting "Soft Construction with Boiled Beans (Premonition of Civil War)" on the cover of this volume.
- Dover Press for permission to cite from Arthur Schopenhauer's *World as Will and Representation, Volume 1*. Translated by E. F. J. Payne. New York: Dover, 1969.

Introduction

This book examines how the philosophical character of "ideas" themselves are re-thought within the changing paradigms of philosophy. At the same time, it picks up on the problem that Thomas Reid had identified in his attempt to rescue philosophy from what he, albeit critically, following Locke, had called "the way of ideas." For Reid, the danger of that way lay in us becoming beholden to abstractions severed from the knowledge that we accrue through social experience and "common sense:" Thus instead of helping our orientation and participation in worldmaking, philosophical ideas all too easily tyrannize us by rendering illegitimate or "unreasonable" insights which do not conform to the strictures that are part of their "way." Reid also understood that once we factor in that our "sense" of the world is socially shaped and is bound up with the insights and decisions that accrue over time and circulate socially through the names, narratives, and appeals we use, we are far less prone to think of reason as something in and of itself.

Prior to Reid, Giambattista Vico had also emphasized, and in far more anthropological and historical detail, the need for philosophy to take account of language and sociality as essential to its enterprise if it is to help better orientate us to our participation in the world.[1] Vico had shifted the philosophical axis into anthropological and socio-historical territory by demonstrating that reasoning is not to be divorced from the people or time or circumstance or form of expression in which it is undertaken. Different ages favor different kinds of speaking and reasoning, and that is closely bound up with the kind of world which people are participating in. By virtue of his formulating questions that required combining philological, historical, and social matters, Vico also made a powerful case that the more figurative speech of an earlier heroic age cannot simply be dismissed as irrelevant to the human story because a later age deploys more general, demotic, or abstract terms. In this respect, Vico was a pioneer of the hermeneutical and dialogical approach to philosophy, which was then further developed, independently, in Germany by J. G. Hamann and J. G. Herder.

In an earlier draft of this book, I had written chapters on the importance of Vico, Hamann, and Herder as pioneers of this hermeneutical and dialogical, or more broadly philosophical anthropological approach. Due to space limitations, I will leave it to a subsequent book to provide a more detailed account of this alternative philosophical path. But here I signal

1

that this alternative path provides an important stock of questions which are drawn upon in my account of the critical history of the modern "idea" and its role in modern philosophy. Although there are numerous works on these and other hermeneutical and dialogical thinkers, this alternative path remains largely neglected, especially in terms of its broader application to social and political philosophy. Philosophers, in the main, work with ideas and reasons and provide arguments for sovereign principles that are untouched by the contingencies which are intrinsic to institutional, historical, and larger cultural matters, especially when "rationality" in *itself*—or, what is now frequently the case, some extension or (surreptitious) *surrogate* such as absolute emancipation, or equality—is being invoked in some argument, at least outside of pure logic. In effect, this means that "reality" is being desiccated so that some principle or model, and its underpinning ideas remain sovereign.

This book starts with the indisputable claim that thought precedes philosophy, and that philosophy is but one way of doing thinking. Moreover, when philosophy severs itself from the rest of human knowledge in an attempt to preside over what is to be tolerated as legitimate knowledge it contributes to the occlusion of ourselves and our world. Further our world and the appeals and values that have been called upon to make it have, until relatively recently, been far more steeped in the figurative imagination than the pure understanding whose role as policeman of the imagination really takes off only in the launching of the new metaphysical attempts to provide a picture of the universe as a law governed "totality" akin, in the first instance, to a machine. As important as Socrates and Plato were in opening up the pathway of philosophy, in premodern times those who trod that path had relatively little social efficacy in a world in which the gods and enchanted powers were still widely revered or, at least, taken seriously within the broader culture. (It is true that philosophy plays an important role in medieval universities, but its tasks were invariably directed by and aligned with theological conundrums and considerations.) The social and cultural significance of philosophy took on an entirely different scale of importance with the cultural victories of modern philosophy and its initial metaphysics. The initial symptom of this cultural victory lay in the Enlightenment spread of Deism, in no small part facilitated by the Masonic lodges, and then atheism, throughout the general population, so that any talk of God or the gods remained outside the legitimate sphere of public truth. To be sure, the Reformation had already drawn truths of the spirit into the interiority of one's own conscience, so it is not difficult to see the "logic" behind Hegel's reading of the history of philosophy as the history of freedom, even if it is still very much an open question precisely what is involved in that freedom as well as the cost involved in it "purchase." Nevertheless, modernity is a very Western creation bringing with it a raft of new problems, as well as a force field in which many old and recurrent ones refuse to go away. In its encounters with non-Western migrants and narratives, the West can no longer simply appeal to its own ultimate powers, beliefs, and drivers; it is forced to reconsider its ways. This book is part of that task of reconsideration.

It also remains the case that philosophers, as well as those working in a number of the human sciences who are servants of some philosophical (usually in the guise of an ethico-political) enterprise commonly ignore the collision between the kinds of truths and appeals that owe more to the figurative imagination, rather than the more abstract understanding, which is seemingly free from contingency. Figurative "truths" are always allied to contingencies, reports, sightings, testimonies, and stories of the sort common to all "religions." At the center of the shift from the figurative imagination to the pure "understanding" is the change involved in how we speak about what are our ultimate appeals. The change can be formulated thus: once our oaths and appeals were to (the) god(s), now they are to an argument or idea. But there is no evidence at all that there is any idea that is robust enough for us to be sure of reality's *essential* nature, so that knowledge absolutely trumps faith. Or to put it another way, and in anthropological terms, our ideas are surrogate divinities to the extent we give them absolute (sacred) status through our appeals. Sadly, I see little evidence that truth in the modern West is more resplendent than ever, and less a matter of authoritarian consensual enforcement than in previous ages, even if the stock of "truths" of a more technical character have accrued aplenty.

If Socrates, as his accusers insisted, did indeed worship "strange new gods," the gods of ideas (or mere clouds, as Aristophanes suggested), it was Plato that provided the ontology of Socrates' great love and who divinized reason. Plato's question in the *Euthyphro* "is something holy because the god wills it, or does the god will it because it is holy?" is indicative of the transformation that occurs with philosophy's origin. Beginning with Plato, we enter into a way, the way of idea-ism, of trying to make sense of life as we order ourselves within the idea that serves as a model or principle guiding right action. Idea-ism is a faith—it is a faith that helps us do what all faith does: do what we would not do, and hence notice what we would not notice without it. But in directing our attention to features of reality which conform to the model or sovereign principle we bring to bear upon reality, it also serves to occlude processes that we may later realize we need to be more conscious of. The history of modern philosophy is also, in large part, a history of the attempt to escape the prison of a previous paradigm by the recognition of important questions that need answers, and that invariably remain unasked within a particular paradigm. Paradigms are destroyed by the pitch and jag of questions that refuse to be suppressed by inadequate answers consistent with a paradigm's perseverance. Hence, too, another important feature of this work is its attempt to demonstrate how the major paradigm shifts in modern philosophy occur through philosophers asking questions which force them outside of the "territory" presided over by a particular sovereign dictatorial principle—the overarching "idea" that they have become subjects of. But once a new paradigm becomes ensconced, the new sovereign-principle all too quickly becomes but another tyrant of reason.[2] Thus, due to its "idea-isms" and paradigmatic character, modern philosophy has spawned an array of dictatorial sovereign principles, and philosophers who eagerly protect *their* "sovereign" from philosophical critique of the sort that enables the acquisition of knowledge of a type, which extends beyond the sovereign's borders, and threatens to bring down its authority and the "truths" under its dominion.

"Idea-ism" in this book is not limited to philosophies which are traditionally classified as "idealist." Hence it is of little consequence for the philosophical hegemony of the idea, and the "idolatrous" response to it, whether the philosophical idea that leads to truth is underpinned by coherence, correspondence, or, as in Deleuze, "construction." Nor is it relevant whether the evidence or focus is ostensibly upon "material" things and processes, as Marx thought it was. For things and processes, irrespective of their initial unifying "ground," once incorporated into a set of claims and generalisations seeking truth status are, from a philosophical view, as Hegel correctly noted prior to Marx crudely recasting him, inescapably idealized.[3] Hegel thought that the concatenation of conceptual relationships which are implicated in ideas are an indication of the unity of reason and its dynamic expansion. One need not share the faith in reason that, as Franz Rosenzweig put it, reaches from "Parmenides to Hegel,"[4] to concur with Hegel's insight that any term of knowledge has to be mediated by other terms; if we know something it is because we know enough about other existents to ascribe meaningful predicates to it; and meaningful predicates are the result of intelligence at work. Thus there is always what Hegel called a "labour of the concept"— even though this "labour of the concept" involves conceptual convulsions or shakeups which ultimately destroy the larger ambitions of Hegel's systematizing, and his certitudes about reason's unity over time. I should also add that Hegel often has brilliant insights that retain their value, and which I draw upon at times, in spite of my criticisms of Hegel's conviction that he has expressed the Absolute idea.

This book, then, does not place primacy of importance upon rational coherence, correspondence, or "constructivism" in themselves as the touchstone of truths (which is not to say it celebrates the incoherent and what bears no connection with our reality), but to our responsiveness, and the revelation and circulation of insights and perspectives that emerge from our social topographies, reciprocities and roles, encounters, historical convulsions, and responses to our present, past and future. Likewise, when truth is considered it is not solely from the perspective of our very selves as mere subjects engaging with and impressed by objects.

We ourselves are also caught within, what the little known German sociologist, historian, and social philosopher Eugen Rosenstock-Huessy, called our trajective and prejective encounters. For while we are pushed by past events that are completely beyond our control, we are also makers of each other and the world, and our calls and commands push us collectively into a future, which is both shaped by us and formative of us.

Philosophy was ultimately an attempt to find the essences that were smothered by the misuse of names and words, and to lead us to the eternal sources of order. But the Jews had, contra to later development in philosophy, proceeded in such a manner that one could infer that God's mysteries are not for modeling, and being made in God's likeness neither are ours. Encounters, surprises, contingencies, miracles, spontaneous acts, and the unpredictable are far more important, far more eventful than our ideas. Here there are truths, but not of the sort that the logos in the Socratic Platonic sense much helps us with. The logos itself becomes flesh—this in large part is because the word and creation and love and salvation are so inextricably tied together. One may well use the logos/argument against this way of participating in life, but the argument does not affect the actual participation, it simply takes into account what the person arguing takes as a higher source of authority and meaning of the logos. But what is made is not unmade because someone provides a reason against its value, let alone existence.

Further, at a more routine and elementary level, ideas emerge out of encounters, though the person engaged in the encountering is invariably socialized and thus brings all manner of predispositions to an encounter as well as a range of pre-existing references—names—in social circulation. A response, though, may require the letting go of the predispositions as well as the names one has brought to the encounter. Sometimes mere survival requires inventions and founding of worldmaking ways heretofore unimaginable.

Every human life is what it is because of who and what it has encountered, and the significance of the who is enmeshed in the why and how, the time and meaning of an encounter, which is to say that our lives are the tapestry of our encounters—thus Martin Buber's pithy and astute declaration "All actual life is encounter."[5] I and you are who we are because of the encountering—however loving, vicious, committed, or casual—beginning with the meeting of our parents, and their parents, and through infinity. The encounter is the knot that ties an infinitude of trails. Encounters are essential to our materializations. They matter every bit as much as ideas—they are the primary conditions of any reflexivity. More, ideas and matter do not suffice to make our world, but are part of our encountering.

Every life is implicated in countless encounters, going back through every moment of social time. Because each encounter gives birth to some aspect of social being, we might be tempted to declare that the encounters prior to birth *determine* a human life—but this metaphysical term *determines* conceals the more appropriate and less metaphysical, and less ominous term, *predisposes*. For it is true that if we generalize we can say anything that happens is dependent upon everything that happens. But saying that leaves us clueless about the weightings and impacts and meanings of all those encounters. To be sure, human beings are frequently caught up in patterns and each habitat has its patterns—and philosophy flourishes in consideration of patterns. But because living patterns and structures are ever unraveling this is only helpful up to a point. We are constantly being made and we are constantly making in our relationships, our engagements, our loves and hatreds. We ravel and unravel, and it is true that large clusters of encounters of a certain "fit" and congruence may well form a prison or a hell from which only revolt, war, or death can provide exit. When a cluster of forces take on such magnitude that they are to a life-world as earthquakes and tsunamis are to the natural world, it is understandable that we have to "start again." Here life has truly bestowed freedom as a dreadful necessity upon us, and such bestowal has little to do with the bravado and enthusiasm of the sort Sartre had conjured up in his ultra-Cartesian depiction of the self.

Each encounter is unique, although there is a repetition of form in encountering and in what comes out of encountering (parenting, being a child, a spouse, a member of a profession, etc.). Martin Buber pointed out that in an encounter with a living creature we are ever coming up against more than an It. The You, he notes, "knows no system of coordinates."[6] The You is alive precisely because it is not an It, is not something that we can stand over. The moment we do that the You is no longer alive—we have killed You through making You an It. If we simply absorb the routines and dictates of office and thereby we ourselves become an It, we will also be incapable of forming a human relationship with You. The I and You relationship is a becoming in which both of us are transformed by virtue of our participation with each other. A relationship is the risk and surrender of the previously known and stable—the becoming more, by each becoming different. The various forms of love always hold out this promise: dissolution into some extra spirit that is beyond what both brought into the relationship. The language of religion will speak of this being miraculous; a more demotic language is likely to miss the fact that life is one creation after another, and the fact that, in large part because our relationships that are themselves but the trails of an infinitude of encounters are involved in creation, our world is unpredictable.

There are all manner of ways in which we are tempted into destroying vital human relationships and cementing them into a mere It-ness. This happens, for example, every time someone defines themselves or others exclusively through a single feature of their being. The person who believes that they or others are only a Christian, a Jew, a Muslim, a communist, a liberal, a feminist, a conservative, a member of a group, or that the world of living souls can be broken up this way, is in denial about their own self as well as others, and on path to negation and dehumanization. Taking the fixed picture of one thing and forcing oneself or others to conform to it, whether that fixed picture is religious or philosophical, is another form of idolatry. For even the servant of the living God, if I may put this in the language of religion, is only serving that God if he or she is astute to God's living power, not the power and command expended and required for yesterday. All fanatics are fanatics because they prefer death to life, even if they don't recognize the preference made manifest in their action. They are sure that they understand what is assured, what God commanded—yesterday, not realizing that today is a new day; a new creation. To be sure, we are forced to face it with what we learned yesterday, what we think we know for sure, but we may also stand with our hearts and minds wide open ready to "leap" into the unknown and "heed" some new decree "from heaven"—or, more prosaically, give attention to some idea heretofore unconsidered.

To be sure, to commit oneself under a name is a way of providing order and structure, meaning and resolve, community and friendship in a life, and that is intrinsic to having a life. But being alive always demands more than the life we already have. Our freedom is constantly called out of us so that the concatenation of names which are intrinsic to who we are is potentially adaptive and expansive. To live in the tensions of the multiplicity of names, to be full of contradictions is a bare requirement of having a soul, being en-souled; having (a) soul, being en-souled is no more a right than having wealth; it is a "miraculous" or spontaneous event, any musician knows when the soul refuses to be in the performance. The expanse of our responsiveness makes us capable of a rich life.

Our knowledge of the world is built out of the uniqueness of an encounter and the generality of the forms in which our encountering takes place. Determinism mistakes the form of encountering for its substance. Forms may become rigid and rigidifying, but if there is anything living within a form it has the possibility of subverting it—this insight was the kernel of Derrida's anti-structuralist reading strategy, but it is as applicable to any form in which we operate. To be a member of the social world does involve roles and processes of distribution, and roles are productive and distributive means of social energy. They may command, but do not determine. We are the creature who can produce the unexpected. But to expect that we can produce it at any time is to fall into another metaphysical trap—viz. voluntarism. And like the determinist, the voluntarist is but another kind of idea-ist.

In a letter to the German sociologist, historian, and social philosopher Rosenstock-Huessy, Jacob Taubes nicely formulated the problem: "perhaps humanity as it is in body and soul in its relationships must be calculated into the question of truth?"[7]

The answer to such a question, then, cannot commence with such stark and anti-anthropological and anti- (yet ultimately very) historical alternatives such as reason and unreason, or superstition and enlightenment. We are indelibly shaped by the stories we tell and insights we have about ourselves, our gods (our idols), and the world insofar as humans, god/s and world "evolve" through those stories and insights. Our philosophical insights have value to the extent they throw some light on our doings, and they assist us in our responsiveness. [8]

Philosophy may help draw our attention to the "dwelling" we inhabit, it can enable us to think about why this and not that dwelling, how this and not that, what is wrong with this, how can it be better, or how can we flee from it, etc., thereby its thinking is, as Heidegger correctly saw, a contribution to "building."

To be sure, we may even hope this may eventually help us to take stock of what we are doing and do some things differently—but this is a far cry from offering the world instruction about what it must become to fit our philosophical insights. Moreover, by the time our insights have any kind of efficacy, the world—constituted as it is by its infinitude of encounters—will have moved on considerably. The struggle of memory and forgetting means that our insights are only as strong as the lines between memory and the future that we are responding and calling to. Opacity is the human lot. And then there is the tragic nature of prophecy itself: when a tragic outcome is in play it is invariably too late to change its course until it has played out.

The kind of philosophizing advanced here is one that is likely to have more currency among practitioners of the human sciences than those who want their philosophy pure, and thus their illuminations not dulled by the opacity and chiaroscuro of motives, relationships, interactions, and encounters. An insight may have its reasons, but reasons alone do not make an insight. The most fundamental dyad of philosophy since Socrates and Plato has been that involving reason and the irrational—even if it persists, as more or less self-explanatory, in such a powerful social scientist as Max Weber.[9] This dyad is not sustainable. Reasoning about human matters always operates with contingencies, and our life's meanings are shaped by the importance we ascribe to certain contingencies—historically momentous actions and actors which supply peoples with meaning and narratives, potencies which generate life-worlds, founding and institutions, which in and of themselves are no more rational or irrational than they are red or blue or cold or hot.

If this work hopes to be a methodological contribution it is to make the case that philosophy is not a completely self-sufficient discipline, but its purpose and development is bound up with lived practices and the modes of knowledge that are generated in our practices. It takes issue with the various "devices" and "stratagems" which take us out of the world in order to judge it—and it takes issue by looking at what *happens in the world* as the various claims about and appeals to the beyond are being made. Ideas, institutions, and peoples are not discrete substances or entities—we cannot identify a people apart from the institutions which modulate their activities and the appeals and venerations, the ideas, they have about themselves, their world, their past, their present, and future. We cannot understand institutions apart from the ideas behind them and the peoples who dwell within them. Ideas are more deceptive. They all too easily take on, as Marx and Nietzsche noted (before succumbing to the same temptation), a reified life of their own, and in their flight return to haunt and defile us precisely because of their *irreality*. An idea is a wisp as much as a building block, a fetish as well as an illumination, a vestige of time well and truly past, as well as a possibility, a promise of the yet to come. We can speak of ideas as if they existed in themselves or as if they dwelt in a pure heaven of reason's own making, and if we are speaking of mathematics such a manner of speaking may not seem inappropriate, even if the paths to the purer worlds occur and evolve in time. But the more we require our ideas to help us socially the more we need to appreciate their connectedness to, or circulatory character within peoples and institutions. Ideas are world- and self-making names. The most important names commence in insight and discovery, love and hate, appeal and veneration, catastrophe and response, not mere description: and for the most part even when we describe, we do so because we have to or want to serve some purpose other than mere or sheer description, when something more primordial than the descriptive disposition is adopted.

Ideas direct the organization of those associations we make when thinking of something. In this important respect, then, it is simply the way things are that we rely upon some kind of ideational hierarchy in our thinking, and hence any "philosophy" insofar as it is a coherent body of associations can be viewed in terms of the underlying orientation that inheres in an idea. Hence it could be said that this book also succumbs to idea-ism. But my argument is not a criticism of the use of ideas and principles for organizing our thoughts. Rather it is directed at thinking that is predicated upon ideas that remain unquestioned. This is why when they are properly noticed and stringently questioned the paradigm that they support will fall apart. The history of philosophy is basically the story of paradigmatic breakdown due to someone posing the right questions to the dictatorship of an idea or cluster of ideas serving as principles or models.

It is obvious that the argument developed here may also be read as resting upon a sovereign idea, viz. the Heraclitian "idea" that life is transformation. I think this is irrefutable because a refutation could be nothing other than a confirmation. The idea that life is transformative has one decisive advantage when it comes to thinking: it says nothing about the pace, nature, or content of transformation. It serves as a heuristic. It is primarily a reminder against dogmatics rather than providing any dogmatics themselves—it need not even rule out possible exceptions such as a Platonic theory of mathematics, though it would also alert us to the change that occurs that would enable us to move from ignorance to knowledge, and make the case that the meaning mathematics may have will depend upon all manner of things other than mathematics. What we may discover as having real value for our lives is fleeting and ever susceptible to changing conditions—life is one trial after another, and, for all our self-consciousness, we are responsive and dependent creatures. It is this that has been lost sight of in the "way of ideas."

NOTES

1. See Ivana Marková, *The Dialogical Mind; Common Sense and Ethics* (Cambridge: Cambridge University Press, 2016), for a discussion of Vico and common sense which also refers to Reid, 39–61.

2. Appeals and commitments, consensuses or paradigms, are too important to remain purely Kuhnian; Kuhn places too much weight upon acts of consciousness, or puzzles and professions and not enough, especially in the foundational moments of paradigms, upon exigencies and responses to social catastrophes, and the family resemblances which move through or even constitute them. Kuhn uses the term in the context of problem solving and thus its social, institutional, and existential sides are downplayed in favor of intellectual inquiry. I am far more interested in the paradigm as a common response to a problem in which groups are activated and institutions changed, and agreements reached about what has to be overcome, which then generates disagreements about how one overcomes *it*. In this respect I can sympathize with J. G. A. Pocock's ambivalence about the term "paradigm." See his *Political Thought and History: Essays on Theory and Method* (Cambridge: Cambridge University Press, 2009), xi–xiv.

3. "[T]he claim that the *finite is an idealization* defines *idealism*. The idealism of philosophy consists in nothing else than in the recognition that the finite is not truly an existent. Every philosophy is essentially idealism or at least has idealism for its principle, and the question then is only how far this principle is carried out. . . . The opposition between idealistic and realistic philosophy is therefore without meaning." G. W. F. Hegel, *The Science of Logic*, translated and edited by George di Giovanni (Cambridge: Cambridge University Press, 2010), 124.

4. Franz Rosenzweig, *The Star of Redemption*, translated Barbara Galli (Madison: University of Wisconsin Press, 2005), 22.

5. *I and Thou*, translated by Walter Kaufman (New York: Simon and Schuster, 1970), 62.

6. *I and Thou*, 81.

7. This letter of 21.7.1953 is available in the Rosenstock-Huessy Archives in the Rauner Special Collections Library, Dartmouth College. I don't think Taubes succeeded in sufficiently living up to this splendid formulation.

8. Rosenstock-Huessy once formulated his own "principle" of orientation against the Cartesian "cogito," thus: "*Respondeo etsi mutabor*—I respond although I shall be changed." Eugen Rosenstock-Huessy, *Out of Revolution: Autobiography of Western Man*, with an Introduction by Harold Berman (Oxford, Providence: Berg, 1993), 753.

9. Cf. "For the purposes of a typological scientific analysis it is convenient to treat all irrational, affectually determined elements of behaviour as factors of deviation from a conceptually pure type of rational action." Max Weber, *Economy and Society: An Outline of Interpretative Sociology*, edited by Guenther Roth and Claus Wittich, translat-

ed Edward Fischoff et. al., 6. What seems to be straightforward in terms of means and ends readily becomes a labyrinth due to the collision of "rationalities" which spawn all manner of irrationalities.

ONE
Ideas and Names—A Philosophical Crossroad

THE PLATONIC TURN TO THE IDEA

In the history of philosophy, any discussion of the term "idea" must take its point of departure from Plato (even if mention is also invariably made of Parmenides for his insistence on the implacability and immobile nature of truth and from which Plato learnt so much.) Unlike Parmenides who certainly valorizes the logos, which may be translated as word, speech, story, and reason, and while Socrates makes disputation essential for understanding the nature of something, it is Plato who lays out the method enabling us to *see* ideas with the mind's eyes. Idea, which is also translated as form, comes from the infinitive of the Greek word to see, *idein* or *eidein* from *eido*, but *eido* is also to know *oida*, "the pf. [perfect tense], I have seen, is used as a pres. [present]. In the sense I know (for what one *has seen, one knows*)."[1]

Visibility is thus critical to Plato's idea of the idea, as well as to his epistemology where the word is a means to the truth of insight. Thus as Paul Friedländer noted: "Plato, as far as we know, was the first to speak of the eye of the soul, and . . . he does so especially in those passages where he envisages the highest stages of his philosophy."[2] The core question for Plato involves the truthful visibility that presents itself to the mind's eye, as opposed to what is merely visible to the material eye or the senses. It has been argued, for example by Laszlo Versényi, that this emphasis upon visibility evolves out of the Homeric epic task which is to render visible the great heroic deeds to an audience.[3] In the *Republic* Plato attacks Homer and Hesiod and the other poets for creating confusion and wickedness in minds and hearts because what they rendered visible was but the copy or image of things. In other words, the poetic tradition provided incoherent glimpses which formed the basis of public opinion and poets valorized what we might call the method of the mere glimpse as opposed to insight. Insight comes not from simply hearing an opinion about something and rendering one's second hand *impression* of it, but from actually knowing it. That Plato sees it as perfectly natural to criticize the poets for their deficiencies in mental "sight," that is for putting too much trust in what they think they know due to not looking behind the appearances, is indicative of an earlier turn of the Greek world itself which made of the poets a means of social orientation. The poet who summons the muse in order to be transported back into the action of which he sings experiences a kind of elevation—the elevation that gives him the panoramic view. Bruno Snell has argued that in contrast to the epic poets, the lyric poets "were the first to voice this new idea, that intellectual and spiritual matters have 'depth.'" [4] That is, in contrast to the epic poets, who take us to the horizon to see battles and homecomings, the lyric poets "peer" into the depths, and plunge us into ourselves: in each case we are, nevertheless, drawn to a reality that is not a visible here and now, but something conjured up by the word that impacts upon the soul itself. The word becomes a means for orientating sight, of bringing it in as well as further out and back.

Contrast this with the Hebrew tradition which dwelled more on what Walter Ong calls "the highly auditory sensorium." [5] In his *Hebrew Thought Compared with Greek*, Thorleif Boman makes the point that: "true being for the Hebrews is the 'word,' *dabhar*, which comprises all Hebraic realities: word, deed, and concrete object." [6] The Hebrew faith in God is also faith in the word. And as Boman says of the lie: "A lie for the Hebrew is not as it is for us, a non-agreement with the truth . . . the lie is the eternal decay and destruction of the word . . . that which is powerless, empty and vain is a lie: a spring which gives no water lies (Isa.58.11, kazabh)." [7]

The Christian equation of God and logos may make the apostle John look a Greek, but the God who speaks existence into being, who only sees and affirms *after* he speaks is a God in which word and deed necessarily precede reflection. Such a God is indicative of a pre-reflexive culture. And a culture formed around such a God defers to the authority of God's word rather than a specific person's own insights. God's humbling of Job from the whirlwind and the rebuke of his chattering neighbors is a reminder of the gulf between the creative power and authority of the God who speaks and the created creature who will never grasp the real whys of existence. Thus too the early Christians enmeshed in cultural and semantic "flows" of Romans, Jews, and Greeks initially retained a suspicion of philosophy which was consistent with the Jewish tradition (cf. Paul *Colossians* 2: 8) with its constant reminder of human dependency upon a power far greater than human beings themselves. We are made is the resounding Jewish "insight" that is affirmed by the word rather than the spectator's "view" that poetry, lyric, and drama all fostered, and which reached its apotheosis in philosophy where God eventually, being perfect, contemplates Himself in his own perfection as intelligence. *That* we need orientation is the existential predicament—*how* social formations and people provide it and what kind of orientations take hold is what differentiates peoples.

The philosophical emphasis upon the mind's power of sight will eventually be the key element of philosophy, particularly once it is conjoined with the much more potent powers that the scientific revolution unlocked. But the quest for a meaningful and satisfying or good life itself may not be one in which reflection and questioning is decisive. Thus, it is all too understandable why the anchorage provided by modes of social orientation in which lives are highly sculptured by reference to revelation and traditional imperatives and proscriptions, rather than one's own reason and choices, has been so fiercely defended for so long by adherents to their traditional faiths.

In the West, the scale of violence of the religious and denominational conflict, triggered by the Reformation, set the stage for a new kind of hope and faith—hope and faith in "rationality" itself, and its creations, "emancipation" and "autonomy," eventually from any kind of domination. That would eventually mean submitting all social mores and institutions to critique: against the flesh and blood struggles of generations, the critical philosopher could appeal to principle and ideal. All that was needed was that flesh and blood conform to the ideas that the modern visionaries and their disciples would instruct them in. Had not humanity been duped by superstitious and crazed imaginings for millennia? But the problem was this: the real truth of a story was not so much in the "facticity" of its origin, nor even the rational coherence of its underlying precepts and components, but in what a people made out of themselves through these stories and precepts. Traditions were not the derivatives of rational principles *tout court*, but the expressions of lives that had their reasons, along with all manner of pressures for survival, and everything else that made people do what they do.

The part "reason" plays in making sense of people's lives cannot be so sharply hived-off from passionate decisions and collective imaginings. That Westerners are forced now to confront this because of Muslims, rather than Christians or (non-orthodox) Jews, whose orthodoxies have largely been cordoned off and sidelined from public disputation, is a relatively recent phenomenon that only highlights how successful the Enlightenment drive has been in dismantling the West's more archaic traditions. But the snag was that as rational moral principles became increasingly inviolable they became ensnared in a contradiction that their advocates were unprepared for: the contradiction was between the principle of cultural respect and the very source of that principle, which, in the first instance, was not culture, but reason. For in the West, culture was a relatively late consideration of reason. And initially reason was used as a means of criticizing the social and political institutions which were intrinsic to the culture, but which were also seen as bulwarks of injustice, and instruments of injustice. When culture became a serious consideration for "reason," as it did in Herder, it was part of a larger consideration of the world's complexity.

To his credit, Herder never shied away from this. He focused upon the tensional reality of humanity as a potential unity constituted by cultural differences. But to achieve this, Herder recognized that there were far more complicated considerations involved that could not be sidestepped by invoking rational universal moral principles as Kant or Fichte had done in their appeal to practical reason. For Herder, whose chief philosophical source of inspiration was always Kant's philosophical *bête noir*, Leibniz, the absolutization of the divorce between reason and sensation is not only philosophically mistaken, but it contributes to a moral culture divorced from the all-important attempt to try and understand why and how we differ culturally and historically.[8]

I mention in passing that Rosenstock-Huessy take an even further step by noting that different types of professions such as monks, doctors, artists, and engineers had their origins with founders who had created new "partitions of time." Thus even the one culture was also inhabited by "dis-temporaries." The great problem, for Rosenstock-Huessy, then, was how to make contemporaries of "dis-temporaries."[9] Our reasons and our social appeals are completely bound up with our lives in and over "lived-time." Herder and Rosenstock-Huessy, among others, provide important grounds for the dialogical and hermeneutical features of reason that need to be factored into any philosophical contribution to achieving greater bonds of solidarity between peoples.

When Socrates and Plato raised their questions and challenges about the good life, they did so in a world, where philosophy was yet untried. Philosophy was a new act of faith. The faith that intelligence (and not just obedience to the gods—for how could we *know* what was really a god and a holy order?) could make us better was fundamental to the founding of philosophy. Like all real faith, it had its own reasons. Socrates and Plato had witnessed how poetry had helped make a people—albeit, they believed, not for the better. But just as poetry was making people act badly because the poets' words failed to meet the truth of what goodness required, they held that true speech could change people's behavior, provided those with (potential) political influence had the ability to understand philosophy, and the character to act upon it.

In their observation of artisans, they could see how design operated in transformation, and design was intrinsic to the proper making of anything. That is why Platonism views thinking as a kind of technique, and this stands in the closest relationship to the significance demonstration holds for Socrates and Plato. For Socrates had started by observing that artisans have a skill, and that skill is something you can either demonstrate or not. A user (say a flautist) may be needed to judge the adequacy of the craftsmanship—but this is largely due to the flautist also having a skill which ultimately benefits from the skilled workmanship of the instrument supplied. In each case skill builds on skill, and skill requires that someone knows what they are doing and why they are doing what they are doing at the moment of their doing. Demonstrability thus becomes intrinsic to knowing. This is why Martin Heidegger finds the root of Western thinking in Plato and its terrifying flower in technicity or calculative thinking. Plato is primarily interested in thinking about the good life, but starting from the artisans and the fact that their knowledge is based on their skill, their *techne*, he is also drawn to mathematical truths as demonstrating the intrinsic nature of the universe, which is also why Platonism remains a serious option in the philosophy of mathematics.

The question of actually knowing what something is as opposed to thinking one knows "what it is" is what unites Socrates and Plato, and it is this question which takes philosophy further along the path originally taken by Parmenides. While the desire is simple, the history of philosophy would suggest that the answer is not so simple. For Plato, the very Socratic question "what is x?" has thus generated the question, which he addresses directly and at length in the *Theaetetus*, "how do I know what x is?" We might say that the question forces us to make another abstraction.

Naming is perhaps the most fundamental operation in social orientation, and hence one of the most elemental social acts of humanity. Names commence their "life" within a collective, and as responses to circumstances, and as such serve all manner of social purposes. Likewise, they grow out of collective experience, and their capacity to both impress and trigger further responses is closely connected with the specific collective in which they have their power. Naming also designates identity and difference (two of the "ideas" which, according to Plato, "the soul grasps by itself").[10] Names proliferate as events emerge and new insights and findings occur. Likewise, names of individuals who "save the day" or betray the group are engraved within the social memory and become fundamental "triggers" of inspiration, hatred, etc. Names vary in their use, but they all designate and apportion (the weight of the glory and shame of the past, as well as the expectation for the future). Designation and apportionment may be connected to one's achievement, one's activity or merely to mark one's presence in the world—though at the time of the designation a personal name may or may not be full of hope and expectation, but throughout the course of the life the achievements (perhaps not even noticed until the death of the name's bearer) may suffice to make that name part of the common stock of names within a practice so that it has historical importance. Our conversations, declarations, behests, and other kinds of "speech" are marked by names because we are appealing not only to each other, but often to others beyond the person to whom we are talking, which is happening every time there is a denunciation or condemnation. A society is, *inter alia*, a vast chain of names, a heroic and sacred record, as well as a record of a day of judgment, of what the group now condemns to hell and what it sanctifies and aspires to be: to call a child Adolf Hitler means something altogether different in 1933 or 1945 than it did in 1889. Names are "tested," "affirmed," condemned, and revised collectively. In a person's own life the concepts follow behind the name—the name does contain an aspect of pre-formation, expectation, as well as the blessing and burden of belonging, but these are subject to change depending upon what becomes of one, what one makes with and of one's name. Naming is, then, *inter alia*, a symptom, cipher, and marker of the transmutation and metamorphosis of life-stages and expectations such as the coming of age, becoming recognized in a profession, or achieving a certain status.

Names are more precise, i.e., individuating, and more general or opaque than concepts (which is the source of the philosopher's preference for concepts and ideas over names), in part due to the haphazard (potential of) application in certain social contexts, and the rationale of a designation, often fading from view and bearing little or absolutely no relation to what people "perceive" by the name.

"Death by Abstraction" was the felicitous title of a draft of the essay by Rosenstock-Huessy which would eventually be published in *I Am an Impure Thinker* under the title "Heraclitus to Parmenides."[11] Rosenstock-Huessy argues that Parmenides was the "scalper of names" and that his grammatical valorization of the pronominal, which, he claims, is repeated in modern times by Heidegger, has taken us away from one of the most important features of worldmaking and knowing—the conferral of and responsiveness to names. Parmenides' desire to see the way of the world led him to place little store in the social significance of our inherited designations: he wished to look over or through or beyond the designations, the names of things, so that he could think about knowing, in the hope he would know the world better by knowing better what knowing was. Parmenides seems to have known one big thing—"Being is." But that knowledge stopped taking on the priority it did as soon as he needed any kind of practical engagement reliant upon knowing who had the qualities to do what, or what was involved in the circumstances of the doing. Then he had to have recourse to names, and naming and names themselves are part of the process of worldmaking. If Parmenides' preference for Being over process was the beginning of the fascination with the implacable and eternal as the source of knowledge, it is, nevertheless, with Plato that the history of philosophy becomes one in which names and hence social designation is largely considered to be irrelevant in comparison to how we understand, really see, and argue for what needs to be known. Plato realized, quite rightly, that the act of naming was very different from the act of "knowing." And he also rightly recognized that if knowing was to be based upon a stringent philosophical method then the philosopher cannot be bound or take orientation from the far more haphazard processes that are involved in the chaos of naming. Names are not clues to knowledge because they have not been arrived at philosophically; they are simply ciphers of the chaos and irrationality that philosophy needs to tame, and they inevitably mislead us about the essence of things. The following passage, from the dialogue that is dedicated to the problem of names, the *Cratylus*, presents a summary of the position that Plato argues for:

> if there is always that which knows and that which is known–if the beautiful, the good, and all the other verities exist–I do not see how there is any likeness between these conditions of which I am now speaking and flux or motion. Now whether this is the nature of things, or the doctrine of Heracleitus and many others is true, is another question; but surely no man of sense can put himself and his soul under the control of names, and trust in names and their makers to the point of affirming that he knows anything; nor will he condemn himself and all things and say that there is no health in them, but that all things are flowing like leaky pots, or believe that all things are just like people afflicted with catarrh, flowing and running all the time. Perhaps, Cratylus, this theory is true, but perhaps it is not. Therefore you must consider courageously and thoroughly and not accept anything carelessly–for you are still young and in your prime; then, if after investigation you find the truth, impart it to me. [12]

To be sure Socrates leaves open the possibility he may be wrong, and Cratylus has not been completely persuaded as he still inclines to Heraclitus. But he has *not* only been unable to adequately refute Socrates, he has already advanced far along the Socratic/ Platonic way, having conceded that:

> How realities are to be learned or discovered is perhaps too great a question for you or me to determine; but it is worthwhile to have reached even this conclusion, that they are to be learned and sought for, not from names but much better through themselves than through names. [13]

Although the *Cratylus* does succeed in identifying why the names themselves do not suffice for achieving what Socrates is looking for, viz. essences, or things in themselves, which are what ideas are for Plato, the fact remains that Plato does not engage in a genuine social exploration of what is involved in naming and what this contributes to our worldmaking and subsequent knowledge of the world we have and continue to make. Indeed the issue is oversimplified by virtue of the fact that Plato, through the persona of Socrates, is fighting against the sophistic tactics of etymology (he also mocks the technique in the *Protagoras*) as part of the sophists' bag of tricks for enhancing their own social status and power through their rhetorical deftness which requires little or no knowledge about the world's truth. Just as Plato, then, had argued the poets dealt in shadows because they merely glimpsed bits and pieces of things and put them together in a haphazard and ultimately stupid and wicked fashion (evil being ignorance being another Platonic/Socratic formulation), he believed orators and sophists deceived people by manipulating speech. Once someone could "see" the truth, then that person could not "un-see" what these shady characters were passing off as truth.

Plato had provided a depiction of the philosopher's way of dealing with things, how he does his business, by comparing him with other social types that had become powerful within the polis—at the opposite end to the philosopher the beast that is the tyrant, a beast, too frequently celebrated in Greeks by the poets who, Plato suggests, themselves draw crowds toward tyranny or, what Plato sees as the pre-tyrannic political form, democracy (*Republic* 568a-c). The same predilection for tyranny, according to Plato, is also fostered by the art of rhetoric (the subject of the *Gorgias*). Plato's championing of what needed to be done to grasp the truth as something over and above the contingencies of any particular social environment was done by setting up the alternative ways of world-making that were very particular, and very Greek. What he wanted to negate—poetic thoughtlessness, rhetorical excess, and eristic trickery—largely "determined" his response. They could all be defeated by dialectical openness and sincerity, natural ability, the right method and genuine philosophical toil. It just happened to be the case that the stability that the philosopher was seeking in order to have knowledge was intrinsic to the very order of things that philosophy could access. The philosopher was seeking a pattern and the universe was formed on the basis of pattern, or model. Thus in the *Timaeus*, the demiurge must look to eternal ideas as models, but it is every bit as essential to his insight into the relationship between artisan and product: the artisan looks to a model which is the idea for every table, chain, shoe, etc.[14] That knowledge can be found among the artisans is thus expanded to the insight of the philosopher, though it involves one key reversal. For in the case of the artisan, while the deed of making confirms that there must be a model to explain the knowing that operationalizes the making, with the philosopher the invocation of the model is undertaken to confirm the philosopher's knowing. It is far from obvious, though, that making souls is really analogous to making flutes, tables, or shoes. For the responsiveness of a soul is far less pliant, and far more elusive, more "spirited," than any material substance. Indeed, the philosopher's intention, plan, or model may have no bearing whatever on the soul of the person receiving philosophical instruction. Further, unlike a shoe or table, what is being made is not so obviously functional or limited in its function: for a person is not philosophical in all respects at every moment, but a table, while perhaps deployable for "un-table"-like purposes, e.g., to wedge against a door to bar entry, as long as it is unbroken or decayed beyond recognition, stays a table. Moreover, whereas the material of a thing created by the artisan is incidental to the larger purpose, it is far from obvious that the "human-ity" (*Menschlichkeit*) of a person is of lesser worth than a philosophical nature. One only has to be around the spouses of philosophers to see (as Xanthippe no doubt experienced it) that the philosophical side of a phi-losopher may wear rather thin in day to day life, and what often really matters are far more elemental and indeed indispensable qualities for fulfilling the various roles that one must take on in a life. Just as becom-ing a philosopher is a sifting process so that some qualities come to the fore in those moments where a philosophical disposition is required, philosophical sight requires sifting out those qualities of reality which are not necessary for a philosophical understanding of something.

Thus too the myriad formations of sociality, which were essential to the very existence of the polis and which were themselves conditions of there being a philosophical type, were only admitted back into the pic-ture once the philosophical method had been sufficiently established with its peculiar form of visibility so that the philosopher could judge the philosophical worth of a regime or the qualities required for the best regime. To be sure, there is much to learn from Plato's dialogues about politics and Greek society, just as we may, for example, learn some things about tribes and family, women and slaves, and especially about the nature and diverse kinds of the polis from Aristotle's *Politics*, but what we learn might well amount to far less than what we would learn from hearing women and slaves and tribal members talking about the relation-ships they are involved in. This, though, would require hearing other voices, not the philosopher surveying and passing down the line what he sees. In other words, the kinds of dialogues which are part of everyday life, and which open us up to all manner of aspects of the human realities we are encountering take on a narrow quality when we are dealing with a philosophical dialogue. And, with few exceptions which have to in-clude Plato, who had a great "feel" for character and drama, most philo-sophical dialogues are utterly wooden because the characters are nothing but extensions of ideas.

While the mind's eye and (in)sight are needed if we are to know things, we must also know how to attune the mind's eye in order to have insight, in order to see the idea that discloses the truth of something. Although the doctrine of ideas is the result of a dialectical disclosure, an insight that is simultaneously a methodological *fabrication*, Plato is ever reminding his readers that the father of dialectic is Socrates, who was executed for doing nothing more than wanting to know things, and wanting to illustrate that those who did not know the most important things about the soul (writ small, i.e., the self, and large, i.e., the commu-nity), especially rulers and educators, were contributing to the passionate behaviors, ignorant and evil decisions of the assembly that ends in chaos, rapacity, and murder. The unphilosophical did not know what they were doing, and they did not know the difference between what was really good and what seemed to be good; they lacked Socrates' character and his ideas. And if they had his ideas they may have had a better character. Which is also to say that ideas themselves, like philosophy (like Socrates), are good. Not only then is knowledge good, but knowledge of what the good is is ultimately what all knowledge strives for. This idea would lead in many directions, not the least interesting being in the neo-Platonic tradition which makes a God of the good.

Plato commences the deification of knowledge and method by which we know. And knowledge is then turned against society itself, insofar as society, as it is, is but a poor replica of the society that can be philosophically understood as being the model for assessing the value of a regime. Let us concede that the polis was sick and this turning was understandable, but Plato does not simply turn against the sickness of the polis but against all that he believes contributes to that sickness, particularly the "real" educators of the Greeks (it is also, as Plato states in the *Apology*, a poet, Aristophanes, whom Plato had accused for being the real accuser of Socrates and thus responsible for his death). But it is not just the educators, but the very beings which held the city together, the known gods, at least as they are poetically depicted. To be sure Socrates himself was brought to court precisely for this move, and before Socrates, Xenophanes had looked to a new kind of god, due to his exasperation with the old ones. Following Xenophanes, Plato, in the *Republic*, having coined the term "theology," replaces Achilles as the model of the hero with Socrates, and hence makes Socrates' heroics outshine Achilles' heroics. Socrates also (in no particular order): examines a range of claims and arguments about the nature of justice; the question of whether it is better to be just or simply appear to be just; provides a model of an ideal polis; lays out the best curriculum for educating philosophers; makes the case that philosophers should be kings; demonstrates why poets and statesmen are incapable of real rulership; sets out the philosophical method; establishes the theory of ideas; demonstrates why the philosophical life is the best life and why the tyrant's is the worst; provides a diagnosis of the pathologies of other constitutional forms; provides a theory of the nature of the soul, as well as an argument for the immortality of the soul. One might say the *Republic* is not only the book which first sets out the idea of an idea but it is full of ideas. And hence in any Western Civilization course, it is generally the first book off the shelf. Also, it is no wonder that it is a book that attracts young scholars and generates an unending number of works and interpretations—though one might think after two thousand years, its content would not need yet another new interpretation. And the fact that it is written as a dialogue, has characters and what may loosely be called a plot, only adds extra layers of interpretation and hence the possibility of ever new ideas about its real meaning. And I am not even thinking about the various types of Platonic interpretation through the ages—to take randomly from different ages and interpretations, the readings by Proclus, Ficino, the Cambridge Platonists, Hegel, Jowett, Heidegger, Strauss—one can barely believe they are reading the same figure. If Plato can be said to teach a method—and it is plain for all and sundry that it does—it is somewhat astonishing that a method that emphasizes the implacable, eternal nature of ideas, and hence the reliability of knowledge can lead to such diverse interpretations by people whose stock-in-trade is the study and discussion of ideas. That I think is an important fact that is often left out of approaches to and discussions of Plato, but it is one that might tell us as much, or even more about the nature of ideas than Plato himself tells us.

THE IDEA AS DISCLOSED THROUGH RIGHT METHOD

In spite of the plethora of interpretative studies of Plato's dialogues, Plato's method is very straightforward and comes down to one core insight: if we wish to have ideas about things we need to observe their many species/sub-species and identify the unity they all share.[15] Such a process invariably involves a discussion—dialectic being the discussion which is not mere trickery—eristic—but a discussion governed by rules of the procedure needed to do this dismembering and assembling. The speakers are thus engaged in an exhaustive analysis, proceeding by way of examining hypotheses and testing them in argument, which leads to a definition. That is also to say that if something can be known it must be definable, and if it is definable it must be able to cover the various cases in which it appears. This contrast between the conclusion which involves the definition that covers the constitutive elements of something and the beginning where we start with a name that does not suffice for much other than to get the show on the road, so to speak. A typical example comes from early in the *Sophist* where the Eleatic stranger says to Theaetetus:

> but now you and I must investigate in common, beginning first, as it seems to me, with the sophist, and must search out and make plain by argument what he is. For as yet you and I have nothing in common about him but the name; but as to the thing to which we give the name, we may perhaps each have a conception of it in our own minds; however, we ought always in every instance to come to agreement about the thing itself by argument rather than about the mere name without argument.[16]

Because signs are prone to misinterpretation, the definition is always in need of modification in the to and fro of discussion (hence the mistrust of writing expressed in the *Phaedrus* [274–79] that Derrida, in "Plato's Phar-

macy" would see as a key to Western *logocentric* metaphysics). But it is
the idea that provides the radiance from which we may assess the value
of the definition, although (paradoxically) it is the definition that points
to that illuminating source. The idea is this unity behind or within or
common to the various members which partake in it. The job, then, of a
philosopher will be to lead people through the various misunderstand-
ings they may have about the ideas that are being discussed, about the
ideas we are seeking to grasp in order to enhance our knowledge so that
we and the world will be the better for it. Whatever one may say about
Plato's theory of ideas even his staunchest critics are hard put to deny
that they write in the hope of achieving something better (even if there
are those like Sade who believe evil is better than good—which is no
disproof of Plato).

The one problem which will come up time and time again in refuta-
tions of the kind of thinking that Plato defends can invariably be traced
back to poetic and religious thinking/speaking, and philosophers from
Hamann to Nietzsche to Heidegger to Michael Polanyi have basically
riffed around the same theme: we actually know all sorts of things that
we cannot adequately define or even articulate in a manner that lends
itself to the dismembering/reassembling method Plato requires. Instinct—a favorite term in Nietzsche—is an obvious case in point. Instinct
enables us to know something swiftly so that we can act swiftly, but if we
"know" some things "instinctively"—e.g., such as, while driving, how to
corner at what speed—this is not the kind of knowledge that is easily
defined so that its various sub-species may be reassembled into an overarching unity that may enable us to rationally apprehend the idea that
illumines the definition. Instinct has little if anything to do with definition and the *logos;* it is the knowledge that comes from multiple rapid
micro-cognitive processes—which is why its best means of conveyance to
someone else may be through mythic, poetic, or other means of evocative
communication.

The Platonic division between opinion and knowledge is the belated
response to the information that is relayed by those micro cognitive processes. By devising a triptych of the soul, Plato relegates that processing
to the irrational, thus enabling reason to free itself from instincts and
have access to the ideas in themselves. With that move Plato establishes a
cognitive division that has been intrinsic to Western philosophy, and it
has been pointed out on occasions how even Freud's tripartite psychic
division is a variant on Plato's initial distinction between the rational and
irrational parts of the soul. It also provides the kind of cleavage which
cannot help but make the soul like a thing or an object to be understood
by an examination of its parts. But what if this is a fundamental mistake
in so far as it commences with what may be "end-states"? Certainly, we
can, up to a point, meaningfully talk about rational and irrational or
conscious and unconscious behaviors, but does this really mean that

there are parts of the soul that correspond to the roots or sources of these behaviors? What if instead of there being such parts—recall Freud's ego-id-superego diagram which suggests distinct locations which, flow into each other—we have a plethora of cognitive processes which may "fail" to adequately relay information "further on up the chain"? Consciousness thus understood is a delayed reflective reaction—with all the advantages and disadvantages of reflection and delay. An opportunity to review, to reconfigure more immediate impressions, but also a time-lag, a loss of balance that might send a tightrope walker over the edge, just as it might also save one from a lifetime of regret.

The significance of micro-cognitive processing was behind Leibniz's monads, those perceptual point qualities, and it would be picked up by Herder and Schelling. I think it is far from obvious that the unconscious of psychoanalysis really has a more compelling case to make about how drives affect us than the philosophers of the "pre-conscious" (and again psychoanalysts are just as much in dispute with each other as philosophers about therapeutical diagnostics and curative means).

The kinds of ideas developed by Leibniz's concerning the continuum between opaque and clear perceptions, connects instinct and reason in a very different way than the Platonic division between reason and unreason. The Platonic legacy, whether consciously adopted or merely replicated, involved making the idea as a model, and this would play a leading role in the metaphysical revolution accompanying the emergence of the mechanical "world picture." Leibniz's account of the idea also allowed for that. But his genius was that he also saw a way of reconciling the dark and the light, the instinctive and the rational, quality and quantity, force and logic. I signal this at the outset, for although Leibniz remains primarily wedded to the paradigm of the new sciences, he, more than any other philosopher working on the new metaphysics, created an arsenal of ideas which would inspire others to look deeper into the depth and range of reason, including reasons of the heart and community, the latter being the speciality of Herder, who (in my opinion) was Leibniz's greatest student.

EXISTENCE AND LOVE, AND A HERMENEUTICAL ALTERNATIVE

The presence of the idea, reached slowly through the process of Socratic inquiry and then, with Plato, through the identification of the methodological nature of that inquiry, is revealed to be essential for knowledge of the entire purpose of philosophy, the good life. The idea that is revealed by the right—i.e., dialectical—method is the very "thing" that transforms philosophy from a speculative activity with seemingly no means of reconciling the vast array of speculations into an activity which holds out the promise of truth of things made visible to the mind's eye. That transformation quickly renders the lived nature of the encounter between disputants a secondary matter. The living are subordinate to their ideas, and it is on the basis of their ideas that we can assess the worthiness or goodness of the living. And yet, while this conforms to the various conclusions that are reached in Plato's dialogues, a tension between the idea and the existential remains a conspicuous feature of the dialogues. For it is all too obvious that Plato loved the living man Socrates. To be sure it was because of who Socrates was, but it was, nevertheless, Socrates himself rather than the idea of Socrates that he loved, even if his appraisal of Socrates' greatness was due to his being able to see how the ideas of goodness, wisdom, justice, temperance, courage, and piety were "actualized" in the man.

If we are to take Plato's method on the terms he presents it, we can put it thus: Plato's setting of the dialogue as an *agon* emphasizes character and context, the living community at work, but his love of truth ultimately trumps his love of Socrates, his love of what is more real than reality, of what illumines reality. That is, his faith in the possibility of what ideas can do is what lays down the future of philosophy. What came second—the (faith in) knowledge—now came first; and what came first, the love of Socrates came second. Yet, Plato loved Socrates for what he did, and what he did was know how little he knew. But how many knowers are subsequently unlovable, and do not contribute to the world's conviviality through their knowledge? Surely another feature of Socrates that Plato loved was his bravery and determination, his willingness to martyr himself for the new way of living that he had opened up. But, however we put it, the love for Socrates, if strictly understood through the *method* Plato attributes to Socrates and the students of Parmenides which he lays down (as opposed to what we have emphasized), is *idea-ized* love.

The tension and the conundrum of the relational nature of love and the particularity of love, by virtue of love being a particular relationship is amply evident in Plato's dialogues on love, the *Symposium* and *Phaedrus*. In both the emphasis is upon love as a movement toward the eternal, the idea of beauty, and particularity is a starting point for the soul's elevation and expansion of its reason. The existential gives way as one opens up to the *ideal-ity*, the eternal and unchanging, the forms themselves. For what is ultimately being sought is the immortality of that part of the soul that is itself depicted in Plato as immortal, its reason.

Plato had believed he had found in philosophy the means for ending the chaos and suffering that came from evil and ignorance. Society had to follow the insight of the philosopher—i.e., society had to be guided and given shape by the ideas accessible to philosophers. While Plato had originally hoped it might take the form of direct rule of a philosopher king, his disillusionment with his protégé Dionysius II of Syracuse left him with the more diminished hope that philosophers might make their contributions less directly, i.e., by means of pedagogical influence upon future statesmen (as evident in the dialogue *The Statesman*), or constitutional crafting along the lines he set out in the *Laws*.

Insofar as Plato and the writers of the Bible dwell upon the suffering that comes from evil, it is understandable why there would be various attempts, commencing with Philo, to see a profound relationship between biblical teachings and philosophical ones. Nevertheless, religion and philosophy invariably part ways over the question of how we make sense of our place in the world, and where suffering fits into that place. Judaism and Christianity (on this point they are unified), for example, and the Socratic philosophical turn are fundamentally divided on the matter of virtue and reason's role in the achievement of virtue.

What the Jews first noticed was that our failures, our "sins," are intrinsic to the woof and warp of life. It is God's power and light, not ours, that provides the possibility of redemption. Within the biblical tradition, the best a person can be is righteous. This should not be confused with virtue. For righteousness comes from obedience to God, not from the elevation and extension of the mind's powers. In large part, this is because the mind itself within this tradition receives no greater weight than anything else of and from God. In part also, this is because the language of the Bible is not grounded in abstraction or argument. It draws heavily, if not exclusively, upon the language of parable and metaphor. And in the context of that language, the miraculous "record" of God and His acts cannot readily evaporate into a more demotic or prosaic understanding of the world and the things of the world, without, at least, removing the sense of awe and wonder—and hence an important aspect of participation within reality—that inspires the writing in the first place. While the Bible is a revealed book, what it reveals is not what is knowable through the mind's analytic inspection, but through one's participation in what is, *inter alia*, an hermeneutical community. The figures and the events depicted in the Bible are meaningful to the community which receives its social and personal orientation from that work and numerous other narratives it motivates, just as the figures and events in Homer, Hesiod et al. were, for the Greeks prior to (and, for many, after) Socrates and Plato.

Moreover, as the example of King David shows: the wrong, i.e., disobedient act does not discount the action in the greater narrative of redemption, but may become a powerful "contribution" to the "covenant." This kind of thinking is not metaphysical, but it is undoubtedly still thinking, irrespective of the disdain anyone may have about how the thinking is done or what is held to be true about it. In this approach, it is neither our will, nor our understanding, but something much larger that is the real source of creation. Irrespective of what one "believes," the lesson we can learn from this is that the choice between our own consciousness and what becomes of what we do requires anthropological and psychological considerations which—if we do not unquestionably accept the Socratic claim that the unexamined life is not worth living—do not automatically enable us to say that the philosophical choice is simply better in what it makes of us or our world. Of this we can be certain: while we can argue that God does or does not exist, what is indisputable is that some kind of insight or understanding of lived experience is in operation in biblical and mythic writings. And we are perfectly at liberty to inquire whether there may be certain features of life experience that are registered by the figurative imagination. This, as Vico grasped, is to suggest that it is possible to translate from the figurative to the more abstract understanding, without having to reduce the former to the later.

Yet, if reason becomes opened up by more considerations of the sort that were originally expressed religiously and mythically rather than philosophically, imaginatively rather than conceptually, and which, nevertheless, can be assimilated to the human sciences, then it is evident that the more narrowly construed philosophical understanding is not apposite. It must "open up" its method to take account of how people understand their lives.

A fateful methodologically driven decision (even if the method was concealed in the original decision) that is conspicuous in the origin of philosophy and reproduced over the millennia lies in the original ontological and metaphysical choice about the ground of reality: is it material (with the pre-Socratics resorting to all manner of speculative possibilities), or is it mental? In the *Phaedo*, Socrates recounts how disappointed he was in learning that while Anaxagoras asserted that "it is mind that produces order and is the cause of everything" (*Phaedo* 97 b-c),[17] in fact, Anaxagoras had "made no use of mind and assigned to it no causality for the order of the world, but adduced causes like air and aether and water and many other absurdities" (*Phaedo*, 98 b-c). Socrates could rightly point to his own circumstance, and make the point that the real reasons he was sitting in prison could not be explained by his sinew and bones, joints and limbs and the like but that he is there "since Athens has thought it better to condemn me, therefore for my part have thought it better to sit here, and more right to stay and submit to whatever penalty she orders" (*Phaedo*, 98d–e). Aristotle would contribute philosophically to a more sophisticated account of causality which would account for mental purpose as well as material conditions (along with the form and producer of anything), though insofar as he retained the human dimension of causation when reflecting upon nature, he was seen by most of the modern physicians as obstructing our understanding of nature.

Dividing the world into two possible sources, material or mental, is a vastly speculative conjecture, which to be sure, like all idea-isms illumines aspects of and connections within reality otherwise not noticed. It stands, as I have suggested, in striking contrast to the Jewish and subsequent Christian insight, that is not originally presented as an argument but as a revelation that our deepest needs are not strictly material nor mental. Thus too the spirit and the soul is no more to be equated with intelligence than with the body. Thus, resurrection in the Christian tradition, with certain Jewish antecedents, is also a resurrection of the body, even if, as Paul suggests, it is a spiritual body. This is indicative of an outlook which while appealing to the spirit or soul's surmounting of the flesh's "warring members," nevertheless retains a sense of unity more consistent with everyday experience than either the metaphysical dualism argued for by Plato, and the more stringent dualisms of modern philosophy, as in Descartes and Kant, or the equally tendentious metaphysical monism of a Spinoza or Hegel.

But this fundamental decision of the Greek philosophers preceding Plato to postulate and then choose a material or intelligible essence of explication and derivation directs us into certain kinds of explanations that either sideline, overlook, or underestimate other questions and insights. An example that I take here which was taken up by Augustine, Pascal, Hamann, Kierkegaard, Max Scheler, Gabriel Marcel—all of whose philosophical thought stands in close relationship to what they see is a rich "resource" for thought that comes from religion—is the issue of the worldmaking power of our loves.

Augustine had provided the formulation that "My weight is my love. By it I am carried wherever I am carried." [18] That formulation stood in the closest relationship to his faith in a triune God, whose Son was the redeemer. Redemption itself was predicated upon a view in which the soul could either be elevated by its willing acceptance of God's grace, or its resolve to be extricated in its own morass of desires that draw it deeper into the depths of itself and its own fallen world. In Augustine free will plays a decisive role in whether the soul is elevated or drawn to the things it desires—"the body tends toward its own place by its gravity." [19] But unlike modern voluntaristic philosophies where the will is a facultative component aiding or hindering the understanding, or the metaphysical drive within the cosmos itself, in Augustine it is a potential aperture for the reception of God's grace and light—hence not my will, but "thy will be done." Thus for Augustine:

> By thy gift, we are enkindled and are carried upward. We burn inwardly and move forward. We ascend thy ladder which is in our heart, and we sing a canticle of degrees; we glow inwardly with thy fire—with thy good fire—and we go forward because we go up to the peace of Jerusalem. [20]

This also stands in close relationship to a view of Augustine about the nature and order of our loves: "there are four kinds of things that are to be loved—first, that which is above us; second, ourselves; third, that which is on a level with us; fourth, that which is beneath us. . . ." [21]

In Augustine it is the "weight" of our loves rather than our understanding, or mental aptitude that is decisive in what we do. Love is incarnatory, and since we are creatures drawn along by our loves, and thus too our hates, we are incarnatory beings: we, like our world are constantly being "fashioned" by the direction and nature of our loves. When we consider ideas as incarnatory, they move beyond being models or primary patterns or development principles, as Plato had argued. Though, insofar as words and names and, taken in its more everyday usage, "ideas" trigger or activate our loves and hates they still have potency. But then the question is, how much do we love or hate these "ideas"?

It is not that Augustine places no importance upon thought or mind, nor the material facets of existence. But his focus attunes us to a very different feature of our existence, i.e., our capacity to love, and it thus also has implications for the kind of questions we may ask. For it is not the reasonableness of a decision, nor the underlying material nature of the world that is the primary concern, but the kind of love that may be detected in action. We saw that while Plato's love for Socrates played a major part in his own activity, that, when it comes to doing philosophy, love is rendered as secondary to what is loved, and that love is for the idea, the thing in-itself. In keeping with this, Plato argues, in the *Symposium* (201d–204 c), that love is the child of resource and need "always partaking of his mother's poverty" (203 d)[22] — that is only truly satiated by the attainment of the idea of the beautiful. Ultimately the beautiful, as with truth itself, is subordinate to the idea of the good. Thus too the contemplative life must take priority over the active life—a position also held by Aristotle.

This too stands in the closest relationship to the idea that the philosophical life is the best or highest kind of life. This contrasts not only with Augustine but the Christian (and Jewish, and, in this instance, the Muslim and Buddhist) view of life, all of which present existence in a way where intelligence is not as privileged in the overall scheme of life, but has to be gauged in a much larger schema of powers and processes and circumstances. Moreover, as we have suggested above, because of this, our respective appraisals and appeals will differ considerably according to whether we accentuate intelligence and understanding rather than the nature or quality of our loves.

One can also make the case that the philosophical binary over the question of worldmaking can, then, be put aside as one raises questions about the lovable nature of the world. To be sure, the question of whether we rightly understand what we love is a legitimate question, and it is one that may occur alongside the emphasis upon our loves. This is very conspicuous, for example, in Dante whose *Comedy* is the most detailed poetic exploration of the "meaning," "direction," and "weights" of our loves, and who makes of love the great moving force of the cosmos itself, or, as he puts it in the final line of the *Comedy*: "By the love which moves the Sun and other Stars." Once hermeneutics is allowed for, the subordination of reason to revelation is not an invitation to "irrationalism," but a taking stock of the limits of what reason can do and what purpose it serves in the greater scheme of life, which presents us—or reveals to us—an array of contingencies whose meaning is not solely tapered to, or in some instances simply not the kind of things that fit, philosophical reasoning, even if they are perfectly understandable to members within a hermeneutical community. We might say members of a hermeneutical community think with their hearts—not to mention guts—as well as their minds.

It is this recognition that we can discern in Pascal's split between reasons of the heart and those of the head:

> We know the truth not only through our reasons but also through our heart, it is through the latter that we know first principles, and reason, which has nothing to do with it, tries in vain to refute them. The sceptics have no other object than that, and they work at it to no purpose. We know that we are not dreaming, but, however, unable we may be to prove it rationally, our inability proves nothing but the weakness of our reason, and not the uncertainty of our knowledge, as they maintain. For knowledge of first principles, like space, time, motion, number, is solid as any derived through reason and it is on such knowledge, coming from the heart and instinct, that reason has to depend and base all its argument. The heart feels there are spatial dimensions and that there is an infinite series of numbers, and reason goes on to demonstrate that there are two square numbers of which one is double the other. Principles are felt, propositions proved, and both with certainty though by different means, it is just as pointless and absurd for reason to demand proof of first principles from the heart before agreeing to accept them as it would be absurd for the heart to demand an intuition of all the positions demonstrated by reason before agreeing to them. Our inability must serve therefore to humble reason which would like to be the judge of everything, but not to confute our certainty.[23]

In keeping with this distinction, Pascal eschewed the fateful move in the development of modern metaphysics that comes from the elevation of the understanding over the imagination, to the detriment of the kinds of contingent truths of the heart which are so closely associated with love, faith, and habit. Such "truths," by virtue of their very contingent nature, are often incapable of being defined as propositions and then axiomatically developed. This is also, as Pascal and later thinkers like Hamann, Herder, and even Nietzsche and Heidegger had grasped, why the poetic thinking of figure is, if understood aright, resistant to metaphysical refutation. Pascal himself had noted in a fragment entitled "Figurative Language in Bible and Human Relations":

> Among the Jews the truth was only figurative; in heaven it is revealed,
> In the Church it is concealed and recognized by its relationship to the figurative,
> The figure was drawn from the truth,

And the truth was recognized from the figure. [24]

Pascal was deeply conscious of the fact that he was part of a greater tradition of thought and action and decisions that had expressed itself in figurative form: and the figurative rendition of specificity and generality does not begin in the kind of coherence of members within an ideational unity, definitional precision, or ideational clarity and distinctness that Plato and Descartes and subsequent philosophers of the "idea" have sought.

From within this alternative tradition we can observe that while reason or the "intellect" is "humbled" (and Christian thinkers like Hamann and Kierkegaard both embrace and take seriously Socrates' more humble statements about his own reason, whilst providing styles of thinking that are anti-Platonic and anti-metaphysical), our intellect, like all other powers of our bodies and soul, is a gift. The purpose of our reason, though, is not exhaustively recognizable to itself, but only revealed through something beyond itself: for these men this was how faith was not the enemy of reason, but its foundation, constant accompaniment, and completion.

Reason like every other power is disclosed or revealed through its doings, operations and achievements. To think that reason can surmount itself to view itself from outside itself as opposed to identifying its activity within the world and itself is to place a weight upon it that does it no justice. This was essentially behind Rosenzweig's (Nietzschean and Jewish) critical account of philosophy in Part One of *The Star of Redemption* where he demonstrates how all attempts to know the "All" inevitably end in failure because the All is not reasonable, and reason is not the All. Reason is something that occurs within life; it may help us get from a to b, but it must always allow for the interruption of contingencies beyond its own making. It is precisely this emphasis upon reason's limits and the accompanying appeal to a loving God's power as well as the power of love itself to transcend limits identifiable by reason alone that originally provided an alternative hermeneutical tradition to the metaphysical tradition within philosophy. The more metaphysically driven philosophies, commencing with Descartes, including even atheistic existentialists, most obviously Sartre, have elevated reason and the understanding to the extent that the limit condition is not so much in *kind* but in *time*. The solution to our greatest problems are essentially a matter of time; i.e., if we have enough time and keep searching, a method will come.

With the modern reinvigoration, reapplication and elevation of the philosophical mind in the process of worldmaking, the axiomatic or "geometrical" (Spinoza) development of ethical, aesthetic, and political ideas or essences became the means by which our aspirations and deeds are primarily to be appraised. And with that, the importance of love as a power that is beyond the exhaustive power of the understanding tends to be relegated to the more mythic and purely personal powers of the imagination and social "channels" of theater, novels, movies, songs, etc. It was precisely this displacement occurring alongside reason's elevation that thinkers like Pascal, Hamann, Kierkegaard, Max Scheler, Rosenstock-Huessy, Rosenzweig, Marcel, and Unamuno responded against. It is well put by Scheler in what is essentially a restatement of Augustine:

> Whether I am investigating the innermost essence of an individual, a historical era, a family, a people, a nation, of an individual, or any sociohistorical group, I will know and understand it most profoundly when I have discerned the system of its concrete value-assessments and value-preference, whatever organization this system has. I call this system the ethos of any such subject. The fundamental root of this ethos is, first, *the order of love and hate*, the organization of these two dominating passions, within a social class which has become exemplary for the others.[25]

This distinctly Augustinian hierarchy also finds an expanded application in Eugen Rosenstock-Huessy's interpretation of the major revolutions of the Western world. His opening gambit—"Our passions give life to the world. Our collective passions constitute the history of mankind"[26]—is soon followed by the citation provided below, which will provide the "method" for his reading of the revolutionary irruptions, fall-outs and emergence of novel creative forms that come from the overthrowing of institutions and relationships that have become so hateful that great groups of people would rather leap into an unknown future in the hope of discovering a world more in keeping with its passions, faith, and loves than abide in their world. The world that they seek flight from, which has become hell, though, was once too founded by loves, as well as the hates directed at a preceding order.

> Now, this work intends to disclose an intelligible sequence in the course of human passions, follies, and beliefs. The history of our era which, at first sight and in our times, may seem a crude encyclopaedia of all possible methods of government and public morals, is at closer inspection one ineluctable order of alternating passions of the human heart. As in individual life, every one of the passions calls for the next. The deeper and truer it is, the more urgently does it call. For such is the noble nature of man, that his heart will never wholly lose itself in one single passion or idol, or, as people call it apologetically, one idea. On it goes from one devotion to the next, not because it is ashamed of its first love, but because it must be on fire perpetually. To fall from Reason, as our grandfathers did, is but one Fall of Man among his many passionate attempts to find the apples of knowledge and eternal life, both in one.
>
> When a nation or individual declines the experiences that present themselves to passionate hearts only, they are automatically turned out from the realm of history. The heart of man either falls in love with somebody or something, or it falls ill. It can never go unoccupied. And

the great question for mankind is what is to be loved or hated next, whenever an old love or fear has lost its hold.[27]

I leave to one side the question of whether Rosenstock-Huessy's work successfully identifies the "intelligible sequence in the course of human passions, follies, and beliefs." More important for what follows is simply to underscore that while philosophy has tended to follow Plato in its idea-ism, what Rosenstock-Huessy above identified as an "idol," another way to view philosophy is to see it as one power among many other powers that enhance our understanding of life, the world, and humanity in general. That has tended to be a path less taken within modern philosophy, as we now follow the dynamic of the major paradigmatic contributions of modern philosophy, as it moves from either idea to idea, or idol to idol.

NOTES

1. *A Lexicon Abridged from Liddell and Scott's Greek-English Lexicon* (Oxford: Clarendon Press, 1977), 195.

2. Paul Friedländer, *Plato, Volume 1: An Introduction* (London: Routledge and Kegan Paul, 1958), translated by Hans Meyerhoff, 15.

3. Laszlo Versényi, *Man's Measure: A Study of the Greek Image of Man from Homer* (Albany; State University of New York Press, 1974). In the section "Homeric Questions" in *Order and History, Volume 2: The World of the Polis* (Baton Rouge: Louisiana State University, 1957), Eric Voegelin focuses upon passages in Homer, Hesiod, and Pindar which "together formulate the great theme of blindness and seeing that recurs in Aeschylus and Plato: Who sees the world is blind and needs the help of the Muses to gain the true sight of wisdom; and who is blind to the world, is seeing in the wisdom of sweet song. The Muses, and through them the poets, are the helpers of man who seeks to ascend from his darkness to light," 73. The tension between blindness and sight is developed throughout the entire volume and the triumph and nature of insight is a central theme of the third volume of *Order and History, Plato and Aristotle* (1957).

4. Bruno Snell, *The Discovery of the Mind: The Greek Origins of European Thought*, translated T. G. Rosenmeyer (Oxford: Basil Blackwell, 1953), 17–18.

5. Walter J. Ong, *The Presence of the Word: Some Prolegomena for Cultural and Religious History* (Minneapolis: University of Minnesota Press, 1967), 12.

6. Thorleif Boman, *Hebrew Thought Compared with Greek* (London: SCM Press, 1960), 56. James Barr, in *The Semantics of Biblical Language* (Oxford: Oxford University Press, 1961), is highly critical of what he sees as Boman's "linguistic determinism," but Boman's more fundamental point about an aural versus visual orientation is important.

7. Boman, *Hebrew Thought Compared with Greek*, 56.

8. It is a great pity that Herder's lengthy, two volume, *Metakritik zur Kritik der reinen Vernunft* is almost unknown outside of Herder scholarship, and more often (and, in my view, mistakenly) dismissed as failing to understand Kant. Herder also devoted another substantial critique of Kant (specifically Kant's third Critique), *Kalligone*. Both are included in Johann Gottfried Herder, *Schriften zu Literatur und Philosophie, 1792–1800*, (ed.) Hans Dietrich Irmscher (Frankfurt am Maine: Deutscher Klassiker Verlag, 1998).

9. Herder, *Im Kreuz der Wirchlichkeit*, Volume 2, 340.

10. See *Theaetetus* 186 a-b. Also *Sophist* 259 a-b, in Plato, *Theaetetus and Sophist*, translated by H. N. Fowler (London: William Heinemann, 1928), and *Parmenides*143–146, in Plato, *Cratylus, Parmenides, Greater Hippias, Lesser Hippias*, translated by H. N. Fowler (London: William Heinemann, 1926).

11. *I am an Impure Thinker* (Norwich, Vt: Argo, 2001), foreword by W. H. Auden, 77–90. A number of philosophers have written on naming, but none has done it with more doggedness and insight than Rosenstock-Huessy, for whom the importance of names drives his numerous writings on "speech."

12. *Cratylus*, 440b–d.

13. *Cratylus*, 439 b.

14. *Timaeus*, 28–29 in Plato, *Timaeus, Critias, Cleitophon, Menexenus, Epistles*, translated R. G. Bury (London: William Heinemann, 1929).

15. The most focused discussions of method, apart from the discussion of the divided line, and the reinvigorated critique of the poets in book X of the *Republic*, are to be found in the *Theatetus, Philebus*, and, most significantly, the *Parmenides, Sophist*, and *Statesman*. The latter two deal with types that have generally played a perverted role within the polis. But whereas the sophists are a type that is a corrupt and shabby simulacrum of the philosopher, and hence are unnecessary, statesmen are necessary types, but they need to know what they are doing — which is to say, in general, they need to be very different from how they have been heretofore.

16. *Sophist*, 218–B-C.

17. *Phaedo*, translated by Hugh Tredennick in *The Collected Dialogues of Plato Including the Letters*, edited by Edith Hamilton and Huntington Cairns (Princeton, NJ: Princeton University Press, 1962).

18. St. Augustine, *Confessions*, in *Confessions and Enchiridion* (Grand Rapids, MI: Christian Ethereal Library, 1955), translated by Albert Outler, chapter IX, Book 12, 235.

19. Ibid.

20. Ibid.

21. *On Christian Doctrine* in *The Works of Augustine Vol. IX*, translated by Marcus Dodds (Edinburgh: T. and T. Clark, 1892), 20.

22. Plato's *Symposium*, translated by Michael Joyce, in *Collected Dialogues including Letters*.

23. Blaise Pascal, *Pensées*, translated by A. J. Krailsheimer, (Harmondsworth: Penguin, 1966), 58.

24. Ibid., 277.

25. Max Scheler, "Ordo Amoris," in *Selected Philosophical Essays*, translated by David Lachterman (Evanston, IL: Northwestern University Press, 1973), 98–99.

26. Eugen Rosenstock-Huessy, *Out of Revolution: Autobiography of Western Man*, 3.

27. Ibid., 4.

TWO

Mechanistic Metaphysics, the "Way of Ideas," and the Understanding's Rule of the Imagination

DESCARTES AND THE CLEAR AND DISTINCT IDEAS OF THE UNDERSTANDING

What in the previous chapter I called micro-cognitive states, or "instincts," do not convey the kind of information that comes from the "setting up" or "construction" of variables which are transposed onto a theoretically designated field. The appearance of Newton or Einstein is the result of multiple explorations that may have little to do with instinct, with one exception—the instinct which may "kick in" once the designated data itself becomes a kind of object of mental play, relations not obviously mapped out are "picked up" by cognition, often when it is more relaxed, not looking, in sleep or daydream. It is essential in reflecting upon knowing to distinguish between constructive modeling and intimation, or "sensing" in the most primordial manner. Contra Kant, whose critique of Leibniz is built round the privileging of the scientific model as the epistemic reality to be explained, Leibniz is correct to identify this process as one of degree rather than kind. On the other hand, constructive modeling focuses attention upon a "problem," which is only possible once a great deal of abstraction has taken place, once a number of conditions and variables are construed with precision and once their meaning has been stabilised within the problematic. This modeling requires processing "data," which Kant classifies as a representation (*Vorstellung*); "representation" is the generic term to cover either an intuition or concept, while the "concept" is what provides a representation with meaning. The term and cleavage are apposite in that they betray an empiricist commitment commensurate with the mechanistic imagination which wipes away the general meanings of the world, and hence of lived experience to reappraise them anew in order to ensure that *this time* our representations convey the reality that is really in conformity to what the laws of nature enable, rather than what our mere imaginings substitute in their place. This is evident time and time again in the various cognitive investigations of the mechanistic metaphysicians.

While Bacon is a major figure in the history of the modern mind, and his identification in the *New Organon*, of the idols of the tribe, cave, market, and theater are invaluable "directions" for freeing ourselves from prejudicial and distorted natural inquiries, his impact remained dominant among thinkers whose observations of the natural were not dictated by nature's numbers, but by its types.[1] Nevertheless, Kant uses a passage from Bacon's *Great Instauration* as the epigraph to the *Critique of Pure Reason* and refers, in the preface to the second edition of that work, to Bacon's "ingenious proposals," which "partly initiated" the discovery of natural science (understood by Kant as mathematical physics).[2] But, as is all too evident in the fact that Kant's transcendental critique is erected around problems of mathematical physics that superseded Bacon, Bacon's views on science were themselves philosophically superseded, though not necessarily by all, in the evolution of the metaphysics accompanying the more mechanistic sciences. Conversely, though, Bacon's writings often retained their importance for those who resisted taking metaphysical and epistemological ideas that only occluded the non-mechanical, and more specifically human side, of the natural. Thus Vico, Herder, and even Hamann saw that Bacon was no enemy of the historical and anthropological dimensions of natural experience that was their focus, and they all cite him as a source of inspiration.

There is then a very sound reason why the opening gambit in modern metaphysics is attributed to Descartes and not Bacon. For it was not Bacon, but Descartes who first saw (a) that the new scientific discoveries in physics were but components of a totality of intermeshed laws, and (b) that the mistaken observations about nature by the philosophers of antiquity were all part of a false picture of the universe that had sprang from their bad metaphysics. He provided a new metaphysics for explicating why all nature, as Galileo had put it, could be read as a book written in the language of figure and number. The new metaphysics required accepting that that book could only be accessed through a complete reworking of how we go about knowing and where our focus of knowledge needs to be directed. Descartes, as we all know, subjects everything to doubt, only to realize he must, even when he doubts everything, still be thinking. That "hyperbolic" moment of doubt has one all-important consequence: reality as we think we know it is dissolved, so that it can be properly "espied," and "de-composed" and "re-composed" for the purpose of more closely aligning cause and effect. This act of subjection of the entire universe is the methodological "moment" which itself provides a model to enable modeling. Nevertheless, and his own vast ambition to the contrary (not ameliorated by the self-deprecatory persona he adopts in *Discourse on Method* to advance it), Descartes no more than anyone else subjects all things to doubt—one simply cannot do it. Or to rephrase that, one can subject the world as object to doubt only by changing it into a model. I can study breathing by objectifying it, but I cannot study breathing if I am not breathing. The act to be studied is only partially "the act"; the study of a process is not identical with the process: the former requires a representation, the latter does not.

The representation of what makes the world—the world being but a totality of laws—is comprehensible (and most lucidly spelled out by Descartes in the first chapter of his *Discourse on Method* and *Rules for Conducting the Mind*) via the break-down of the particular phenomenon to be understood into its smallest components, which will gradually be reassembled as each part in its relationship to others has been understood. Descartes's purpose, as evident in his works on analytic geometry, meteorology and optics, is to break complex phenomenon down into simple models. While Descartes's epistemological orientation hugely contributed to changing the very nature of philosophy, his scientific "solutions" only rarely successfully combined the two essential components of the "new science"—experiment/modeling and mathematics. But he certainly knew that this pairing held the keys to the new kingdom. So did Galileo, but his focus is directed to bodies in motion, while with Descartes, the study of bodily substances will provide a full picture of the "world"; though what the study of bodily substance cannot disclose are the cognitive functions we deploy methodologically to know the world.

The recognition by figures such as Galileo that what we call nature had to be broken up into what we see and think to be true and what we know to be true, that is the old Platonic distinction between appearance and reality (and the various cognates of reason versus unreason, opinion versus knowledge, etc.) had led to a distinction between primary and secondary qualities, that is, the realities of the world and the mere everyday (mis)perceptions.[3] Descartes's universal act of doubt was a grand gesture of philosophical theater which magnificently represented the *meaning* of the new science, at least with respect to how we needed to view our everyday experiences with suspicion if we wished to improve our lot. But if Descartes's contribution to the scientific method and to popularizing it had ensured him international repute (and in some quarters infamy), philosophy was embroiled in questions about two of the most fundamental "elements" that were intrinsic to this revolutionary way of thinking about the world (which to be sure had had distant antecedents, and were known to do so, in antiquity, particularly in Stoic and Epicurean accounts of the universe).

It may seem strange that philosophers who were so committed to understanding the world around them would become so enmeshed in metaphysical problems, which seen from outside may be as bizarre as scholastic disputes about the nature of angels, but the problems they grappled with were the inevitable result of the demand for stringency and precision. Even more importantly questions that had emerged simply out of the way nature was to be conceived were seen as touching the very core of what a human being was and thus what society should be. The fact that Christendom had been so vehemently fractured by religious wars plays no small part in the huge importance that metaphysical claims drawn from the study of nature were taking on by philosophers and theologians.

That Descartes was such a pivotal figure in making the problems of scientific inquiry part of a greater metaphysical canvass is undeniable. The question of dualism in Descartes (which he only too willingly seizes on metaphysically as a demonstration of religious sincerity) emerges from the extension of his doubt coming up against the resistance point of thinking. Thinking and spirit/mind are identical—thought is nothing but an amalgam of operations, "a thing that doubts, understands, affirms, denies, wills, refuses, and that also imagines and senses."[4] It cannot be an extended thing, as is evident if we put to any of these operations questions of the sort that we would put to natural objects—e.g., how many inches wide or what color is my doubting what I have just heard? If one takes Descartes at his word and follows his prescription not to "accept any opinion in my writings or elsewhere as true, unless they very clearly see it is deduced from true Principles"[5]—the all-important distinction between *res mentis* and *res extensa* simply comes down to function: the function of methodological orientation requires that the mind not be confused with the extended substance to be known.[6] That is what his argument genuinely establishes methodologically. But when it came to demonstrating that the metaphysical implications of his teachings were thoroughly consistent with traditional Christian metaphysics, Descartes will play up the old vocabulary of soul and spirit in an environment of great hostility to someone who is rendering as nonsensical all that precedes the great all-encompassing methodological act of doubting with what is going on in the material world—while being cautious enough to emphasize his obedience to the laws and customs of his country (chapter 3 of the *Discourse*). This suggests that Descartes was fully cognizant of the enmity that he was provoking.[7]

While more overtly materialistic philosophers such as Hobbes could not abide Descartes's dualism, the overwhelming legacy of Descartes lay less in his metaphysic being able to satisfy all committed to the common project of trying to discover the laws of nature to improve the lot of human beings than in the decisive philosophical shift he had achieved. With Descartes the new philosophical emphasis was upon questions that were implicated in nature being a totality of potentially discoverable laws, and in the methodological demand for clarity and distinctness in perception. This in turn involved the privileging of mathematical and geometrical relationships and scientifically verifiable models as the means to approach the proper order of causation.[8] The more general insight that we cannot trust our mere perceptions, but only methodologically sound ones is behind Descartes's insistence that "since I now know that even bodies are not, properly speaking, perceived by the senses or by the faculty of imagination, but by the intellect alone, and that they are not perceived through their being touched or seen, but only through their being understood"[9] holds as much for Newton's *Principia* with its defense of the principle so anathema to Descartes and his followers, of there being "action at a distance," as it does for Descartes's own intended forays into natural science. For the understanding here does not mean logical understanding—this is precisely why Aristotelianism can no longer be tolerated when it comes to discovering nature—but "the light of reason," insofar as it provides a sound understanding which is primarily concerned with mathematical and experimental models. Newton's famous riposte to the Cartesians—"Hypotheses non fingo" ("I do not deal in hypotheses") is precisely an appeal to the understanding in which observation, model, and mathematics all line up—in spite of a mystery that is posed by the mind wanting a logical coherence that could only be satisfied were material relations, not what they are demonstrated by Newton to be. Not surprisingly, given this philosophical movement away from logic to observable quantifiable models, Descartes's flaw was to let his own imagination do too much of the work to help make sense of the data.

Nevertheless, when it comes to Descartes's metaphysical treatment of the soul and God, while there is, at the very least, a case for being somewhat incredulous about the ease with which Descartes moves an epistemic operation of absolute radicality to a metaphysic of ostensibly such staunch traditionalism,[10] it was the case that as the mechanistic view of life spread it was very quickly defended by philosophers who wanted to demonstrate the compatibility of the modern style of metaphysics with more traditional metaphysics. Thus, for example Henry More, in his *An Antidote Against Atheism* marshals Descartes into an army of ostensibly like-minded souls who include Moses, Pythagoras, Plato, Philo, and the cabbalists. For all his appeals to the Christian faith, More in his invocations of the ancients and Jews against scholasticism and atheists is a traditionalist only insofar as he is also a modern syncretist. Malebranche also focuses upon the metaphysical "fallout" and possibilities of mechanism and with some tweaking finds fundamental symmetries between Augustine and Descartes, which we discuss in a later chapter. In this respect Descartes had provided a clue to a link in that his argument from doubt was a replay of Augustine—but with one all important difference, the thinking self in Descartes is not just a passing point of reference as it is in Augustine, who places the thinking self with all his anxiety under the dominion of the almighty God and his commandments. In Descartes this thinking self becomes a fulcrum for rethinking the world. The metaphysical grounding of the subject takes place in a work where all authority other than its methodologically sound deliberations and observations (i.e., what conforms to the analytic/synthetic method) is merely custom. And the real Cartesian ethics is an extension of physics—mere deference to custom and authority is, within a consistent Cartesian approach, provisional and nothing to do with truth.

Irrespective of the different metaphysical "solutions" proffered by philosophers after Descartes, the role of the mind and its operations in knowing, which Descartes saw as in need of fundamental explication given that nature hides and common sense deludes, would be central to much of the philosophical tradition committed to understanding the totality of nature's law culminating in Kant.

Objects, knowledge, and the mind's operations were all part of the one problematic that converged around what Spinoza would call "the idea of everything that is caused depends on a knowledge of the cause, whereof it is an effect," which for Spinoza is but a proof of the proposition that "the order and connection of ideas is the same as the order and connection of things,"[11] and "the ideas" being "the mental conception which is formed by the mind as a thinking thing."[12] Although Spinoza is embroiled in the matter of method and cognitive operations every bit as much as Descartes, he seeks to clear up the latter's dualism by claiming "that substance thinking and substance extension are one and the same substance comprehended now through one attribute, now through another."[13] In my view (albeit not the standard one) Spinoza is reaching the same solution that Descartes has—but he is clearer about it: Descartes had (I think deliberately) conflated talk of the soul so that it could appear under one or the other optic. For in Descartes's *Passions of the Soul* it is obvious that once the soul is being explored without any need for representing cognitive operations or functions within the context of method, the narrative is utterly materialist, and the psychology is a pioneering work in behavioral psychology. The pineal gland which is ostensibly the location of soul that animated bodily activity is clearly *res extensa* posing as *res mentis*. On the other hand, when Descartes speaks of cognition in the context of method he does not invoke the pineal gland. When Descartes dons the scholastic posture to engage in tradition metaphysics he does indeed make the slippage from assemblage of cognitive functions to a substance—but having unequivocally divided substances into two kinds, he rules out the more traditional Christian understanding of the soul, which is neither mind nor body, but something else altogether, which has nothing genuinely in common with Descartes's cognitive bundle constituting *res mentis*. Likewise, the Christian view of the body had nothing in common with Descartes's *res extensa*. And the same is the case when one considers Descartes's "God." If the nature of Descartes's God bears little resemblance to Yahweh and the father, it can hardly be a surprise that what exactly Descartes proves by the existence of "God" has little to do with the lives of those who are faithful to their God, and who do not await some philosopher providing validation of a power who they see as their creator. The question that must be posed is what exactly does Descartes's proof deliver? And that most accurate answer is that Descartes's metaphysical proof for the existence of God serves no other philosophical function than to ensure that the universe is law-like, and hence not miraculously interfered with (which is, of course, yet one more break with the traditional Christian view of God and His relationship to us and our world). Nevertheless, the proof of God's existence is represented by Descartes in the *Meditations* as somehow a great demonstration of faith and conviction. I think, to put it mildly, that there is all the difference in the world between the motives behind the metaphysics of the Cambridge Platonists and Descartes. But as my previous comment about Henry More suggests, the Cambridge Platonists are not traditionally Christian either. Both (and this is also as true of Berkeley and Malebranche as of Hobbes, Spinoza, Bayle et al.) are symptomatic of a new style of philosophizing and theologizing: the new style of theologizing may immerse itself in "traditional" arguments about God, the world and reason, but this God no longer has the same institutional alliance with the Church: for these thinkers there is no Church as such anymore. Philosophers no longer serve the Church but God directly (whether they are ostensibly Catholic is irrelevant) as an "object"/idea of rational inquiry—or if they do not believe in this object/idea they turn away and face nature itself. If Plato had demanded that all knowledge must be of ideas, I think it fair to say that even though the kind of modeling preoccupying the mechanistic thinkers was far from anything he had in mind, the preoccupation with materiality did not diminish in the philosophical mind the need to identify what ideas were.

Again let us consider Descartes. For the question of knowing the *res extensa* would end up being not only as much for the nature of nature as for the nature of ideas. For the knowledge of the former—as opposed to an immediate encounter, a view, or bump, etc.—could simply not be acquired without proper orientation. Descartes would pose the problem thus:

> good order seems to demand that I first group all my thoughts into certain classes, and ask in which of them truth or falsity properly resides. Some of these thoughts are like images of things; to these alone does the word "idea" properly apply, as when I think of a man, or a chimera, or the sky, or an angel, or God. Again there are other thoughts that take different forms: for example, when I will, or fear, or affirm, or deny, there is always something that I grasp as the subject of my

thought, yet I embrace in my thought something more than the likeness of that thing. Some of these thoughts are called volitions or affects, while others are called judgments. Now as far as ideas are concerned, if they are considered alone and in their own right, without being referred to something else, they cannot, properly speaking, be false. For whether it is a she-goat or a chimera that I am imagining, it is no less true that I imagine the one than the other. Moreover, we need not fear that there is falsity in the will itself or in the affects, for although I can choose evil things or even things that are utterly non-existent, I cannot conclude from this that it is untrue that I do choose these things. Thus there remain only judgments in which I must take care not to be mistaken. Now the principal and most frequent error to be found in judgments consists in the fact that I judge that the ideas which are in me are similar to or in conformity with certain things outside me. Obviously, if I were to consider these ideas merely as certain modes of my thought, and were not to refer them to anything else, they could hardly give me any subject matter for error.[14]

Getting the right idea so that one may have the correct judgment is decisive. The metaphysical bifurcation over the matter of mind and body,—most famously Descartes, the Cambridge Platonists, Leibniz, Berkeley, on the one hand, Hobbes, Spinoza, Gassendi, Locke, on the other—and the (even more questionable) epistemological one of rationalists versus empiricists, tends to obfuscate the fact that the disputes that arise from the bifurcation between rationalists and empiricists arise because of a shared commitment to a common set of elements and procedures.[15] For the world has been reconfigured as an infinite body that may also be rendered as a body of infinites, or, as Descartes preferred leaving the designation of infinite to God, "indefinites." The fact of orientation remained as Spinoza put it—and in a manner completely in keeping with Descartes above which is a rejection of any logicist residues of the sort they generally (Leibniz excepted) attributed to Aristotle's unfortunate legacy—one of idea and method:

> method is not identical with reasoning in the search for causes, still less is it the comprehension of the causes of things: it is the discernment of a true idea, by distinguishing it from other perceptions, and by investigating its nature, in order that we may thus know our power of understanding, and may so train our mind that it may, by a given standard, comprehend whatsoever is intelligible, by laying down certain rules as aids, and by avoiding useless mental exertion.
>
> Whence we may gather that method is nothing else than reflective knowledge, or the idea of an idea; and that as there can be no idea of an idea—unless an idea exists previously—there can be no method without a pre-existent idea. Therefore, that will be a good method which shows us how the mind should be directed, according to the standard of the given true idea.[16]

LOCKE'S ATTEMPT TO PROVIDE GREATER CERTAINTY ABOUT THE NATURE OF IDEAS FOR THE UNDERSTANDING

The attempt to "lock down" precisely what is involved in having a healthy grasp of reality led to numerous "rigorous" analyses which came to completely antithetical solutions. Let us briefly compare the attempts by Locke and Malebranche (although we shall return to Malebranche in more detail in the next chapter), both of whom think that people's minds are, not to put too fine a point of it, full of rubbish because they have been misled by the imagination. For Malebranche, "Imagination is a lunatic that likes to play the fool. Its leaps and unforeseen starts distract you, and me as well."[17] Though, he adds, "if you are determined to curb your imagination you'll meet no obstacles to entering the place where reason gives its responses; and when you have listened to it for a while you will find that what has appealed to you up to now is negligible, and (if God touches your heart) you will even find it disgusting."[18] The purpose of Locke's *An Essay Concerning Human Understanding* is not so different from Malebranche's metaphysical inquiries, even if the conclusions are antithetical, and their metaphysical proclivities differ in accordance with their temperaments: "to inquire into the original, certainty, and extent of human knowledge, together with the grounds and degrees of belief, opinion, and assent."[19] And the way he will achieve this is:

> First, I shall inquire into the original of those ideas, notions, or whatever else you please to call them, which a man observes, and is conscious to himself he has in his mind; and the ways whereby the understanding comes to be furnished with them.
>
> Secondly, I shall endeavour to show what knowledge the understanding hath by those ideas; and the certainty, evidence, and extent of it. Thirdly, I shall make some inquiry into the nature and grounds of faith or opinion: whereby I mean that assent which we give to any proposition as true, of whose truth yet we have no certain knowledge. And here we shall have occasion to examine the reasons and degrees of assent.[20]

Locke's view of the mind is an instrumental one, so is Malebranche's, though Malebranche is more overt in making a concordance between what he takes as the spiritual ends of life and what our knowledge is for. Had either said "up until now none has really quite grasped exactly how to breathe or use our arms or legs or hands" it would be hard for anyone to take either seriously. But insofar as both are talking about "cleaning" up how we use our minds, they remains firmly in the Platonist tradition and its preoccupation with ideas in themselves. Thus for Locke: "Every man being conscious to himself that he thinks; and that which his mind is applied about while thinking being the ideas that are there."[21] Locke and Malebranche are attempting to "make sense" of the reality they discern, and the means of discernment or understanding, as revealed by the advances in the mechanistic science places them very much within the same camp. Both are also very conscious of the broader cultural and social impacts that flow from how reality is "pictured," and endeavor to contribute to a richer understanding of how we should live with each other, and what life is all about. But they are antithetical in what they see as providing the certainty that they argue they have. In much the same way as the earliest speculative philosophers into the origin of the universe, having accepted the idea of an overarching unity of existence, had divided over all the possible original sources they could conceive, Locke and Malebranche present two of the antithetical positions spawned by the mechanistic metaphysical paradigm.

Not the least reason for their inability to reach agreement about how to ensure the certitude guaranteed by the understanding has to do with their respective conceptions of the most basic element of the narrative: the nature of the idea itself. Both take their cue from Descartes on the importance of clear and distinct ideas, though Locke suggests that the terms "clear" and "distinct" would be clearer were they nominated as "determinate" and "determined," respectively.[22] Both can also be seen with good reason as reacting critically to Descartes's theory of mind and ideas. Locke's "first book" of the *Essay* declares "Neither Principles nor ideas are innate," that is anything that does not have its basis in experience. In his appeal to experience, Locke is no more—nor less—committed to experimental science than Descartes was. It was just that Descartes did think that it made little sense to speak of a broad range of metaphysical, mathematical, logical "entities" such as "God, himself, thing, thought, truth, mind, body, triangles, and the number three"[23] as deriving from the senses, mainly because they were (as Kant would more elegantly formulate the problem of epistemic and cognitive filters) the conditions for understanding experiences. To be sure, compared to Kant, Descartes's innate ideas look something of a grab bag, but Locke's response, for all its aspirations, and allowing for the fact that Locke enters into a more elaborate discussion on the nature of words and addresses the problem of moral knowledge, was no more compelling than Descartes's. (Descartes treats ethics very cursorily—as custom, which, for the sake of convenience, one would be advised to conform to, and, philosophically, as a branch of physics, whose details he leaves to others.) As Hegel points out, in spite of Locke's intention, Locke's philosophy does not end up being any less dualist than Descartes's.[24] From the outset, Locke is stuck with the dualism of the human understanding and sensory experience. He then concedes—in a curious apologetic manner—that he cannot get off the ground without speaking of ideas:

> But, before I proceed on to what I have thought on this subject, I must here in the entrance beg pardon of my reader for the frequent use of the

word idea, which he will find in the following treatise. It being that term which, I think, serves best to stand for whatsoever is the object of the understanding when a man thinks, I have used it to express whatever is meant by phantasm, notion, species, or whatever it is which the mind can be employed about in thinking; and I could not avoid frequently using it. I presume it will be easily granted me.[25]

Having granted this much—i.e., that the very term which is supposed to be demonstrated to be a derivative now turns out to be an essential condition for our understanding—the *Essay* transports the reader straight to the reef of the very divide he ensures us he will cross. Thus having announced there are no innate ideas, and that there is "one word" (viz. "experience") that answers the question: "How comes it [the mind] to be furnished? Whence comes it by that vast store which the busy and boundless fancy of man has painted on it with an almost endless variety? Whence has it all the materials of reason and knowledge?" he then immediately divides ideas into two classes:

> In that all our knowledge is founded; from that it ultimately derives itself. Our observation employed either, about external sensible objects, or about the internal operations of our minds perceived and reflected on by ourselves, is that which supplies our understandings with all the materials of thinking. These two are the fountains of knowledge, from whence all the ideas we have, or can naturally have, do spring.[26]

It is evident that Locke generally takes experience to be what exactly conforms to the "objects" of mechanical philosophy, which, we recall from Descartes (also Malebranche), is precisely what we cannot trust the senses to convey to us. That is, he is addressing "method-dependent" experiences. Moreover, Locke defending another dualism—that between qualities in bodies and ideas, which he indicates is essential for his undertaking because without the distinction "it were impossible to discourse intelligibly"[27]—begs pardon to "this little excursion into natural philosophy."[28] But this entrance into natural philosophy, which is introduced as if it were an aside, is really at the center of the undertaking. Just a few pages earlier—again the move is made with Locke's impeccable manners as he engages the reader's forbearance—in order to discover the nature of our ideas better and—again—"to discourse of them intelligibly,"[29]

> it will be convenient to distinguish them as they are ideas or perceptions in our minds; and as they are modifications of matter in the bodies that cause such perceptions in us: that so we may not think (as perhaps usually is done) that they are exactly the images and resemblances of something inherent in the subject; most of those of sensation being in the mind no more the likeness of something existing without us, than the names that stand for them are the likeness of our ideas, which yet upon hearing they are apt to excite in us.[30]

Locke certainly wants to extricate all the bits and pieces of mind and sensation, just as he wants to make experience the basis of knowledge. But every step he takes further implicates method and sensation within the paradigm that guides the entire endeavor: that he did not see this as a problem is hardy the point. Not surprisingly, he appeals to "original or primary qualities" — "solidity, extension, figure, motion or rest, and number,"[31] and secondary qualities such as "colours, sounds, tastes," "qualities which are nothing in the objects themselves but powers to produce various sensations in us by their primary qualities."[32]

In turn Locke will argue that all complex ideas are composed of simple ideas, which he sees as reducible to three types: modes, substances, and relations.[33] That the complex ideas Locke then analyzes by examining their constituent simple parts (including his take on good and evil being "nothing but pleasure and pain")[34] is dictated by the undertaking and the terms that compose it.

Locke knows that in the main human beings do not think of themselves in mechanistic terms—and this is part of the problem that Locke wants to rectify. On the other hand, he also recognizes that there are important matters which do not lend themselves to mechanical resolve. Morals are such a case—for the explanation of what is ostensibly moral is, as we just said, traceable to sensations of pain and pleasure, and yet a society needs a moral code—in large part to inflict pain on those whose behaviors do not conform to its agreed-upon principles. Locke's moral constructivism anticipates Kant, but while Kant has undertaken a most elaborate circumnavigation of what Strawson felicitously calls, in his book of this name, "the bounds of sense," in Locke the dualism between the operations of the mind and "experience" find, as Ernst Cassirer once put it, no bridge between them.[35] What Locke overlooks is what Kant grasped: that if the world is going to be thought through in completely mechanistic terms, and if the human understanding is something in-itself which is identifiable in a manner severed from experience, then there had to be a "fit" between mathematics and geometry and world. Kant believed he supplied this "fit" by arguing that mathematics/geometry was a construction undertaken in time upon space and that both time and space were forms of intuition—the very same intuition with the same forms that were essential conditions of any sensory object being potentially knowable.[36] The "fit" that Kant finds between the mind via its forms and functions (the categories of the understanding) of experience is what enables him to also make the case that the metaphysical ideas of God, soul, and freedom are products of the mind's own dialectic, the expansion of the categories beyond their theoretically legitimate application (to experience). But Kant is also able to provide a far more coherent elaboration of the moral realm precisely because when he does invoke the dualism of ought and is, he had (or, more precisely, thought he had) more carefully construed the "seams" of his dualism. The fact that Locke simultaneously gives a cultural account of moral behavior, a constructivist account of moral rules, and a mechanistic account of the poles of moral evaluation is indicative of the lack of systemic rigor plaguing the *Essay*: experience easily becomes everything and nothing. In contrast to Locke, Kant remains true to the transcendental conditions of his dual metaphysical pillars (experience and morality) by insisting that moral goodness cannot be a matter of pleasure, but it cannot be considered as beholden to any material affectation or condition.

As yet the question of exactly how old the human race is, remains something of a conjecture, but it appears to be in the two to three hundred-thousand-year ballpark—though such a duration was not typically ascribed to the existence of the species in the seventeenth century. Nevertheless, by contrast the paradigm that Locke participated in and contributed was not much more than half a century old. Now it is true that the kinds of "discoveries" about nature that the experimental mathematical model disclosed took technological applications to an unprecedented level, and the way for the industrial revolution was prepared by the commercial and scientific revolutions. And Locke played an important intellectual role in formulating the significance of both. Yet Locke's epistemology, for all its talk of experience, is not about experience at all—it is about a certain kind of *filtering* and *contrivance*, an *understanding* of experience, which facilitates other filtered/contrived "experiences."

Sartre's insight that Being is predicated upon the capacity we have to (make) Nothing of things, i.e., in order to foreground we transform a vast array of phenomena into a kind of nothingness or "white nose" of background, is what the new science and new metaphysics turned into a virtue. And most remarkably of all, this seemingly most general and clear word—"experience"—is the means that Locke uses to ensure the dominance of the understanding over the imagination. Leo Strauss's reading aside, Locke is not the kind of person one would generally accuse of duplicity, but his reasoning does contain a significant "trick": experience is invoked so that we better sort out the sound use of the understanding, yet it is the sound use of the understanding (unimpeded by wild imaginings) that identifies an experience.

This substitution of a contrivance *constructed* of "simple ideas" as the means to understand reality is not only taking place within the realm of nature qua nature, but is also applied by Locke, as it was by Hobbes before him, to the human world, and political society. Just as the natural philosopher uses the understanding to clear away the chaos of sensation to better focus and conduct experiments to identify nature's laws, the new political philosophers will substitute their own reductive version of pre-political nature in order to identify a political model which conforms to the nature that is prescribed to it. But whereas the physicists were dealing with material that did not "talk back," and which could be "observed" in proportion to the end of the understanding itself, when it came to analyzing social and political experience, the problem was that there was little more than consensus that one could rely upon, and the mediation between polarized consensuses had nothing to defer to other than historical experience. But this was precisely what the new reductive model had sought to rescue people from. In other words, while a group of natural philosophers might well take their bearing from an experiment where agreement about the method and means might well require putting interest in the result to one side, in political matters even our abstractions have a heritage and require institutional sanction, and our various dispositions are as psychologically as sociologically shaped. One only has to think of the role that fear plays in Hobbes, and its absence in Locke, to see that two ostensibly "scientific" approaches to politics are governed not only by concerns that for all their similarities are different from the outset, but derive from different psychological dispositions, which in turn lead them to emphasize different social (and historical) qualities and experiences.

That reason or the mind will be invoked as a means for better understanding experience by others such as Malebranche, Leibniz, and Berkeley, who differ with each other every bit as much as with Locke, is done primarily for the same reason as Locke is doing his labors: to eliminate the phantasms that lead our knowledge astray. All desire to improve our knowledge of the things of the world and our behavior within it. What they really disagree about is what the process involves. And like Plato they all trust the mind rightly attuned more than language. Locke's case against language runs:

> The chief end of language in communication being to be understood, words serve not well for that end, neither in civil nor philosophical discourse, when any word does not excite in the hearer the same idea which it stands for in the mind of the speaker. Now, since sounds have no natural connexion with our ideas, but have all their signification from the arbitrary imposition of men, the doubtfulness and uncertainty of their signification, which is the imperfection we here are speaking of, has its cause more in the ideas they stand for than in any incapacity there is in one sound more than in another to signify any idea: for in that regard they are all equally perfect.[37]

Locke's claim that language is to be understood by something he calls its "chief end" helps expose the problem as much as does his invocation of reason for a process that entangles us in the very "aspect" of existence that mechanism has to ignore to make headway—viz. meaning. That is, the mechanism must completely wipe away (Descartes's doubt again) all the meanings achieved heretofore not only because speech falsifies but so do the senses if not espied correctly (another viewpoint that Locke, Malebranche, Berkeley all share). One of the other great "monsters" that the mechanists had to clear out of the universe in order to have us view it aright was (as I have said on a number of occasions) Aristotle; and one of his major "crimes" was the ascription of final causes to natural processes. We recall Descartes balked at a completely mechanical view of human beings because of language—thus too the infamous Cartesian distinction between the soulless machines (animals) and humans with souls (their cognitive capacities) and free will. In the *Essay* there is a marvelously honest moment when Locke says:

> I first began this Discourse of the Understanding, and a good while after, I had not the least thought that any consideration of words was at all necessary to it. But when, having passed over the original and com-position of our ideas, I began to examine the extent and certainty of our knowledge, I found it had so near a connexion with words, that, unless their force and manner of signification were first well observed, there could be very little said clearly and pertinently concerning knowledge: which being conversant about truth, had constantly to do with proposi-tions.[38]

That Locke did not even think about words as important when he started his exploration is once again an example of the philosophical faith in "the mind" as the store of "truth" and words as the instruments to help it.[39] We can also add that mechanism continues in this philosophical tradi-tion, even as it positions itself in so many ways against classical philoso-phy (Plato is as committed to final causes as much as Aristotle). That he would also see the "connection" between world, truth, and clarity in terms of "propositions" exactly as Frege and Russell would later do is in no small part due to the narrowly functionalist view they have of lan-guage. In spite of their belief that language is a medium of meaning, to call language's "chief end" communication is at best tautological, i.e., the means of communication exists for communicating. But this amounts to saying that language is a means for relaying ideas in one's mind to some-one else so that together we may compare our ideas, and adequately convey the sensations we have. Locke aside, this particular kind of com-municating is hardly a clue to communication. Communication is not an end in-itself (except for the aspiring writer who knows not what they want to say but desperate to say it); we communicate because we have ends, and those ends extend far beyond merely understanding the sensa-tions (regardless of whether simple or complex). In most of our commu-nications understanding is the least of our concerns—we assume it; understanding is not an end, even though it is a condition of there being an end.

Locke had sought the bedrock of ideas in experience, but as confident as he is in his belief he had achieved his goal, the fact was that he could not convince other philosophers of his success. To take but three, Male-branche, Berkeley, and Leibniz would each find that the new understand-ing of nature opened up a number of metaphysical quandaries that led them to take what they each considered the most reasonable "solutions." And each in their way sought some new indispensable certitude or bedrock that would satisfy their intellectual as well as spiritual inquiries. The diversity of their answers is very instructive, and one can only marvel all the more at the "critical solutions" provided by Kant's transcendental idealism as one appreciates his attempt to deal with all the "elements" that are "thrown up" by the metaphysicians of the new world. But he is part of the new metaphysics that has created a view of "experience" which must conform to, what (at least prior to Kant) were still generally identified as "ideas," that fit the new philosophical view of the mind and the world.

NOTES

1. Ernst Cassirer in his chapter on Bacon in *Das Erkenntnisproblem in der Philosophie und Wissenschaft der neueren Zeit. Zweiter Band* (Berlin Bruno Cassirer, 1922), rightly points out that for all Bacon's importance as an empirical scientist, his method is still driven by the search and cataloguing of qualities that is contrary to the great breakthrough in science in which secondary qualities are read through the great totality of laws: "Nature for Bacon is not an ordered whole of lawful transformations, but rather the exemplar of self-consisting 'entities'," 11.

2. Immanuel Kant, *Critique of Pure Reason*, translated by Norman Kemp Smith (New York: St. Martin's Press, 1929), BIII, BVI.

3. Galileo was very conscious of his debt to Plato. And Plato was invoked by many philosophers trying to find a more satisfying spiritual account of what the new science meant. See, for example, Douglas Hedley and Sarah Hutton (eds), *Platonism at the Origins of Modernity: Studies on Platonism and Early Modern Philosophy* (Dordrecht: Springer, 2010).

4. René Descartes, *Meditations, Objections and Replies*, translated by Roger Ariew and Donald Cress (Indianapolis: Hackett, 2006), 15.

5. Descartes, *The Principles of Philosophy*, translated by V. and R. Miller (Dordrecht: Reidel, 1983), xxvii.

6. Cf. Ernst Cassirer, *Substance and Function* (Chicago: Open Court, 1923).

7. Vico would simply and accurately state: that Descartes metaphysics did not "yield any moral philosophy suited to the Christian religion. Certainly the few things he himself wrote on the subject do not constitute such a philosophy, and his *Passions* is more useful to medicine than to ethics. Even Father Malebranche was unable to work out from them a system of Christian morality." Giambattista Vico, *The Autobiography of Giambattista Vico*, translated by Max Fisch and Thomas Bergin (Ithaca: Cornell University Press, 1944), 130.

8. "I now seem able to posit as a general rule that everything I very clearly and distinctly perceive is true." *Meditations, Objections and Replies*, 19.

9. Ibid., 18–19.

10. A number of works, such as Hiram Caton, *The Origin of Subjectivity: An Essay on Descartes* (New Haven: Yale University Press, 1973), have made the case for Descartes "feigning" his faith. But I think the strongest case (also recommended by Caton) is Cornelio Fabro's magnum opus *God in Exile: Modern Atheism: A Study in the Internal Dynamic of Modern Atheism from Its Roots in the Cartesian Cogito to the Present Day*, translated by Arthur Gibson (Westminster, MD: Newman Press, 1964). Fabro goes beyond a merely textual analysis of Descartes and his interlocutors and does a genealogy of his impact upon the history of modern atheistic thought.

11. Spinoza *Ethics*, part II, Proposition 7 in *The Ethics*, in *Works Volume 2: On the Improvement of the Understanding, the Ethics Correspondence*, translated R. H. M. Elwes (New York: Dover, 1955), 86.

12. Ibid., Part II, III, 82.

13. Ibid., Part II, Note to Proposition VII, 86.

14. *Meditations, Objections and Replies*, 20–21.

15. Kant reproduces it unquestioningly. But to believe that Spinoza and Descartes belong to the same epistemological team of rationalists, while they are so metaphysically divided on the question of dualism and monism, only serves to show how dubious these distinctions are, and how much is being made of the arrangement of elements *within* an assemblage or problematic.

16. "On the Improvement of the Understanding," *Spinoza, Works Volume 2*, 12.

17. Nicolas Malebranche, *Dialogues on Metaphysics and Religion*, translated by Jonathan Bennett, p. 1. http://www.earlymoderntexts.com/pdfs/malebranche1688.pdf last viewed December 5, 2014.

18. Malebranche, *Dialogues*, 2.

19. John Locke, *Locke's Essays: An Essay Concerning the Human Understanding, and A Treatise on the Conduct of the Understanding* (Philadelphia: Troutman and Hayes, 1850), 33.

20. Ibid., 34. Locke also wants to "discover the powers thereof; how far they reach; to what things they are in any degree proportionate; and where they fail us; I suppose it may be of use to prevail with the busy mind of man to be more cautious in meddling with things exceeding its comprehension; to stop when it is at the utmost extent of its tether; and to sit down in a quiet ignorance of those things which, upon examination, are found to be beyond the reach of our capacities." Ibid.

21. Ibid., 75.

22. Ibid., 15.

23. Deborah Boyle assembles this list from the Third Meditation and a letter to Mersenne and Conversations with Burman in *Descartes on Innate Ideas* (London: Continuum, 2009), 1.

24. In his *Lectures on the History of Philosophy*, Hegel had, correctly, the absolutization of the finite, whether it be the mind or sensation, as the dualism that is at the basis of modern metaphysics.

25. *Locke's Essays*, 35.

26. Ibid., 75.

27. Ibid., 97.

28. Ibid., 97.

29. Ibid., 93.

30. Ibid., 93.

31. Ibid., 94.

32. Ibid., 94.

33. Ibid., 202.

34. Ibid., 171, 235.

35. Ernst Cassirer, *Das Erkenntnisproblem in der Philosophie und Wissenschaft der neueren Zeit, Zweiter Band*, 260.

36. When we consider later some of the critiques of Kant, we should clarify that the "bridging problem" is only a problem where we have a substantive divide between the world and relations of experience and those of mind. Those who stay closer to Leibniz, such as Hegel and Herder, for all their respective differences, see the problem as one that already implicates reason is a fallacy.

37. *Locke's Essays*, 310.

38. Ibid., 316.

39. For a more detailed account of how Locke's philosophy of language is largely focused upon the imperfections of language, see Paul Guyer, "Locke's Philosophy of Language," in *The Cambridge Companion to Locke*, edited by Vere Chappell (Cambridge: Cambridge University Press, 1994), 115–45.

THREE

Metaphysical Quandaries along the "Way of Ideas"

BERKELEY'S ALL-ENCOMPASSING UNDERSTANDING OR *ESSE EST PERCIPI*

The new metaphysics creates new range of problems concerning ideas and experiences which are manifest in the philosophies of Berkeley, Malebranche, and Leibniz, and which ultimately feed back into the new metaphysics itself.

Berkeley is often and easily counter-posed to Locke as his antithesis insofar as he ascribes to the mind the same certainty that Locke had lent to experience. His distrust of language, his interest in the natural world, particularly its visual peculiarities, his experiential emphasis, his acceptance of what Locke, in continuation of the Cartesian emphasis upon the mind's transforming sensation into an object for itself, had called "the way of ideas" in his dispute with Edward Stillingfleet, was every bit as intrinsic to his metaphysics as it was to Locke's. It is true, as it would be for Malebranche and Leibniz, that Berkeley prided himself on being able to block off the path to atheism which he thought materialism supported.[1] But while the cultural implications of a particular metaphysic were not insignificant, the philosophical commitment to a universe that was lawful seemed to strengthen the idea of intelligence at work in the world, and that we would not have ideas of anything were we not perceiving/intelligent beings. His formulation *esse est percipi* does not come from an inattention to experience, but rather from the fact that any experience we have is due to our having some perception and thus idea of it.[2] Further his argument (taken up by Hume) against Locke's theory of abstract ideas, that "an idea, which considered in itself is particular, becomes general by being made to represent or stand for all other particular

ideas of the same sort" is (again as Hume saw) more consistently empiricist than Locke's too hasty move to abstract generalities, which suggests
giving too much ground to the Platonist realists who held these "generalities" to be real.[3]

To speak of objects outside of an understanding to which they conform is, Berkeley argues, meaningless. Kant's appeal to the thing-in-itself
as an idea preceding the specific object that the mind identifies will be his
concession to Berkeley, as he tries to rescue what he thinks is a more
reasonable understanding of experience. Yet Berkeley, with good reason,
sees himself fighting against abstraction and defending the certitudes of
"our own ideas or sensations."[4] To the Lockean argument that our ideas
are resemblances or copies of things which exist, Berkeley not unreasonably replies:

> an idea can be like nothing but an idea; a colour or figure can be like
> nothing but another colour or figure. If we look but ever so little into
> our thoughts, we shall find it impossible for us to conceive a likeness
> except only between our ideas. Again, I ask whether those supposed
> originals or external things, of which our ideas are the pictures or rep-
> resentations, be themselves perceivable or no?[5]

The point is made further as he sees the distinction between primary and
secondary qualities only confirming his position: for while the new science has dissolved all qualities into "nature" as such, with nature itself
seen as materiality, Berkeley points out that those qualities which enable
us to understand its laws (those same characteristics which were essential
for Locke's simple substances)—namely, extension, figure, and motion
"are only ideas existing in the mind, and that an idea can be like nothing
but another idea, and that consequently neither they nor their archetypes
can exist in an unperceiving substance." The consequence he draws from
this is that matter is a mere chimera, and that we would all think more
clearly if it were banished.[6] The importance of the model and kinematics
and the role of the observer is essential to the argument he is making; but
whereas the application of number to what is ostensibly the *source* of
knowledge creates a deal-breaking contradiction for Locke, Berkeley's
claim that "number is entirely the creature of the mind" only reinforces
the link between the metaphysics and the world as it is "modelled" metaphysically.[7] This does not alter the fact that Berkeley's thought is counter–intuitive in a way which Locke's is not; Samuel Johnson's famous
riposte of the stone kick—"I refute it *thus*"—is the "common sense" response to the metaphysics of Berkeley. But Johnson's "common sense" is
an act of defiance that carries little weight within the criss-cross of narratives that have required the kind of disposition and orientation which
radically doubts common sense. In contrast to Johnson, Berkeley's metaphysics feeds off the counter-intuitive orientation which enables the mechanistic revolution in the first place. This is no less the case with Male-

branche, whose metaphysics is at once a metaphysics of mechanism, an affirmation of God, and an attempt at a synthesis between Augustine and Descartes.

MALEBRANCHE TIGHTENING THE UNDERSTANDING'S GRIP ON THE IMAGINATION BY GREATER RELIANCE UPON GOD

Although Malebranche can be openly critical of Descartes, he is also capable of portraying himself as "Descartes's true heir."[8] It is certainly the case that Malebranche's starting point is strictly dualist in the manner of Descartes, that sensory information needs to be properly understood as the building blocks of science, and this requires understanding our mental operations, moreover that we remain aware of the damage done by the imagination, especially strong ones which are "extremely contagious,"[9] and are spread through books (his more detailed examples are of Tertullian, Seneca, and Montaigne) and folklore and other means that only a penetrating grasp of the understanding can rectify. Any suggestion that he is less well disposed toward science than Locke would be ludicrous. But it is true that his social or cultural motives are overtly theological and that this impetus in his thinking is decisive in the ultimate shape that it has, leading as it does to God's importance for knowledge. Whereas Descartes had argued that the very idea of God—as an infinite perfect being—was proof of his existence (an argument also in Malebranche), Descartes had nevertheless no God other than the idea of God. This, far more than Malebranche's criticism of Descartes physics,[10] is behind Malebranche's major metaphysical difference with Descartes. To repeat an earlier point: the fulcrum of the Cartesian system is the cogito, while the idea of the God it has innately within itself serves to ensure that the deceptions that occur due to the senses' opacity and the imagination not following rules for directing the mind is a guarantee that once clarity and distinctness of ideas takes over God will not deceive. This simply means that the laws of the universe are constant. The observation about this constancy and the way this is related to the creator is both metaphysical and theological. The metaphysics and the theology ultimately *serve* the physics, no less than the rules for directing the mind, and the dualism of *res cogitans* and *res extensa*.

Nevertheless, as we have indicated, with Malebranche a major shift of purpose has taken place: the physics serves to direct us to the beauty and intelligibility of creation and to the creator behind the creation. Thus in the first of the *Dialogues on Metaphysics*, Malebranche's philosophical "hero" Theodore says:

> Don't think that what I am saying now is new. It is the opinion of St Augustine. If our ideas are eternal, unchangeable, necessary, you plainly see that they have to exist in something unchangeable. It is true,

> Aristes, that God sees intelligible extension–the model that is copied by
> the matter of which the world is formed and in which our bodies
> live–in himself, and (I repeat) it is only in him that we see it. Our minds
> live entirely in universal reason, in the intelligible substance that con-
> tains the ideas involved in all the truths we discover. [11]

This is a neat summary of the argument laid out in the *Search* which
proceeds by identifying errors: from the errors of the senses, to the errors
of the imagination, to the errors of the understanding or pure mind, to
the errors of inclination and the errors of the passions. Once Malebranche
identifies the true nature of the pure mind it is then and only then that
the central importance of God's intelligibility is made clear: for the
mind's power, according to Malebranche, is dependent upon God's power, the natural light receiving its light from the divine light—"God is truly
the mind's light and the father of lights." [12] Thus in the opening of Book
Three, Part Two of the *Search* he writes:

> our mind's immediate object when it sees the sun, for example, is not
> the sun, but something that is intimately joined to our soul, and this is
> what I call an idea. Thus, by the word *idea*, I mean here nothing other
> than the immediate object, or the object closest to the mind, when it
> perceives something, i.e. that which affects and modifies the mind with
> the perception it has of an object. [13]

From the outset Malebranche emphasizes that the understanding is a
passive quality of the soul, [14] and that the "*senses* and the imagination are
nothing but the understanding perceiving objects through the organs of
the body." [15] Of itself, the understanding does not err—all of its operations are nothing but "*pure perceptions*" [16]—it is the will that is the source
of our error: the understanding for Malebranche is a passive faculty, the
will active. The will, for Malebranche, cannot arrest an impression, but "it
can in a sense turn it in the direction that please it, " thereby distorting its
significance, and confusing what the understanding makes of its perceptions. [17] The problem of error stands for Malebranche, then, in the closest
relationship to the problem of freedom—we are free, but our freedom is
corrupted. The difference with Descartes is indicative of the kinds of
shifts which run through Malebranche.

Descartes's philosophy is essentially utilitarian in conception, a philosophy for the building of a new technologically better world; Malebranche's philosophy, on the other hand, though not disputing the desir-
ability of mechanical benefits, is based on an appreciation and genuine
interest in the infinite marvels of what nature can do, and the divine
design/structure that makes that possible, [18] but he is determined to demonstrate the compatibility of nature as it really is with the spiritual meaning of our existence. It is thus indicative of the "totality" of his problematic that his discussion of error is allied with arguments about the nature of
Adam and sin and divine purpose. Thus whereas Descartes considers the

evidence of the senses untrustworthy—until a true method has been established—Malebranche subtly but significantly shifts the diagnoses of
the "root" of the problem of sensory delusion. "Our senses," he argues
"are not as corrupt as might be imagined; rather it is the most inward
part of the soul that has been corrupted. . . . The senses would not plunge
us into error if we used our freedom properly and if we did not rely on
their reports in order to judge matters too precipitously." [19] Having "established" this, he then returns to a rule that is utterly compatible with
Descartes—"*Never judge by means of the senses as to what things are in themselves, but only as to the relation they have to the body* because, in fact, the
senses were given to us, not to know the truth of things, but only for the
preservation of our body." [20]

The step from Cartesian physics to Augustinian metaphysics is central
to Malebranche's undertaking—but it is contentious whether Malebranche's Augustinian "moment" is as straightforwardly Augustinian as
Malebranche seems to think. It is the arguments he provides about cognition that facilitate the transition from the mind as the indubitable seat of
knowledge of the world and ideas to a perception of a sort that is uncon-
strained by "ideas." Malebranche draws upon another dualism—viz. the
modes of the soul's perceptions—those things it perceives in-itself and
those outside itself. According to Malebranche, it is those things that exist
outside the soul, things "that cannot be intimately joined to the soul" that
can be perceived "only by means of ideas." [21] Spiritual realities "can be
revealed to the soul by themselves and without ideas." [22] Moreover,
Malebranche argues that the soul does not have the power to make real
beings, and ideas are real beings, even if they are "spiritual" realities. The
matter of the dependency of a created being has all the hallmarks of the
seal of orthodoxy: human finitude, God's omnipotence, omniscience and
love. But things take an important turn as Malebranche attempts to show
that every mind is dependent upon God. His reasoning is that since God
existed before the world and that "He could not have produced it without knowledge or ideas; consequently, the ideas He had of the world are
not different from Himself, so that all creatures, even the most material
and terrestrial are in God, though in a completely spiritual way that is
incomprehensible to us." [23]

Whereas Plato had the creator god looking at models/ideas, Malebranche appeals to the seemingly Christian orthodox position of not tol-
erating any being, even an "idea," higher than God. Malebranche wanted
to consolidate an understanding of our nature with a metaphysical
understanding consistent with what he sees as intrinsic to the Christian
faith, and this also means, for him, connecting our divinely ordained
purposes with the world, which has been revealed to be run along mechanistic strictures. His solution has to keep the alpha and omega of the
Creator in the "picture," but because "created minds . . . can see in themselves neither the essence nor the existence of things," because they "can-

not contain all beings as does God,"[24] the idea they have of the infinite confirms for Malebranche the soul's knowledge of its dependence upon God at all times in a manner that is analogous to his view of motion as caused at all times not by the bodies of the world themselves but by God's will.[25] What, though, appears to be a hybrid of neo-Platonism and Augustine, ends up looking alarmingly Spinozian, as creature and creator all end up "together," as a shift from dependency to union takes place. For Malebranche the idea we have of the infinite is the greatest and most beautiful proof of God's existence. Moreover, it is only by virtue of union with God that we have "a very distinct idea of God."[26] That a number of Malebranche's critics accused him of ultimately having a position indistinguishable from Spinoza's is hardly surprising when we read in *Search*:

> the mind perceives nothing except in the idea it has of the infinite, and far from this idea being formed from the confused collection of all our ideas of particular beings (as philosophers think), all these particular ideas are in fact but participations in the general idea of the infinite . . . every creature is but an imperfect participation in the divine being.[27]

One great challenge of the mechanistic world picture was not to have all particularity swallowed up in the infinitude of God or nature, and Locke's response to Malebranche's making the infinite the condition of finite beings glides easily from mathematics to everyday experience:

> I do not observe, that when I would think of a triangle, I first think of all beings; whether these words all beings are to be taken here in their proper sense, or very improperly for being in general. Nor do I think my country neighbours do so, when they first wake in the morning, who, I imagine, do not find it impossible to think of a lame horse they have, or their blighted corn, till they have run over in their minds all beings that are, and then pitch on Dapple; or else begin to think of being in general, which is being abstracted from all its inferior species, before they come to think of the fly in their sheep, or the tares in their corn. For I am apt to think that the greatest part of mankind very seldom, if ever at all, think of being in general, i.e., abstracted from all its inferior species and individuals.[28]

Locke's point about his country neighbors, though, could be applied to all the mechanists who are wrestling to make sense of a universe in which everything is construed as law-governed and constituted by masses and forces in motion, and who all see that misplaced faith in the primacy of the common sense world of secondary qualities. Perhaps even more demanding than Berkeley and Malebranche in its break with common sense in order to supply an accurate metaphysics of existence is Leibniz, who, in a book-length refutation of Locke in his *New Essays on the Human Understanding*, argued that the mind is "veined" like marble rather than a blank sheet, contributing its own powers to our understanding of reality.

LEIBNIZ'S "LOGICIZING" OF THE WORLD AND IDEA

Unlike the figures thus far discussed, Leibniz sees that thought and reality are so interpenetrative that the problem of the nature of reality requires us to find a principle that is also genuinely logical. Whereas Locke's simple qualities remain "physical," Leibniz's argument about substances being the complete (i.e., infinite) totality of possible predications that can be made about them infinitizes both logic and empirical data so that the world, as he himself realizes, once again resembles at least some of the features of the scholastic/Aristotelian doctrine of substantial forms that the entire tenor of the mechanistic metaphysics was united against: that the world, and all in it, is a real quality, and not merely an accident or epiphenomenon of extension—and hence a qualitative composition. Each thing is an operative metaphysical power that is not the result but the condition of mathematical-material relationships. [29] Moreover, far from seeing the revival of neo-Platonist and Aristotelian elements as a slight on his metaphysical solution, Leibniz saw conciliation as confirming that he was on the right path. [30] Moreover, it was precisely the desire to break with overly logicizing experience to the detriment of understanding the world that had been behind the animosity directed at Aristotle and the schoolmen—an animosity that was already prevalent among pre-mechanistic humanists such as Erasmus. For Locke, making experience the bedrock of reality led him to the position that logical elements are nothing more than the set of the mind's interior operations. Leibniz certainly has no "bridging" problem, and he sees his concept of substance as the logical "source" of all predications as serving the mechanical world no less than the logical world. [31] In both, the principle of sufficient reason and the law of non-contradiction apply. And his commitment to them applying equally to a logical and mechanical world enabled him to switch between the purely logical to the mechanistic, or what, in his parlance, is a dynamic world. If philosophy from its very inception had made materiality and design/intelligence the two contending metaphysical *archai*, it is perhaps not surprising that at times philosophers will, as Leibniz does, find a metaphysical "moment" (Schelling will do it again with the point of indifference) in which these substances are seen to make "sense" only through their relationship to each other. How he does so is put neatly by Deleuze who describes what he takes as the "operative function" of the baroque in general, whose great exemplar is Leibniz, as treating of the folds of the real by differentiating them as "moving along two infinities, as if infinity were composed of two stages or floors: the pleats of matter and the folds in the soul." [32] Leibniz's metaphysics concedes everything to the idea of causation so that everything is literally implicated in everything. As for Locke's argument about the ideas of the understanding being built up by simple qualities, Leibniz argues:

the ideas of size, figure and motion are not so distinctive as imagined, and that they stand for something imaginary relative to our perceptions as do, although, to a greater extent, the ideas of colour, heat, and other similar qualities in regard to which we may doubt whether they are actually to be found in the nature of things outside of us.[33]

While Leibniz's position is completely in keeping with the mechanistic view of life and the modelling that is needed for experimentation, this does not exhaust Leibniz's purview, which differs from that of his contemporaries in how he understands perception itself as well as the dynamic metaphysical source of nature. A key to this lay in his recognition that the principles of mechanism are not themselves to be found within mechanism, an insight that of itself might not put him obviously in dispute with other metaphysicians of his age, but which leads to an altogether different position and role for metaphysics. In a letter to Remond de Montmort Leibniz writes: "When I seek for the ultimate reasons of mechanicalism and the laws of motion I am surprised to discover that they are not to be found in mathematics and that we must turn to metaphysics."[34] Thus too, as Paul Janet in his incisive and sympathetic introduction to *Leibniz's Discourse on Metaphysics and Correspondence with Arnauld and Mondadology* says: "It is in metaphysics that mechanicalism has found, not its contradiction, but its completion through the doctrine of dynamism."[35] That is, Leibniz was convinced that his metaphysic contributed to a better understanding of the operations of the dynamic nature of the world, and he saw it as also providing as indisputable arguments for God as a providential source of creation and the soul as immortal. God and the soul were not merely to be understood as metaphysical incidentals— so that science and metaphysics could be separately compartmentalised by the mind—but essential ideas for a dynamic (yet law-governed as with the mechanistic) account of nature.[36] The following from a draft of a letter to Arnauld below provides an elegant summary of Leibniz's metaphysics, and the axial shift it contains.

> since the soul is an individual substance it must be that its concept, idea, essence or nature involves all that will happen to it, and God, who sees it perfectly, sees there what it will do or endure forever and all the thoughts which it will have. Therefore, since our ideas are only the consequences of the nature of the soul and are born in it by virtue of its concept, it is useless to ask regarding the influence of another particular substance upon it. This aside from the fact that this influence would be absolutely inexplicable. It is true that certain thoughts come to us when there are certain bodily movements and that certain bodily movements take place when we have certain thoughts, but this is because each substance expresses the whole universe in its fashion and this expression of the universe which brings about a movement in the body is perhaps a pain in regard to the soul.[37]

It also illustrates why Leibniz's theory of knowledge simultaneously smashes the more common-sense divisions of the soul or mind being "impressed" by experience, as he argues that the sovereignty of the substance means that it is not affected by any other substance: as he puts it in the *Monadology*—the monad is a living mirror of the universe that has no windows. For Leibniz, the more common sense empirically "realist" approach blinds us to the realities of the constitutive infinitudes of life which we are all participants within, and contributors to:

> It is customary to attribute the action to that substance whose expression is more distinct and which is called the cause, just as when a body is swimming in water there are an infinity of movements of the particles of water in such a way that the place which the body leaves may always be filled up in the shortest way. This is why we say that this body is the cause of the motion, because by its means we can explain clearly what happens. But if we examine the physics and the reality of the motion, it is quite as easy to suppose that the body is in repose and that all the rest is in motion conformably to this hypothesis, since every movement in itself is only relative, that is to say, is a change of position which cannot be assigned to any one thing with mathematical precision; but the change is attributed to that body by means of which the whole is most clearly explained. In fact, if we take all phenomena, great or small, there is only one single hypothesis which serves to explain everything clearly. We can therefore say, that, although this body is not an efficient physical cause of these effects, its idea is at least, so to speak, the final cause of them, or, if you prefer, a model cause of them in the understanding of God; because, if we wish to ask what reality there is in motion we may imagine that God desires expressly to produce all the changes of position in the universe exactly the same as that ship was producing them while going through the water. Is it not true that it happens exactly in the same way, for it is not possible to assign any real difference? If we speak with metaphysical precision there is no more reason for saying that the ship presses upon the water in order to make that large number of circular movements because of which the water takes the place of the ship, than to say that the water itself exerts pressure to make all these circles and that it therefore causes the ship to move conformably. Unless we say, however, that God expressly desired to produce such a great number of movements so well fitted together, we do not give any real cause for it, and as it is not reasonable to have recourse to divine activity for explaining a particular detail, we have recourse to the ship, notwithstanding the fact that, in the last analysis, the agreement of all the phenomena of different substances comes about only because they are productions of the same cause, that is to say, of God. Therefore, each individual substance expresses the resolves which God made in regard to the whole universe.[38]

Leibniz's view of reality requires that anyone thinking seriously about reality must at every second think micro- and telescopically—thus his beautiful "Every portion of matter may be conceived as like a garden full of plants, and like a pond full of fish. But every branch of a plant, every member of an animal, and every drop of the fluids within it, is also such a garden or such a pond."[39] The other most telescopic of metaphysicians was Spinoza. But Spinoza's dissolution of all individual substances into the one and only substance in which all individuations function merely as modes renders talk of an extrinsic source of creation meaningless—as the more traditional philosophical God had been conceived. Leibniz's metaphysics makes us think of an infinitude of distinct entities each with their own perspective which never touch so that something is needed to provide a larger coherence for the mind, within which diverse perspectives may occur.[40] That something is God. And, unlike Spinoza, for whom God's immanence and inseparability from nature, eclipses any importance God may have as independent from His creations, in Leibniz's metaphysics the closed infinitudes of substances mean that God and nature can never be one—the same is true of the soul and nature. Thus in Leibniz, God is required in his system to make the universe intelligible. And as we have seen, the entire emphasis upon clear and distinct ideas (a formula repeated by Leibniz on many occasions) stresses the need for intelligibility in the new thinking. In Leibniz's case, though, as with the Cartesians, the Newtonian action at a distance is seen as defying intelligibility, and being unintelligible it is not incorporated into the metaphysics: a position which ultimately only damaged Leibniz's reputation.

That Leibniz's investigations into physics were so dependent upon his metaphysics was something that he was delighted by: for he believed it reconciled the pious, so that they need "not fear reason," and men of reason, who can now "return to grace with piety; with which it used to be in all too little agreement."[41] For Leibniz, the workings of the universe were so intricately beautiful they were inherently miraculous, so much so that the more progress one makes in philosophy,

> the more he acknowledges divine power and goodness; and . . . that person is no stranger to revelation or to the things we call miracles or mysteries, since he can demonstrate that certain things are near enough miracles happen every day in nature. For no revelation would seem more extraordinary and in conflict with the senses than for a thing to be annihilated and created, or for there to be an actual infinity of parts in a finite thing.[42]

Although himself often involved in experimentation, Leibniz saw that the metaphysical underpinnings of nature posed a major difficulty for those who were now trying to proceed solely by virtue of sensation and imagination. And to ward philosophers away from such practices he writes:

> And, let philosophers in their turn, stop referring everything to the imagination and figures, and stop declaiming as trifles and fraud anything that conflicts with those crass and materialistic notions by which some people think the whole nature of things is circumscribed. As they

will recognize when they reflect on these matters properly, motion itself is not at all subject to imagination, and certain metaphysical mysteries of a truly spiritual nature will be found contained in it.[43]

As we have seen throughout the desire for intelligibility meant that metaphysics increasingly becomes a philosophical end, while in Descartes, as I have stressed, it was but a means; Descartes had advised his followers not to spend too much time, as Gary Hatfield puts it, "rummaging about down there in the 'roots' of metaphysics."[44] It is this desire for intelligibility by philosophers that would lead so many philosophers away from taking the natural world as the horizon of reality and back into the metaphysical quandaries that go to the heart of thought qua thought, rather than thought as primarily directed to understanding nature. To be sure, Leibniz's entire metaphysics is in large part an answer to those who draw upon metaphysics primarily in relationship to nature, but it has drawn logic back into the enterprise as an essential contributor to the enhancement of our understanding, as opposed to something that needs to be treated with suspicion. But the metaphysics also has all manner of theological implications. That the very nature of space and time—so important in the debate with Newton via Clarke whether they are absolute (Newton/Clarke) or purely relational (Leibniz)—took on such theological importance is indicative of the transformation taking place theologically. Nevertheless, we also need to keep in mind that we are a universe away from the theological disputes that embroiled Catholic apologists, Luther, Zwingli, and Calvin about the location and nature of God's presence in the host. That Leibniz will be the major inspiration for Hermann Samuel Reimarus who would argue that the natural religion of reason could be marshalled to disprove the supernatural origins of Christian revelation (and, astonishingly, thus making Leibniz compatible with a Spinozian historical approach to the bible) would be the unintended consequence of Leibniz's ecumenicalism. Thus adding some credibility to the accusation by Leibniz's less rationalistically inclined evangelical compatriots who nicknamed him *Löve-nix* [believer in nothing].

The interrelationship between the physics, metaphysics, and theology also explains Leibniz's pride in reconciling his metaphysical solutions to problems in mathematical physics, epistemology, and theology. Though, as with the majority of the mechanistic metaphysicians, the metaphysical deferral to God's role in creating or maintaining the machine increasingly render the existential relationship between God and the individual soul, traditionally strengthened through the ritualistic self-fashioning, more of a matter of intelligibility of the universe as such than a personal answer to one's inner most needs. Further, the substitution of the cold clarity of this metaphysics for the more heated passions of traditional faith went hand in hand with a view of life in which the everyday world of experience seemed to fade into a mystery so extraordinary that it no longer seemed a fit dwelling place for anyone other than the philosopher. That Leibniz's metaphysics was perhaps the most extraordinary, the most remote from how we tend to make sense of the world in our daily life seems to have been the position of Arnauld, who comments to Count Ernst von Hessen-Rheinfels: "I find in his thoughts so many things which frightened me and which if I am not mistaken almost all men would find so startling that I cannot see any utility in a treatise which would be evidently rejected by everybody."[45]

More than any of the other metaphysicians, including Spinoza, Leibniz's metaphysics attempts to reconcile force and perception. The problem is that Leibniz's philosophy requires an even more radical break with how everyday experience is viewed, which in turn places a degree of importance upon metaphysics far beyond what either Descartes or Locke, or even Spinoza envisaged. Nevertheless, he leaves an important legacy which is picked up by Schelling and Herder (who also take inspiration from Spinoza). That legacy also extended to the entire field of aesthetics in Germany, which was deeply indebted to Leibniz. Nevertheless, Leibniz also hailed, by way of reaction, a return to the more familiar world of "common life," or common sense.[46]

NOTES

1. According to Berkeley "the enemies of religion lay so great a stress on *unthinking matter*, and all of them use so much industry and artifice to reduce everything to it; methinks they should rejoice to see them deprived of their grand support, and driven from that only fortress, without which your Epicureans, Hobbists, and the like, have not even the shadow of a pretence, but become the most cheap and easy triumph in the world." *Principles of Human Knowledge in Principles of Human Knowledge and Three Dialogues*, edited, introduction, and notes by Howard Robinson (Oxford: Oxford University Press), 65.

2. Ibid., 25.

3. Ibid., 13–14.

4. Ibid., 25.

5. Ibid., 27.

6. Ibid., 27.

7. Ibid., 29.

8. Nicholas Jolley, *The Light of the Soul: Theories of Ideas in Leibniz, Malebranche and Descartes* (Oxford: Oxford University Press, 1990), 6.

9. Nicholas Malebranche, *The Search After Truth*, edited by Thomas M. Lennon and Paul J. Oscamp (Cambridge: Cambridge University Press, 1997), 161.

10. See Ibid., 510–26.

11. *Dialogues on Metaphysics*, 10.

12. *Search*, 231.

13. Ibid., 217.

14. Ibid., 3.

15. Ibid., p 3.

16. Ibid., p 7.

17. Ibid., 4–5, 9.

18. Cf. "Nothing in nature is despicable, and all the works of God deserve to be respected and admired, especially in on notices the simplicity of the ways in which

God makes and preserves them. The tiniest gnats are as perfect as the largest of animals, and it even seems as though God has willed to bejewel them in compensation for their lack of size." 31.

19. Ibid., 23.
20. Ibid., 24.
21. Ibid., 218.
22. Ibid., 218.
23. Ibid., 229.
24. Ibid., 229.
25. Ibid., 225.
26. Ibid., 232.
27. Ibid., 232, also see 237. In their "Introduction" to their edition of *Search*, Thomas Lennon and Paul Olscamp point out that Dortuous Mairan (a former student of Malebranche), Noel Aubert de Versé, and Antoine Arnauld ("at least implicitly") all saw that there was no difference between Malebranche's position and Spinoza's, xix.
28. John Locke, "An Examination of P. Malebranche's Opinion of Seeing all Things in God," in *The Works of John Locke, Volume II*, with a preliminary essay and notes J. A. St. John (London: Bell and Daldy, 1872), 430–31.
29. See Leibniz proposition XI of Correspondence with Arnauld.
30. Christia Mercer correctly takes Leibniz's desire to harmonise philosophical systems—what she calls his "conciliatory methodology," 13—as the key to his metaphysics, *Leibniz" Metaphysics: Its Origins and Development* (Cambridge: Cambridge University Press, 2004).
31. Cf. Jürgen Lawrenz, "Leibniz's *Kehre*: From Ultradeterminism to the Philosophy of Freedom," *The European Legacy*, 23:5, 479–89.
32. Gilles Deleuze, *The Fold: Leibniz and the Baroque*, translated by Tom Conley (London: Athlone, 1993), 3
33. Proposition XII of G.W. Leibniz, *Discourse on Metaphysics* in *Discourse on Metaphysics, Correspondence with Arnauld and Monadology*, introduction by Paul Janet, translated George Montgomery (Chicago: Open Court, 1902), 17.
34. Letter to Remond de Montmort (Erdman, Opera Philosophica, 702) in "Introduction" to *Discourse on Metaphysics*, ix.
35. Paul Janet, "Introduction," *Discourse on Metaphysics etc.*, viii.
36. The importance of Leibniz in Kant's first *Critique* cannot be overstated: for it is Leibniz's endless continuum of perception and the role of God as a necessary component *for understanding* the laws and qualities of experience that Kant sees as a major source of philosophical confusion. For Kant, this can only be rectified through a scientific metaphysics that forecloses any talk of God, when it comes to the world of experience, other than as a *regulative idea* for providing a more systemic totality of nature's laws for our reason.
37. Draft of the letter of Nov. 28–Dec. 8 to Arnauld, in G. Leibniz, *Discourse on Metaphysics, etc.*, 149–50.
38. Leibniz, *Discourse* etc., 150–51.
39. Leibniz proposition 68 of *Monadology* in *Discourse etc.*, 266.
40. The following is a classic analogy from the *Monadology* (proposition 53, 273) "And as the same city regarded from different sides appears entirely different, and is, as it were, multiplied perspectively, so, because of the infinite number of simple substances, there are a similar infinite number of universes which are, nevertheless, only the aspects of a single one, as seen from the special point of view of each Monad."
41. G. W. Leibniz, "Pacidius to Philalethes: A First Philosophy of Motion," in *The Labyrinth of the Continuum: Writings on the Continuum Principle, 1672–1686*, translated, edited, and introduced by Richard Arthur (New Haven: Yale University Press, 2001), 219.
42. Ibid., 219.
43. Ibid.

44. To Elizabeth, Descartes confided that metaphysics should be pursued "once in one's life," see his letter to Elizabeth of June 28, 1643. Étienne Gilson had also noted Descartes only turned to metaphysics a decade after he had been working on mathematical physics. See Gary Hatfield, "Descartes's Physiology and Its Relation to Psychology" in *The Cambridge Companion to Descartes*, edited by John Cottingham (Cambridge: Cambridge University Press, 1992), 336.

45. *Discourse etc*. Letter March 13, 1686, 73. This assessment is similar to Thomas Reid's relatively brief critical discussion of Leibniz—Reid is generally positive toward Arnauld.

46. This would be closely related to his emphasis upon the intrinsic harmony and perfection of things. See, e.g., "From the Ethical and Legal Writings 1639–1700," No. 111. On Wisdom," in Gottfried Wilhelm Leibniz, *Philosophical Papers and Letters*, translated and edited Leroy E. Loemker (Dordrecht: Kluwer, 1989), 425–26.

FOUR

The Return of the Idea to the Everyday World

In comparison to Leibniz, David Hume represents a return to the solidity of the everyday world—while both were employed for much of their lives as librarians, if every great insight of Leibniz seems to come out of the end of a microscope, Hume's appear to come from the man seated in his armchair in his library marveling at the (predominant) folly and (occasional) wonder of human beings. Nevertheless, Hume commences his early great work *A Treatise on Human Nature* with the natural reality to be explained being the reality opened up by mechanism.[1] Thus, for him, whatever solidity there is comes from compounds, and the defect of our senses is that they give us "disproportion'd images of things, and represent as minute and uncompounded."[2] Moreover, Hume also factors in the "experimental method" as a central feature of the scientific—thus does he (by analogy) wish to extend it to our "understanding of morals." It is fair to say, then, as Martin Bell does that "[b]y the use of the experimental method Hume means the attempt to discover causal laws on the basis of observation and experience rather than on the basis of supposed rational insight into the essence or nature of things."[3] But in spite of Hume's various references to "modern" (i.e., Newtonian) physics, what is so conspicuous is that the methodological strictures which shape both the observation and the kind of experience that typifies modern mechanistic philosophy do not assert themselves throughout. Further, in his writings on politics, and conjectures on human nature, Aristotle was not a whit less "experimental" than Hume; what is lacking in Aristotle's experimental method is the laboratory condition enabling variable control, which is also absent in Hume's moral "experiment." On the other hand, Hume definitely wants to eliminate any need for a supernatural source to render our knowledge meaningful. But this valorization of the experimental method hardly serves as an adequate engagement with those philosophers who were no less attached to the experimental method as a modeling process isolating variables than Hume, and who were nevertheless persuaded that our "ideas" could not all be explained by "experience." Hume's desire to find a philosophy adequate for "common life" helps explain why he thinks he can safely ignore any rigorous engagement with Leibniz, and hence why his blithe discussion of innate ideas takes no cognizance of the objections raised by Leibniz against Locke in the *New Essays*. Indeed, apart from Hume's hostility to metaphysics, nothing in the *Treatise* or *Enquiries* suggests that Hume had a real grasp of why, after Descartes, there was a serious ontological disputation about the nature and source of ideas to be had in the first place. Hume's remark that "Locke was betrayed into this question by the schoolmen, who, making use of undefined terms, draw out their disputes to a tedious length" indicates how wrong-headed he thinks much of the search for the "source" of ideas had been.[4] If his resolution of the dispute about the origin of ideas cited below is anything to go by, it is hard to believe that he had seriously taken an antithetical position to Locke—whereby intelligence or mind is the source of experience and not vice versa. For whatever one thinks of this explanation it can hardly be said to address the arguments put forward by Leibniz in his *New Essays*:

> I should desire to know, what can be meant by asserting, that self-love, or resentment of injuries, or the passion between the sexes is not innate? But admitting these terms, impressions and ideas, in the sense above explained, and understanding by innate, what is original or copied from no precedent perception, then may we assert that all our impressions are innate, and our ideas not innate.[5]

The sense of Hume's position lies in the distinction he makes between the more forceful and lively perceptions that are impressions and the "fainter" reflections and resemblances that are ideas. Locke's great flaw, Hume announces early in the *Treatise*, is his failure to have made this distinction.[6] And for Hume, we must take our orientation from impressions so that we get our ideas aright. In an analogous fashion to Locke who argued that the truth of complex ideas must come from the reality of our simple ideas, Hume claims that all simple ideas and impressions resemble each other; and "as the complex are formed from them, we may affirm in general, that these two species of perception are exactly correspondent."[7] Though, in "The Skeptic" he also emphasizes "the value of every object can be determined only by the sentiment or passion of every individual, we may observe, that the passion, in pronouncing its verdict, considers not the object simply, as it is in itself, but surveys it with all the circumstances, which attend it."[8] And even more forcefully: "Objects have absolutely no worth or value in themselves. They derive their worth merely from the passion [with which he pursues it]."[9] The derivation, then, of the idea from impressions makes the subject and its constitution as much an object as a subject—there is no simple substance that is the self, and all attempts to "espie" it fail, as one can only ever "stumble on some perception or other."[10]

While, then, Hume can be said to be continuing in Locke's tracks of basing the human understanding upon experience, his existential motives behind his framing of "experience" are part of a larger task of understanding what a rational overhaul of human intelligence will require. It is in this light that Hume finds Locke's commitment to "experience" too weak, and why he needs to redefine the source of ideas with more precision. Locke's ostensible empiricism still leaves a cluster of metaphysical elements—power,[11] substance,[12] God, and the soul—that Hume argues give us a false sense of our knowledge, and thus a false kind of orientation consistent with the superstitious view of life which Hume's congenial skepticism is meant to counter.[13] Hume's attempt to resolve the metaphysical quandaries that are opened up by an imprecise analysis of the human understanding far more so than Locke's is an attempt to circumscribe the bounds of human reason (if this formulation sounds Kantian, it is an indication of the importance of this part of Hume's project to Kant). The importance of his analysis of causation, and the role that custom and habit play in the accumulation of our knowledge, is that it lays bare the "deficiency in our ideas" when "we desire to know the ultimate and operating principle" of "that energy in the cause, by which it operates on its effect."[14] The Achilles heel in this analysis was his claim that "Even mathematical truths are probabilities."[15] It was precisely this kind of conclusion that was pounced upon by Kant, and it was the kind of claim that Leibniz would not have countenanced seriously for a second. Hume's failure to deal with the difference between the apodictic sciences and others is a serious one. Thus the conclusion he draws that "Since therefore all knowledge resolves itself into probability, and becomes at last of the same nature with that evidence, which we employ in common life, we must now examine this latter species,"[16] betrays the fact that Hume has fallen prey to his own quarry.

Yet Hume's analysis of the understanding's subversion of itself when it acts alone is to prevent that subversive activity disclosed through the metaphysical conundrums being transferred to general or common life.[17] But the breach that was required with common life for the mechanistic revolution to transpire was not so easily smoothed over simply because a philosopher (Hume) realized the importance of affirming "common life" against abstractions which have arisen out of the metaphysical conundrums emerging from the philosophy of mechanism. Indeed, Hume's philosophy is conspicuous by the oscillation it participates in between the constructed/modeled particularizations typical of experimental science and mechanism, on the one hand, and common life, on the other. This is all too evident, for example, if we consider Hume's theory of the self as "a kind of theatre, where several perceptions successively make their appearance; pass, re-pass, glide away, and mingle in an infinite variety of postures and situations,"[18] and his conclusion that "there is properly no simplicity in it at one time, nor *identity* in different; whatever natural propension we may have to imagine that simplicity and identity." These are the kind of philosophical conclusions that can only be reached by adopting a most "uncommon" disposition within "common life."

The great paradox of Hume is that he simultaneously advances that attack upon the "common life" of his time, particularly in the area of the lived faith of common people, while appealing to experiences of "common life" to cut philosophy down to size. As in Locke, and as in Husserl (for whom it can be reasonably argued Hume is an important precursor), "experience" is shaped (in Husserl through a non-naturalist phenomenology) by the intention that is brought to bear upon it. Of crucial philosophical importance is what question supports the intention. In Hume, far more than Locke, the intention was to free people from superstition, and the underpinning question was "can we know of God's existence?"[19] A question is, though, itself only an aspect of a greater disposition, emerging from a plethora of contingencies and circumstances, events, accumulated decisions, traumas, discoveries, commitments, practices, interactions, probing, and too much else to itemize. The same question about God's existence, for example, could be born out of despair and religious turmoil—but this is simply not the case with Hume. Whenever God appears in Hume, the charge/assumption of superstition is always close at hand—for it is the terrible effects of superstition that is his real problem—and one cannot eliminate superstition if one allows fantastical beings to be treated as if they are real. Impressions, for Hume, provide the cure to the ailment of superstition.

For Hume, we have no impression of God, the arguments for God's existence are all based upon (dubious) inferences from design, and evil exists. There is, in other words, for Hume, little reason to accept His existence. Not surprisingly, then, his reputation as a skeptic put him in the same camp as the "atheistic" duo of Hobbes and Spinoza.[20] Nevertheless if Hume's philosophy was considered by more traditional minded theological philosophers to be a philosophy that "has done great harm," as, "that bigotted silly Fellow,"[21] and nemesis, James Beattie had claimed,[22] the fact was that the metaphysics of the mechanistic philosophy had shifted theological disputes far beyond any biblical and ritualistic concerns, and hence far beyond the socio-historical contingencies that had played such an important role in cultivating the peoples and practices of Europe.

The biblical terrain is inhabited by personalities and transformative acts—God's creation and commands, and the relationships and responses that transpire over time between Him and his creatures, the various acts of obedience and dissent, of founding and destruction, of battle and of prophesy, of lamentation and prayer, of the covenant, of sinners and God's servant, and deeds great and horrific (genocide) and tiny (the widow's mite), and of stories told by God's own son, as well as the stories of his witnesses and martyrs; the philosopher's theological speculative parameters, on the other hand, were those of mind and nature. Although numerous mechanistic philosophers could lay claim to be good Christians, philosophers had nevertheless—whether believers or not—as a group shifted theology all but completely away from Christianity as a social practice grounded in a plethora of contingent events and specific divine commands and personal relationships. To be sure medieval theology had already continued the ancient philosopher's interest in rational theology, but it swam in a culture of the cross, the cloister, the penitent, the pilgrimage, holy days, sacraments, and the mass. With the deism and theism of the mechanistic metaphysics, the stripping away of visible signs of God's presence that had been such an important part of the Reformation were all dissolved into the infinitude of machines, and the infinite spaces and times of the philosopher's "purified" imaginations. To the extent that the great mechanistic philosophers were believers, they believed (as we saw with Malebranche and Leibniz above) in the marvelousness of creation and the marvelousness of reason—an intrinsic orderliness that they thought could only be adequately explained by a supreme intelligence—"God"—overseeing creation. The best the speculative theologians could achieve was an ecumenical God—and after such a protracted period of religious wars this was a significant achievement, which figures such as Leibniz and Bayle were astutely aware of. Hume knew that the wrathful Yahweh and the God who sacrificed his only begotten Son were largely irrelevant in the conundrums of rational theology. Thus too his argument was not with traditional Christians—they were, in his mind at least, already on the losing side of history.

If Descartes had hinted that the transformation of a culture for the new philosopher to thrive on must be slow (and we recall that his works were placed upon the Catholic index and forbidden texts at the University of Paris), and Spinoza knew that the body politic would have to be reconstituted so that men who taught the kinds of things he did would be protected, for his part Hume knew that while science offered human benefits, the human world was not just the "science world," and what mattered to those inhabiting the world could not be exhausted by mechanical science. He was far from alone in recognizing this, and the case for the essential contribution of aesthetic and moral experience to the human condition (something never forgotten by the philosophers of antiquity) had been remade, *inter alia*, in the writings of the Earle of Shaftesbury and Frances Hutcheson.[23] The full title of what Hume would later call his "juvenile" and inadequate work *A Treatise on Human Nature: Being an Attempt to Introduce the Experimental Method of Reasoning into Moral Subjects* highlights the anthropocentric core of his work. It also indicates that Hume was in many ways closer in spirit to these moralists and aestheticians than to the progeny of Descartes or the fraternity of Newton. Likewise, the anthropocentric core of Hume's thinking separates it from the more mechanical pictures of the universe and "man" in which ethics (as in Descartes, Spinoza, and Hobbes) is but one further branch of physics. In this respect John Danford is correct to argue that all the key moves in Hume's philosophy from his discussion of the nature of causation and the foundations of science, to his analysis of the forms of skepticism, to "his consideration of the nature of religious faith, and his inquiry into the foundations of morals, centre around his discovery of the tension between philosophic reason and common life"[24]—and his resolution through establishing the concordance of common life with philosophic reason, once philosophic reason is cleared of its excess faith in reason.

Hume's philosophical critique of philosophy's failure to grasp the true nature of experience, to "save" common life from false metaphysical speculation, invokes experience as a yardstick. Discrimination—rewarding, condoning (overtly or tacitly) or disapproving, punishing this behavior/action rather than that behavior/action—is indeed an intrinsic aspect of social reproduction, but the argument that it is experience as such that provides the touchstone for truth raises the question: What exactly are we talking about when we defer to experience? That our delusions are experiences was as important an insight for Plato as for Descartes. A mere appeal to "experience" would hardly shake the foundations of either's system—it was because experience was so confusing that philosophy existed in the first place. We can only appreciate why appealing to experience could "matter" if we appreciate that, just as Platonism generated much obfuscation in spite of answering questions, the same was the case with the new metaphysics and the new science. Hume was critical of what a surfeit of reason—i.e., reason detached from experience—had spawned. Hume's skepticism is a rational response to too much reason; his enlightened disposition is a response to insufficient reason. His chief criticism of philosophers is that they are not sufficiently grounded in experience—they are too rationalist; his argument against the unenlightened is that they are not sufficiently rational—their experiences have not been adequately classified.

First, his insistence upon the primacy of experience and impressions leads Hume to uphold two tenets of Descartes that had largely fallen out of favor within the new metaphysicians: custom and skepticism. For the Cartesian, customary perception was precisely the problem that required launching a new method, and skepticism was a "moment," not a solution, in the bid to overcome the limits of custom.[25] In Hume, custom is the answer to the problem of cause and effect—the problem that launched Kant's great metaphysical journey—and skepticism is primarily adopted as an invitation to the good manners of knowing one may not be correct in one's hypothesis about causal relations, and thus the means for providing a dialogical opening of inquiry.

But Hume, in breaking open the division between common sense and philosophical rigor from a philosophically acceptable rigorous point of view, implicates it in the kind of skepticism that is better rescued by common sense than philosophy—which is the antithetical mode to that of Descartes and so much of modern philosophy. The purpose of this, as suggested above, is to salvage the other areas of life for rational inquiry that do not conform to the mechanistic model. Although Descartes and Locke are certainly among the important founders of the Enlightenment, as the Enlightenment evolved it was increasingly obvious that the new philosophy was not solely about studying the mechanisms of the natural world, but a thorough exploration of the rational nature and character of human behavior and institutions more generally. Thus the kind of undertaking done by Hume and those who shared this expansive application of reason generally are crucial to the Enlightenment. The entire thrust of the *Treatise* and *Enquiries* is to improve the human understanding when it is dealing with human affairs where moral behaviour really matters. Now Hume knows this, which is why he insists upon moral experiment in the opening of the *Treatise* being different in kind to natural experiment. So although Hume must work with the philosophy of nature, the enterprise requires that he walk a fine line between accession to the truths that are compelling within it, and depicting its limits.

General life does not need philosophy to carry on—"the reflections of philosophy are too subtle and distant to take place in common life, or eradicate any affection"[26]—thus Hume's famous line about how cold, strained, ridiculous and off-putting his philosophical speculations feel after dining, backgammon, lively conversation, and merriment with friends.[27] But Hume believes that general life can, nevertheless, benefit from philosophy—provided the philosophy is one that has something to offer and hence can connect with general life. And this, as he perceives it, is the problem that the metaphysics of the new science has created: the hiatus it has established between its speculative insights in the attempt to render explicable the grounds and nature of the new physics when applied to general life look quite crazed: Berkeley's and Malebranche's metaphysical arguments are, for Hume, two cases in point. Speaking of Berkeley, Hume says "all his arguments, though otherwise intended, are, in reality, merely skeptical," for "they admit of no answer and produce no conviction. Their only effect is to cause that momentary amazement and irresolution and confusion, which is the result of skepticism."[28] Whereas Hume concedes that "the ultimate force and efficacy of nature is perfectly unknown to us, and that t'is in vain we search for it in all the known qualities of matter,"[29] and thus concurring ontologically with Malebranche, he finds the metaphysical appeal to God by Malebranche and the Cartesians as the source of motion of the universe to explain how matter—as an extended substance—must receive its motion from somewhere to be contrary to the very condition of knowledge: viz. that there is an impression providing an idea.[30]

It is significant that Hume the historian—yes Leibniz was also a historian, but his refusal to compromise his metaphysics with pre-philosophical knowledge (i.e., common sense) kept his metaphysics pure from historical affect—can warmly welcome historical memory into an epistemological argument that is ostensibly about experience as such. But the custom that Hume actually invokes is not the real custom with its pre-enlightened semantic and existential foibles (the superstitions which the congenial enlightened Hume hopes to cure humanity from), it is the custom of epistemic subjects who have transformed their impressions into ideas and ideas into knowledge. Thus, for example, as mentioned above, Hume thinks that belief in "God" is essentially an answer to a question and an ill-thought-through response to trying to understand the cause of existence; but this has no basis at all in our historical and anthropological knowledge. As far as we can tell peoples around the world invoked gods long before there was any speculative reflexive culture; the gods were just part and parcel of the way things were.

In making his case for common life, Hume, in spite of his emphasis upon impressions, had "piggybacked" on what Locke had called "the way of ideas."

In the philosophical arc from Descartes to Hume we can discern why the rationalization of the complete dissolution of the world of common sense by Descartes to shore up the certainty of scientific observation leads to a new set of metaphysical explorations which changes the way philosophers talk and think about God and humanity. Prior to modern philosophy philosophical talk of human beings and society rarely operated in a context in which the relationship between God(s) and humans was not also of major relevance. Even a mechanistic metaphysics such as that advanced by the Stoics was a testimony to a divine intelligence and cosmic master plan (to be sure this was not the case with the Epicureans). Hume's philosophy was by no means the first to sever the relationship between God and humanity on the basis of reason, but the way he does it is novel in its play-off between philosophy and common life, in how he checks philosophy by appealing to common life, and how he philosophizes common life so that it is not really common. That Hume in his analysis of causation also makes the imagination—the faculty which the earlier mechanistic metaphysicians saw as the bane of the world so long as it operated without the oversight of the understanding—as the central faculty of our worldmaking or orientation, is indicative of how far modern philosophy had succeeded in shaping the modern world and the modern imagination. In this respect Hume's importance is towering. Yet the philosophical brilliant and influential responses to his work by Thomas Reid and Immanuel Kant draw out very different key weaknesses in his philosophy.

THOMAS REID'S CRITIQUE OF "THE WAY OF IDEAS"

The philosophical crossroads reached by Hume and the different directions taken by Kant and Reid would be decisive for the fate of modern philosophy. Yet while Kant's critique of Hume is a momentous event in modern philosophy, providing the impetus for his "critical" philosophy, Reid's critique is generally forgotten. Nevertheless, his critique not only of Hume but what he saw as a tradition that culminated in Hume was an extremely important source of inspiration for Johann Georg Hamann, Friedrich Jacobi, and Johann Gottfried Herder, who all threw out a fundamental challenge to the philosophical direction Kant had hoped to ensure with his critical philosophy and its transcendental idealism.[31] Hamann and Herder did this by emphasizing common features of life (in different degrees and measure—language, tradition, contingency, and existential faith) that defied the Enlightened diremption of the rational and irrational. Hamann, who had helped with the publication of Kant's *Critique of Pure Reason*, possessed a French translation of Reid's *Inquiries*. And, as Kuehn also convincingly argues, it is highly unlikely that Hamann's enthusiasm for Reid's work would not have arisen in conversation with Kant—just as Kant's colleague and friend (until they fell out) Johann Krauss had read it with admiration. Moreover Reid's *Inquiries* (as well as the works of Oswald and Beattie) had not only been widely reviewed in Germany, but was frequently cited by contemporaries of Kant such as Christian Garve, Johann Feder, Johann Eberhard, and Johann Tetens.[32] Moreover, while we can find certain "elective affinities" in the works of Reid and Kant, overemphasizing occasionally similar critical formulations easily obfuscates far more significant and fundamentally antithetical narratives about what philosophy is at its best and what it should be doing.

It seems that while Reid was unaware of Kant's work, Kant was familiar at least with the gist of Reid's position, even if he did not know it well.[33] And he criticizes Reid, as well as his followers James Oswald and James Beattie, along with the non-Reidian Joseph Priestley, in the Preface (part II) of the *Prolegomena* for failing to understand the point of Hume's great achievement.[34]

While Reid continually invokes common sense against philosophy, he is still, after all, a philosopher. But his is a philosophy driven by deep sensitivity to the role of language and sociality as much as everyday experience, and an awareness of the dangers of using philosophy as a kind of vantage point offering not only a God's-eye view outside of the world, but a special place of greater safety that protects the philosopher from the kind of vagaries that plague the rest of us. Nevertheless, while Reid demonstrates how the removal of philosophy from common sense ultimately led it into labyrinths far worse and far more dangerous than the common deficiencies in human knowledge it hoped to surmount, he appreciated (like Kant) that any explication he gave of knowledge had to account for its greatest success in the study of nature, which is to say in the work of Isaac Newton, and the method and means that underpinned that work. Whereas Kant draws upon the success of Newtonian physics to identify what Hume pointed toward but did not grasp himself, and explores the cognitive source and epistemological nature of the principles of Newton, Reid provides an explication of Newton which renders the metaphysical arc reaching from Descartes to Hume as fundamentally erroneous (in spite of Reid conceding Newton's pivotal role in the formation of modern natural philosophy and metaphysics).

For both Reid and Kant, Hume's claim that mathematics is probabilistic was indicative of a major flaw within his system. But whereas Kant continues in the philosophical tradition in which common life is ultimately subordinate to philosophically rigorous "filters" of observation and legitimation, Reid takes Hume's cue by siding with common life against philosophy in those areas where philosophy overextends its reach, while at the same time opening up common life for philosophical instruction in those areas where it builds upon and improves common life. It can be plausibly argued that the reason that Reid (who was enormously popular in his life time and for a brief while after his death) would ultimately be completely overshadowed by Kant is because of the dazzling systematic quality of Kant's account of the forms of judgment deployed in metaphysics, experience, morals, aesthetics, and natural and historical purpose. Certainly, in comparison to Kant, Reid's philosophical voice is far more modest and his analysis can be repetitive to the point of tediousness.

The weakness in Reid's philosophy that cannot be avoided is insufficient attention to the historicity of common sense — so that common sense tends to look like what an extremely well read, curious, and thoughtful Scottish clergyman says it is. His appeals to the Supreme Maker as a source of social orientation fails to account for the malleability of common sense, with its various cultural and socioeconomic modulations — something altogether obvious when we consider how much easier it is today for a contemporary "Brit" to simply leave God out of any "common sense" picture of reality, than it is for a (non-academically educated) American (whether from the US or below its border). Nevertheless, this weakness does not suffice to nullify Reid's brilliance, evident in the thoroughness and complete dismantling of the philosophical way of ideas — a way he sees as stretching back to Pythagoras and from there to Plato and Aristotle, in antiquity, and being reinvigorated in modern times by Descartes and culminating in Hume's skepticism. The way of ideas, in other words, for Reid is ultimately the substitution of an image of the real crafted by the philosophical mind at the expense of the real that we make with words and deeds.[35] Yet Plato's original solution for ensuring that a stable form from which knowledge could take its bearing, and which also served the purpose for refuting sophistic relativism, becomes as much a means of disputation about the nature of knowledge and of the mind and universe as a means for the reconciliation of different opinions. As Reid says:

> Philosophers, notwithstanding their unanimity as to the existence of ideas, hardly agree in any one thing else concerning them. If ideas be not a mere fiction, they must be, of all objects of human knowledge, the things we have best access to know, and to be acquainted with yet there is nothing about which men differ so much.[36]

Thus, for Reid, philosophy needs to come to terms with having taken a wrong turn by deviating its focus away from reality—the full force of its consequence, for Reid, being evident in Hume's skeptical arguments.[37] Hume had wanted to identify the philosophical limits of our knowledge, but his skepticism had robbed both the philosopher and the common person of any real knowing. Whether fair or not, Hume's probablism was interpreted by Reid and many of his contemporaries as a pernicious skepticism depriving us of any genuine orientation within the world. Nevertheless, Hume's one certainty—that knowledge is probabilistic—is reached by retaining the philosopher's low regard for common sense, and then showing how philosophy not only fares no better by doing this, but, by so doing, renders itself largely, if not completely, redundant. Unlike Hume, Reid does not assume that common talk of God is superstition, nor that the common stock of knowledge exhibited in language may be all erroneous—as in the manner that modern philosophers have generally approached the subject by requiring a philosophically agreeable implacable foundation. Reid accepts from the start that, with the exception of axiomatic knowledge such as mathematics, our knowledge is contingent upon our limitations. Thus "everything that exists has a real essence, which is above our comprehension; and therefore we cannot deduce its properties or attributes from its nature, as we do in the triangle."[38] But, he argues that the mistake of modern philosophers was to follow Descartes (and Plato) in exaggerating the error of the senses, when "all the human faculties are liable, by accidental causes, to be hurt, and unfitted for their natural functions, either wholly or in part . . . there is no more reason to account our senses fallacious, than our reason, our memory, or any other faculty of judging which Nature hath given us."[39] It is our activities and needs that first motivate human designation, and the knowledge of common life does not require certitude of the sort that is required for mathematics and what Descartes also required for philosophical inquiry. Thus too where Descartes, Locke et al. see words as impediments to our understanding because of their lack of clarity and distinctness, Reid sees words as the storehouse of common knowledge. Moreover, words are not themselves primarily intended as pure definitions of essences—rather they relate to each other just as we relate to them and each other and the world. Language is part of a great praxeological concatenation (Reid is not to be confused with Saussure by talking of a "system" of signs) in which our activity can already be assumed. By the time anyone has any facility with their language, the quest for pure or original definitions is meaningless—"every word cannot be defined; for the definition must consist of words and there could be no definition, if there were not words previously understood without definition."[40] Although Reid's primary philosophical achievement is his critique of philosophy, that critique is predicated upon the philosophical failure to take human sociality and action sufficiently seriously to see its own activity within a greater context.[41] Thus Reid asks the simple but salient question:

> Why have speculative men laboured so anxiously to analyse our solitary operations, and given so little attention to the social? I know no other reason but this, that, in the divisions that have been made of the mind's operations, the social have been omitted, and thereby thrown behind the curtain.[42]

The close association between thought, and sociality is possible because we are speaking creatures. When Reid observes that it "was one of the capital defects of Aristotle's philosophy, that he pretended to define the simplest things, which neither can be, nor need to be defined; such as time and motion,"[43] he has an eye to the difference between the pragmatics of social communication and the precision of the solitary thinker wishing to find watertight definitions to mount compelling truth claims. In the two examples here identified by Reid (and this is no doubt the reason for taking them as his examples) we are confronted with precisely why Aristotle's physics had to be overthrown if a genuine science of bodies in motion could occur. Even Descartes, who did so much to topple Aristotle's influence in understanding the physical world by identifying number and empirical modeling rather than definition and logic, would succumb too readily to the speculative temptation. If action at a distance did not make rational "sense"—as clearly it didn't—yet could still be confirmed through observation and quantification, then so much the worse for rational "sense." Descartes's physics with its plenum, its contiguities, and its planetary vortices was ultimately as irrelevant to the truths uncovered by modern mechanics as Aristotle's. To be sure, its errors are vastly different to Aristotle, but the Newtonians (and hence Reid) grasped that because something happens for inexplicable reasons does not mean it is not true. For the new science was not about explication but identification—its truths were not reached through definition but by tracking the relationships between phenomena.

While it is obvious enough to Reid where modern and ancient philosophy divide, he, nevertheless, identified the enduring legacy for philosophy as the process of abstraction, which he sees as going back as far as Pythagoras. The forms perceived by the senses are spiritualized

> so as to become objects of memory and imagination, and, at last, of pure intellection. When they are objects of memory and of imagination, they get the name of phantasms. When, by farther refinement, and being stripped of their particularities, they become objects of science; they are called intelligible species.[44]

This, argued Reid, was the model that—in spite of all anti-Aristotelian attacks upon final causes—became subsequently adopted in the history of philosophy. While then the ontological difference between Plato, Aristotle, Descartes, and Locke is frequently represented as a conflict between empiricism versus rationalism, this is of less interest to Reid than the way in which the intellectualized entity (irrespective of where the root of that intellection is) that is philosophically identified and then argued about becomes the object of the philosopher's inquiry.

By contrast to this clear-cut division between subject and object, Reid argues that the process of understanding is not due to solitary abstractions initially taking place before being shared, but to social interactions in which our senses are involved and communicated. This does not rule out solitary reflections rectifying mistaken beliefs about the things of the world—but even then the solitary person is, by virtue of drawing upon the common store of names and concepts, digesting and expanding upon insights that have been collectively assembled.

Reid's critique of modern philosophy is, to repeat, not an attempt to obstruct the advancement of "natural philosophy" (i.e., modern physics). But, in addition to wanting to accurately identify its constitutive processes, he is all too aware of the dangers of its rationalist excesses—in particular, he does want to halt the subsequent skepticism and atheism which he sees as the inevitable consequence of that excess. He is equally alert to the dangers of naturalistic reductionism for all human activities—one of many concerns he shares with Kant. Hence while he is unstinting in his defense of Newton and in his deployment of Newton against modern philosophers, he also writes:

> There are many important branches of human knowledge, to which Sir Isaac Newton's rules of Philosophizing have no relation, and to which they can with no propriety be applied. Such are Morals, Jurisprudence, Natural Theology, and the abstract Sciences of Mathematicks and Metaphysicks; because in none of the sciences do we investigate the physical laws of Nature.
>
> There is therefore no reason to regret that these branches of knowledge have been pursued without regard to them.[45]

While Reid's critique of the "way of ideas" may be seen as suggestive of the post-Hegelian emphasis upon human experience and action, Reid is more invested in preserving what past experience has accumulated and passed on through language and social institutions. That is, there is no great new human project, as in Marx or Nietzsche, nor any existential probing of the sort and height that can be found in Kierkegaard. And there is certainly no new great metaphysical breakthrough as in Schopenhauer and Nietzsche. Rather there is a reconciliation with the world we have made as a world of common sense and with what Reid repeatedly refers to as the Supreme Maker.

NOTES

1. David Owen goes so far as to say that "Hume, like Locke, was dazzled by the success of seventeenth century physics, culminating in Newton," David Owen, *Hume's Reason* (Oxford: Oxford University Press, 2002), 65.
2. *Hume's A Treatise on Human Nature*, edited by L. A. Selby-Bigge (Oxford: Clarendon Press, 1888), 28.
3. Martin Bell, "Hume on Causation," *The Cambridge Companion to Hume*, edited by David Norton and Jacqueline Taylor (Cambridge: Cambridge University Press, 2009), 148. The "downsizing" of the discussion of space and time in the *Enquiries* from the *Treatise* suggests to me that although Hume's mind-set is certainly informed by Newtonian mechanics, the more he tried to draw out his own originality the less he needed to dwell on the essential conditions of the physics.
4. Hume's *Enquiries Concerning the Human Understanding and Concerning the Principles of Morals*, edited by L. A. Selby-Bigge (Oxford: Clarendon Press, 1888), footnote 1, 22.
5. *Enquiries*, 22.
6. *Treatise*, 1.
7. Ibid., 4.
8. "The Skeptic," *The Philosophical Works of David Hume, Volume 3* (Edinburgh: Adam Black and William and Charles Taite, 1826), 194–95.
9. Ibid., 188.
10. *Treatise*, 252.
11. "We never have any impression, that contains any power or efficacy. We never therefore have any idea of power," *Treatise*, 161; see also *Enquiry*, section VII, parts 1 and 2, and 350.
12. *Treatise*, sect 111, part IV.
13. Cf. Stephen Buckle, *Hume's Enlightenment Tract: The Unity and Purpose of An Enquiry Concerning Human Understanding* (Oxford: Oxford University Press, 2001), vii and viii.
14. *Treatise*, 266–67.
15. Ibid., 181.
16. Ibid., 181.
17. Ibid., 267–68.
18. Ibid., 253.
19. Hume's reputation as an atheist and skeptic was closely related to his deep antipathy toward what he saw as superstition. While the importance of his opposition to superstition may be gauged from the entire tenor of his philosophy, a clear indication of its importance comes from Hume's conversation with Adam Smith shortly before he died where the reason he gives to the mythical ferryman of Hades, Charon, for wanting to live longer is so that "I may have the satisfaction of seeing the downfall

of some of the prevailing systems of superstition." Letter from Adam Smith to William Strahan, November 9, 1776, in *Letters of David Hume to William Strahan*, edited by G. Birkbeck Hill (Oxford: Clarendon, 1888), xxxvii.

20. See the comparison with Hobbes in Paul Russell, "Hume on Religion," *The Stanford Encyclopedia of Philosophy* (Winter 2014 Edition), Edward N. Zalta (ed.), http://plato.stanford.edu/archives/ win2014/entries/hume-religion / last viewed January 30 2015.

21. See J. Y. T. Greig (ed.), *The Letters of David Hume* (Oxford: Clarendon Press, 1932), ii. 301.

22. James Beattie, *An Essay on the Nature and Immutability of Truth* (Edinburgh: Denham and Dick, 1805), 13.

23. Cf. for example see Ben Mijuskovic, "Hume and Shaftesbury on the Self," *The Philosophical Quarterly*, 21. (85), 1971, 324–36, Dabney Townsend, *Hume's Aesthetic Theory: Taste and Sentiment* (London: Routledge, 2001), Peter Kivy, *The Seventh Sense: Frances Hutcheson and Eighteenth Century British Aesthetics* (Oxford: Clarendon, 2003).

24. John Danford, *Hume and the Problem of Reason: Recovering the Human Sciences*, (New Haven: Yale University Press, 1990), 8. Danford's chapter "Science and Truth" correctly emphasizes the turning away from common sense in the new philosophy of science.

25. David Norton's very insightful piece "An Introduction to Hume's Thought" makes the claim that Hume is a post-skeptical philosopher, *Cambridge Companion to Hume*, 9.

26. "The Skeptic," 196.

27. *Treatise*, 269.

28. *Enquiries*, 155.

29. *Treatise*, 159.

30. Ibid., 159–60.

31. See Manfred Kuehn, *Scottish Common Sense in Germany, 1768–1800: A Contribution to the History of Critical Philosophy* (Kingston and Montreal: McGill-Queen's University Press, 1987), 141–166.

32. Ibid., 167–207.

33. Manfred Kuehn concedes that most philosophical scholars don't think there is enough evidence to confirm that Kant knew Reid's work in any depth. See, *Scottish Common Sense in Germany, 1768–1800*, 167.

34. It is odd that Kant places Priestley in this company insofar as Priestley had subjected Reid, Beattie, and Oswald to criticism, as well as Hume. See his *An Examination of Dr. Reid's Inquiry into the Human Mind, Dr. Beattie's Essay on the Nature and Immutability of Truth, and Dr. Oswald's Appeal to Common Sense in Behalf of Religion* (London: J. Johnson, 1775 [2nd ed]). See also Paul B. Wood, "Thomas Reid's Critique of Joseph Priestley: Context and Chronology," *Man and Nature*, 4 (1985), 29-45, and J. H. Faurot, "Reid's Answer to Joseph Priestley," *Journal of the History of Ideas*, Vol. 39, No. 2 (Apr.–June, 1978), 285–92.

35. The point is made repeatedly, but this from *Essays on the Intellectual Powers of Man* contains the nub of his belief is the central false belief uniting ancient and modern philosophers: "from Plato to Mr. Hume, agree in this, That we do not perceive external objects immediately, and that the immediate object of perception must be some image present to the mind." Thomas Reid, *The Work of Thomas Reid with an Account of His Life and Writings by Dugald Stewart, Volume 2* (Charlestown: Samuel Etheridge, 1814), 24.

36. Ibid., 228.

37. "His [i.e. Hume's] *Treatise of Human Nature* is the only system to which the theory of ideas leads; and, in my apprehension, is, in all its parts, the necessary consequence of that theory." Thomas Reid, *The Work of Thomas Reid with an Account of His Life and Writings by Dugald Stewart, Volume 3* (Charlestown: Samuel Etheridge, 1815), 129.

38. Thomas Reid, *Works, Volume 3*, 16.

39. Reid, *Works, Volume 2*, 322.

40. Ibid., 2.

41. Ibid., 55–56, 71–74.

42. Ibid., 73.

43. Ibid., 4.

44. Ibid., 13.

45. *Thomas Reid on the Animate Creation: Papers Relating to the Life Sciences,* edited by Paul Wood (Edinburgh: Edinburgh University Press, 1995), 185–86.

FIVE

Transcendental, Subjective, and Objective Idealisms

A Matter of Absolutes

KANT'S TRANSCENDENTAL IDEALISM

While Reid provides an essentially Baconian apology of Newton, Kant sees the problem in such a way that any such direct appeal to experience as such is blocked, and it was Hume's account of causality, mistaken as it was, that tripped the switch for him. Further, while Kant's appeal to the cognitive sources of our various claims about reality (from metaphysics, to knowledge of experience, to morals, to taste, purpose, and faith in progress) has generally had the far greater philosophical impact than Reid's emphasis upon sociality and language, ultimately, Kant's critique of Hume depends upon one fundamental insight: Hume's identification of the importance of causality opened up the question of synthetic *a priori* judgments—which are the basis upon which modern physics is possible, while Hume reduced the *a priori* to the probable. This was due to an elementary error that involves blurring the conceptual distinction be-tween the content of a law of nature and the form of a law of nature, in which *inter alia* causality figures. This distinction required, Kant argued, that elements, which are intrinsic to the form of the laws of nature, have to be constituted *a priori* by the understanding, while the specific causal explanation for observable phenomena, i.e., the content of the laws, is what we can only "read" out of experience. Kant's discussion of phenom-ena being subject to laws is based upon the causal account of strictly isolated variables. That is to say, we can establish that "b" always follow "a" under certain experimental or laboratory conditions which enable us to isolate variables and "block-out" other causal intrusions or forces. But the universe is unknown and, as a totality, unknowable in-itself, so the interplay of variables at any time outside the laboratory has to be hypothetical because a "pure" phenomenon is a construction of the imagination "peeling" away extraneous features/factors of the real that obstruct a clearer understanding of what we wish to know. Hume conflates causes in the world with causes that have been stripped back by the mind's intervention. He seems to be doing this so that he can make the point about the mind's (or rather the imagination's) role in making the connections between perceptions (much like Kant will), but the discussion constantly draws the argument to the goings-on in the world, and the impossibility of predicting exactly what will go on precisely because we don't grasp the exactitudes of existents in the world. This is correct, but it is Kant's insight that scientific advancement has to be looked for in the subject which poses questions to nature. This is also why Kant can rightly credit Hume's importance in his own philosophical development, but also why it is Kant not Hume who truly grasps the conceptual significance of the cleavage between subject and the world of objects and thereby undertakes the Copernican turn in philosophy.

The entire language of subjects and objects is the language of metaphysics directed toward the "laboratory" of the imagination shaped by the understanding, not of common sense, let alone custom. This is a key insight behind Kant's *Critique of Pure Reason*.

In spite of what I said above about a common commitment to the model uniting Plato and Descartes and most other metaphysicians of the new science up to Kant, one must also bear in mind the great shift that has taken place with respect to what knowledge means. When the ancients speculated about the metaphysics of nature, they had no laws of motion, no infinitesimal calculus, no gravitational forces, no Newtonian laws to contend with. It never occurred to Aristotle to think that his categories could only be verified if they could be "schematised," i.e., that they be shown to conform to the strictures of a mechanistic view of time so that they could also function as principles enabling the science of physical nature.

The importance of the fit between scientific modeling and Newtonian physics was also central to Kant's critique of Leibniz. In the first instance, Kant was able to point to certain shortcomings in Leibniz's view of space. Thus against Leibniz's claim that space is predicated on empirical relations, Kant uses the example of the same relationships reflected in a mirror.[1] Further, Kant's dissection of the different sources of the elements of cognition targeted Leibniz's cognitive continuum, which was based on distinctions of degree (more or less clear), and not as Kant argued on distinctions of *kind*. Once the emphasis is upon kind rather than degree, the distinction between what counts as (scientific) experience and what does not is epistemological, but the epistemology, as we have said, is built around the idea of having a fit between model and experience, the principles of pure reason and the physics, from which the principles have been derived. Likewise, Kant's cognitive apparatus is also tailored to the Newtonian model of experience he commences with—thus intuition (*Anschauung*, which he himself renders in the Latin *intuitio*)[2] is already severed from the kind of microprocessing which *precedes* a judgment. Although intuition mostly operates in tandem with our understanding because we generally "intuit" and understand (classify) simultaneous-ly—indeed they are each in "need of each other" when knowledge of experience is at issue—Kant makes intuition and understanding distinct faculties of the mind. In other words, the distinction between intuition and understanding is purely the result of a set of epistemological com-mitments that are based upon a methodological decision. Yet they appear in Kant as cognitive *faculties* or *capacities* as real in their way, and as *distinct* from each other as our limbs.

Kant's critique of Leibniz is dependent, in other words, on a certain understanding of knowledge in which proof and disproof, which is to say consciousness as opposed to the non-conscious (i.e., what is entirely empty of the consciousness of the subject), is essential to the process. The process only exists in Kant insofar as it is the cognitive interactions he himself has authorized to "deal with" the problem. For Kant, Leibniz's central error is that he does not introduce the cleavage between intuition and intellection, thus he has a God's-eye view—intellectual-intuition.[3] But intellectual intuition is precisely what we do have when we "micro-process"; the distinction Kant makes only makes sense at a certain reflec-tive moment taken up below, where we model. Kant, of course, speaks of instincts in a variety of places, especially in the context of his moral philosophy, but when it comes to "theoretical reason," and hence to the acquisition of knowledge, instincts are completely lacking. Indeed, while Kant's moral philosophy only addresses reason in order to ensure that moral judgments are never evaluated as moral if any instinct can be demonstrated to inform them, Kant's theory of "theoretical reason" also requires that instinct play no role. What is preserved is the purity of reason, and hence the purity of the problem and representations, what is questionable is whether casting the problem of reason thus is really in-structing us about reason's nature.

Leibniz's imbuing the universe as such with consciousness—all the way up and all the way down—was generally in agreement with the more religiously concerned Cambridge Platonists—and they were all op-posed to some of the metaphysical and atheistic implications of the new science rather than the science as such. In the more reductivist mechanis-tic world picture, though, consciousness was an epiphenomenon not a ground. But the problem was whether what was an epiphenomenon was also such a distinctive feature of human reasoning that it made little sense not to separate consciousness and its reasoning processes from what it was that our consciousness sought to understand. Descartes's dualism and the representation of cognition as a "bundle" of cognitive functions or capacities was one way of dealing with the problem. Locke and Spinoza wanted none of the dualism, but they could not avoid the problem of us being able to distinguish between conscious subjects and a world of "objects." Descartes had compounded the problem by bringing in what he called innate ideas,[4] thereby setting philosophy down a path to what Kant would later classify as *a priori* functions of the understanding ("concepts"), and principles of reason, i.e., the "ideas" that serve to help us better understand nature's mechanisms.

In sum, the first *Critique* was designed to resolve (and in doing so provide a scientific basis to) the metaphysical quandaries that mechanism had spawned by virtue of our modelling being based upon the questions we pose to nature.[5]

The circularity involved in Kant's view (as a model requiring a fit between the mind's representations and reality) and his facultative "logic" is also evident in how Kant formulates the central problem in the *Critique of Pure Reason*—"how are synthetic judgments *a priori* possible?" Again, the comparison with Leibniz is apposite for seeing what is happening. For Leibniz, every substance contains everything within it, which amounts in Kant's terminology, to all judgments being analytic judgments—i.e., all predications are logically contained in the "subject." The problem for Kant with this is that if this is so, then experience is unnecessary for knowledge—we could know everything on purely logical grounds. If this is so, then Leibniz is also the archetypical rationalist, and it is understandable why, if philosophy is to help secure us in our knowledge, Leibniz has to be completely refuted.

For his part, though, Leibniz never for a moment suggests that reason and logic are meant to displace knowledge gained from experience, they are meant to help us investigate experience (Herder found Kant's treatment of Leibniz completely exasperating). The very example of an analytical judgment that Kant provides—i.e., "all bodies are extended"[6]—only further highlights his antipathy toward Leibniz's way of thinking; for it was precisely the idea that extension was of the essence of a body that Leibniz denied. And Kant's decision to reinvoke it, although compatible with the general tenor of mechanistic philosophy, does not suffice as an argument against Leibniz.

Another core problem that shapes Kant's procedure in the first *Critique* is his objection to the Platonist "glide" from mathematical entities to empirical entities or appearances. Now Plato, Leibniz and Kant agree that there is a connection between nature and number, or in modern parlance sense data is quantifiable. Given that is the case, then this is not a problem as such for Kant, what is the problem is that he thinks that the rationalists (Plato, Leibniz et al.) will conflate mathematics as such with experience. Again, it is very difficult to argue that Leibniz is actually guilty of this. Moreover, Kant's attempt to save "mathematical experience" founders on his theory that mathematics is a constructive science grounded within the inner sensibility of the subject. For Kant, the question of *how* the apodictic science of mathematics and the contingencies of the world could be brought into unison in one science was all important. Moreover, his solution brings time and space and the number line into unison and hence fulfills the requisite explanatory conditions required for the level of geometry and calculus in Newton's physics. But for all its brilliance, the theory of mathematics in *The Critique of Pure Reason*, bears about as much relationship to a contemporary philosophy of mathematical science as a steam train does to a microchip. Moreover, ultimately it reproduces, albeit at a more sophisticated level, the kind of problems which befall the cruder empiricist reductions of the origin of mathematics, a position which Kant himself critiques by distinguishing between Euclidean geometry and early Egyptian geometrical measurements.[7] The reproduction is obvious as soon as one must concede that (a) it is pointless to make irrational numbers beholden to the number line (b) that irrational numbers are as essential to modern physics as "rational numbers," and (c) that aspects and dimensions of physical reality, such as those uncovered by Einstein's deployment of curved space in the general theory of relativity, and quantum mechanics are dependent upon non-Euclidean geometry. Reid, by the way, who argues that mathematics is axiomatic,[8] does not come up against this problem. Instead he argues that:

> The clear and accurate notions which geometry presents to us of a point, a right line, an angle, a square, a circle, of ratios direct and inverse, and others of that kind, can find no admittance into a mind that has not some degree of judgment. They are not properly ideas of the senses, nor are they got by compounding ideas of the senses: but, by analyzing the ideas or notions we get by the senses into their simplest elements, and again combining these elements into various, accurate, and elegant forms, which the senses never did nor can exhibit.[9]

In other words, Reid argues that while qualities may commence with the senses, the subsequent analysis of geometrical and mathematical qualities enables an axiomatic construction which is dependent upon the qualities suggested by, but not grounded in, nature. The question of the *fit* between the axiomatic and the natural system is thus one of precision which can only be verified by trial and error. This is why Reid insists that Newton is correct not to try to explain rationally defiant, yet real, phenomena such as action at a distance. To be sure Reid is invoking the mind in this process—but it is precisely because he does not draw a sharp line between the mind and the senses as Kant does that he does not have a two-world theory. As in common sense—having sense does not mean dispatching the mental from the sensory, but rather appreciating the mystery of the interpenetration between sensation and thinking. Kant and Reid are both devoted to preserving science from rationalism, but Kant treats the mind and world or nature as strictly dual (every bit as much as Descartes), and it is this underlying dualism that leads him to adopt his solution, and hence his dogged determination to shake off the specters of Plato and Leibniz.

Reid would have no doubt that just as Plato is an early exponent of the way of ideas, along with Aristotle, Kant too takes the same way as Descartes, Malebranche, Locke, Berkeley, and Hume. In other words, the dyad of rationalism versus empiricism, while of such importance to Kant, is only of secondary importance for Reid. Reid commences with (and blasts away at) the far greater unity shared by philosophers who have elevated the mind and its ideas outside of the reality of common sense, instead of appreciating that while science does indeed require a closer scrutiny of phenomena, through the laboratory and mathematics, than people undertake with their common sense, there is not so much an absolute breach with common sense, as it is with Descartes and his progeny, but a modification and attenuation of what is required by common sense when dealing with certain kinds of phenomena. This is also why he does not dismiss ideas in the everyday sense they are used, but only refutes philosophical ideas as grounded in the sceptical disposition of the philosophers who have so substantialized mind that they make their disposition the only means of access to reality.

Kant, on the other hand, has to postulate the reality of the inaccessible thing-in-itself (as a theoretical requirement) that has to be left behind so that we can know *our* reality, the phenomena. This is reinforced by Kant's commitment to moral judgments as also being purely rational. Being purely rational, moral judgments and dignity itself are founded in noumena; for Kant phenomena and noumena must be different in kind. Hence the problems of mathematical origins, *a priori* forms and functions of experience and moral ideals must be carefully compartmentalized so that the rational existence of the one (morals) is not seen as a mere extension of the contingencies of the natural world or phenomena. And as I have said, in doing this he remains committed to what Reid calls "the way of ideas"—which in the case of Kant involves combining the *a priori* elements of reason and the representations (*Vorstellungen*) which he depicts as deriving purely from the observational disposition. Stated otherwise, subject and object are strictly severed, even though our objects are, nevertheless, transcendentally subjectivized. But we go awry if we confuse transcendental subjectivism with empirical subjectivism. There is, then, for Kant, a transcendental logic that must be complied with if we want to properly understand the world. The question is which transcendental conditions govern which kind of judgment. That transcendental logic is not purely rational, though it is of the mind's own making, is also why Kant is convinced that the failure to grasp the source and nature of this logic is also at the basis of the kind of logicism exhibited by Plato and Leibniz.

When I mentioned above that Kant had to cut Leibniz/Plato off at the mathematical pass, it was not simply because he saw an epistemological defect in Leibniz's/Plato's metaphysics of the physical world (which he did). Most importantly, he knew that Platonism had to be defeated, if he were to provide an absolute fissure between moral judgments and judgments about (Newtonian) experience in order to make the case that freedom was absolute and not conditioned in any way by our physical appetites and needs. In other words, the primary *motivation* behind the epistemology of the first *Critique* is *primarily* anthropological, and the anthropology is an idea-ized view of what defines us: viz. our moral freedom.

Just as Plato had wanted to talk about ethics and found himself thinking about mathematics—so much so that the philosopher in the *Republic* has to have mathematics as part of his education, Kant had to dismantle Plato's theory of mathematics so that the duties of moral freedom he wished to defend could be grounded in freedom rather than nature. Yet the one aspect of Plato Kant retains is the idea that morality is to be understood first and foremost as an *idea*.[10] And hence while Kant's metaphysics is so closely bound up with the nomenclature of his cognitive components, he retains the Platonic term "idea" for what is the product of reason's own making, the most important of which is moral freedom. In both Plato and Kant, it remained the case that it was the ethical that was the prime driver of their philosophical choices. Moreover, Kant was insistent that mathematics does not, as Plato thought, assist us in grasping an idea in the way that one can speak of the idea of moral goodness (Kant's not Plato's term). On the contrary, mathematics is important, for Kant, not because of its intrinsic demonstration of (divine) intelligence in the cosmos, but, as we suggested above, because it discloses something *only* about the physical world. If we could not represent the physical world mathematically, the problem of mathematics might have interested Kant as an aesthetic problem, but not as a decisive one for crafting his metaphysics. And we note, Kant only belatedly realized that aesthetics (and teleology) posed problems for the metaphysical pillars of experience and morality, and how they might relate, that he needed to address.

For a brief moment Kant could bask in the glory of his philosophy having finally "found" the elusive philosopher's stone—by establishing a scientifically reliable metaphysic once and for all;[11] his metaphysics of experience was the culmination of metaphysics tailored to mechanistic science; his practical reason was defined, in turn, by what it was intended to be in opposition to, natural forces, instincts and whatever else sullied the absoluteness of human freedom. But he had to watch in horror how it was all wrecked by the temerity of Fichte and the outrageous "enthusiasm" of Schelling—not to mention the less well received, though no less well mounted criticisms of Hamann and Herder, which, for Kant, only confirmed that they were not real philosophers. Kant was convinced that his critics were all just reproducing the errors of the "pre-critical" metaphysicians.

I have said that Kant started with a core distinction between intuition and conceptualizing or understanding, but he had also used another important term that precedes that distinction—the term "representation" (*Vorstellung*, which is invariably rendered in English translations of Schopenhauer's *Die Welt as Wille und Vorstellung*, as either representation or idea). The Kantian subject is confronted with a representation which is then authenticated by the appropriate match up of its marks by the fit between our intuition of it and our concept of it. Again, we see how Kant has set to work, in the manner, even if not in the precise result, common to all mechanists, of interpreting what he calls experience in such a way that experience is already modified by a very precise experience, mainly the experience of studying nature in order to gather scientific laws. A major flaw in what he is doing is evident in what might seemingly be overlooked as being completely innocuous or trivial, that is in the semantic choice he makes in his cognitive distinctions and the ensuing philosophical results and demarcations. For Kant, while representations (*Vorstellungen*) are the vagaries which then need to be adequately conceptualized in conformity with our view or intuition of them, and our judgments of experience are what he calls the synthesis of concepts, our ideas (*Ideen*) are what we achieve through the syllogistic capacity or reason. That is, Kant deploys cognitive terms in which he eschews any talk of ideas (*Ideen*) except in a technical sense, i.e., in the sense of reason's own creations as it absolutizes or finalizes through the syllogistic process. These ideas are then further demarcated into those which have a regulative or heuristic use for expanding our knowledge, and those which have a moral use. By the time of his last critical work, the *Critique of Judgment*, that expansion of knowledge will also be linked to a sense of historical progress.

While, on the one hand, then, we can see how the evolution of modern philosophy from Descartes to Kant has refined its cognitive terminology, the refinement in no way brings the matter of how we classify back (to use Hume's term) common life, or Reid's common sense. Kant does indeed provide a space for common sense within his aesthetic theory. But the relegation of common sense to what is but a subjective sense having no bearing on real knowledge ensures that he still has philosophy being beholden to the insight of the observer who correctly intuits and conceives a composite of relations (a manifold). Concomitantly, the solitary thinker who wishes to be sure of their knowledge is at liberty to review the phenomena. Not surprisingly we have the dyad of truth and falsity, and not far away is good sense and superstition. Hence Kant's critical philosophy for all its rigor is really the consolidation of a worldview which will eliminate all the collective wisdom of millennia unless it can conform to the strictures of "experience" by becoming a mere object which can be understood by this mere inquiring subject.

The culture of scientific inquiry creates a new kind of community of disinterested observers, at least for all of us (I suspect rather few) who don't let career, grant money, corporate incentives, etc. interfere with disinterestedness. This is as remarkable an achievement as the actual advances made in the full gamut of the natural sciences. But we are still the creature who can undertake explorations at far reaches of the universe, while still not knowing how to prevent everyday acts of neighborly squabbling, let alone the ferocious social explosions of mass violence. Kant's great contribution to classifying the latter kind of event was that we can classify certain intended acts as immoral! And what was most pressing for Kant, as it is today for moral philosophers in countless university departments around the world, is to find the right principles for being *really* moral.

For all his efforts in defining the "bounds of sense," making room for faith in moral freedom, and identifying how our aesthetic and teleological judgments act as a bridge between our faith in freedom and experience of necessity, Kant, nevertheless, left largely untouched what the phenomenologists would call our "life-world." Moreover, while his attempt to identify the forms of certain kinds of judgment is dazzling, his solutions would all come asunder. It was, though, a great pity that Hamann's and Herder's arguments that philosophical reasoning grows out of collective (historical) experience, insights and language, and is not *sui generis*, were drowned out by the more idea-ist criticisms of Kant's idealist progeny.[12]

FICHTEAN AND HEGELIAN IDEALISMS

Kant's rational faith had established a cognitive hierarchy which reflected Kant's anthropological horizon of man as a creature who is driven to answer the questions of what man may know, what he should do, and what he may hope for.[13] Although establishing the circumference of the conditions of knowledge must be done first—and this is an indication of the limits of our possibility as creatures enmeshed in the natural world—it is the commitment to what we should become, to our moral purpose that Kant sees as giving us our distinctive human purpose: a purpose that only makes sense insofar as we are not only appetitive creatures, but rational beings. The corollary of this is that were we merely natural creatures driven only by instincts and appetites, our life would be as worthless as that of other non-rational creatures. We can see how remote Kant's view of natural creation is from the traditional Jewish and Christian depiction of a God who loves his creation and his creatures.

Just as the real core of our faith is morality, Kant's view of God and the soul as immortal are primarily operative in the moral orbit in which they are construed, though the possible existence of the soul and of God also serve as heuristic ideas for gathering more knowledge. Our most *valuable* representations (*Vorstellungen*), those representations which enable us to think of ourselves as members of a moral rational commonwealth, a rational kingdom of ends, are our moral ideas (*Ideen*)—they are "mere" ideas. They are fragile (i.e., not experientially confirmable), yet they are unconditioned. The idea of the total system of knowledge, the "absolute whole of all appearances" had been a product of reason divorcing or freeing itself from the legitimate constraints imposed by intuiting and understanding our experience.[14] Like all the principles and "ideas" of reason, "the absolute whole" is "transcendent" and oversteps the "limits of all experience."[15] Yet Kant also concedes that as an idea that holds out the promise of our knowledge forming a complete unity the idea of this "absolute whole" also has heuristic value in increasing our knowledge. But we could never *know* or *understand* it in the same way that we know or understand something that occurs within the realm of appearances. With respect to this absolute, we are in a relationship in which we are ever striving to comprehend something that is beyond the bounds of our comprehension. In this respect, and this is a point that Hegel recurrently refers to in his criticisms of Kant, it is analogous to our moral predicament: we are ever striving to live up to the maxims of our own moral absolutes, the unconditional ideals that are the products of reason itself. For Kant our entire dignity, then, rests on nothing more, nor less, than us having and subordinating ourselves to these ideas of reason. But as their existence cannot be disproven, they serve a practical/moral purpose, they are merely objects of a rational faith.

It is this sense of freedom, dignity and faith in the will that catches afire in Fichte's thinking. Wherever we turn in Fichte we see the triumph of the self-postulating willful subject: whether it be the nature of man as outlined in the *Determination of Man*, or the nature of right and the *System of Ethics*, or the nation in *Speeches to the German Nation*, or the state in *The Closed Trading State*. One and all they rest upon a view of the willful subject (repeatedly "deducted" in the multiple versions of the *Wissenschaftslehre*). Fichte, as we discuss below, had argued that what is circumscribed by our theoretical reason, i.e., our understanding of nature, is a construction of the self-postulating "I," and hence not restricted to Kant's categories of the understanding, nor the (Newtonian) principles that Kant had drawn upon to provide his transcendental schemata and the principles of pure reason. In other words, the Fichtean self was far more expansive and ultimately far freer in its constructions than Kant had envisaged in his moral writings. Conversely, Fichte was not so willing to place our moral freedom under the oppositional metaphysics, and hence constraints and limits of what nature is dogmatically taken to be. For Fichte, the "dispute between the idealist and the dogmatist is, in reality, about whether the independence of the thing should be sacrificed to the self, or conversely, the independence of the self to that of the thing."[16] For Fichte, then, dogmatism and materialism (which is a merely a form of dogmatism) were the deadly enemies of human freedom and dignity.

Hegel would say that Fichte's philosophy (especially in its more popular expression) with its emphasis upon acting out of one's innermost conviction in order to achieve the highest purpose and realize "the good" had sparked "a revolution" in Germany.[17] And while the philosophical climate had changed considerably by the time of the neo-Hegelians, Fichte had undoubtedly helped create the kind of moral climate in which social and political institutions would be seen as being in need of a radical overhaul more in keeping with our freedom. It was precisely the kind of climate in which the more philosophically minded and energetic would seek to shape the society to their own wills that Hegel had hoped to prevent. Unlike the various modern morally driven philosophies, of which Fichte's was just one offshoot, and in which the subject pitted itself against, or over the object of its will and intentions, Hegel saw the subject itself and its reason forming an *identity* with its world. For Hegel, Kant and Fichte were, then, part of a larger problem of the age, an age in which philosophy was taking upon itself the role of comprehending the spirit and meaning of the times, and the practices and institutions that defined and were defined by the times. This kind of philosophy was itself the expression of a spirit of an age and all the "labor" of reason that had formed it.

One cannot underestimate the impact of the horror that Hegel saw as the disjuncture between the aspiration for a republic of virtue and the actualization of that republic as it had been played out historically in the "terror," and which Hegel would philosophically depict in the *Phenomenology of the Spirit*. The erroneous "idea" that was operative in this event was the miscomprehension of the relationship between knowledge and our world, a miscomprehension that would be the centerpiece of Hegel's philosophy, and the vantage point from which he would criticize other contemporary philosophies. That miscomprehension, for Hegel, lay in the most fundamental error about the nature of reason and mind or spirit themselves: that the disjuncture between us and our world are total, that the finitude of our understanding and the infinitude of reason (and all that it has generated) is such that they must remain unreconciled, that this requires us having *faith* in a *beyond* as we *infinitely* strive to reconcile the desires of our own reason with the world. This would be the central theme of the first work in which Hegel had presented himself as a philosopher in his own right, *Faith and Knowledge*, which was devoted to identifying the common spirit that was shared by Kant, Fichte, and Jacobi. (Until *Faith and Knowledge*, Hegel had appeared as Schelling's philosophical accomplice.) To an important extent this disjuncture between faith and knowledge, which also replicated itself as a cleavage between the institutions of our ethical life and the abstract moral reasoning, which posits rational principles in opposition to existing ethical life, has been the result of an Enlightened approach to the world. The Enlightenment, for Hegel, was characterized by its own finitude positioning itself against the actual infinite of reason.

> The *living ethical* world is Spirit in its *truth*. When Spirit first arrives at an abstract knowledge of its essence, ethical life is submerged in the formal universal legality or law. Spirit, which henceforth divided within itself traces one of its worlds, *the realm of culture*, in the harsh reality of its objective element; over against this realm, it traces in the element of thought the world of *belief* or *faith*, the *realm of essential being*. Both worlds, however, when grasped by Spirit—which, after this loss of itself, withdraws into itself- when grasped by the Notion [concept— Begriff], are confounded and revolutionized by the insight [of the individual] and the diffusion of that insight, known as the Enlightenment; and the realm which was divided and expanded into *this world* and the *beyond*, returns into self-consciousness which now, in the form of morality, grasps itself as the essentiality and essence as the actual self; it no longer places its world and its ground out-side of itself, but lets everything fade into itself, and, as *conscience*, is Spirit that is certain of itself. The ethical world, the world which is rent asunder into this world and a beyond, and the moral view of the world, are thus the Spirits whose process and return into the simple self-consciousness of Spirit are now to be developed. [18]

That approach, though, has also brought in its train the expansion of freedom and hence also reason itself, for freedom and reason, for Hegel, are, when properly understood, one and the same. Thus Hegel also sees Descartes as the initiator of modern philosophy,[19] the first who really grasps that that "principle in this new era is thinking, the thinking that proceeds from itself," and that "the universal principle now is to hold fast to inwardness as such, to set dead externality and sheer authority aside and to look upon it as something not to be allowed."[20] But, the fact that Descartes was so focused upon using his metaphysics to support the empirical, i.e., mechanical, sciences, also leads Hegel to observe that "the reflective treatment [*denkende Betrachtung*] of the empirical is what predominates in this philosophy."[21] It is, for Hegel, this one-sided dominance that forces thought, spirit, to escape its incarceration in such a limit of its potentiality, and inner drive and purpose. For Hegel, the history of modern philosophy is the working out of spirit's self-realization and actualisation in and for-itself, and the respective emphases that philosophers, all responding to the condition of which they are a part, systematically develop.

Hegel, then, is deeply attuned to what he sees as the dangers of the one-sided emphasis upon the finite understanding and the Enlightenment invocation of the Absolute in the "beyond." He also accepts that there can be no retreat to an earlier age, or to any kind of thinking bound up with a previous age. Further, he also sees Kant's transcendental idealism as a watershed in modern philosophy. Kant's philosophy (and the metaphysical quandaries Kant attempts to solve) is the culmination of the metaphysical tradition in which the finite and infinite remain pitted against each other. Of course, among the pre-Kantians, Spinoza and Leibniz already provide some of the impetus for how Hegel proceeds. Kant also, unwittingly, provides the impetus for the breakthrough that philosophically leads from Fichte's "subjective idealism," with its center in the subject's free action, to Schelling's "objective idealism," with its identification of a point of "indifference" that mediates between subjective idealism and a philosophy of nature, to Hegel's own "absolute idealism," with its provision of a complete system of reason. That system aspired to identify all the elements, or thought-conditions, in their dynamic development, which overcome the dualisms of reason and world, subject and object, freedom and necessity.

Hegel sees Fichte's importance in having identified the central weakness of Kant's philosophy. But he also sees him as providing a solution which, by virtue of its retaining a number of key dualisms that are but variations of Kant, makes him "the completion of the Kantian philosophy," rather than the founder of a philosophy that really addresses what the age most needs.[22] Both Kant and Fichte, as we indicated above, are philosophies of "endless striving"; both are caught up in "a bad infinite." That is, both fail to come to grips with and hence provide a philosophy that fully grasps reason in its absoluteness, and hence the full extent of its freedom and development: they do not know how to reconcile knowing itself with the absolute condition of their knowing—which, though, was the promise both philosophers held out. But Fichte did have one great thought, viz. that Kant had not achieved what he set out to do, and that he had drawn upon elements from a "system" he did not himself provide. Kant, he says, in the "Second Introduction to the Science of Knowledge,"

> by no means *proved* the categories he set up to be the conditions of self-consciousness, but merely said that they were so: that still less did he derive space and time as the conditions therefore, or that which is *inseparable* from them in the original consciousness and fills them both: he never once says of them, as he expressly does of the categories, that they are such conditions, but merely implies it. . . . However, I think I also know with equal certainty that Kant *envisaged* such a system: that everything that he actually propounds consists of fragments and consequences of such a system, and that his claims gave sense and consequence only on this assumption.[23]

Kant had, as we have suggested above, conveniently used a "bundle" of cognitive faculties to solve his problems, but he had not explained how he could be sure that what his consciousness had identified as the cognitive conditions of experience could themselves be known. Indeed, his entire account of what knowing involved could hardly be convincing when the entire philosophy rested upon his defiance of the principles he had laid down. Fichte saw that what was really lacking was the very pivot that Kant had claimed to provide in the "transcendental deduction" but didn't because he did not take the necessary step to provide the more preliminary deduction. Kant should have deduced all conditions of knowledge from one principle: the all-important act of consciousness, what Kant had identified in the "transcendental deduction" as the transcendental act of apperception, which Fichte in a move harkening back to Leibniz and pointing forward to Schelling also identifies as requiring an act of "intellectual intuition." Once this is done, however, it is evident that Fichte is doing more than merely a "clean up" operation on Kant's behalf. And the more obvious it was that his philosophy was not just Kant slightly repaired, the more Kant's importance moved from that of philosophical "savior" to that of philosophical "prophet" of the new philosophy, which Fichte himself would provide. Its centerpiece was its *act of decision*, the fact-act that the I as act is the condition and expression of knowledge *and* freedom. For Fichte this original act of self-postulation cannot be derived from other concepts, but it is the condition of there being any concepts at all. The knowing is in the doing, and to try and explain it further would be as much a waste of time as explaining color to a blind person.[24] Our *knowledge* and moral world are all, then, the expression of this absolute "I" that is a self-positing, fact-acting "I." To be sure, it is an I that is, as Günther Zöllner rightly says, "not a specific I but an I in the generic sense of a structure or a set of formal conditions . . . [which is]not characterized by consciousness—neither by the reflective awareness of itself, or self-consciousness, nor by the self-consciousness of objects."[25] It is consciousness as conditioning and act.

While, then, Fichte's philosophy was developed from the clues provided by Kant, but which Kant himself did not adequately think though, in the "transcendental deduction"—viz. the unifying and dynamic act of the subject's sovereign role in the sciences and the moral realm, it is important to emphasize that Fichte was not interested in solving the same puzzle that Kant had set himself to solve on the basis of the fit between the *a priori* principles of experience dug out from Newton. Indeed there is no evidence that Fichte had construed the problem of the categories as requiring a metaphysics that was completely congruent with the *a priori* underpinnings that Kant had detected as operative in Newton's *Principia*.[26] But, to repeat, Fichte's recognition that Kant had not philosophically "deduced" how and why the elements of cognition would become the bridge between a philosophy that had sought to find the solid ground for knowledge of experience and moral freedom to a philosophy dedicated to *faith* in man's capacity to *act*. Kant's philosophy, in other words, was the philosophical culmination of an age; Fichte's the commencement of a new one. This new philosophy did not require what Kant had called a "transcendental critique," but a "Science of Knowledge," which would provide "a genetic derivation of that which occurs in consciousness."[27] And, insofar as the sciences were dependent upon the self-postulating "I," and hence "the science of knowledge" furnishing "the ground of all experience,"[28] there could no longer be a radical separation between form and content.[29] But, as we recall, for Kant, it was Hume's failure to distinguish between the form and content of the laws of nature that was the original spur to Kant's transcendental idealism. Kant's transcendental idealism had been built upon the distinction between synthetic *a priori* functions, judgments and principles and *a posteriori* ones, but for Fichte this only served to show the limits of Kant. For Fichte: "For a completed idealism the *a priori* and the *a posteriori* are by no means twofold, but perfectly unitary: they are merely two points of view, to be distinguished solely by the mode of our approach."[30] In turn we can see the larger philosophical ambitions at work in the "Science of Knowledge":

> The science of knowledge should, however, not only give the form of itself, but it should give the form of all possible sciences, and establish with certainty the validity of this form for all sciences. This can only be conceived under the condition that everything which is supposed to be a proposition in a science should already be contained in a proposition within the science of knowledge, and that the proposition is already set out in its appropriate form.[31]

Given what it was Kant was trying to prevent, his response in his "Explanation in Relation to Fichte's Science of Knowledge" should have been no surprise to Fichte:

> Pure science of knowledge is nothing more nor less than mere logic, which, with its principles does not search for the material of cognitions, but as pure logic, abstracts from their content, from which a real object is vainly picked out.[32]

Ironically, Hegel's critique of Fichte was that he had failed to recognize that it was precisely the "labour of the concept" that only a *Science of Logic* could provide. That is, Hegel concurred with Kant up to a point: Fichte had re-opened the question of metaphysics in such a way that only a logic could solve it. But, for Hegel, Fichte had not realized what he had done. Nevertheless, as Hegel saw it, after Fichte there was no turning back: Fichte's "great merit" lay a) in recognizing that Kant had been philosophically unjustified in adopting "thought-determinations, the categories, empirically, just as they have been worked out in [traditional] logic, that is, just as the universal forms are found in the [table of] judgments," and b) he rightly "called for, and sought to complete, the derivation or construction of the categories of thought from the I, and he did in part carry out this project."[33] More, Fichte was the "first" who had "posited philosophical consciousness or the aim of philosophy as the knowing of knowing."[34] For Hegel, then, Fichte was absolutely correct to see philosophical knowledge as concerned with a totality of inner connected dynamic and living totalities. But while Hegel also agrees that Fichte is right to see a fundamental unity between the sciences (i.e., the totalities of our knowledge) and our world, he thinks that the principle that Fichte settles upon was incapable of achieving what is required of it. That is, for Hegel, the Egoic centerpiece of Fichte's philosophy is but another illustration of the very dualism that this new kind of idealism had rightly sought to vanquish, and, as we will pick up later, he sees that Fichte merely transposes the source at the basis of Kantian dualism, the thing-in-itself, to the "not-I." In this respect Hegel agreed completely with Schelling's critique of Fichte: his philosophy was merely a one-sided, subjective idealism. And as long as it did not a) provide a philosophy of nature and b) clarify how nature and freedom were genuinely unified philosophically, it was, to put it brutally, a failure. What was needed was as Schelling, implying that he had completed what Kant and Fichte had opened the way to, a *System of Transcendental Idealism*. Although, in the next chapter we will discuss in detail why Schelling was unwilling to have his philosophy be but a moment in Hegel's development, it is the case that this insight of Schelling's, and what he also called the "philosophy of identity" with its point of indifference, was absolutely essential to the development of Hegel's own system.

For a brief time, though, Schelling and Hegel were allies in rejecting Fichte's one-sidedness. In their insistence upon the unity of the world and the Absolute both joined in the revival of Spinoza that Herder and Goethe had been active in. Yet by incorporating the dynamism at the heart of Fichte's subjective idealism and the importance of the "deduction" into his account of reason, Hegel's philosophy was not merely Spinoza redux. (Nor as we shall discuss in the next chapter is Schelling's.) More, for Hegel, Spinoza's greatness was not, as others at the time emphasized, in its dynamic and totalizing organicist view of nature, but in his very understanding of the infinite. The infinite was not the counter-concept to the finite, but it was the genuinely absolute. If the finite existed apart from it, it could not be infinite. Spinoza had realised that the infinite must contain the finite as immanent, and it cannot be made up of an extensive series of finites. As Spinoza wrote,

> My statement concerning the infinite, that an infinity of parts cannot be inferred from a multitude of parts, is plain when we consider that, if such a conclusion could be drawn from a multitude of parts, we should not be able to imagine a greater multitude of parts; the first-named

multitude, whatever it was, would have to be the greater, which is contrary to fact. For in the whole space between two non-concentric circles we conceive a greater multitude of parts than in half that space, yet the number of parts in the half, as in the whole of the space, exceeds any assignable number.[35]

Another example, is that of the fractional representation of repeating decimal—the fraction provides the infinite as a unified totality, while a recurrent decimal is always in "progress." For Hegel this is precisely the distinction between a "bad infinite" in which one is held prisoner, as it were, to the sequence of a series that is never fully grasped, and the absolute infinite which is the productive power operative within the finite moments of the sequence. For Hegel, this insight of Spinoza was not extended far enough by Spinoza himself, who did not grasp "that in and for itself the idea contains within itself the principle of movement or of vitality, the principle of freedom, and hence the principle of spirituality"[36] (*Geistigkeit*, which in Hegel needs to be understood in terms of thought, the mental spirit.) But it provided the insight that enabled Hegel himself to see that the underlying fundamental error plaguing modern philosophies that played itself out in the countless dualisms which are bandied about as little absolutes: finitude and infinitude, understanding and reason, the *a priori* and *a posteriori*, synthetic and analytic, phenomena and noumena, morality and nature, freedom and necessity and so forth. Once, though, we recognize that thought thinks itself, that its dualisms are *its* dualisms, then they lose their finite intransigence and can be rightly seen as they are, i.e., aspects of reason's own operations. This is also why metaphysics, for Hegel, reaches its conclusion by returning to its real grounding in logic, not logic as an absolutely formal science—for thought and logic precede the recognition of its forms—but as a *forming* science, and hence as reason as substantiating. For this is what thought does: it transforms and brings into being, it moves and makes, it acts and devours, posits and negates, creates diremptions and reconciles—it grasps and conceives. Its summit is in its self-recognition as Absolute idea, as what coordinates and brings into union the diverse components of its own constitution. Thought and its ideas are alive.

For Hegel, then, reason is a substance that is also a subject and as the Absolute idea bears all within. Thus the great problem for Hegel lies in philosophy reconciling philosophy with itself. For different philosophies are but aspects, or, more accurately, "moments" of reason in its development. To identify how its different ideas, inherent rational totalities, cohere over the ages, or even appear as diremptions within a common spirit of an age, is to identify philosophy not only as absolute spirit, but to salvage reason itself. As a subject, reason develops in time; reason is a spirit of travail. As the subject in-itself that drives the world and our knowing and existence within it, philosophy and history are not two utterly distinct fields. Because the world and the self are constituted by the very same reason, a major error of those like Kant and Fichte, is to see the world either as morally empty, neutral, or even bankrupt, awaiting the imposition of philosophically formulated moral dictates. For Hegel, there is no legitimate way to transport oneself into a beyond of reason from which one can then act as a kind of God over creation. Nor are we left ever striving (again as in Kant and Fichte) against the obstacles to our moral will—we are surrounded by institutions directing our ethical life. The world does not, to repeat, await the philosopher's decree to be as it should be, rather the world discloses a reason that the philosopher should grasp/conceptualise because the way of the world and the way of reason are one.

We are also, then, for Hegel, as much outside of ourselves as inside of ourselves. Both the outside and inside are historical and neither was a sheer there, a mere manifold, as Kant would have it, because he takes another dualism intuition and understanding as essential. When Heidegger dwells upon *Dasein* one cannot but hear the designation as a deliberate break with Hegel, and the emphatic assertion of a being who is thrown, but not historically captive to the detriment of its own authenticity—which is why Heidegger could also be adopted by the left as well as the right: for both groups want confirmation of themselves as activists. Hegel, on the other hand, provides little solace for those leaping into a beyond, not because he does not understand transformation and the dying of the old—he certainly "tarries with the negative" (to adapt the title of a Lacanian treatment of Hegel by Žižek—though Žižek then uses this "tarrying" "moment" to twist Hegel into a much more radical figure than he is). Hegel tarries with the negative because he sees any future as bearing its own mediations of infinitude and finitude. Modern radicalism strives after and promises an infinite freedom from the restrictions of social and historical finitude, which is why it is ever a negation—and while Hegel was fully conscious of the power of the negative, he always stressed resolve and reconciliation as the achievement of freedom.

Hegel also saw that by making the founding question about the "fit" between mathematics and the physical world, and the possibility of *a priori* synthetic judgments being intrinsic to experience, Kant had also made the Newtonian world equivalent to the world as such. Our world, though, is shot through with Spirit and Spirit does not simply gather itself under Newton's cloak—i.e., what Kant calls theoretical knowledge. (One cannot underestimate the importance that Goethe's critique of Newtonianism was having upon the generation of which Hegel and Schelling belonged.) That is, Hegel had grasped that what is knowable is skewed from the outset in Kant by his mechanistic commitments and framings. While Hegel jettisons the facultative logic, he still retains the idea of reason as a sphere, which Kant had also deployed, and thus he concludes his *Encyclopaedia* with Aristotle's reflection in the *Metaphysics* on mind contemplating mind. Theologically expressed, God is mind and mind is God and the world but the effects of the causes of the mind of God. One does not need to be remotely theologically inclined to see that Hegel had absolutized or divinized the mind, and his philosophy provides his reasons for doing so.

We have seen how Kant's account of the transcendental conditions of a metaphysics of (Newtonian/ mechanistic) experience stands in the closest relationship to his designation of the cognitive faculties and their *a priori* elements. It should not be surprising, then, that having rejected Kant's opening gambit within the mechanistic metaphysics, Hegel will review the cognitive terminology to enable him to provide a more adequate account of reason's dynamism.

In his aspiration to show the real resources of spiritual replenishment that come from the rationality intrinsic to our life and world, Hegel, as we have indicated, retains the idea (*Idee*) as the most valuable epistemic term which he then also treats ontologically—a move that stands in the closest relationship to his disparagement of what he sees as the empiricist prejudice (and naivety) behind Kant's "refutation" of the ontological argument.[37] But the value can only be appreciated if the dualism which makes of the idea (*Idee*) a mere species of representation (*Vorstellung*) in Kant is negated and representation (*Vorstellung*) identified as but an "immediate," "unreflective," "isolated," "approximate," "general," and "preliminary" type of cognition. The idea's (*Idee*) elevation at the expense of representation (*Vorstellung*), in Hegel, also involves assembling "feeling, intuition, desire, will" (and he adds "etc.") and it involves a complete rethinking of thinking.[38] Thus the very opacity of the term, which comes from our original not knowing, is seen by Hegel as indicative of its lesser cognitive status; as we come to know things, we dissolve their *Vorstellungen*—they are literally grasped by us as concepts (*begreifen* to conceive builds upon *greifen* to grasp). In other words, what Kant had simply *identified* (one might say as Fichte and Hegel did, he merely "found" them) as a set of cognitive functions, the means of processing what we know, and what we *believe* as rational creatures, is reassembled in a *rational* manner by Hegel. Thus the highest act of rationality must be implicated in the very knowing, and not, as Hegel sees it in Kant, as being simply added on.

This rational reassembling of the process of knowledge is the key to Hegel's system, indeed the key to why for him philosophy can only be a system. And its grandeur, for Hegel, lies in the triumph of the incorporation of the idea over the lesser, but essential contributing determinations of intuition (*Anschauung*) which Hegel sees as the cognitive power operating in art, representation (*Vorstellung*) whose manifestations are evident to us, according to Hegel, in religion where symbol, ritual, rite and the like arouse feelings and hopes and desires etc. without ever rising to the clarity and consistency of conceptual knowledge. There are echoes here of Leibniz's view of cognition as a continuum, but in Hegel this takes on socio-praxological dimensions as specific spiritual activities—art, religion, philosophy—are seen as expressions of consciousness. Philosophy itself is dedicated to tracking the "labour of the concept," the dynamic development of thinking as it grapples with and reaches a more comprehensive grasp of the relationships within a process. The idea is the purpose as revealed by thinking to itself—the meaning inherent in any cluster of conceptual relationships. Whenever we are analysing something our primary referent is the idea; without it we are simply moving in the bad infinite, an endless tracking that seems to be going nowhere, because we have literally no idea about the underlying idea which is pushing us from one incident or factor to the next, and hence we are incapable of grasping the pattern that is right before our eyes, but not in the manner we expect it to be. For Hegel this is the only way that we can genuinely make sense of knowledge and ourselves. Note that in this move Hegel has not only completely distanced himself from any privileging of mechanism, but he has done it long before Husserl will attack naturalism. With Hegel the importance of the Absolute as encompassing the logic of its own conditions and expression and the History of its development means that rather than following Kant in speaking of the relative fragility of the idea in relationship to the more robust experiences we have of nature—(as Kant would say, "mere Ideas")—we should not think of "ideas" as so bare and vulnerable. On the contrary, it is nature that *means* almost nothing without our predications, without the content that we bring to it through the historical accumulation of our knowledge in our concepts and the sciences under the dominion of their driving principles, their immanent ideas. Nature's "distinct characteristic is its positedness, its negativity," says Hegel near the beginning of the *Philosophy of Nature*.[39] Logic and history have been elevated, logic has become and thereby replaced metaphysics,[40] but the logic is nothing without the sciences it generates; and the sciences are sciences, for Hegel, precisely because of their genetic development which is the development of thought. Any science would be impossible without the logic which inhabits it, but each science is but part of a chain, or rather a train of reason's movements. That this way of thinking still takes seriously the initial insight of Kant, that the science cannot be peeled away from the systemic posits of cognition, as well as the sheer questions we ask of nature (recall Kant's comments on Galileo, Toricelli, and Stahl's experiments) which frame data. But it takes cognizance of humanity's historical being defying the pure naturalism that was the reductionist view of those like Helvétius who represent humans and society as mechanisms. The Hegelian system is the system of all sciences, which is why it so impossible to maintain his Absolute. And that it was impossible was evident by the immediate response of the next generation: there were disciples like Michelet, and

Rosenkranz, but who, apart from students of Hegel's legacy, remembers them?

Having opened up the problem of the applicability of the *a priori*, Kant had opened up the far greater problem of the constituents of thought and their permeation of the world as such. Hegel's proud moment was in identifying the growth and scope of those constituents—from the barest nothing of being to the most triumphant achievements of Absolute Spirit—and pretty well everything else he could manage to fit in in between. But what is ostensibly Hegel's greatest moment ends up with the Absolute's explosion from its own all encompassment—its ever expanding girth. For in demanding that the Absolute be not merely formal, but actualizing, and demanding that the task of philosophy was to present a scientific system of reason's self-actualization, he faced an insurmountable problem. He had to know absolutely everything; if he did not, then his philosophy would just be another exercise in the formalism of thought of the sort he had persistently criticized in others. The ask made the task impossible. We have only touched the surface of Hegel's philosophy, and it is in so many of its moves that it is both at its most dazzling (so much of the logic especially when applied to the history and dialectics of modern philosophy), and at its weakest, "exhibit A" being pretty much the entire *Philosophy of Nature*, which fared far less well even than Schelling's attempts at a philosophy of nature. Certainly what Hegel had done, though, would once and for all demonstrate the intellectual flaws inherent in any dogmatic naturalism/empiricism or dogmatic moralism, which seek to address reality as such while ignoring the socio-anthropological and historical dimensions of knowledge.

If Hegel might be simultaneously viewed as a high point and end of a metaphysical pathway culminating in a philosophy of the Absolute, his former ally and mentor Schelling had been working assiduously, though not publishing, as Hegel's philosophy had taken on such prominence. While Hegel thought he had accounted for Schelling, Schelling had very different ideas on this matter, just as he had different ideas about the Absolute and the future and direction of philosophy itself. Moreover, while the generation that comes after Hegel cannot improperly be seen as post-Hegelian (even if was not always based upon conscious opposition or even a thorough knowledge of Hegel, as was the case with Nietzsche), the value and purpose of Schelling's philosophy (mercilessly derided in his later years) would remain largely waiting to be discovered by theologians and philosophers of the next century.

NOTES

1. Immanuel Kant, *Prolegomena to Any Future Metaphysics That Will Be Able to Present Itself as Science*, translated and edited by P. Gray-Lucas (Manchester: Manchester University Press, 1953) para. 13, 42.

2. The invocation of intuition is both indicative of a connection with Descartes and the shoring up of a solution which tries to rescue the mind from the metaphysical morass that Kant wants to clear up. In the third Rule for the Directions of the Mind Descartes makes the "self-evidence and certainty of intuition" a requirement for "any train of reasoning whatsoever." "Rules for the Direction of the Mind," 14 in *The Philosophical Writings of Descartes, Volume 1*, translated by John Cottingham, Robert Stoothoff, and Dugald Murdoch (Cambridge: Cambridge University Press, 1985).

3. *Critique of Pure Reason*, B72, B159, B308ff.

4. Seeing motion *in* matter itself is, I think, the crucial distinction between Descartes and the Cambridge Platonists and Leibniz who make consciousness or mind a real activating substance or force.

5. Kant refers to Toricelli rolling balls down inclined planes. Immanuel Kant, *Critique of Pure Reason*, BXI-BII.

6. *Critique of Pure Reason*, B 11.

7. *Critique of Pure Reason*, BXI.

8. *Collected Works of Thomas Reid*, Volume 1, 18.

9. *Collected Works of Thomas Reid*, Volume 3, 91.

10. *Critique of Pure Reason*, 370–75.

11. *Prolegomena*, 3–5.

12. Richard Kroner's magisterial *Von Kant Bis Hegel* (Tübingen: H. Laupp, 1921) is indicative of how philosophers position Kant and his aftermath. Kroner devotes chapters to Jacobi, Karl Reinhold, and Salomon Maimon as transitional philosophers between Kant, Schelling, Fichte, yet he bypasses Hamann and Herder altogether. They are also absent from Kuno Fischer's even more majestic *Geschichte der neuern Philosophie* ("History of Modern Philosophy"); 6 vols., Stuttgart-Mannheim-Heidelberg, 1854–77; new edition, Heidelberg, 1897–1901). They do, however, appear in Frederick Beiser's excellent study *The Fate of Reason: German Philosophy from Kant to Fichte* (Cambridge Massachusetts: Harvard University Press, 1987).

13. *Critique of Pure Reason*, B 832–833

14. Ibid., B 384.

15. Ibid.

16. J. G. Fichte, "First Introduction to the Science of Knowledge" in *The Science of Knowledge with the First and Second Introductions*, translated by Peter Heath and John Lachs (Cambridge: Cambridge University Press, 1982), 14.

17. G. W. F. Hegel, *Vorlesungen über die Geschichte der Philosophie, III, Werke, Bd. 20*, eds. Eva Moldenhauer and Karl Markus Michel (Frankfurt am Main: Suhrkamp, 1971), 414. Although R. F. Brown makes a good case for the importance of his translation and edition of the 1825–1826 lectures, some of the formulations in other versions of Hegel's *Lectures on the History of Philosophy* better encapsulate in a sentence or two ideas that Hegel expresses in many places with greater prolixity. Where possible references are to Brown's translation. Georg Wilhelm Friedrich Hegel, *Lectures on the History of Philosophy Volume 3: The Lectures of 1825–1826*, Ed. by R. F. Brown, translated R. F. Brown and J. M. Stewart with the assistance of H. R. S. Harris (Berkeley: University of California Press, 1990).

18. G. W. F. Hegel, *Phenomenology of Spirit*, translated by A.V. Miller, with Analysis of the Text and Foreword by J. N. Findlay (Oxford: Oxford University Press, 1977), 265. Unfortunately for those who read philosophy in English the enormous importance of the cognitive dispute taking place from Hegel toward Kant is often lost in translation, as words which are identical in the German in Kant and Hegel—and thus central to the problem they are attacking—are not uniformly translated. Take the simple term concept—*Begriff*—in a number of translations of Hegel it is rendered as "Notion"—though not always consistently—(Petry, Miller, Findlay, Baillie), one will scour long and hard to ever see the term Notion in an English translation of Kant; yet Hegel is using exactly the same word as Kant in German. Rendering it as Concept (as Knox does) at least retains the word but the capitalization (which of course has no equivalent in German which capitalizes all nouns) suggests a difference that does not

exist. A similar difficulty appears with the word Kant translators inevitably render as representation— *Vorstellung*— Knox when translating Hegel, for example, takes *Vorstellung* as "idea" to distinguish it from *Idee*, which he translates as "Idea." What is extraordinary with these translators, who are excellent scholars in many respects, is that it does not seem to have occurred to any of them that the cognitive names deployed by Hegel have a pedigree and that his arguments with his predecessors and contemporaries is predicated upon the terms in which it is pitched: to have to say this about Hegel seems to be stating the very obvious. Rather than reproduce the error and when using a translation from Hegel, I will add what I think is the more suitable word in square brackets along with the German.

19. *Lectures on the History of Philosophy Volume 3: The Lectures of 1825–1826*, 131–32.

20. Ibid., 131–32.

21. Ibid., 149.

22. *Vorlesungen über die Geschichte der Philosophie, III*, 387.

23. J. G. Fichte, *The Science of Knowledge with the First and Second Introductions*, 51.

24. Ibid., 38.

25. Günther Zöllner, "From Transcendental Philosophy to *Wissenschaftslehre*: Fichte's Modification of Kant's Idealism," *European Journal of Philosophy*, 15:2, 249–69, 253.

26. Andrea Poma sums it up neatly: "Since Fichte's philosophy had lost touch with Newton's science of nature, self-consciousness, Fichte's transcendental, was no longer a criterion but an organ of the *a priori*." *The Critical Philosophy of Hermann Cohen*, translated by John Denton (New York: SUNY, 1997), 74.

27. "Concerning the Concept of the *Wissenshaftslehre*, or, of So-called "Philosophy," in *Fichte: Early Philosophical Writings*, translated by Daniel Breazeale (Ithaca: Cornell University Press, 1988), 30.

28. "First Introduction to the Science of Knowledge," in *Science of Knowledge*, 6.

29. "Concerning the Concept," 66.

30. "First Introduction," in *Science of Knowledge*, 26.

31. "Concerning the Concept," 52.

32. Immanuel Kant, *Gesammelte Schriften: Akademieausgabe*, Band 12. Herausgegeben von Ottot Schöndörffer (Berlin: Walter de Gruyter, 1922), 371.

33. *Lectures on the History of Philosophy Volume 3: The Lectures of 1825–1826*, 229–30.

34. Ibid., 231.

35. Benedict de Spinoza "Letter to. . .," LXX (LXXI) in *Improvement of the Understanding, Ethics and Correspondence*, 413. See "Remark 1 *"the conceptual determination of the mathematical infinite"* of Hegel's *Science of Logic*, 204–14—Hegel then applies this insight to other problems of mathematics. Also *Lectures on the History of Philosophy, Volume 3*, 156–58.

36. *Lectures on the History of Philosophy, Volume 3*, 162.

37. See the *Science of Logic*, translated by George di Giovanni, 64–65. Kant, of course, had dismissed the ontological argument with the claim that the representation or idea of 100 thalers (rendered by di Giovanni as dollars) does not mean one actually has the money. To which Hegel responds: "these dollars are indeed an empirical content, but cut off, without connection or determinateness as against *something else*; their form of immediate self-identity deprives them of external connection and makes them indifferent to whether they are perceived or not."

38. *The Encyclopaedia Logic (with the Zusätze): Part 1 of the Encyclopaedia of the Philosophical Sciences*, translated with Introduction and notes by T. F. Geraets, W. Suchting, and H. S. Harris (Indianapolis: Hackett, 1991), paragraphs 1, 3, and 20.

39. "Remark" to Paragraph 248 of the *Encyclopaedia*, in *Hegel's Philosophy of Nature*, translated, edited and introduced by M. J. Petry (London: Allen and Unwin, 1968), 209.

40. See the "Introduction" to the *Science of Logic*, esp. 42 in George Giovanni.

SIX

Schelling on Thinking *and* Being

An Absolute to End All Absolutes

HEGEL VERSUS SCHELLING ON THE ABSOLUTE

With the possible exception of Schelling, no philosopher had up until this moment in history provided a more systemic and penetrating critique of the grounding ideas and their development of modern philosophy than Hegel. And none had so systematically subjected the movement of reasoning to such philosophical scrutiny of the fields of its expansion— though, as we indicated, his treatment could only be as good as *his* knowledge of natural science, history, law, art, religion, etc. Philosophically he had, with significant debts to Fichte and Schelling, and Hölderlin (who had with he and Schelling worked on the original program of systematic idealism), provided a thoroughly idealist critique of the ideas— the idea-ism—of modern philosophy itself, by providing an idealism that was ostensibly developed out of the restlessness of mind or spirit in its most elemental substantiating movements, reaching out into knowledge of the natural world, culminating in spirit's subjective, objective, and absolute knowledge.

In *Faith and Knowledge*, Hegel, had demonstrated his brilliant ability to provide a dialectical critique of Kant, Fichte, and Jacobi. It was obvious that, with one exception, Hegel was addressing the most important philosophers and ideas of the age. The exception was Schelling, and Hegel's silence about him in that work was deafening. Unlike the *Difference* writing, *Faith and Knowledge* provided nothing to suggest that he was still the junior partner in Schelling's enterprise. Hegel was still developing his own system, and it was not until 1807 when he presented what was intended to be his introduction to his system, *The Phenomenology of Spirit*, that Hegel could lay serious claim to be a philosopher with his own unique voice and vision. *The Phenomenology* was frequently brilliant, but often impressionistic, or simply impenetrable. As if in recognition of its deficiencies, Hegel himself abandoned his intention of having the *Phenomenology* serve as an introduction to his system, and he would rework the best parts into his *Encyclopedia of the Philosophical Sciences*, as well as use much of it in his various lectures and writings on right, art, religion, history, etc. Hence it was not until 1812 with the *Science of Logic* that Hegel had really achieved his ambitious alternative to, or, as he saw it, philosophical rectification of traditional metaphysics and the new transcendentally grounded forms of idealism that stretched from Kant through Fichte to Schelling. Insofar as Hegel could rightly claim that his philosophy did indeed build upon materials supplied from metaphysics generally and transcendental (and post-Kantian) idealism, in particular, it was not unreasonable for him to present himself as having philosophically superseded his "precursors." By this time Fichte's and Schelling's fame had peaked, in 1806 and 1809, respectively, with Fichte's *Addresses to the German Nation*, and Schelling's short but dazzling *Investigations into the Essence of Human Freedom*. While Fichte would die in 1814, Schelling retreated into relative obscurity, until returning to the larger philosophical stage, having taken up the chair of philosophy in Berlin after Hegel's death. With the exceptions of two minor works, a polemic against Jacobi in 1812, *Denkmal der Schrift von den göttlichen Dingen des Herrn Jacobi (Memorial on the Divine Things of Mr. Jacobi)*, and his study on mythology, *Über die Gottheiten zu Samothrake (On the Divinities of the Samthracians)* of 1815, Schelling's philosophical endeavors were restricted to public lectures in Munich, Erlangen, and Berlin. Indeed, Schelling's career can be said to consist of two halves: the one of a precocious young man who cannot stop himself flying into print to disclose each new development of his philosophy to the public; the other, far more mature and reserved, a perfectionist who restricted himself to lecturing because he was still wanting to find the most compelling formulations to convey the insights that his philosophy had into the relationship between the Absolute/God and humanity. When Schelling's philosophy is considered in its entirety, it provides a powerful alternative vision of the Absolute to Hegel's. We can also understand why Schelling never accepted that Hegel had provided an adequate philosophy of the Absolute, let alone an adequate critique of his own account.

In spite of the tremendous renaissance of interest in Schelling in the last two decades, Schelling scholarship has not impacted greatly upon the broader understanding of the history of philosophy, and hence in the "shoot-out" over the Absolute, Hegel's importance tends to eclipse Schelling's, as it had in the first half of the nineteenth century, before itself fading largely from view in Germany, though having something of a life in Scotland and the United States. For his part, outside of a short intense period of interest among some prestigious natural philosophers such as J. M. Ritter, Heinrich Steffens, and H. C. Ørsted, Schelling's impact on the direction of the nineteenth century was almost non-existent, though C. S. Pierce and Coleridge were notable exceptions.[1]

Further, if Hegel was at least seen as sufficiently philosophically significant to be worthy of being criticized by the next generation, when Schelling gave public lectures in Berlin, after taking up the chair of philosophy upon Hegel's death, he was perceived as a museum exhibit from another age. His aspiration to demonstrate finally that he was the real summit of the tremendous philosophical activity that had transpired in Germany from Kant onward was generally dismissed with derision. I doubt if any philosopher has ever given a series of lectures to an audience consisting of such historically significant figures as Schelling did in Berlin. His audience included the neo-Hegelians Ludwig Feuerbach, Friedrich Engels, August Cieszkwoski, and Marx's early associate Arnold Ruge, the Russian anarchist Mikhail Bakunin, the great explorer Alexander von Humboldt, the historians Jacob Burckhardt and Leopold von Ranke, the legal theorist Carl Savigny, and Søren Kierkegaard.[2] Sadly, for Schelling, the general consensus was summed up by Kierkegaard (who originally was genuinely enthusiastic about what Schelling's "positive philosophy" might offer): "Schelling talks the most insufferable nonsense."[3] One of the more interesting comments that strongly puts the case that Schelling's anti-Hegelianism was most definitely not to be equated with the concerns of the neo-Hegelians comes from Marx, who seeing Schelling as a mouthpiece of reaction, implored Feuerbach to provide a critique of Schelling, adding "Schelling is an anticipated caricature of you, and as soon as reality confronts the caricature, the latter must disappear into thin air."[4]

It is only when we get to the twentieth century that we see a serious interest in and application of Schelling—in Tillich's theology, for example,[5] and in Rosenzweig's analysis, in the *Star of Redemption*, of the relationship between nothing (nought) and something (aught) which is pure Schelling, as is the way he mounts the case for the distinction between creation and revelation. Further, the way Rosenzweig understands Christianity as a historical and revelatory power moving through the three ages of the Petrine, Pauline, and now Johannine Age is straight out of the conclusion of Schelling's *Philosophy of Revelation of 1841/2*.[6] Jaspers also wrote a book on Schelling treating him as an important figure within existentialism, while Eric Voegelin's diagnosis of spiritual defiance and social suicide is, in spite of Voegelin's reservations about the theosophical and gnostic residues he discerns in Schelling, deeply reminiscent of Schelling.[7] Whether Heidegger was conscious of it, there is a far deeper elective affinity between Heidegger after the *Kehre*, when he dispensed with his own emphasis upon willful action, than is to be gauged by simply reading Heidegger's rewarding study of Schelling's *Freedom* essay.[8] Deleuze and Žižek have also found material in Schelling they see as forays into areas suited to their own projects, although their admiration conceals far deeper divergencies that stem from their respective radical political projects and the view of human beings and human action upon which their politics is predicated than Schelling's far more traditional philosophy and his suspicion of political salvation (discussed below).[9]

Like Hegel, Schelling is symptomatic of an end of philosophy, a project that is meant to be open yet is so tailored to the quest and preoccupations, the mind and knowledge of one person that it could not help but lead to another dead end insofar as he brings a certain kind of philosophical reason to a demise.[10]

Together Schelling and Hegel had successfully drawn attention to the key flaw in Fichte's philosophy, its self-negation demanding too much of a subject as Absolute, when they turned their critical attention to each other, even though both seemed oblivious to the fact, each would be fatally wounded in the "cross-fire."[11] For each had rightly hit upon the key weakness of the other, though both carried on "producing" long after their fatal wounds. In both cases, their greatest thoughts were to show what others had done wrong—and both had defended a dynamic Absolute against the philosophical roots of mechanism, moralistic voluntarism, and the desiccated self-understanding that had become increasingly commonplace within modernity, and, indeed, would become even more commonplace after their own personal and philosophical demise. To this extent both retain salient vantage points for assessing what Schelling would call the "spiritual sickness in mankind" that comes from the dominance of reflection. For Schelling this sickness occurs

> where it [reflection] imposes itself in domination over the whole man, and kills at the root what in germ is his highest being, spiritual life, which issues only from Identity. It is an evil which accompanies man into life, and distorts all his intuition even for more familiar objects of consideration. But its preoccupation with dissection does not extend to the phenomenal world; so far as it separates the spiritual principle from this, it fills the intellectual world with chimeras, against which, because they lie beyond all reason, it is not even possible to fight. It makes the separation between man and world permanent, because it treats the latter as a thing in itself, which neither intuition nor imagination, neither understanding nor reason, can reach.[12]

The "shootout" between them was over one thing—indeed the big thing—the Absolute, and the path to it. In this sense, in spite of their respective insights which are still worth thinking with, they truly brought to an end all talk of the Absolute—and even though metaphysics persists after them, few, if any, have the temerity to still talk of the Absolute as being the subject/object of their philosophical endeavor.

Aside from Hegel's and Schelling collaboration on the "First System Program of Idealism," a program though written in Hegel's handwriting, is deeply steeped in Schelling's thought as well as ideas from Hölderlin, Schelling and Hegel also worked jointly on the *Critical Journal of Philosophy*. Further, in what is commonly recognized as his "first distinctly philosophical work and the first original essay that he published,"[13] *The Difference between the Fichtean and Schellingean Systems of Philosophy*, Hegel had come down firmly on the side of Schelling against Fichte, arguing that the core problem with Fichte's philosophy is its one-sided, and hence incomplete treatment of reason as the Absolute: "Identity," he writes, "has been constituted in Fichte's system only as a subjective Subject-Object."[14] By contrast: "the principle of identity is the absolute principle of Schelling's entire system: philosophy and system coincide, and identity is not lost in the parts, much less in the result."[15] In his next major work, *Faith and Knowledge*, Hegel had continued his critique of Fichte, along with Kant and Jacobi, as philosophers who all—albeit in different variegations of the one underlying principle or spirit—postulate reason (the Absolute) as so deficient that it needs to defer to a beyond of faith that is outside and above reason itself, thereby rendering reason as powerful (yet, in fact, Hegel observes, impotent) precisely because it is a beyond.[16] While, as we noted above, Schelling is conspicuous by his absence in *Faith and Knowledge*, the deficiency that Hegel ascribes to Kant, Fichte, and Jacobi, would soon be directed at Schelling for his failure to make a genuine science of philosophy, and—for Hegel this is tantamount to the same thing—a genuine system of reason. When read in light of Hegel's eventual "shootout" with Schelling, however, there are intimations in the *Difference* writing that while Hegel endorses Schelling against Fichte, he identifies what he will later bring to the fore as the central weakness of Schelling's philosophy: "the absolute principle, the only real-ground and firm standpoint in Fichte's as well as Schelling's philosophy is intellectual intuition," he notes in passing. There are all manner of places that one might cite to illustrate what Schelling means by "intellectual intuition," but the following formulation from *Further Presentation of My System* is probably as good an account as any: "to see the plant in the plant, the organ in the organism, in a word to see the concept or indifference within difference is possible only through intellectual intuition."[17] The idea of intellectual intuition makes sense for Schelling in the context of the necessity of a unity beyond the dualism required by Kant between intuition and understanding. Schelling also sees this dualism as redolent of the core philosophical divide between realism and idealism, which itself can only make sense in light of the absolute unity that enables the division in the first place. Thus the underlying unity is not merely posited as an abstract inference, rather it is a condition of the recognition of an antithesis. In other words, there is an immediacy about this akin to the immediacy that is intrinsic to anything that is empirically observed in

space and time. To be sure, Schelling is not following the Kantian stricture of the transcendental aesthetic and transcendental analytic. But this
is largely because such a stricture is indicative of Kant's own dogmatic
refusal to allow for "intellectual intuition" that results in, what for Schelling, as with Fichte and Hegel, is the Kantian philosophy's failure to deliver on the promise of a transcendental deduction by not adequately drawing out the implications of what Kant calls "the act of transcendental
apperception." More so than Fichte, Schelling seizes on the issues of differentiation, and opposition, that is evident in the most archaic and elementary of philosophical distinctions between the form of knowledge,
thought, and the what of knowledge, being. And again, the difference
points to a more fundamental unity that enables the division. Thus
Schelling says "the absolute unity of thought and being, of the ideal and
the real, not differentiated from its essence, is the Absolute's eternal form,
the Absolute itself."[18] Realism and idealism are, then, for Schelling, not
so much antithetical philosophical grounds as such, but rather the inescapable designations of the contrary starting points we confront because of
what the world is and how we must interact with it mentally. Thus, from
one starting point, viz. idealism, it is the cognitive form that dictates the
knowable, and thus may be predicated as absolute because our system of
knowledge could not occur without such form:

> But cognition is not yet cognized as absolute if one views it in antithesis
> to being and does not also recognize it as absolute reality. Realism
> alleges that it starts from an absolute being, but if this being is really
> absolute, it directly follows that it is a being located in the ideas, and as
> simply absolute, in the idea of all ideas, in absolute cognition. This
> relationship is what we have called the relation of indifference [not
> some inane synthesis, as many have represented it].[19]

As, the above citation about "the plant in the plant" indicated, the oppos-
ing ontologies that point to a unity beyond and operative within themselves are but one further illustration of the most elemental feature of
identification of something as something, as a = a:

> In this identity or equal absoluteness of the unities that we distinguish
> as particular and universal resides and is found the innermost mystery
> of creation: the divine identification (imaging) of original and copy that
> is the true root of every being. For neither the particular nor the univer-
> sal would have a reality for itself if the two were not formed into one
> within the Absolute, i.e., unless both were absolute.[20]

Finally, on this point, the idea of intellectual intuition is the condition of
philosophy itself, for it enables identification of the absolute indifference;
but conversely without absolute indifference there could be no intellectual intuition. Thus he says: "Whatever else the particular form {of error}
may be, when one overlooks or ignores the absolute indifference of cog-

nition and being, or of form and essence, intellectual intuition is lost and with it philosophy itself." [21]

Schelling finessed, but never abandoned, this position. Likewise, once Hegel crafted the problem of the Absolute, hence of mind and world, as a concatenation of predications disclosed by our knowledge of it, and hence as a logical problem of the "genetic" relationships of fields and subjects of knowledge, he was adamant that the reliance upon "intellectual intuition" was a serious philosophical weakness. For the original promise of philosophy as a science simply could not rest upon a singular act of consciousness—and intellectual intuition, as it was functioning in Schelling, and as it also did in Fichte, was like the last of the Mohicans of the facultative logic having survived the long trail from Descartes to Kant and Fichte. For, as Hegel saw it, any idea of the Absolute in which the activity of the Absolute is so fundamentally severed from the labor of the concept so that it simply tramples over the rational processes inherent in the development of the sciences must be deficient. Thus, in Hegel's *Lectures on the History of Philosophy*, Schelling is said to have gone awry by not devoting himself sufficiently to the labor of the concept—the logic: he "presupposed" the "point of indifference . . . but he did not follow it through in a determinate, logical fashion." [22] More cuttingly—and turning Schelling's own words against him—he had placed his faith in his own genius and thereby posited "cognition on the basis of immediate knowing, of what pops into one's head." [23]

This assessment had originally been directed against Schelling throughout the *Phenomenology*. In what is among the most famous one line polemical put-downs in the history of philosophy, and picking up on Schelling's claim in *Further Presentations from the System of Philosophy* that "most people see in the essence of the Absolute nothing but empty night and can discern nothing in it," [24] Hegel referred to a "monochromatic formalism" which "palm[s] off its Absolute as the night in which . . . all cows are black." [25] Almost as famous was his reference to "a pistol-shot of illumination aiming straight at absolute knowledge." [26] But two other passages perhaps better encapsulate the line of irreconcilable philosophical difference with Schelling as perceived by Hegel. In one he compares his own philosophy with the vagaries of common sense and with a philosophy which originates in "the conceit of genius" thus:

> True thoughts and scientific insight are only to be won through the labour of the Notion [concept]. Only the Notion [concept] can produce the universality of knowledge, which is neither common vagueness nor the inadequacy of common sense, but a fully developed cognition; nor the uncommon universality of a reason whose talents had been ruined by the conceit of genius, but a truth ripened to its properly matured form so as to be capable of being the property of all self-conscious Reason. [27]

The reference to the "conceit of genius" had essentially reiterated a point he had made a page or so earlier, which none familiar with Schelling's philosophy could take as anything other than an attack upon Schelling:

> Genius, we all know, was once the rage in poetry, as now is in philosophy; but when its productions made sense at all, such genius begat only trite prose, instead of poetry, or getting beyond that, only crazy rhetoric. So, nowadays, philosophizing by the light of nature, which regards itself as too good for the Notion [concept], and as being an intuitive and poetic thinking in virtue of this deficiency, brings to market the arbitrary combinations of an imagination that has only been disorganized by its thoughts, an imaginary that is neither fish nor flesh, neither poetry nor philosophy.[28]

That Schelling would recognize himself is not surprising, given that Hegel manages to combine so many essentials of Schelling's philosophy in his damning critique: the philosophy of nature, intellectual intuition, poetry (art), and genius. For Schelling, as he writes in the *System of Transcendental Idealism*: "Philosophy attains, indeed, to the highest, but it brings to this summit only, so to say, the fraction of a man. Art brings *the whole man*, as he is, to that point, namely to a knowledge of the highest, and this is what underlies the eternal difference and marvel of art."[29] And when Schelling writes that "this absolute contingency in the highest power of self-intuition is what we designate by means of the idea of *genius*,"[30] he is indeed laying down a task for philosophy that is completely antithetical to the direction and means of Hegel. The line of divide between the two are the notions of the irreducibility of being to the concept, and the irruptive and absolute nature of freedom, and concomitantly the free and even personal nature of the Absolute. Hegel had identified the fact that Schelling was not so much a man of science, but a seer. It is hard to argue against this, for while Schelling is often dazzling, the dazzling nature does not change the fact that the connections he deduces are acts of great audacity and originality, rather than compelling conclusions. In part this is because he revives and develops metaphysics, and liberates it from the stringent conditions that Kant had applied in the first *Critique*. But liberated metaphysics ultimately carries the burden of all metaphysics: the solitude of being accessible only to the thinker who can storm its citadel, and who is unable to provide a sufficiently compelling methodological map for anyone else who wishes to enter the citadel. Hegel was one of the last to propose a map. But Schelling thought Hegel had only the map, while he himself had been to where the map was representing. But who could be sure of this? Nevertheless, even if Schelling was deluded, what he saw about the age and its conditions was sufficiently luminous to be remembered; his philosophy was a great fire, a blaze of insights into life.

SCHELLING'S ABSOLUTE: THE FIRE OF CONTRADICTION

Schelling's philosophy is built around a number of different starting points and ends that can be counterposed as dualisms, but are intrinsically related to each other and hence co-dependent—knowledge *and* being, subject *and* object, idealism *and* realism, criticism *and* dogmatism, nature *and* freedom, philosophy *and* poetry, and, eventually, negative *and* positive philosophy, mythology, *and* religion. These dualisms all testify to the fact, as Schelling sees it, that "All life must pass through the fire of contradiction. Contradiction is the power mechanism and what is innermost of life."[31] But that fire of contradiction that drives all life is nothing less than the Absolute, i.e., God.[32] Hence in each of his philosophical investigations, he is ever seeking a more comprehensive and systemically integrated, yet at the same time open and dynamic account in which we expand our knowledge of the real object of all philosophical concern, the Absolute. And, for Schelling, nothing can be genuinely philosophical that does not concern itself with the Absolute, for it is the Absolute itself which is the real subject of all activity: "Being is essentially God or the Absolute, or rather, God is himself Being, and there is no being save God."[33] And

> The whole universe is in the Absolute . . . not as . . . the particular unity, but as absolute unity. It is first within appearances, where it ceases to be the whole, where the form pretends to be some-thing for itself and steps out of indifference with essence, that each becomes the particular and the determinate unity.
>
> No aspect of the particular entity, therefore, not even its species or natural kind, is within the Absolute. There is no plant in itself or animal in itself; what we call plant is [not essence, substance, but] mere concept, mere ideal determination. All forms obtain reality only because they receive the divine image of unity, but, owing to that, they themselves become universes and are designated ideas; each ceases to be a particular entity in that it enjoys the double unity in which absoluteness consists. Therefore the philosopher does not know distinct beings, but only one being in all the original schematisms of world-intuition; he does not construct the plant or animal, but [the absolute form, i.e.,] the universe in the figure of a plant, the universe in the shape of an animal.[34]

Thus too:

> Everything we can know is a fragment of the absolute essence of the eternal principle, only cast in the form of appearance. But philosophy considers only what everything is in itself, i.e., in the eternal.[35]

As is evident here, the absoluteness of which Schelling speaks is real and ideal and it is this reality-ideality that is the condition for any particular thing. From this position, Kant's identification of the Absolute as a heuristic and hence regulative "idea" involved a fundamental philosophical

incoherence that any true philosophy had to rectify. Nevertheless, although Schelling retreats to pre-critical metaphysics he never deviated
from the conviction, underscored in his Berlin Lectures, that he would
"have to dispute the opinion that any position can be advanced that is
completely removed from a connection to Kant."[36] In large part, as he
says shortly after, this is because "Kant's *Critique of Pure Reason* is the
source for the vast majority of the contemporary philosophical vocabulary."[37] As such it is also plays a decisive role in bringing about what
Schelling would call philosophy's "final crisis,"[38] a crisis in which a philosophy of the living pits itself against what he saw as the arid and
vacuous spiritual world that the mechanistic philosophies, which includes the Kantian, and even idealist post-Kantians, had settled for.
Nevertheless, it was Kant who provided the initial problem of the
transcendental subject and the problem of the *a priori* conditions of experience that open the door for Fichte's idealism, and the need, as Schelling
(repeating Fichte) puts it, for a more rigorous transcendental deduction
than that supplied by Kant:

> Kant's deductions tell us at first glance that they presuppose superior
> principles. Thus Kant names the only possible forms of sense percep-
> tion, space and time, without having examined them according to a
> principle (as for instance the categories according to the principle of
> logical functions of judgment). The categories are set up according to
> the table of functions of judgment, but the latter are not set up accord-
> ing to any principle.[39]

Although scholars dispute the extent to which Schelling was ever completely a disciple of Fichte, Fichte's critique of Kant's inability to provide
a complete transcendental deduction, i.e., one that would explain the act
of consciousness making the initial synthesis to justify Kant's claim that
the *a priori* elements he hits upon are indeed the totality of elements of
pure reason, undoubtedly inspired Schelling's own precocious philosophical undertakings. Originally, Schelling saw the task in Fichtean
terms as breaking beyond the barrier between the world and knowledge,
which presupposed a confinement of the self's assertion and power within reality, instead of identifying the self's identity with reality. Further,
Schelling's youthful work of 1794, "On the Possibility of a Form of All
Philosophy" thanks Fichte for directing his own thoughts "toward a
more complete development of the problem,"[40] viz. "of establishing a
principle that would not only furnish an original form as the root of all
particular forms but also give the reason for its necessary connection with
the particular forms that depended on it."[41] But very quickly Fichte's
philosophy is seen as justifying a position which must be negated if one is
truly to account philosophically for the creative unity of nature and spirit.
Indeed, while the very title "Of the I as the Principle of Philosophy or On
the Unconditional in Human Knowledge of 1795" suggests an essential

commitment to the Fichtean program, and while Schelling states that he is toppling Spinoza's system to build what he refers to as a "counterpart to Spinoza's *Ethics*," [42] he never explicitly says that his idealist defense is identical to Fichte's—because, in spite of appearances to the contrary, it wasn't. [43] More importantly, although Fichte thought this was a confirmation of his own light being shone further by his disciple, Schelling had already identified the ontological conundrum and the fundamental insight that would possess him his entire life: "*the principle of being and thinking is one and the same.*" [44] To be sure in the earliest writings of Schelling this might look straightforwardly idealist in the Fichtean sense of the role of the active self-postulating subject in any kind of knowledge. And "Of the I as Principle" proclaims that "the ultimate to which philosophy leads is not an objective but an immanent principle of preestablished harmony, in which freedom and nature are identical, and the principle is nothing but the absolute *I*, from which all philosophy has emanated." [45] Nevertheless, nagging questions and asides keep bursting through the surface of "Of the I as Principle," including the claim that "the moral law, even in its entire bearing on the world of sense, can have meaning and significance only in its relation to a higher law of *being*, which, in contrast to the law of freedom, can be called the world of nature," [46] and in his *Philosophical Letters of Dogmatism and Criticism*, in spite of still signaling a commitment to the critical project that reached from Kant to Fichte, Schelling emphasizes that the realism of the dogmatists poses problems he cannot simply avoid. As Schelling increasingly speaks of the Absolute, and God as the Absolute, it is evident that the I as Absolute, as with nature as original ground, are but different starting points with their respective potencies of the Absolute. That is, God as free creative subject is also an I, and insofar as Schelling argues that the Absolute is constantly active, we might say, absolutizing itself, this earlier formulation is not so much, from the position of the more developed Schelling, wrong, just one-sided. For the distinctive characteristic of Schelling's philosophy is that each of the elements of "being and thinking" (including the "and") are to be taken in their unity with each other. Schelling would never cease gnawing on the bone of "being and thinking." Thus, more than fifty years later, his diaries of 1848 are full of entries (jostling alongside daily weather and health reports, and political observations) where he is still reflecting on philosophy, especially Kant and Aristotle (by now much admired by Schelling). To take a rather typical entry of that year in which he is rereading Aristotle with great care:

> But what is the existent (*das Seiende*)? Here is the question with which philosophy itself begins;—for it has no presupposition other than only reason itself, which no longer recognizes any authority beyond itself, and which proceeds only from what it itself set, or has something directly to be placed, but now has existence (*Seiende*). That self-ruling science that proceeds only by itself! And from no other authority. [47]

By the time of *Ideas for a Philosophy of Nature*, Schelling had adopted a position in which a break with Fichte and the Kantians was impossible to avoid, no matter how much he stressed the importance of the "and" (the identity) between being and thinking. By the time Schelling proclaimed that he had the key to a system of a philosophy of nature (rather than the system itself which he says "does not yet exist") philosophy "is nothing other than a natural history of our mind"; it "becomes genetic; that is, it allows the whole necessary series of our ideas to arise and take its course as it were, before our eyes. From now on there is no longer any separation between experience and speculation."[48] What is also conspicuous in the change of emphasis is the attack, referred to above, upon the divisions of reflection which transform us from participants in reality to mere objects of reality subject to the subject's reflective scrutiny.

Like Fichte, Schelling cared little for Kant's compulsion to tie his transcendental conditions of "theoretical reason" to the aligning of Newtonian physics, Aristotelian/logic, and Euclidean space that provide the baseline of the first *Critique*. Indeed, Kant's "theoretical reason" was predicated upon the principles of pure reason being *a priori* operative in the mechanistic sciences, while Schelling's philosophy of nature, probably prompted by his encounter with Goethe,[49] was largely mounted in open opposition to what he saw as a fundamentally mistaken philosophical view in which the dynamism of nature and the polarities that run through it are displaced in favor of a "dead object." For Schelling the living cannot be explained by the dead, and, hence too, the organic and inorganic must be unified via dynamic forces. Nature is a constructive and productive process, pure immanence, "its own legislator,"[50] "absolutely active,"[51] "every material is thus nothing other than a determinant degree of action, no material is originally mechanically aggregated."[52] And a philosophy of nature must demonstrate how this is so, moving as it does through the major levels of natural organization from the inorganic to organic, from the material to the spiritual.

The other crucial dimension of this is that for Schelling: "Where physical forces divide, living matter is gradually formed; in this struggle of divided forces the living continues, and for that reason alone we regard it as a visible analogue of the mind."[53] So there is a congruence between the dynamics of differentiation and the development of the mind and its ideas, and nature itself. In this respect nature has to be seen as *a priori* as well as empirical, ideal as well as real.

Ironically, insofar as Kant himself in the chapter on dynamics in his *Metaphysical Foundations of Natural Science* had argued that attractive and repulsive forces pertain to the essence of matter, Schelling is at once a Kantian, as well as a post-, and anti-Kantian. Kant's emphasis upon a procedure in keeping with the epistemic framework that is the defining foundation of the critical philosophy and the dualism at the base of the procedure and epistemology is illustrative of the weakness Schelling detects in Kantian metaphysics. Concomitantly, it will also be the source of his breach with Fichte. And that divide is succinctly summed up in this claim that "the system of Nature is at the same time the system of our mind."[54]

What is on the surface an epistemological move requiring the metaphysical disjuncture between subject and object, which is so definitive of modernity, is ultimately, for Schelling, an ontological error which brings in its train a series of other even more terrible errors about what we are, and what we can or should do. Thus it is that the original opposition that Schelling would work upon was that between the philosophy of the I and the philosophy of nature. His answer to the problem, as indeed all subsequent problems, was: the Absolute/God is the condition and creator of all being, and is itself a being and beyond being, both immanent and transcendent, eternal and historical, mind and nature, rational and irrational, and so forth. Likewise, he would ever seek to identify the point of indifference as well as identifying the polarizing powers or potences which are immanent in the process of natural and cognitive differentiation. All difference is identity of opposition. Hence Schelling requires that we think idea/form and reality each through to the point of their indifference. In this respect the philosophy is both and neither—absolute idealism and absolute realism. The reconciling of opposites is in keeping with another aspect of Schelling's philosophy: it is a philosophy that brings out the truth within other philosophies so that they all may be reconciled within the greater truth. Thus although his lectures on the history of philosophy as well as his own adaptations and integrations of metaphysics is very different from Hegel, Schelling shares with Hegel the conviction that it is the Absolute itself that is being expressed through philosophy, in general, and his philosophy, in particular. This dimension of Schelling not infrequently gives rise to the idea that he is a pluralist or "relativist" in the Nietzschean sense; but this is to miss the key point that Schelling himself has hit upon the means of conciliation between disputants; having followed the Absolute into its very viscera, we may say, he is developing a system that brings all systems together.[55] And while it is the case that the integration and deployment of other metaphysical systems develops as Schelling's own system develops, the following provides a brief summary of Schelling's metaphysical inspirations or borrowings.

Plato's *Timaeus* had left a deep impression at the very commencement of Schelling's philosophical education, and by affirming that the ideas are archetypical ultimate realities, of which individuals are imperfect instantiations, Schelling revives Plato ("Plato risen from the grave" is how Michael Vater describes Plato's presence in *Bruno*);[56] insofar as all is God, Schelling revives Spinoza; insofar as each individual is the instantiation of the Absolute, he revives Leibniz; insofar as he insists upon the spiritualisation of nature and matter he revives the neo-Platonists and theosophy of Jacob Böhme; insofar as he follows the formalism of the *a priori* to its founding egoic source of unity he is Kantian and Fichtean; insofar as he makes being an absolute condition (an indivisible remainder) that is not to be folded within the epistemic formalism, he revives Aristotle. What is unique to Schelling is the critical qualification and combination he makes of each of these revivals and applications so that ways of thinking advanced (in opposition) to each other can be combined and applied in one philosophical system. If one is patient and willing enough to persist with Schelling in his seemingly interminable deductions, it is hard not to be in awe of the achievement—it is an achievement of genius, and Schelling is not wrong to identify philosophy in general, but by inference very specifically his own philosophy as the result of genius, and intellectual intuition. To be sure, his initial turn against Fichte is bound up with the philosophy of nature, and later generations would find it grotesque— Schelling "die-hards" call it "suggestive," or rich in potential," a turn of phrase that most would see as a way of avoiding the fact that something is rich in ambition but terrible in execution. Indeed along with Kant's *Metaphysical Foundations of Natural Science*, and *Opus Posthumum*, Schelling's and Hegel's philosophies of nature are about as relevant to real science today as Newton's alchemical scribblings. Likewise, just as the idea behind Hegel's *Logic* is intriguingly brilliant but comes with a tortured and turgid, and frequently baffling or downright unconvincing "execution," the brilliance of the idea driving Schelling's deductions of idealism and philosophy of nature is inevitably accompanied by the leaden chains of the deductions themselves. Indeed much of both Schelling and Hegel is to philosophy what Joyce's *Finnegans Wake* is to literature—a brilliant idea relentlessly fleshed out that leaves us more aware of an author's erudition than the world outside it. Again, as with their respective philosophies of nature (for this is as true of Hegel's *Philosophy of Nature* as Schelling's), most of Hegel's and Schelling's moves, outside of their more general dialectical approaches remain unrepeated and unrepeatable. Schopenhauer, whose work shows genuine familiarity, if not much sympathy with Schelling's writings, expresses, with his typical bluntness, what had become a rather common response to Schelling:

> the writings of the school of Schelling, and . . . the constructions . . . are built up from such abstractions as finite and infinite-being, non-being, other-being-activity, hindrance, product-determining, being determined, determinateness-limit, limiting, being limited-unity, plurality, multiplicity-identity, diversity, indifference-thinking, being, essence, and so on . . . but because an infinite amount is thought through such wide abstractions, only extremely little can be thought in them; they are empty husks. But in this way the material of the whole of philosophizing becomes astonishingly poor and paltry; and from this results the unspeakable and tormenting tediousness characteristic of all such writings. If I were to call to mind the way in which Hegel and his

companions have misused such wide and empty abstractions, I should necessarily be afraid that both the reader and I would be ill, for the most sickening and loathsome tediousness hangs over the empty bombast of this repulsive philosophaster. [57]

To a large extent the problem stems from the claim that there is a congruence between the system of "nature" and system of "thinking" and that every essence we study is a potence, absolute for itself, hence too a "member" of God and the universe (which are but "different views of one and the same").[58] Whether we philosophically investigate thought, nature, art, or history we are, for Schelling, still investigating the only object of genuine philosophical inquiry, the Absolute—albeit, as it expresses itself in the form or potence of thought, nature, art, or history.[59] Each "object" of inquiry thus, has its own inherent ideational structure that expresses the dynamic polarization of its absoluteness as well as its place in the larger idea of the Absolute. The following from Schelling's Jena lectures of the Winter system 1802–1803 clearly illustrate how philosophy, art, and mythology align philosophically in the light of the respective potences of philosophy, art, and mythology:

> Whereas philosophy intuits these ideas as they are in themselves, art intuits them objectively. The ideas, to the extent that they are intuited objectively, are there-fore the substance and as it were the universal and absolute material of art from which all particular works of art emerge as mature entities. These real or objective, living and existing ideas are the gods.[60]

The universal symbolism or universal representation of the ideas as real is thus, for Schelling, given in mythology. For, the gods of any mythology are nothing other than the ideas of philosophy intuited objectively or concretely. Schelling will even say, "all possibilities within the realm of ideas as constructed by philosophy are completely exhausted in Greek mythology."[61]

WILLFUL FREEDOM AND HUMAN ESTRANGEMENT

In his Berlin lectures Schelling's speaks of the incomprehensibleness of humanity and its world driving him "to the final desperate question: Why is there anything at all? Why is there not nothing?"[62] The relationship between the incomprehensible nature of human beings—and its wretched condition—and the metaphysical question is an important cipher about what largely drives and defines Schelling, viz. a deep sense that in our willful or free separation of ourselves from the Absolute (God), we have failed to live up to our possibility. Ironically, few, if any, people have been more conscious of their alienation than the moderns who have surpassed all previous peoples in their scientific development, and consciousness of their own freedom. Like Hegel and Heidegger, Schelling's excursus into metaphysics is deeply connected to his search for an answer to the problem of modern estrangement. Thus as he would say in his Berlin Lectures:

> However, if I see in philosophy the means for healing the fragmenta-
> tion of our time, then I do not thereby mean a feeble philosophy that is
> a mere artifact. I mean a robust philosophy of the type that can meas-
> ure up to life and that—far from feeling powerless in the face of life and
> its awesome reality or being confined to the miserable business of only
> negation and destruction—takes its vitality from reality itself, and for
> this very reason brings forth something that is again efficacious and
> enduring.[63]

It has been said that "Schelling, even more explicitly than Kant, submits theoretical to practical reason,"[64] and "the philosophy of nature is an expressly ethical project."[65] Such an observation is apposite for Schelling's earlier writings, which include his own foray into a deduction of natural right that though anticipating some of his later ideas is, neverthe-less, broadly Fichtean and Kantian. But ultimately Schelling's view of the dynamic of nature leads him to a position that has little in common with the moral objectives of Fichte or Kant—and hence with any philosophies which replicate their essential impositions upon reality.[66] In this respect, Schelling's philosophy of the Absolute paradoxically involves taking a stance against idea-ism.

It is very tempting, and not uncommon, to see Schelling's analysis of human estrangement in Marxian terms, and it is true that Marx, from Schelling's perspective, would not be seen as wrong in seeing how the drive for capital accumulation and modernizing leads to estranged hu-man relationships, although Schelling was horrified (as we discuss be-low) by scientific communism and the idea that "property is theft." The core difference, though, lies in the fact that Marx, in complete opposition to Schelling, believes the way out of such estrangement can be politically achieved, and that his program is also predicated upon economic ad-vancement, albeit in a form of accumulation generated by socialism. Moreover, underlying the Marxian belief that the surpassing of oppres-sive social and economic systems will instigate a natural tendency for human social cooperation is an underlying faith in human goodness, and the belief that suffering can be essentially overcome. Both positions are, for Schelling, metaphysical and absurd. As the Freedom essay, discussed below, illustrates, evil exists because we have free will—ultimately faith in a socioeconomic formation that will guarantee un-alienated relations is to require "heaven on earth";[67] but "[s]uffering is universal, not only with respect to humanity, but also with respect to the creator."[68] Such a belief, from Schelling's point of view, if widely acted upon, will lead to a metaphysically created hell.

When viewed from Schelling's perspective one conspicuous feature about Marxism is that, at a metaphysical level, it lends itself to being broken down into a Hegelian and a Fichtean element, each of which is then pulled by Marx in his own direction. The Hegelian element lies in the emphasis upon totality, and Marx's analysis of capital provides, in Hegelian terms, the infinite by means of which the finite conditions of life under bourgeois society are to be identified; the Fichtean element lies in the willful activation and imposition of (the socially designated) free agents who, through revolt and the elimination of classes create a better future based upon their natural cooperation and harmony of interests. Both accounts, from Schelling's perspective, requires not only transporting people out of the Absolute as it is as nature, history, and even spirit, but it involves a fundamental failure to understand the nature of freedom in its relationship to God and hence our own nature as we seek to impose a non-reality, an abstract view of what we are and can be upon the reality that is only revealed through our history and by the Absolute/God.

Turning more specifically to Schelling's critique of Fichte, we can see it is illustrative of the kinds of ethical projects that have become such a commonplace symptom of modern idea-ism, and what today goes under the name social critique, akin to the idea-isms we discuss later in the chapter on anti-domination philosophies. The following criticism was made when Schelling was underscoring how he differed from Fichte and relates to the central thought that we have to see ourselves in light of the Absolute, then primarily (though not exclusively) seen in its relationship to nature.

> What does this deficiency produce in natures that only rely on the power of the own individuality and are inner directed? In fact, nothing other than a life-undermining and hollow moralization of the whole world, a real disgust with all nature and life other than that of the subject, a crude praise of morality and moral teaching as the only reality in life and in science. . . . He who seriously attempts, in a scientific way, to maintain a morality without taking any account of nature is sure to become quickly aware how little account it takes of him. . . . Infinitely more lies above and beyond the limits of this morality, not merely that which [is] a free life in nature and in art, but rather the divinity of the disposition itself which is our release from law and reconciliation with the divine, to which we were formerly subject.[69]

What human beings have done is not, then, something contrary to their nature, but part of their nature, and the idea that this nature can be short circuited by institutional transformation is what Schelling disputes. Moreover, both Fichte's and Kant's practical reason are predicated as an antithesis to mechanism, but the very antithesis derives from a consciousness of reflection in which polarities are pitted against each other, as one must be eliminated for the triumph of the other. The principles of duty and freedom that are to be found in Kant and Fichte are, from Schelling's point of view, the desiccation of lives due to a lifeless approach to life itself and the living powers of truths which are revealed through life.

With both Kant and Fichte, moral philosophy morphs into a philosophy of right by virtue of a compromise of inner intention with external factors. But Schelling sees something more deeply troubling in the expansion of dependency upon the state as well as the concentration and intensification of powers required to facilitate behaviors of right. This point was sharply formulated in his Munich lectures where he criticized Hegel for deifying the state, a position he saw as very much an expression of a spiritual flaw of the age, and not merely something idiosyncratic on Hegel's part:

> this philosophy ends with the deification of the state. . . . But even in this deification of the state, this philosophy shows itself as being fully trapped in the immense error of [our] time. The state, [no matter] how much it includes that which is positive within itself, still belongs to the side of the most negative forces that are against all that is positive, and against all manifestations of the higher spiritual and ethical life. The state is but the carrier of a higher life. The state is the organism that is determined to support a higher, spiritual, ethical, and religious life. And just as the body is more healthy when it is less aware of its organism, so are those peoples, who have to fight for their external organism [the state], denigrated to a lower level of life. The true, but greatly misunderstood task of our time is to shrink the state itself . . . in every form. Thus whoever makes the state into the absolute highest, has a system which is essentially conservative, in that he subordinates everything that is higher [in life] to the state.[70]

Modern philosophy had become a symptom of modern idolatry: the unreal, i.e., merely formal, self (a product of negation and abstraction) sought succor not in the products of the spirit, but in the laws and regulations, i.e., in the authority of the state, which negate freedom to protect it. This stands in close relation to Schelling's more general political views. He was not an economic liberal—indeed he takes little if any interest in economics, he was deeply afraid of the events of the forces unleashed by the revolution of 1848 seeing it as an occasion for the entrenchment of "genuine despotism like the Russians."[71] At one point he notes with some prescience the struggle that would transpire for modern political salvation:

> The most recent revolution has the great advantage of having brought men, who previously thought themselves unfairly excluded from the conduct of affairs, onto the stage. Now they have their chance, their inability is made manifest.
>   The time [will come] when it's a crime to own something . . .— burning of manorial castles—expulsion of the Jews.[72]

In his introduction to Schelling's *Tagebuch* (Diary) of 1848, Hans Jörg Sandkühler, having made the point that Schelling, in spite of favoring monarchical government, because he thought it less intrusive, was not merely a reactionary as the neo-Hegelians claimed, provides an insightful assessment of where politics fits into the greater scheme of life, for Schelling.

> Schelling's political thinking is simultaneously anti-revolutionary and anti-utopian. It would be a mistake to see it as nothing but the re-legitimization of the past, the reactionary feudal return to the old social and political *ancien régime*, or the rehabilitation of the myth of an order recognized by God that is now threatened by the bourgeoisie and so-cialists. Schelling was a political philosopher in the sense that he in-cluded the political in order to abolish it in the idea of a self-organizing history of the Absolute, which fulfils itself, that can be made political only at the price of a break with being, the fall from God: politics is anti-history. Schelling pleads for an alternative kind of human emanci-pation than those of the present; he does not want regression, but rath-er anticipation; his philosophy is the construction of a paradox-of the still pending origin. An open historical future can only be thought of as a new quality of the "as yet un-thought (*unvordenklichen*)" being of God.[73]

While, then, Schelling may well be considered something of an anti-polit-ical thinker, to the extent that he did not believe politics alone could provide the spiritual freedom that was most important in human devel-opment, as Arnold Ruge (so critical of him in other respects) had ob-served, Schelling was not only not in favor of censorship, but very ready to engage in dialogue with the neo-Hegelians and liberal opponents.[74]

All of this stands in close relationship to three aspects of Schelling's thought which became increasingly prominent as his ideas developed: his account of freedom; how that account then contrasts with what he saw as the deeply mistaken philosophical direction undertaken by ideal-ism; and his self-identification as a Christian philosopher in the broader context of what he ultimately sees as the role of what he formulated as "philosophical religion."

Just as Schelling sees the mistaken belief that human reflection can counterpose itself to the world, he opposed any elevation of human be-ings on the basis of what he takes as the fact of their freedom. Originating in the dark ground of the abyss, the "preceding darkness," freedom has the potential to displace us from own spiritual grounding in God. For the essence of freedom ultimately originates from the fact that even God Himself has a dark ground. This ground is "inseparable, yet still distinct from him,"[75] "the yearning of the eternal that "wants to give birth to God, that is unfathomable unity, but . . . not yet unity . . . considered for itself, also will . . . not a conscious but a divine willing whose divining is the understanding."[76]

After the eternal act of self-revelation, everything in the world is, as we see it now, rule, order and form; but anarchy still lies in the ground, as if it could break through once again, and nowhere does it appear as if order and form were what is original but rather as if initial anarchy had been brought to order. This is the incomprehensible base of reality in things, the indivisible remainder, that which with the greatest exertion cannot be resolved in understanding but rather remains eternally in the ground. The understanding is born in the genuine sense from that which is without understanding. Without this preceding darkness creatures have no reality; darkness is their necessary inheritance. God alone–as the one who exists–dwells in pure light since he alone is begotten from himself.[77]

[C]orresponding to the yearning, which as the still dark ground is the first stirring of divine existence, an inner, reflexive representation is generated in God himself through which, since it can have no other object but God, God sees himself in an exact image of himself. This representation is the first in which God, considered as absolute, is realized [*verwirklicht*], although only in himself; this representation is with God in the beginning and is the God who was begotten in God himself. This representation is at the same time the understanding–the Word–of this yearning and the eternal spirit which, perceiving the word within itself and at the same time the infinite yearning, and impelled by the love that it itself is, proclaims the word so that the understanding and yearning together now become a freely creating and all-powerful will and build in the initial anarchy of nature as in its own element or instrument.[78]

It should be evident that Schelling's account of the emergent loving God is in no way a radical departure from the philosophy of nature or the system of transcendental idealism, but a "deduction" of God's own emergence, freedom and power—for only "such a divinity befits nature."[79] Further, God's laws and representations are of him, yet revealed. God and his creations—nature and self—are all dynamic, and all in "procession," "a self-revelation of God."[80]

"Man" is himself caught up, in this self-revelation and becoming of the eternal/God, his yearning and love, and hence exists in the relationship between dark and light. Humanity's response to this circumstance is what provides spiritual elevation or fall, whether "his" attitude is one of wilful surrender to the divine, or outright defiance in which the self's elevation comes at the expense of the entire order and true meaning of creation, which nevertheless requires the very condition of the fall in order that there be spiritual elevation:

The arrogance of man rises up [sträubt sich] against this origin from the ground and even seeks moral reasons against it. Nevertheless, we would know of nothing that could drive man more to strive for the light with all of his strength than the consciousness of the deep night from which he has been lifted into existence.[81]

The "self-will" is the "pure craving and desire" that pertains to "creatures." It is grounded in the dark, but when it takes itself as "the *centrum*," it becomes, according to Schelling, the root of human evil, and misery.[82] It is enclosed in its nature and its laws, and yet it wants to exert itself and its desire over nature and spirit. Seen thus human freedom is not the elevation into light which is part of the divine becoming, but a fall into the darkness, into evil. This is why, for Schelling, freedom is the source of sin, and its absoluteness is predicated upon a false understanding of the relationship of condition and conditioned, Absolute and creature.

While the *Investigations* show the influence of Spinoza (whom Schelling sees as caught up in his own contradictions and blind to God's freedom)[83] as the "deduction" unfolds it is essentially a theosophical explication (redolent of Jacob Böhme and Franz von Baader) of God as a person, and evil being rooted in the self's own self-love—"not my will, but thy will be done" is the traditional Christian formulation.[84] In the third version of the *Ages of the World*, Schelling writes, "Everything only rests when it has found its proper being, its support and continuance, in the will that wills nothing. In the greatest restlessness of life, in the most violent movement of all forces, the proper goal is always the will that wills nothing. Every creature, especially every person, actually only strives toward the state of no conation [*das Nichtwollen*]."[85] Against the self's determination to increase its freedom—its satanic defiance—which is the source of its own hell as it descends further into evil and hence away from the light, Schelling provides a metaphysics commensurate with a Christian anthropology that he will develop most fully in his *Philosophy of Revelation*.[86]

While the *Freedom* essay provides a philosophical account of what was essential to the Christian worldview, it is also a counter attack upon the direction of the philosophical spirit of the age. Ironically, Hegel when chastizing Schelling in his *Lectures on the History of Philosophy* for starting with the position of immediate knowing, from "intellectual intuition," had drawn attention to the fact that "immediate knowledge of God as a spiritual being exists only for Christian peoples."[87] That is to say, he had made the point that Schelling was the heir of a spirit that he had failed to account for. Given that Hegel's God was not a person, and, as Schelling not unfairly pointed out "Christian dogmas were but a trifle for this [i.e., Hegel's] philosophy,"[88] Hegel's invocation of Christianity as a basis for mediation meant little if the "actuality" of Christianity was something to be merely subjected to his own (in Schelling's terms) "negative" philosophy. Hegel did represent himself not only as a Christian but, more specifically, as a Lutheran. More, Hegel is emphatic that Christianity is an event of momentous importance in world history. Indeed, without it, he sees that not only the medieval, but the modern world, with its uniquely philosophical shape and power would not have occurred. For Hegel,

"God is grasped as selfdifferentiating, as concrete, and the mediation or coherence with what we have termed 'consciousness' consists in humanity seeing its own root within God,"[89] and "the Christian principle contains within itself the highest summons to thinking, because in it the idea has a wholly speculative content."[90] That Hegel here is not only describing Christianity but core components of his own thinking does lend support to Schelling's more general point that Hegel's at best scanty treatment of actual Christian dogmatics (and Church history) in favor of a philosophical reconstitution of the meaning of the Christian religion ultimately means that once Christian spirits are poured into Hegel's "bottles," little is left over from Christianity that is not Hegelian.[91]

Whereas a Catholic "priest read prayers over the Lutheran Schelling's open grave,"[92] Hegel saw the spirit of philosophical truth and progress carried exclusively within the Protestant principle, a point of view rightly criticized by Rosenzweig in his *Hegel und der Staat*, for rendering him blind to the geo-political importance of Catholic Austria.[93] In contrast, then, to Schelling, who, if anything is deeply suspicious of any tendency to equate God's might with social or political "progress," Hegel's philosophical convictions led him to see that all that really matters, in terms of both *deserving* and *having* a future, as transpiring within the Protestant world. The Hegelian system has as little place for a personal God, as it does for personal salvation. In this respect, Hegel is at one with the entire thrust of modern philosophy, which is is triggered, for Hegel, by Descartes's philosophical insight that "the unity of the idea, or of the concept, and what is real, is in God alone,"[94] "the unreal" becomes what does not fit within this "unity of the idea," and the God that has become equivalent to the "idea." Hegel knew that he had completely equated God and idea, and he had placed himself in subservience to the idea he had devoted his life to. The difference, as we shall see later, between Hegel and the post-Hegelians is not so much that the latter are no longer in obeisance to a sovereign idea driving their thinking, but they are no longer interested in providing such an elaborate conceptual coherence of the identity between thought, in the logic of its determinations, and action.

Schelling's retention of the idea of God as a person drives him in a very direction to Hegel, and ultimately it is one in which faith in our capacity to think with reason's ideas remains constrained by what is not us (from Hegel's position this is a continuation of the Kantian, Fichtean failure to overcome dualism), but what is not merely impersonal.

While Christianity along with mythology had been a subject of great importance to Schelling even at a very young age, he would devote himself increasingly to ensuring that his metaphysical deductions were neither merely bounded by thinking qua philosophy and being qua nature, but also attentive to the historical experience of the spirit as a reality, and that included, as was evident from the *Freedom* essay and subsequent writings, conceiving of God, in a traditional Christian sense, as a person.

But, unlike the more overtly cultural anthropological investigations of Herder, the metaphysics of the undertaking remain of central importance. Thus in the Berlin lectures where Schelling was directly addressing the matter of revelation he also claimed he was presenting a philosophy—"the positive philosophy" that was "an empirical *Apriori* . . . the empiricism of what is *a priori* insofar as it proves that the *prius per posterius* exists as God."[95] This was not to be confused with a philosophy concerned with providing reasons about the nature of reason, the reason of nature or even the freedom of both (much of his philosophy had been devoted to exactly that) that would invoke the super-sensible God as a necessary condition. Rather it was intended to be illustrative of the Absolute/God in action. In other words, for Schelling, what had to be deduced was *how* the personal God was a fact of consciousness, and a reality—to be sure, a fact of a specific people's consciousness—and the product of revelation. Thus he also saw that just as he had to provide deductions for the self, for nature, for freedom, he would have to do so for religion (and mythology) in general, and the revelation of Christian peoples in particular.

Further, unlike what he had classified as negative philosophers, Christianity "required a God with which they could begin something, that allows God to be conceived as the founder of the world, and particularly revelation."[96] Moreover, insofar as faith in this God has been a force impacting upon the European world, and hence also the greater world by virtue of Europe's expansion, Schelling states that:

> As one would now declare any philosophy incomplete that had excluded nature from itself, so too would a philosophy in no way be complete that could not comprehend Christianity. For Christianity is one of the greatest and most significant phenomena of the world. It is in its way just as good a reality as nature and has the right, just as every other phenomenon, to be left in its singularity and not to be misrepresented only in order to be capable of the next best thing, that is, of applying to it an explanation accessible to everyone.[97]

Indeed so important, for Schelling was the facticity of Christianity and its presence in the world that he would say:

> Christianity in its purity is the archetype (*das Urbild*) towards which philosophy should direct itself. I am not saying this in order to defend myself against those who hold my philosophy to be irreligious or not upstanding—there is, in fact no irreligious philosophy, for philosophy without religion is a non-thing (*ein Unding*)—but instead because I would consider it to be unworthy cowardice not to declare that I have drawn my contentment (*Beruhigung*) from the New Testament and that I hope that others will find the same. The decisive name for my philosophy is Christian philosophy, and I have grasped this decisive element with seriousness. Christianity is thus the basis of philosophy.[98]

Schelling's view of Christianity also cannot be divorced from his more general recognition of the importance of mythology as a fundamental feature of human development. While dissatisfaction with the Enlightenment's diminishment of the importance of figurative imagination, in general and hence mythology and religious rite and ritual is an important source of Romanticism, and not something unique to Schelling, the typical critique directed at Romanticism is that its passion for the past tends to inspire reactionary delusions about what is valuable in the present and needed for the future. However, the fact remains that modernity has not simply created a world in which religions and mythologies have simply evaporated into the deistic or humanistic secularized reality that the philosophes and, later, neo-Hegelians and such like thought would happen. On the contrary, people have generally becoming increasingly conscious of other religions and mythologies by virtue of the sheer contiguity that modernization has facilitated. Schelling's awareness of this process led him to see his philosophical work as preparatory for a new amalgamation of philosophy and religion. For, as Bruce Matthews has rightly noted, the real importance of the "positive philosophy" lay in its desire to "communicate the inner truth of all religions–from the mythological, to the revealed, to the philosophical–without, however, doing injury to their unique and enduring truths."[99] Matthews also provides an excellent summation of the rationale behind what Schelling would call "philosophical religion":

> This inclusive philosophical consciousness must, of course, address religious phenomenon, becoming, as it were, a requirement for developing a "framework in which Christianity is also an essential member, but precisely only a member" (WMV, 84). As he says in the Berlin lectures of 1842, due to the historical reality of an emerging world culture, which includes both Eastern and Western philosophical and religious traditions, he is "compelled" to call for a wider philosophical consciousness in order get beyond the parochial nature of the European Weltanschauung. Citing "the virtually unrestricted expansion of world relations," he argues that "the Orient and the Occident are not merely coming into contact with one another, they are being compelled, as it were, to fuse into one and the same consciousness," a consciousness that has not yet been realized, but one that must be cultivated and "expanded into a world-consciousness!" (II/3, 4).[100]

The task of philosophy, then, was, *inter alia*, to better disclose the truths of the Absolute that had evolved through the mythological and all revelatory and religious traditions. "Philosophical religion" was thus not to be confused with making a religion of philosophy, nor with the Enlightened project of seeing religion and mythology as immature attempts to express the truths which philosophy (or its empirical scientific offshoots) alone is equipped to grasp properly. Rather philosophy in its study of the Absolute is able to move across the different essences disclosed by the Absolute and the development of the different potences that pertain to each of these essences so that it can assist the public in seeing the "positive" features—the realities and ideas—that inform the world's religions. As Wayne Hudson rightly puts it. Schelling's "vision" was of a

> philosophical religion for all humanity, derived not from reason, but from the factual history of mythology and revelation. This religion would be faith become intelligible and worldly, a synthesis needing no external authority, which all would access freely–a truly public religion of all humanity in which humanity would find the supreme knowledge.[101]

The difference between Schelling's view of a philosophical religion and Hegel's view of the relationship between religion and philosophy is spelled out in his *Philosophy of Revelation* of 1841/1842:

> Only that philosophical religion will be the true one, which contains the elements of all religions, and hence is capable of seeing the truth in mythology and revelation without, however, sublating the authenticity of this truth. The true religion of reason (*Vernunftreligion*) should not then push mythology and revelation aside, or, as with *Hegel*, ascribe something else to it. For even the former is to be preferred, to those who throw the positive content completely away. Hegel gives us invalid paper currency for stolen treasure; a single historical fact is more valuable than his entire Logic, because we are initially directed to *history*. Instead of breaking away from metaphysics and reacting to it with self-reliance, the philosophy of religion has always held itself within metaphysics and general philosophy.[102]

It was ever Schelling's intention to draw his readers into the spiritual integrity of life, and as evident for example in *Clara*, Schelling would show a genuine interest in the kind of phenomena of spiritual life that is more commonly left to occultists. Also, along with his attempt to demonstrate the integrity in thought, nature, art, mythology, and religion, Schelling had also become increasingly conscious of the way in which our relationship to time carries with it a different cognitive bearing on our part. As he puts it in the opening of the third draft of *Ages of the World*: "the past is known, the present is discerned, the future is intimated. The known is narrated, the discerned is presented, the intimated is prophesied."[103] The importance of this distinction lies in the fact that each, in its own way, is a "conduit" of the Absolute. Thus to focus exclusively on one modality of time is once again to be entrapped in the kind of estrangement that Schelling saw as intrinsic to the age of Enlightenment. We need, in other words, if we wish to free ourselves from the estrangement that has such a hold over us and our age, to be aware that any kind of spiritual and important human truth will require not only a narration of the past, and a discernment of the present, but an intimation of the future. That is, indeed, a task that should humble us when placed before the Absolute. At a time when the post-Hegelian philosophical generation was summing up the meaning of the past and proposing the kind of world we should be making in the future, Schelling was reminding his audience of the enormity of our ignorance and warning:

> Then just as all history is not just experienced in reality or only in narration, it cannot be communicated, so to speak, all at once with a general concept. Whoever wants knowledge of history must accompany it along its great path, linger with each moment, and surrender to the gradualness of the development. The darkness of the spirit cannot be overcome suddenly or in one fell swoop. The world is not a riddle whose solution could be given with a single word. Its history is too elaborate to be brought, so to speak, as some seem to wish, to a few short, uncompleted propositions on a sheet of paper.[104]

It was not that Schelling retreated from the idea he had expressed as a much younger man in the *System of Transcendental Idealism* of humanity being co-creators and artists of creation, but rather that if our creations are in defiance of the laws of the spirit, of what is revealed, and is primarily the product of abstract thought from first principles (negative philosophy), then they are but entrapments and sources of even greater suffering. This is also at the very core of Schelling's hostility to what he saw as contemporary idealist philosophy—its draining off of the truths of the Christian heritage and pouring them into its pallid and ultimately insubstantial forms, which are incapable of providing spiritual sustenance.

> this idealism that has appeared among us is just the expressed mystery of the entire direction that has been for a long time more and more prevailing in other sciences, in the arts, and in public life. What was the endeavor of all modern theology other than a gradual idealization and emptying of Christianity? Character, competence, and force are getting less and less in both life and public opinion, but so-called "humanity," for which the above qualities would have to serve as ground, counted for everything. Likewise, this age could only avail itself of a God from whose concept all power and force had been removed. This is a God whose highest force or expression of life consists in thinking or knowing and which, besides this, is nothing but an empty schematizing of itself. This is a world that is still just an image, nay, an image of an image, a nothing of nothing, a shadow of a shadow. These are people who are nothing but images, just dreams of shadows. This is a people that, in the good-natured endeavor toward so-called Enlightenment, really arrived at the dissolution of everything in itself into thoughts. But, along with the darkness, they lost all might and that (let the right word stand here) barbaric principle that, when overcome but not annihilated, is the foundation of all greatness and beauty.[105]

The mature Schelling was a man out of time, as was evident by the hostility he encountered by those already to launch the great projects of the nineteenth century which, for worse as well as better, still very much shape our own age. Many of Schelling's warnings about the dangers of the age's incipient idealism retain their relevance, stemming, as they do, from a thoughtful distillation of what may be philosophically gauged from human experience when we think through the unities and dynamic polarities that have shaped the ages that we are heirs to. Nevertheless, it was also the case as Michael Vater, an astute, sympathetic but not uncritical reader of Schelling, observed, that in spite of his "positive philosophy" Schelling nevertheless was "insufficiently historical, cross-cultural and empirical," on account of "assuming that social empiricism or cross-cultural study will verify the initial assumption of one universal culture of reason or provide a point of Archimedean support for the hope in a philosophy of history with a single narrative thread."[106] Likewise, although Schelling's later work, as Emilio Brito claimed, can rightly be identified as steeped in Christian anthropology,[107] Alan White correctly observed that

> Schelling continues to strive to produce a comprehensive system grounded in God; he does so not out of perversity or obstinacy, but rather because he is convinced that nothing else can satisfy the demands of philosophy. He cannot turn from theology to philosophical anthropology, because he is convinced that anthropology not grounded in theology cannot possibly be philosophical.[108]

Thus although Schelling's "philosophical religion" has much in common with the kind of culturally hermeneutical, and dialogical project of Herder (whom indeed he admired) and subsequently Rosenzweig (who, as we have noted, took much from Schelling) and Rosenstock-Huessy, Schelling's immediate, if not ultimate, fate was to have contemporaries who disappeared with him, and to be mocked and ignored by the next generation. His uniqueness and genius was in the dogged determination to think through the most fundamental oppositions of philosophy to their inner unity, to discover their identity and point of indifference, all the while relating everything to the Absolute, and claiming he could bring his reader into the heart of the Absolute, not only as rational in-itself, but as productive and free, dynamic and developing. Schelling had claimed that those implacable sources of illumination that Plato had designated as ideas, were philosophically accessible and the Absolute remained Absolute. In this he remained Hegel's twin, albeit each twin saw in the other a repellent mirror image of what he himself was: a bearer of the distorted Absolute.

It was, however, a fractured absolute or the absolutization of contingency which largely defined the next generation of philosophers, albeit, not infrequently through the surreptitious reestablishment of another absolute—whether Kierkegaard's solitary individual, Schopenhauer's will, Marx's proletariat and communism, or Nietzsche's superman—each of which require an act of willful defiance of the modern condition, when, in fact, as we have emphasized, Schelling saw willfulness of the self as both a condition of its freedom and the source of its fall. The crisis we moderns face, according to Schelling, is a crisis of satanic defiance and spiritual isolation from the source of life itself. It is a religious problem, and philosophy's role, for Schelling, was ultimately a religious one.

NOTES

1. I am sceptical of the claims made by some Schelling scholars such as Bowie and Snow about Schelling's influence upon Feuerbach, Kierkegaard, Marx, Schopenhauer, Nietzsche (who probably never read more than a few pages of Schelling), etc. See Andrew Bowie, *Schelling and European Philosophy: An Introduction* (London: Routledge, 1993), 4. Dale E. Snow, *Schelling and the End of Idealism* (Albany, NY: SUNY, 1996), 1. John Elbert Wilson, *Schelling und Nietzsche. Zur Auslegung der frühen Werke Friedrich Nietzsches* (Berlin: De Gruyter, 1996) attempts to build a case for Schelling's influence on Nietzsche, but the problem is that Nietzsche's references are few and generally do little more than echo Schopenhauer's take on Schelling.

2. Manfred Frank has provided an invaluable appendix collating reports, articles and letters surrounding Schelling's Berlin lectures. "Dokumente zu Schellings erstem Vorlesungszyklus in Berlin: Hörerberichte, Zeitschriftensartikel, zeitgenössische Brief- und Tagebuchäusserungen)" in 495–581, in F. W. J. Schelling, *Philosophie der Offenbarung 1841/1842*, Herausgegeben von Manfred Frank (Frankfurt Am Main: Suhrkamp, 1977).

3. See Kierkegaard's letter to his brother Peter Christian in *The Concept of Irony with Continual Reference to Socrates Together with Notes of Schelling's Berlin Lectures*, Edited and translated with introduction and Notes by Howard Hong and Edna Hong (Princeton, NJ: Princeton University Press, 1989), 17.

4. From Marx, Engels, *Collected Works* volume 3 (London: Lawrence and Wishart, 1975), 349–50.

5. Paul Tillich, "Schelling und die Anfänge des existentialistischen Protestes," in *Zeitschrift für Philosophische Forschung*, 9 (2): (1955), 197–208.

6. On Rosenzweig and Schelling see Elsa Freund, *Franz Rosenzweig's Philosophy of Existence: An Analysis of the State of Redemption* (Dordrecht: Springer, 1979), 15–46.

7. See Jerry Day, *Voegelin, Schelling and the Philosophy of Existence* (Columbia, Missouri: University of Missouri Press, 2003). In spite of Voegelin's reservations about Schelling, Schelling most definitely has no sympathy for those who would pass themselves off as the mouthpiece for the Absolute.

8. See Lore Hühn "A Philosophical Dialogue between Heidegger and Schelling" in *Comparative and Continental Philosophy*, 6:1, 16–34, 2014.

9. Žižek's Schelling is mediated through Hitchcock, Lacan, Marx and a host of others. The concluding question(able claim) from his "The Abyss of Freedom" tells us much more about Žižek than Schelling: " When Lacan conceives the conclusion of the cure as the moment when the subject, by way of its own destitution, changes into a "being of drive" and becomes its own cause, does this, then, not point towards the Schellingean Reconcilation?," Slavoj Žižek "The Abyss of Freedom" in *The Abyss of Freed/ Ages of the World: An Essay by Slavoj Žižek with the text of Schelling's Die Weltalter (second draft, 1813)* in English translation by Judith Norman (Ann Arbor: University of Michigan Press, 2004), 87. Schelling's answer to that question, by the way, would, as I hope will be clear from this chapter, be an emphatic "No!" Žižek calls Deleuze, a "great Schellingean," Ibid., 61. Whether true or not, Deleuze commends Schelling for his philosophy of powers, and bringing "difference out of the night of the Identical," though he also criticizes Schelling (along with Schopenhauer and Nietzsche's) idea of groundlessness not being able to "sustain difference." See *Difference and Repetition*, translated Paul Patton (London: Continuum, 2004), 240 and 346. Ultimately, the differ-

ence comes down to the fact that in Deleuze the self is endlessly inventive and volun-taristic so that it can create a world of its own wanting, its own freedom. In this respect Deleuze, as I argue in the chapter on anti-domination philosophy, is typical of his generation and their (Fichtean) approach and faith in politics. This, however, is not Schelling: the construction in Schelling is from and of God or the Absolute which is freedom itself. Schelling's philosophy is a philosophy of will, but not of human will-fulness. Marx was not wrong to pick up on Schelling's conservativism. One idea that is fairly common among conservatives is radical evil, and their judgment that while the world as it is is generally neither very just nor virtuous, order is to be preferred to the tumult that will accompany the unleashing of human volition in the relentless search for virtue. For all the difference between Hegel and Schelling, there is concurrence on this point.

10. In this respect it is not wrong to speak of Schelling bringing idealism to an end, as Dale E. Snow's title *Schelling and the End of Idealism* suggests or as Esposito put it, Schelling "probably took idealism as far as it could go," Joseph Esposito, *Schelling's Idealism and the Philosophy of Nature* (Lewisburg: Bucknell University Press, 1977), 9.

11. That much modern thought, invariably unwittingly continues on the Fichtean path, or more precisely abstraction that can only be taken seriously by those oblivious to the death of the metaphysical God is an altogether different matter. See David James, *Fichte's Social and Political Philosophy: Prosperity and Virtue* (Cambridge: Cambridge University Press, 2011) for a sympathetic account of Fichte's application of right to the sensible world. But the problem is not, as James reasonably enough argues, that Fichte's thought proceeds obliviously to historical circumstance, it is that it ever returns to the dubious metaphysical precept of the self as a free being and a commu-nity as a construction of such freedom so that reality is ever a willed and hence idea-ized determination. It is this idea which still has such common currency today that overwrites the greater complexities of the diversities of circumstance, contestable fu-tures, and the inevitable undertow and "tail" that accompanies human action and gives rise to a world which will ever be a creation, at least *inter alia*, of unintended consequences. The enormous number of philosophical narratives that are operative today tells us far more about how social and personal interests are institutionally and culturally instantiated and replicated than the philosophical quality of the ideas in circulation. That is, to make the claim that Hegel and Schelling are philosophically superior to Fichte does not mean that they have greater social and cultural efficacy: societies and cultures are ever an admixture of the living or flourishing and the "dead" or decaying—of good and bad rules, practices, and ideas.

12. F. W. J. Schelling, *Ideas for a Philosophy of Nature as Introduction to the Study of This Science 1797 Second Edition 1803*, translated by Errol Harris and Peter Heath with an Introduction by Robert Stern (Cambridge: Cambridge University Press, 1988), 11.

13. *Hegel: The Difference between the Fichtean and Schellingian Systems*, translated by Jean Paul Surber (Atascadero, CA: Ridgeview, 1978), v.

14. Ibid., 72.

15. Ibid., 71.

16. *Faith and Knowledge*, translated by Walter Cerf and H. S. Harris (New York: SUNY, 1988), 56.

17. "F. W. J. Schelling: Further Presentations from the System of Philosophy," in *The Philosophical Forum*, translated by Michael Vater, Volume XXXII, No. 4, Winter 2001, 373–97.

18. Ibid., 381.

19. Ibid., 383.

20. Ibid., 386

21. Ibid., 384.

22. Hegel, *Lectures on the History of Philosophy Volume 3*, 263.

23. Ibid., 260.

24. "F. W. J. Schelling: Further Presentations from the System of Philosophy," in *The Philosophical Forum*, Volume XXXII, No. 4, Winter 2001, 373–97.

25. G. W. F. Hegel, *Phenomenology of Spirit*, 9.

26. Ibid., 498.

27. Ibid., 43.

28. Ibid., 41.

29. F. W. J. Schelling, *System of Transcendental Idealism (1800)*, translated by Peter Heath, introduction by Michael Vater (Charlottesville: University of Virginia, 1978), 233.

30. Ibid., 236.

31. F. W. J. Schelling, *The Ages of the World (Fragment from the handwritten remains Third Version c 1815)*, translated with an Introduction by Jason Wirth (Albany, NY: SUNY, 2000), 90. The constant references to fire in Schelling as well as his emphasis upon opposites are indicative of Schelling's deep affinity with Heraclitus.

32. Ibid., 53.

33. F. W. J. Schelling, *Statement on the True Relationship of the Philosophy of Nature to the Revised Fichtean Doctrine: An Elucidation of the Former*, translated with an introduction and notes by Dale E. Snow (Albany, NY: SUNY, 2018), 28.

34. "Further Presentations," 386–387.

35. Ibid., 388.

36. F. W. J. Schelling, *The Grounding of Positive Philosophy: The Berlin Lectures*, translated with introduction by Bruce Matthews (Albany, NY: SUNY, 2007), 110.

37. Ibid., 111.

38. *Grounding of Positive Philosophy*, 110.

39. F. W. J Schelling, "Of the I as Principle of Philosophy," in *The Unconditional in Human Knowledge: Four Early Essays (1794–1796)*, translation and commentary by Fritz Marti (Lewisburg: Bucknell University Press, 1980), 64.

40. "On the Possibility of a Form of All Philosophy (1794), in *The Unconditional in Human Knowledge: Four Early Essays* (1794–1796), 38.

41. Ibid., 39.

42. "Of the I as Principle," Ibid., 66, 69.

43. A number of studies have mined this question. In her *The Romantic Absolute: Being and Knowing in Early German Romantic Philosophy, 1795–1804* (Chicago: University of Chicago Press, 2014), Dalia Nassar provides a good overview of the scholarship, 161–86.

44. "Of the I as Principle," Ibid., 72.

45. Ibid., 126.

46. Ibid., 99. The significance of this sentence is noted by Marti in his introduction to the essay, 27.

47. F. W. J. Schelling, *Das Tagebuch 1848: Rationale Philosophie und demokratische Revolution*, 44.

48. F. W. J. Schelling, *Ideas for a Philosophy of Nature as Introduction to the Study of This Science 1797, Second Edition 1803*, 30.

49. For Goethe's influence upon Schelling, see Dalia Nassar, in *The Romantic Absolute*, 195–97.

50. *First Outline of a System of the Philosophy of Nature*, translated and with an introduction and notes by Keith Peterson (Albany, NY: SUNY, 2004), 17.

51. Ibid., 18.

52. Ibid., 23.

53. *Ideas for a Philosophy of Nature*, 177.

54. Ibid., 30.

55. Schelling's philosophy was ever systematic in its aspiration—as is evident in the very titles of a number of his most important works: *First Design of a System of Natural Philosophy* (1799), *System of Transcendental Idealism* (1800), *Presentation of My System of Philosophy* (1801), *Further Presentations from the System of Philosophy* (1802), *System of the Entire Philosophy and Natural Philosophy in Particular* (1804), and *Systems of the Ages of the World* (1827–1828). But he always saw the Absolute itself, as well as systemic philosophical articulations of it, as developmental, and hence a philosophical system

that was adequate to the task had to be a dynamic and an open system, which is how he represented his "positive philosophy" in opposition to the more closed systems of "negative philosophy." See *The Grounding of Positive Philosophy*, 182–83.

56. "Introduction" to F. W. J. Schelling, *Bruno or On the Natural and the Divine Principle of Things*, 1802, edited and translated with an introduction by Michael Vater (Albany, NY: SUNY, 1984), 73.

57. Arthur Schopenhauer, *The World as Will and Representation, Volume 1*, Translated by E. F. J. Payne (New York: Dover, 1969), 84. For a more charitable, though still critical, comment on the Schelling school see Ibid., 143.

58. F. W. J. Schelling, *The Philosophy of Art*, Edited, translated and introduced by Douglas W. Stott, Foreword by David Simpson (Minneapolis: University of Minnesota Press, 1989), 14.

59. Cf. Ibid., 15–16.

60. Ibid., 17

61. Ibid., 41.

62. F. W. J. Schelling, *The Grounding of Positive Philosophy*, 94. The question had been central to Leibniz.

63. Ibid., 96.

64. "Translator's Introduction" to F. W. J. Schelling, *First Outline of a System of the Philosophy of Nature*, xvi.

65. Ibid., xxxiii.

66. I agree with Ian Hamilton Grant's (*Philosophies of Nature After Schelling*, [London: Continuum, 2006]) objections to those who wish to deploy Schellingian moves for an ethical project. Grant's work is an often brilliant and thoroughly erudite display of scholarly exegesis of Schelling's natural philosophy—although I do not share Grant's aspiration to reignite the core thrust, if not the particulars of the philosophy of nature. For all the book' considerable merits, Grant errs by equating the philosophy of nature with materialism, and he ignores the importance of the religious and mythological— i.e., the spiritual—in Schelling's thought.

67. Hans Jörg Sandkühler, "Einleitung," Schelling *Tagebuch 1848*, xxxiv.

68. *Ages of the World Third Version*, 101.

69. F. W. J. Schelling, *Statement on the True Relationship of the Philosophy of Nature to the Revised Fichtean Doctrine*, 14–15. Cf. "God is something more real than a merely moral world order and has entirely different and more vital forces in himself than [what] the desolate subtlety of abstract[ions] [that] idealists attribute to him." F. W. J. Schelling, *Philosophical Investigations into the Essence of Human Freedom*, Translated and with an Introduction by Jeff Love and Johannes Schmidt (Albany, NY: SUNY, 2006), 26. (I have slightly amended the translation, due to what must be a proofing error in their text.)

70. F. W. J. Schelling, *Grundlegung der Positiven Philosophie: Münchener Vorlesung WS 1832/33 und SS 1833*, ed. Horst Fuhrmans (Turin: Bottega D'Erasmo, 1972), 235.

71. F. W. J. Schelling, *Das Tagebuch 1848: Rationale Philosophie und demokratische Revolution*, 139.

72. Ibid., 45–46. He specifically mentions the dangerous consequences of "scientific socialism" and the idea that "property is theft" being seen as normal, 45.

73. Hans Jörg Sandkühler, "Einleitung," Ibid., xxxiv.

74. For Ruge's comments see Sandkühler's "Einleitung," Ibid., xxxvii. A very valuable discussion on Schelling's "anti-politics" that also canvasses the contrary approaches to Schelling and politics can also be found in the doctorate presented to the Humboldt-Universität, Berlin 2014 by André Schmiljum, *Zwischen Modernität und Konservatismus: Eine Untersuchung zumBegriff der Antipolitik bei F.W.J. Schelling (1775–1854)*. Also see Martin Schraven, "Schelling und die Revolution von 1848," in *Philosophie und Literatur im Vormärz: der Streit um die Romantik (1820–1854)*, Herausgegeben von Walter Jaeschke (Hamburg: Felix Meiner, 1995), 193–206.

75. F. W. J. Schelling, *Philosophical Investigations into the Essence of Human Freedom*, 27.

76. Ibid., 28–29.

77. Ibid., 29.

78. Ibid., 30

79. Ibid., 18.

80. Ibid., 18.

81. Ibid., 29.

82. Ibid., 32–34.

83. Ibid., 13.

84. Love and Schmidt's translation of the Freedom essay provides apposite selections from Böhme, von Baader, as well as Lessing, Jacobi, and Herder, which well illustrate the elective affinities between Schelling and his precursors and contemporaries.

85. *The Ages of the World Third Version*, 24–25. This is the position that Heidegger will adopt after his disastrous excursus into political matters. The same point of view is already in Meister Eckhart.

86. For a pithy overview of "Schelling and Christian Metaphysics" and his Christian anthropology, see John Laughland, *Schelling Versus Hegel: From German Idealism to Christian Metaphysics* (Aldershot: Ashgate, 2007), 139–42.

87. Hegel, *Lectures on the History of Philosophy, Volume 3*, 260.

88. *Grounding of Positive Philosophy*, 145.

89. *Lectures on the History of Philosophy, Volume 3*, 21.

90. Ibid., 49.

91. The point has also been made by numerous others including Charles Taylor who writes of Hegel: "he only accepted a Christianity which had been systematically altered to be a vehicle for his own philosophy," *Hegel* (Cambridge: Cambridge University Press, 1975), 102. See also Laughland, *Schelling versus Hegel*, 142–43.

92. Laughland, *Schelling versus Hegel*, 150.

93. Franz Rosenzweig, *Hegel und der Staat, Zweiter Band, Weltepochen (1806–1831)* (München: R. Oldenbourg, 1920), 210–17.

94. *Lectures on the History of Philosophy, Volume 3*, 151.

95. *Grounding of Positive Philosophy*, 181.

96. Ibid., 165.

97. Ibid., 186.

98. Cited and translated in *Hegel versus Schelling*, 140, Schelling, *System der Weltalter* (1827–28), 2. *Vorlesung*, 9.

99. Bruce Matthews, Introduction," *Grounding of Positive Philosophy*, 83–84.

100. Ibid.

101. Wayne Hudson, "Aporeitic Schelling" in Wayne Hudson, Douglas Moggach, and Marcelo Stamm, *Rethinking German Idealism* (Aurora, CO: Noesis, 2016), 74.

102. F. W. J. Schelling, *Philosophie der Offenbarung 1841/42*, 379–80.

103. *The Ages of the World Third Version*, xxxv.

104. Ibid., 4.

105. *Ages of the World Third Version*, 106.

106. Michael Vater, "Friedrich Schelling" in *The History of Western Philosophy of Religion*, Volume 4, edited by Graham Oppy and Nick Trakakis (New York: Oxford University Press, 2009), 61–79.

107. Emilio Brito, "L'anthropologie chrétienne de Schelling," *Revue théologique de Louvain*, 18 (1987), 3–29.

108. Ibid., 145.

SEVEN

Post-Hegelianism — or the Idea in Our Action in Nineteenth-Century Philosophy

HEGEL AND FICHTE (AGAIN), AND THE "ANTI-IDEALIST" IDEALISM OF THE YOUNG HEGELIANS AND MARX

While Schelling found almost total hostility among the next generation of intellectuals who heard him lecture in Berlin, many, nevertheless, repeated the essential element of his critique of Hegel, viz. that being precedes conceptualization. In their different ways, the post/anti-Hegelians were all done with philosophy as it had been conceived from Plato until Fichte, as the truth made accessible via the contemplative life. The post/anti-Hegelians all, again in different ways, exerted themselves and their actions over any systemic account; though oddly Marx, having sided with Feuerbach in his youthful attacks on Hegel, ends up replicating a truncated version of Hegel's Absolute on the "material plane" by requiring that the socioeconomic world was in fact a system with its own logic (its germ cell being the commodity); thereby preserving the concept of totality or Hegel's absolute infinite. Thus, as Lukács correctly argued in *History and Class Consciousness*, the Marxist concept of totality is formed by its identification of the laws of capitalist production and the social relations that are constitutive of capitalist production. According to Lukács, it is precisely Marx's concept of totality that "is the decisive difference between Marxism and bourgeois thought."[1] Thus too, he claims: "the primacy of the category of totality is the bearer of the principle of revolution in science."[2]

In spite of Hegel's eschewing of the prospect of rendering the Absolute in the more humble manner advocated by Kant as a heuristic command of Reason, and his determination to articulate its major moments, Hegel had, nevertheless, brought not only history but sociality to the fore of philosophy. Of course, Vico, Montesquieu, Hume, Reid, Ferguson, and Herder, in different ways were also doing this, but none in a way that so tightly integrated logic and history as Hegel had done in the *Phenomenology of Spirit* and *Encyclopaedia*. Marxism would follow up by making the match between the logic and history of political economy—though its neo-Hegelian anti-institutionalism, which Marxists have never outgrown, ultimately meant that it had a very limited social conceptual stock to work with. With one foot in the beyond of a future communist society that is its enduring faith, theoretically Marxism was destined to ever do critique. The political problem of how to broker peace between groups so that they won't go to war to settle and/or satiate their irreconcilable interests, was displaced by a view of politics in which all social conflict would dissolve, along with the classes that had made it possible.[3] For Marx, like Rousseau, demanded a concordance of interests that earthly men and women rarely exhibit: that communism would be a great time of reckoning—an end of the "pre-history" of human society, as he says in Preface to a *Contribution to a Critique of Political Economy*.[4] Hegel, on the other hand, like Montesquieu before him, grasped the importance of the idea having flesh: the spirit of a time and place being the expression of a people in its institutional configurations and mediations. Thus, unlike Marx, there is not a trace of utopianism in Hegel. Of course, Marxists will rightfully respond that the critique of political economy enables them to avoid the false consciousness of those who are duped into thinking that the reality that they are part of is one worth being part of. Marx's insistence upon the scientific status of his analysis seems to occlude Marx himself from realizing that the revolutionary was a person of faith. The irresolvable contradiction between the revolutionary aspiration for the goal, and the scientific soundness of the method and analysis, which is what Marx constantly referred to as the difference between his socialism and that of the mere utopians ultimately meant that Marxists would eventually have to accept that the activities of the scientist and the revolutionary were irreconcilable. That the most revolutionary of Marxism, in the form of Leninism, and academic Marxism, would be a completely voluntarist style of politics and worldmaking, often, as in Leninism, draped in a thoroughly "deterministic" and materialist metaphysic, was indicative of the problem of wanting to make the world a certain way, while claiming one knew exactly how it was essentially. Ultimately the Marxist remains full of hope and faith in the species (once its delusory, deforming class forms have been blasted away by proletarian victory) and what it can achieve in the future: Marxism is, as Walter Benjamin rightly saw, a secularized form of messianism; though Marx's view of communism was embedded in a model of technological "progress," to be spearheaded by the proletariat, while Benjamin's view of revolution expanded to include those Marx referred to as "the scum (*Lumpen*) proletariat."

Hegelianism, on the other hand, is a much more dull (sober?) acceptance of the perpetual requirement for the mediation of conflictual life. In this sense there is some truth in Hegel's insistence upon the union of the rational and the actual, at least within his system. While Marx's totalizing analysis of capital replicates the monadic "logic" of the Hegelian absolute infinite, Marx's revolutionary impetus is far closer in nature to Fichte than Hegel: the world becomes the expression of the fact-act of consciousness. There is a strong case for arguing, as Lukács did, that the politics of the young or neo-Hegelians was always Fichtean.[5] And the claim by the neo-Hegelian, August Cieszkowski, that "Being and thought must dissolve in action" is pure Fichte.[6] Moreover, the more conspicuous the gap is between the structural story Marx tells and the actual revolutionary movements, the more Fichtean Marxism becomes. Likewise, attempts to reconcile Marx and Hegel by making Hegel a kind of revolutionary, as in Marcuse's *Reason and Revolution*, owe far more to Fichte than Hegel. This is inevitable when one downplays the moment of conciliation in Hegel elevating the importance of the moment of dialectical negation. The centrality of reconciliation within philosophy, which would remain with Hegel his entire life, was powerfully put in his early writing on *The Difference Between the Fichtean and Schellingean Systems of Philosophy*:

> Diremption is the source of *the need for philosophy*, and, as the culture (*Bildung*) of the age, it is the unfreely given side of the form. In culture, that which is the appearance of the Absolute has isolated itself from the Absolute and has fixed itself as something independent. At the same time, however, the appearance cannot disavow its origin and must proceed to constitute the multiplicity of its limitations as a whole. The power of this limitation, the understanding, attaches to its edifice, which it erects between man and the Absolute, all the forces of nature and of its talents, and extends it into infinity: herein can be found the entire totality of limitations but not the Absolute itself. Being lost in the parts, it drives the understanding on to its infinite development of multiplicity. In striving to expand itself to the Absolute, however, the understanding endlessly produces only itself and makes itself ridiculous. Reason attains the Absolute only because it steps out of this manifold partial existence.[7]

For Hegel, diremptions are but the understanding's productions. The great mistake modern philosophies keep making, and which Hegel fights against, is their elevation of a multiplicity of finitudes that are not only posited in an irreconcilable antagonism with each other, but in opposition to the infinite totality (reason) of which they are but thought determinations, or members. For no "thing," for Hegel, is in- and of-itself, but it is always a member of a greater totality. Likewise, nothing we understand is completely, i.e., rightly, conceptualized when it is not grasped in terms of the totality of the idea of which it is but a constituent. This, for Hegel, is evident in the most simply definition or statement, and in *The Difference Between Fichte's and Schelling's System of Philosophy* he had pointed out that "a=b = a= not a = a = b," precisely because reason immediately moves beyond identity and establishes differentiation by virtue of its absoluteness as dynamic.[8] In other words, the simplest kind of knowledge claim "a = b," of the sort that is typically put forward by "empiricists" or those invoking common sense (without acknowledgment of the sociality of language involved in that sense) is, for Hegel, simply not "true" in itself, but rather conditioned by a deeper set of conceptual connections that are hidden beneath the surface of the claim and are implicated in a system or whole, the Absolute. The Absolute is a system that cannot be composed by the gathering of subject-predicate propositional truths in and of themselves, but by disclosing the dynamic negation of any kind of propositional identity which impedes the full recognition of the underlying operation of the system itself. That is, the Absolute is only grasped through the speculative philosophy which is capable of identifying the inter-relationships, and reciprocal, yet developmental, dynamics of the totality. And this is substantive even in its most seemingly innocuous formal claim "a = a." Were "a" simply "a," it would, says Hegel, be nothing, because nothing would have been disclosed about it other than its sheer (stark and mute) identity. Thus the opening gambit of Hegel's *Logic* "being" = "nothing," hence it is also "becoming" insofar as it is anything. From this opening triadic movement within thought, Hegel then proceeds to identify the massive dynamic architecture. These include all the most elemental terms which thought may understand itself or be deployed within any science including such basic terms and its constituents as quality, quantity, measure (to take just the first three sections of the *Science of Logic*), as well as the conceptual dynamic that is constitutive of what Kant had identified (but, for Hegel, failed to "deduce") as the kinds of judgment and syllogisms essential to "subjectivity" as well as the thought determinations of objectivity (mechanism and teleology) through to the Idea itself. This provides the basis of what, for Hegel, is to be an *Encyclopedia of the Philosophical Sciences*.

Whenever we wish to have real knowledge of something, then, we must follow its predications, and not simply provide a word as if somehow the things of the world announced themselves in their immediacy, and as if our knowledge was but the collation of these immediacies and "announcements." A thing is its predications, and its predications are only recognizable as such in so far as the subject is understood by us as generative. Moreover, insofar as we are subjects, we seek knowledge. Hence, the real knowledge of identity of subject and objects that, Hegel, argues neither Fichte nor Schelling had adequately grasped, is not only substantive and generative, but *logical*. The logic is dynamic, and its dynamism comes from what it is not, and what it negates being discernible to reason through its own negations. That is, reason is dialectical, and can only ever grasp things properly if it understands the dialectical identity of reason and its world: it must grasp/conceive its own restlessness as well as its unity of infinitude and finitude. For Hegel, Kant stumbled onto the dialectic, and Fichte and Schelling advanced it, yet ultimately still stumbled around within it. Their failure to make logic the basis of metaphysics, and their failure to provide a "science of logic" in relationship to the sciences of nature and the world of spirit, all goes back to the problem of the age: ("natural") oppositions—"spirit and matter, soul and life, faith and understanding, freedom and necessity etc." have all become part of the understanding, the basic truth and realities of a culture. "They have," he adds, "passed over, in the course of culture, into the form of the contrasts of Reason and sensibility, intelligence and nature, and, for the universal Concept, of absolute subjectivity and absolute objectivity."[9] For Hegel, Schelling had done the most to fight against this, but ultimately he reproduces the dualism, as we saw in the previous chapter, by invoking the concept of intellectual-intuition, and thereby denying the most fundamental identity between logic and idea, reason and systematic knowledge, the infinite and its finite members: the Absolute is stormed by faith and not known. The curse of the age is the curse of the oblivion of reason under the mantel of the absolutization of "understanding."

It is, then, precisely against what Hegel sees as the false triumph of the understanding—the same false triumph he would immediately detect in such new left philosophies as Marcuse, or Žižek—that he then states his own endeavor:

> It is the sole interest of Reason to sublate such hard and fast contrasts. The meanings of this interest of Reason is not to be viewed as if it were to posit itself in general over against the opposition and limitation, since the necessary diremption is one factor of life which eternally constructs itself in opposition, and since the totality in its greatest vitality is possible only through restoration out of the most extreme division. But Reason sets itself over against the absolute fixation of the diremption of the understanding, and all the more so, if those things which are absolutely opposed have themselves sprung from Reason. [10]

By contrast, Fichte's philosophy is a philosophy in which the ego must constantly negate what is beyond itself by drawing it into itself—the non-I (*Nicht-Ich*) is the *Anstoss*, the check or bump that is the occasion of the I's further expansion.[11] For historical creatures this requires acts of heroic wilful imposition in service to the Idea. Thus, according to Fichte:

> I proposed, in the first place, to show you by your own nature, that you could not help approving, admiring, and respecting in the highest degree the sacrifice of the enjoyments of life for the realization of an Idea; that hence a principle upon which this judgment was founded must exist indestructibly within you; a principle namely to this effect,—that

> the personal life *ought to be* given up for the Idea; and that, strictly
> speaking, personal existence *is not,* since it should thus be sacrificed;
> while, on the contrary, there in the Idea alone *is,* since it alone *ought to
> be* maintained.[12]

That the Idea is both the height of the I's activity or postulation as well as
what comes from the I's activity is central to Fichte. For Hegel, Fichte,
and all false idealisms depict a Self in endless pursuit of actualisation—
thus, for example: "In Fichte, this subjectivity of yearning is itself turned
into the infinite, it is something thought, it is an absolute requirement,
and as such it is the climax of the system: the Ego *ought* to be equal to the
non-Ego. But no point of indifference can be recognized within it."[13] For
Hegel, the problem with the view of the self as one involving infinite
striving is that this requires seeing the self as doomed to perpetual misery; it is never able to be reconciled with a world that should—by right—
be recognizable as its own. Hegel could no more abide the politics of
infinite striving and ceaseless resistance, than he could abide threadbare,
i.e., vacuous, concepts of freedom, which would tear down with the
slightest brush of the ironic (or "know-it-all") understanding that had
taken centuries to build.

But it was the fact of not having a place in their world that united the
neo-Hegelians—and that lack of a place was palpable in the fact that,
though, intellectuals, they generally could not gain university employment. Further, the pillars of order, most notably church and state, property and family that Hegel's philosophy had demonstrated as the very font
and verification of freedom were, in the main, the very powers that the
young Hegelians were convinced had to be overthrown. They set about
their attacks in different ways, and with different voices: David Strauss's
moderate voice rendered religion the equivalent of theater and the coffee-
house,[14] while the more belligerent Bruno Bauer saw in Hegel a battering
ram against religion,[15] arguing that political reform without the reform of
consciousness and religious criticism was doomed to failure. Feuerbach,
on the other hand, argued that humanity had to take back into itself its
own essence whose powers had been let fly into the ethereal beyond of
religion. In the *Essence of Christianity,* he attempts to disclose the human
truth and power that has been rendered theologically and ascribed to
God. Others like Arnold Ruge and Moses Hess, and Marx and Engels
fought, respectively, for a more liberal political system (Ruge), or socialist
(Hess), and, eventually, in Marx and Engels, a communist one. And then
there was Max Stirner, mercilessly pilloried by Marx and Engels in *The
German Ideology,* while admired (and, some argue, appropriated) by
Nietzsche, who saw society as composed of artifices which should not be
impediments to that which is most sacred: one's own creative self.[16] In
the main what is of conspicuous importance if one wants to situate them
philosophically, is how they generally tend, in different ways, to be driv-

en by an urgency to radically overhaul the world to fit their ideas. Conversely, they also have stepped out, or, more accurately, lost touch with the driving questions and issues that gave birth to modern philosophy. Not surprisingly, for example, they have little interest in how Hegel became Hegel. Thus, one looks in vain in Marx and Engels for evidence that they read Hegel's work prior to the *Phenomenology* (which in the case of his unpublished *Jena* writings deeply anticipated them on the problem of alienation); nor is there any evidence that they had read Kant with any care. Similarly, there is no indication that they displayed any interest in the philosophical "fit" between the mechanistic view of life and the metaphysical principles which established its parameters. To be sure, Feuerbach is the neo-Hegelian who addresses metaphysics in-depth. But his analysis confirms the point just made: for Feuerbach sees modern metaphysics as theologically driven from the outset. Further, his critique of Hegel rests upon the immediacy and implacable "thereness" of natural existing things,[17] while ignoring so much of the philosophical edifice and conceptual apparatus of modern metaphysics that moves from Descartes through to Hegel, which is the essential backdrop for Hegel's claims about the congruence between Reason and History, and the sciences and our institutions.

Feuerbach's interpretation of all modern metaphysics from Descartes through to Hegel as mere theology (see his *Preliminary Theses on the Reform of Philosophy*) as if all philosophers who preceded him were insensitive to the existence of the world and humanity, is indicative of his impatience with modern philosophers for not adequately taking the anthropological turn which he believed his own reading of religion instigates. Feuerbach is oblivious to the fact that his positing a correspondence between the essence of the human subject and God comes at the steep price of ignoring the kind of alterity which is central to a theology or philosophy that accentuates our finitude in the context of forces that ever precede and exist beyond us, and only have meaning insofar as they also help draw us into our own finitude and limits.

Marx and Engels would concur with Feuerbach's positing of the material reality against the ideal. But they would add that the material reality to be fathomed was not mere nature, but the economic conditions that sculpted our "nature." The primary issue to be considered was not the mere end product, the bloom of ideas, but the material economic tree; the base of production and reproduction not the ideational superstructure, which philosophers heretofore concerned themselves with. Nevertheless, Marxists and political economists still had to deal in ideas, though ideas of economic action; and the question of the quality of the ideas about economic action was not as easily circumvented by an appeal to communism as Marx thought. Moreover, the language of materialism versus idealism would be used time and time again by Marxists (Benjamin, Adorno, Jameson, Williams, et al.) who, in spite of tirelessly appealing to their own materialism against the deluded idealists that surrounded them, all too-frequently restored culture and ideas to the primacy of what had to be studied to achieve a socialist society.

If we inspect Marx (and Engels) more closely to see what he makes of ideas, we see that there is no real sense of continuity anymore with the cognitive terms and metaphysical and associated philosophical problematics that had culminated in Kant, only to be exploded by Hegel as naturalism was forced to give way to consciousness of the centrality of historicity in knowledge and being. This suggests that Hegel had been so successful in making the case for historical conscious and social being that Marx and the other neo-Hegelians were completely insensitive to the importance of the links between modern mechanics and the metaphysical conundrums that had led from Descartes to Kant and Hegel's critique. We can see this, for example, in *The Holy Family* where Marx and Engels side with the English and French materialists against the metaphysicians, whom, they think, beginning with Descartes are advancing a speculative anti-scientific spirit; Descartes's metaphysics is said to be completely separate from his physics.[18] The metaphysical shift required in construing nature as quantifiable forces in motion, the requirements of restricting the imagination in the act of constructing models in which variables can be isolated and selected or neglected in order to identify more finely honed causal relations—these are the very processes which were behind the great metaphysical consensuses and disputes of the mechanistic philosophies. But they play no role at all in the ontological sketches drawn in *The Holy Family*. The same goes for *The German Ideology*, where Marx (and Engels) settle their accounts with the neo-Hegelians, all of whom are ultimately victims of ideology. However, here their concept of ideology would be a decisive contribution to their philosophy of action and the political program that philosophy served.

The word ideology can be traced back to Destutt de Tracy, an aristocratic whose political involvements in the French Revolution and its aftermath place him alongside Talleyrand as one of the great historic weathervanes and survivors of changing political fortunes. He had coined the term "ideology" to designate an exhaustive account of the formation of ideas that would serve as "a comprehensive study of human action" for the purpose of social improvement that he and his fellow "ideologists" were developing.[19] Although, for de Tracy, "ideology" referred to what was essentially a philosophy accounting for feelings or sentiments and their mental genesis and formation, and hence the alignment of ideas, its highpoint was in the still relatively new discipline of political economy. And it would be this aspect of his thought that would deeply impress not only Thomas Jefferson, who would translate the section of de Tracy's work dealing with political economy, but Pavel Pestel who, as a leader of the Decembrists, would help set in motion some of the forces that would eventually explode Russian autocracy.

Although Marx shared de Tracy's belief that science was fundamentally opposed to religion and metaphysics, Marx was generally contemptuous of de Tracy as a bourgeois economist. And Marx and Engels used the words "ideology" and "ideological" in a highly negative sense, indeed in exactly the same way as they saw morality, metaphysics, and religion, i.e., as the inverted understanding of the real processes of living "men." As they write in the *German Ideology*: "in all ideology men and their circumstances appear upside-down as in a camera obscura."[20] Ideology, they claim, is to be found in the civil histories of philosophers, lawyers, and politicians who, having divorced ideas from the individuals and empirical relations which serve as the basis of their ideas,"[21] see the world as a theory and the history of pure thought. More bluntly, for Marx, the ideologist is a victim of idealism. For Marx's notion of ideology was but a restatement of his claim in his critique of Hegel's *Philosophy of Right* that Hegel logicizes everything, and that, contra Hegel, things are not to be confused with the "logic" of things. Thus having previously hailed Feuerbach as providing the pathway for philosophers not merely interpreting the world but changing it, after his discovery of the social importance of political economy, Marx would use ideas (originally derived from Feuerbach!) to equate German philosophy with ideology.

However, Marx could not escape the fact, in spite of his own critical use of the term "ideology," that if he were to provide a sound methodological defense for the superiority of communism over bourgeois ideology, he would have to invoke superior "ideas." Having known the superior social end before its actualisation,[22] what might well have been the definitive critique of idea-ism (as ideological critique) became just another variant of it: as the entire program was erected upon the basis of an extremely vague sovereign idea, viz. communism/a classless society. The vagueness is due to the incoherence at its source: viz. the very condition of classes and economic development is, as Marx knew, the division of labor, but communism will (mysteriously/impossibly) retain economic growth without classes, which is to say without the division of labor. Marxists seem oblivious to the issue because they fail to put two thoughts together: (a) that classes are the manifestation of the division of labor, and (b) hence elimination of classes means eliminating the division of labor, which is the essential condition of large scale production.

But Marx did not treat his work as if it were a theory requiring closer scrutiny and testing to identify what it had missed. Thus the critique of ideology in Marx was but one more means for bolstering up his own "ideas" by ridiculing alternative or competing philosophies and ideas, which he believes are rotten at the very core of their formation. Thus in the *German Ideology*, unlike in the *Communist Manifesto*, Marx contrasts *Ideen* and *Vorstellungen*: *Ideen* are fantasies, bad ideas, merely false *Vorstellungen*.[23] As Marx developed his own theory of capital, the matter became one of (his version of) science versus (Hegel's) "logicism"/ idealism, even though he conceded the great breakthrough Hegel had made in recognizing that a system is constituted by the oppositions that cohere, dynamically develop, and dissolve into ends providing greater concordance. Communism would provide the great concordance; it would end the great conflicts that had previously been such a violent curse upon the species. Why, though, the world's problems are such that they lend themselves to philosophical solutions is as much a dogma as a mystery that obfuscates more fundamental questions about method and what constitutes a satisfactory theory and adequate knowledge. Nevertheless, insofar as Marx recognized the value of the dialectic, i.e., insofar as he saw material and economic reality driven by antagonisms, he would say that his dialectic is materialist, and thus the inverse of Hegel's idealist dialectic: giving rise to the famous quip, in the afterword to the second German edition of *Capital*, "My dialectic method is not only different from the Hegelian, but is its direct opposite. . . . With him it is standing on its head. It must be turned right side up again, if you would discover the rational kernel within the mystical shell." [24] Marx himself claimed that his method was that of the natural scientists because it combined analysis and synthesis. His analysis of capital commenced with the simplest cell and then moved on to explain the social phenomena that this cell had generated. [25] Thus it was, for Marx, that the study of Great Britain in *Capital* serves as the laboratory model. He would also acknowledge his debt to Hegel (which became expressed with increasingly levels of fondness for the "old fellow" as he and Engels became older). And while he insisted that "the ideal is nothing other than the material world reflected by the human mind, and translated into forms of thought" (thus retaining the Lockean epistemology expressed in *The Holy Family*), [26] his method was one which sought to disclose the intrinsic dynamic tension and contradictions within the economic form he was studying: the tensions between exchange value and use value, capital and wage-labor, the forces of production which are riven by their emancipatory and alienating tendencies, capital which is both privatizing and socializing, and absolute and relative surplus value, all of which, for Marx, were expressions of underlying laws.

The young Marx had insisted that Hegel's problem was that he mistook the idea for reality, but he himself could not but *name* the reality he was studying in order to identify the underlying laws: so what exactly does it mean to juxtapose the ideas of material science against ideas about ideas? We are still speaking of ideas. Having opened up Reason to its historical and social dimensions, Hegel had left himself open to the retort that if Reason was everything, it ultimately counted for next to nothing. In Marx's case, by arguing that the economic phenomena of a social system were intrinsically law-governed, he was no less implicated in a metaphysic than the mechanistic metaphysicians whose metaphysical conundrums came from holding that the universe must be a certain way so that it could be law-governed.

In spite, then, of all Marx's belligerence and self-assurance about the revolutionary future, the problem awaiting Marxism from its very inception was its own incipient idealism—ironically given Marx's materialist/idealist dyad, and that the epithet "idealist" was always used pejoratively by Marx. Nevertheless, there is no reason apart from the initial underlying postulate or observational rule that the concatenation (to use a term favored by Marx) of social contingencies need to conform to a set of laws unless at their basis they have some inner underlying essence, i.e., law. This is, of course, exactly what Marx says capitalism is; but what he does not prove is that capitalism is ever anywhere a pure process of production. But the question of whether the laboratory model exists anywhere (given Marx's early critique of Hegel's "*Rechtsstaat*" there is much irony in this) was but a variant of the question that the theologian Heinrich Paulus had put to Hegel: Where exactly is this "law"/state, the "Rhodes," as Hegel insisted, that must be real if it is to be really danced around (i.e., to be correctly understood for what it is)?[27]

It should hardly be necessary to state the obvious, i.e., that any comparison between what is essentially a thought-model with a laboratory experiment is purely analogous, and not substantive. The *idea* of capital in Marx is something that is based upon laws derived from empirical observation and analysis, but which, in turn, can only be proven to be correct by testing it against empirical data. It is akin to what Weber would call an "ideal type." In fact, Marx's model of capital is to Great Britain, as Hegel's idea of the *Rechtsstaat* is to Prussia, i.e., the empirical impetus for the model-building.[28] What hangs on the criticism is not simply whether Marx was right or wrong about his diagnosis of capitalism (as we can easily tally up a number of rights and wrongs); but, rather, whether Marx actually applies adequate nomenclature for us to appraise the socioeconomic forces in the world we live in. For, as Marx knows, we are speaking of processes, not things and processes are constantly penetrated by and giving birth to other processes. In spite of his insistence upon his possessing a socio-historical sensitivity lacking in Feuerbach, in *Capital*, Marx remains caught within the epistemological horizon of metaphysical naturalism, as his writings on his method demonstrates, in order to identify the stable underlying essence of the economic, social, and political forces whose origin, direction, and ultimate purpose he claims to understand. There is nothing wrong with remaining within a particular horizon if the questions one is posing "fit" the processes one is studying. But the problem with Marx is that the human world does not operate along the same lines as the natural world; and no amount of blustering and bullying (and Marx was a notorious blusterer and intellectual bully) will change this. Human sociality is shot through with symbols and signs, which enable unpredictable openings of human possibilities that a mere force does not have available to it. Indeed, even the language of social "forces" is a carry-over from a metaphysical paradigm that is preoccupied with things that affect us, but which are not totally like us.

Ultimately, there is nothing more "material" about the *science* of economics or the *science* of physics than there is in the discipline of philosophy or cultural analysis. And this was a point understood by Hegel. When he had argued that the complex of concepts constituting a science gravitate under the idea (the original organizing principle) that makes them possible, he was not saying anything refutable by Marx, even if Marx might have been right in claiming that political economy is more important for the study of society than the study of politics or literature. On the matter of science constituting a body of genuine knowledge, it is very difficult to simply dismiss Hegel. To put it another way, Hegel identified something powerfully important about how we systematize information and the systematicity of information that is not just a clump of randomly chosen contingencies. On the other hand, the social forces at work that push and pull the what and wherefores of our orientation do not become more readily visible to us by remaining dogmatically entrenched in a totality. Further, Hegel's entire edifice was ultimately driven by an important number of questions and problems, above all the destructively mechanizing, and alienating nature of modern life, with its substitutions of abstractions for real relationships. Thus one of his most insightful questions was about how to overcome the power of diremptions of modern life that leave us so alienated from our own creations that we search for freedom in a beyond instead of through the institutional processes which may make our lives more spiritually meaningful. If Hegel's answer to that problem bore little in common with the young Hegelians, both he and they, nevertheless, recognized that this lack of purpose was *the problem*. However, his readiness to rationalize or cooperate with the state whose authority he recognized existentially (to the extent of providing him with a salary and post) was not shared by the young Hegelians, let alone Schopenhauer who, not altogether unreasonably, saw this as symptomatic of what was so wrong about Hegel's philosophy.

Marx's intellectual fate was divided three ways—between: 1) the social democratic tradition, which would end up divorcing him completely; 2) bolshevism, which replaced the primacy of the working class with the party, and which inverted the relationship between politics and economy so that socialism could be politically created in circumstances that defied the theoretical "science" of Marx's own predictions; and 3) in academic Marxism, whose praxis ended up in a complete severance from Marx's designated agent of revolution (the proletariat) and became the spur to student led new-leftism. But academic Marxism was and remains a hybrid and ever essentially the confirmation of what Marx himself never realized: that Marxism was a means by which the intelligentsia and "a new class" of political managers, as Milovan Djilas correctly designated them, and not the living breathing proletariat, could grab political power.[29] And this is why Marxism as a narrative could not only continue but institutionally thrive through the application and mastery of its narrative emphases by becoming a means for state employment—and hence also a means of social induction of university students within the modern— or in Marxian terms—bourgeois state. For the bourgeois state, and indeed the various Marxist states that came into being were ultimately controlled by professional classes who had imbibed the ideas by means of which society would reproduce itself. This modern state is "ideocratic" in nature, a term coined by Beatrice and Sydney Webb.[30] In keeping with this, the end goal of communism served as an idea, vague as it was and is, for judging the oppressive socioeconomic conditions that exist in the here and now. Marx believed he had been able to predict the immanent social form that would be born through the socioeconomic contradictions inherent to bourgeois society and capitalism. Furthermore, his economic claims were plagued with problems. He had postulated rather than *proven* the labor theory of value, i.e., the idea that the exchange value of a commodity is determined by socially determined labor time[31]—even if he claims that "in the midst of all the accidental and ever fluctuating exchange relations between the products, the labour time socially necessary for their production forcibly asserts itself like an over-riding law of Nature."[32] Nor, had he *proven* that "[a]s exchange values, all commodities are merely definite quantities of congealed labour-time."[33] Nor had he *proven* that:

> in proportion as capital accumulates, the lot of the labourer, be his payment high or low, must grow worse. The law, finally, that always equilibrates the relative surplus population, or industrial reserve army, to the extent and energy of accumulation, this law rivets the labourer to capital more firmly than the wedges of Vulcan did Prometheus to the rock. It establishes an accumulation of misery, corresponding with accumulation of capital. Accumulation of wealth at one pole is, therefore, at the same time accumulation of misery, agony of toil slavery, ignorance, brutality, mental degradation, at the opposite pole, i.e., on the side of the class that produces its own product in the form of capital.[34]

Nor had Marx *proven* that crises of capital are caused by overproduction (as opposed to credit expansion, and dangerous levels of debt accumulation, or financial leverage and capital flight). Nor, as he argued at length in the posthumously published third volume of *Capital*, that the falling rate of profit must lead to the breakdown of capitalism.

Marx was making these claims just as a revolution was taking place, spearheaded by Jevons, in the discipline of economics. Central to this revolution was the doctrine of marginal utility theory, and the dispensation of the objective theory of value: the only thing we could effectively measure was price—what someone is willing to pay for something—not what effort has gone into it. The revolution effectively "killed" the labor theory of value. For all his hostility to metaphysical entities Marx's theory of value requires speculation about a reality (the real value) that exists outside and apart from the world of actual prices. Whereas in Marx supply and demand are secondary features of value, and, for Marx, pricing itself obfuscates the inner reality of value, but the economic revolution requires that pricing as *primarily* a demand and supply matter, triggers economic action. Seen thus labor—as one other thing to be priced—is simply one factor of production; subjective theory of value also shifts attention to quality—albeit a quality has a price.

The implications of this are extremely significant when it comes to the political organization of the economy. Markets are, *inter alia*, a means for the social and personal selection, through pricing, of those talents and skills which consumers may want at a given time, but in a Marxian-based political economy, the price mechanism is based upon an arbitrary figure, or if strictly in accord with Marx's own theory, a formula intended to gauge the number of hours needed for providing the worker with the goods and services seen as socially necessary for his or her reproduction plus the allotted surplus for the society as a whole. Any formula is pure guess work made by planners. Because the specific skills and qualities one brings to market for consumption are reducible to the quantity of (average) labor-time that goes into their formation, there is no trigger to activate one skill more than another other than what a planner thinks. In a nutshell, this was the reason why Marxist economies were so hopeless at supplying consumers with anything other than the more obvious and basic goods that a planner could identify. It is also obvious that the elimination of the market and price-system goes hand in hand with eliminating any place for the entrepreneur.

While there are limits to what economics can do—something many modern economists would gladly concede—if there is any requirement for the large-scale excavation, production and distribution of resources, the only alternatives to the marshaling of forces for these tasks is either political fiat (and employment by the "government," or whatever analogous kind of officialdom is operative within a "society"), or the market, or, as is commonly the case, a combination of the two. In fact the relationship between the modern market and modern state is utterly dialectical, as their interests are so interpenetrated that any artificial severance between them is bound to be disastrous.

All of these bad ideas in Marx can be traced back to the fact that his first principles and model took precedence over what was a far more impure historical process. And in spite of all Marx's talk about science, he eschewed any sceptical scrutiny of the ideas he wanted to be true. This lack of scepticism means that Marx never adequately deals with the historical fact that voluntary and spontaneous *self-organization* of labor is more of a historical rarity than the norm when any large-scale division of labor is involved. To be sure, when he first hit on the idea of communism as the solution to human alienation, Marx had seen the division of labor itself (which as he could not fail to appreciate) is the condition of alienation *and* industry. But having argued that communism would more efficiently run large scale production and hence provide a higher standard of living than bourgeois society, he could no longer seriously dispense with the division of labor, satisfying himself (tucked away in a footnote of the posthumously published third volume of *Capital*) instead with reducing the length of the working day.[35]

But there were other bad ideas that Marx had accepted that affected his historical understanding. He had had also largely ignored the fact that the free exchange between a laborer and a personal employer was far more widespread in antiquity and the Middle Ages than he allowed, and far from being something unique to bourgeois society (even if free exchange were more prevalent as urbanization and industry develop). Marx's division of societies into slave, feudal, and modern was also a shockingly simplistic division that allowed him to overlook the more elemental facts: 1) that—with rare exceptions—people work out of necessity, either to subsist, or because they are physically forced, or paid to work; and 2) if they are paid, the employer has, inevitably, been either the state (or some other communal unit of authority backed up by force), or a private employer (the other major employer in Europe had, of course, been the Church, which by Marx's time was becoming a distant third ranked and increasingly irrelevant employer in comparison to the other two). Marx's call for the elimination of a class of private employers and investors, in other words, only left the state—but he had insisted that there would be no state. Again, the problem was that there was no compelling reason to believe that humans could interact on any kind of large scale, or organize activities without a state, or some larger command structure with punitive backup.

In traditional philosophical parlance, in spite of all Marx's appeals to materialism and science, his theory was very much an exercise in rationalism, in the use of inferences carried out upon empirical claims that had come to serve as principles. It was a new kind of idea-ism; one which was ostensibly anti-idealist, and one which was not beholden to the kind of metaphysical stringencies that typify the philosophies which extended from Descartes to Hegel. Famously, the call was to change rather than understand the world. But insofar as the call was made on the basis of what, not unfairly, can only be called "bad" economic ideas, a highly questionable psychology (at best), and an extremely selective reading of history—in which the far more typical horizontal conflicts are occluded by more vertical types of conflict—it is difficult to see how it could have ever ended well. It would, though, be among the most powerful of all the modern idols of the idea.[36]

THE SUBJECT'S LIVING TRUTH: KIERKEGAARD, SCHOPENHAUER, AND NIETZSCHE

The other great post-Hegelian reactions of the nineteenth century are from Kierkegaard, Schopenhauer, and Nietzsche (even though there is little evidence Nietzsche actually read much of Hegel, or Kant for that matter). Of the three it was undoubtedly Kierkegaard who had the deepest knowledge of Hegel's philosophy, and who was most dogged in his critique of the importance of any appeal to objectivity when it came to choosing how to live one's own life.

Like Hamann, Kierkegaard's deep admiration for Socrates is not due to what Plato worked up into a system in his theory of ideas, but the existential occasion—"[f]rom a Socratic perspective, every temporal point of departure is *eo ipso* contingent, something vanishing"[37]—which ultimately defies inclusion within any kind of rational sphere as such. "All decision, all essential decision," he writes under the mask of Johannes Climacus, in his most comprehensive critique of the philosophical, "lies in subjectivity,"[38] and "Subjectivity is truth; subjectivity is actuality."[39] This truth of subjectivity is the lived truth—one in which the concept at best plays catch up forever, and, at worst, forever annihilates what is unique to the subject's becoming by objectifying its qualities and thus extracting the residues of its dissipation into the idea under which it is subsumed and judged.

> While objective thought invests everything in result, and helps all mankind to cheat by copying and rattling off result and answer by rote, subjective thought invests everything in becoming and omits the result; partly just because this belongs to him, since he possesses the way, partly because as an existing individual he is constantly coming to be, which holds true of every human being who has not let himself be fooled into becoming objective, into inhumanly becoming speculation.[40]

The struggle we moderns face is to be so caught up in "thought existence," in abstractions about who and what we are, that we end up so beholden to the second order reality of abstraction that we become blind to our own reality which is formed through our decisions. The following two passages from *Concluding Unscientific Postscript* powerfully bring out Kierkegaard's critique of this process of reification as well as how he sees it as a particular blight upon the modern soul.

> The good, the beautiful, the ideas are in themselves so abstract as to be indifferent to existence, and indifferent to anything except thought-existence. The reason why the identity of thought and being holds true here is that, in this case, being cannot be understood as other than thought. But then the answer is an answer to something that cannot be asked where the answer belongs. Now surely a particular existing hu-

man being is no idea; and surely his existence is something other than the idea's thought-existence? Existing (in the sense of being this individual human being), though no doubt an imperfection compared to the eternal life of the idea, is a perfection compared to not being at all.[41]

And,

> Human existence has idea in it but is nevertheless not an idea existence. Plato gave the idea second place as the link between God and matter, and as existing the human being must of course participate in the idea, but is not himself the idea.—In Greece, as in philosophy's youth generally, the difficulty was to win through to the abstract and to leave behind the existence that always yields the particular; now the difficulty, conversely, is to attain existence. For us, abstraction is easy enough, but people withdraw more and more from existence, and pure thought is the furthest from existence.—In Greece, to philosophize was an action, and the philosopher therefore someone existing. He knew but little, yet the little he did know he knew to some purpose, because he busied himself with the same thing from morning to night. But what is it nowadays to philosophize, and what is it nowadays that a philosopher genuinely knows anything about?—for that he knows everything I do not deny.[42]

By morphing into a diverse "bunch" of characters (as Hamann had done before him), the masked Kierkegaard unmasks the inhumanity and thoughtlessness of abstract philosophical thinking as he places his philosophy in service to his own life, and the faith which provided meaning for his life. Thus he dedicated his life as an author to doing battle with the dull and numbing, yet tyrannical, routine comforts of bourgeois existence, and the new faith of the passionless, "reflecting" age in which torpor ensures that "no one is carried away to great exploits by the good, no one is rushed into outrageous sin by evil."[43] It is also the age in which the single individual is engulfed and ultimately loses his or her soul to "the crowd." For Kierkegaard:

> The individual must first of all break out of the prison in which his own reflection holds him, and if he succeeds, he still does not stand in the open but in the vast penitentiary built by the reflection of his associates, and to this he is again related through the reflection-relation in himself, and this can be broken only by religious inwardness, however much he sees through the falseness of the relation.[44]

Reminding his readers of such fundamentals of life as inwardness, suffering, love, sacrifice, anxiety, and the various stages and temptations of life, including the aesthetic and even the ethical demands, which seduce us from exploring the absolute meaning that our own lives might provide us with, Kierkegaard relentlessly attacks the age and the problems which define it: the tyranny of abstraction, numeration, the system, the public and all else which extinguishes the potential of the single individual. In summing up his life's work he would write in *On My Work as an Author*:

> The single individual must personally relate himself to the uncondi-
> tional. This is what I to the best of my ability and with maximum effort
> and much sacrifice have fought for, fighting against every tyranny, also
> the tyranny of the numerical.[45]

For Kierkegaard, the larger critique he makes of the various philosophical means and stratagems which usurp the absoluteness of our existence
in itself is how it has become complicit in forming the reflective and
spiritually deadening age.

One of the innumerable paradoxes of the greatest philosopher of paradox is that Kierkegaard's attack upon modernity was so of its moment,
and hence so modern—yet its Christian solution to the meaning of existence was so archaic. Not surprisingly Marxists would frequently just
dismiss it as bourgeois decadent individualism gone mad.[46] Although
they came to different conclusions, the same paradoxical relationship between the modern formulation of existence and the archaic solution to
that existence can be said of Schopenhauer and Nietzsche—the former
harkening back even further than Kierkegaard to the Vedanta, while
Nietzsche returned to the Greeks and Romans and Hindu caste system as
presented in the Book of Manu. And while Marx undoubtedly pushes
onto the future, communism is also part modern revival of what Marx
took as the most primordial mode of production (and hence the least
alienated from our nature), combined with the artisanal view of work as
in the medieval guild. But whereas Marx and Nietzsche take the problems of their world as requiring decisive socio-political action (economi-
cally driven in Marx, while culturally driven in Nietzsche), Kierkegaard
(as with Schopenhauer) is too mistrustful of collective action for any such
faith.

Few authors are so powerful and insightful as Kierkegaard about the
inner life. And insofar as he thought that life was being sapped dry by the
forces of the age, his philosophy remains an invaluable corrective to so
much of what he deservedly critiqued. Yet, there is also something so
completely one-sided about Kierkegaard's absolutizing the single individual—albeit in relationship to the Absolute of God—that it cannot be
ignored. This, ones-sidedness was recognized by Rosenstock-Huessy
who made two comments about Kierkegaard which, when taken together, provide as good a commentary on Kierkegaard as can be found in any
thicker tome. For Rosenstock-Huessy, Kierkegaard, was at once a "seis-
mograph of catastrophe,"[47] and "that grim and grizzly monster without
confession and without Church."[48] Rosenstock-Huessy has no problem
with Kierkegaard's diagnosis of the spiritual ailments of his age, but
when Rosenstock-Huessy, wrote the latter observation, he was a soldier
in the First World War, and he was deep in a problem that would occupy

him his whole life—how not to squander the peace, and thus how to escape the recurrent descent into hell that has hitherto been human-kind's lot.

What Rosenstock-Huessy, not completely unlike Hegel (but without the pan-logicism), and hence in contrast to Kierkegaard would constantly emphasize is the historical and social bonds and forces which form and also threaten us with extinction. There is no real escape from this. This also is indicative of the distinction between how Rosenstock-Huessy and how Kierkegaard approach their Christian faith.

While Kierkegaard is a Christian, it is not the "good news" of the apostles and earliest disciples that defines Kierkegaard's faith, but the burden of finitude in its infinite relationship to the Absolute. The disci-ples had built a Church, but Kierkegaard looks at Christendom and sees nothing but a travesty of Christ. Were the situation as bleak as Kierke-gaard paints it, the question may well arise whether Christ had as the singer John Prine once put it in his magnificent lyrical portraiture of the junkie ex-serviceman, Sam Stone, supposedly died for nothing. Kierke-gaard is a Christian without a Church, a man of faith without any sup-ports—other than God, and the real possibility of his own derangement and self-delusion (i.e., the problem of Abraham).[49] For him

> the particular individual who, after he has been subordinated as the particular to the universal, now through the universal becomes the individual who as the particular is superior to the universal, for the fact that the individual as the particular stands in an absolute relation to the Absolute.[50]

No wonder, then that for Kierkegaard: "Anxiety is freedom's possibil-ity."[51] The prospect of bonds of solidarity outside of the Absolute itself makes him the perfect contrast to Hegel. It would also be what would connect him with the philosophers of existence, as they would be called by Heidegger, in the next century. What would vary was the answer which gave one's existence its authenticity—Sartre would eventually "choose" Marxism; Heidegger Nazism (when his philosophy still bore traces of Kierkegaard's influence). Kierkegaard had made a kind of abso-lute of the subject. Had it, though, not been for modern metaphysics, the self would not have found itself at once as total and, yet, so completely abstract. If we compare for a moment the monastic tradition (likewise the yogic tradition) with its extraordinary men and women who subject the self to all manner of torments in search of purification and beatitude, we can note one all-important difference between them and characters such as Kierkegaard. They do. The modern existential philosopher though re-flects on and *writes* about the doing. It is as if the idea of the doing so completely displaces the act that the act itself is of relatively little conse-quence in comparison to the discussion of the decision. In this respect, Kierkegaard's life and the age he does so much to criticize and to try to overcome are far more of a piece than his philosophy would lead anyone to believe.

While there are few philosophers I admire as much as Kierkegaard, Kierkegaard's philosophy downplays too much, and hence occludes, a great deal about what is important in any life—the bonds of sociality and the larger historical forces of past and present that swirl around and position us.

Like Kierkegaard, Schopenhauer provides a personal/subjective response to the world, and like him he largely ignores history, but he does not ignore the more naturalistic and metaphysical aspects of the objective. At the center of his thinking is the will, which becomes the metaphysical wellspring of our world and its representations, Schopenhauer announces in the first line of the opening chapter to *The World as Will and Representation* that: "the world is my representation is a truth valid with reference to every living and knowing being."[52] This truth is, he adds shortly after, "by no means new. . . . It was already recognized by the sages of India, since it appears as the fundamental tenet of the Vedanta philosophy ascribed to Vyasa."[53] Thus while Schopenhauer is at once wanting to open his reader to the greatness of Eastern, specifically Hindu and Buddhist wisdom, he also casts the problem in philosophical terms, noting that his insight into the world as my representation "was to be found already in the sceptical reflections Descartes started. But Berkeley was the first to enunciate it positively."[54] For Schopenhauer the congruence between the world and its representation is a fundamental given: "We started neither from the object nor from the subject, but from the representation, which contains and presupposes them both; for the division into object and subject is the first, universal, and essential form of the representation."[55] It is, at the very least, questionable that Schopenhauer's philosophy succeeds in providing a philosophy that is not beholden to its own dualism of subjectivity and objectivity. For, on the one hand, while the "whole world of objects is and remains representation," and is "wholly and for ever conditioned by the subject; in other words, it has transcendental ideality,"[56] and while he insists that this thus refutes "materialism," his depiction of the subject is materialist. Although, he seems oblivious to the contradictory implications of his own statement, as is evident in the following:

> the fundamental absurdity of materialism consists in the fact that it starts from the objective; it takes an objective something as the ultimate ground of explanation, whether this be matter in the abstract simply as it is thought, or after it has entered into the form and is empirically given, and hence substance, perhaps the chemical elements together with their primary combinations. Some such thing it takes as existing absolutely and in itself, in order to let organic nature and finally the knowing subject emerge from it, and thus completely to explain these; whereas in truth everything objective is already conditioned as such in

manifold ways by the knowing subject with the forms of its knowing, and presupposes these forms; consequently it wholly disappears when the subject is thought away. Materialism is therefore the attempt to explain what is directly given to us from what is given indirectly. Everything objective, extended, active, and hence everything material, is regarded by materialism as so solid a basis for its explanations that a reduction to this (especially if it should ultimately result in thrust and counter-thrust) can leave nothing to be desired. All this is something that is given only very indirectly and conditionally, and is therefore only relatively present, for it has passed through the machinery and fabrication of the brain, and hence has entered the forms of time, space, and causality, by virtue of which it is first of all presented as extended in space and operating in time. From such an indirectly given thing, materialism tries to explain even the directly given, the representation (in which all this exists), and finally even the will, from which rather are actually to be explained all those fundamental forces which manifest themselves on the guiding line of causes, and hence according to law.[57]

What in Kant is genuinely constitutive of a "transcendental logic" in Schopenhauer is materialist and idealist (logical), but certainly not transcendental in Kant's sense. Although he repeatedly speaks of his inspiration from Kant, he eliminates all the categories except causality (and space and time from the transcendental aesthetic), and replaces the Kantian transcendental elements with his four principles—of which he says "[t]here is absolutely no other perfectly pure rational knowledge"—identity, contradiction, the excluded middle, and sufficient reason of knowledge.[58] That what we have is a materialized kind of idealism is also conspicuous in how Schopenhauer discusses causality, where he writes:

the body is for us immediate object, in other words, that representation which forms the starting-point of the subject's knowledge, since it itself with its immediately known changes precedes the application of the law of causality, and thus furnishes this with the first data. The whole essence of matter consists, as we have shown, in its action. But there are cause and effect only for the understanding, which is nothing but the subjective correlative of these. The understanding, however, could never attain to application, if there were not something else from which it starts. Such a something is the mere sensation, the immediate consciousness of the changes of the body, by virtue of which this body is immediate object.[59]

For Schopenhauer, causality is not unique to "rational beings": "all animals, even the most imperfect, have understanding, for they all know objects, and this knowledge as motive determines their movements."[60] Kant had used the transcendental elements of the understanding as providing the fundamental conditions of the *ideas* of reason itself. And in the transcendental dialectic he had sought to demonstrate how when our capacity to make an inference (to reason) takes the *a priori* conditions of the understanding as if they were substances in themselves this creates a number of metaphysical quandaries—the paralogisms, and antinomies of pure reason—which cannot be scientifically solved (i.e., by resorting to the legitimate conditions that are required of any experience). But while purely rational ideas pose a potential danger if we treat them as if they actually told us about us or our world, they are, for Kant, also the source of our dignity and purpose. Schopenhauer's move, on the other hand, brings down any idea that there is a "sphere of reason" which is completely untouched by experience and its drives or mechanisms. Thus too while, as we argued earlier, Kant's theoretical reason is predicated on the centrality of the understanding supplying a model for the imagination in order to identify the laws of nature, this plays no role at all in Schopenhauer. That is, even though Schopnhauer is interested in the sciences, the problem of the fit between the axiomatic system of mathematics and Newtonian physics and logic does not loom in Schopenhauer. He takes bits and pieces from Kant for his own purposes, and he is either oblivious, or indifferent to a core component of Kant's problem concerning the nature of experience. This is also to be seen in how he treats "the thing-in-itself."

Kant's dualism of phenomena and noumena rests upon the "thing-in-itself." For the thing-in-itself is the most immediate reminder of the finitude of our understanding: concomitantly, its content can only be *purely rational* and hence limited to practical reason. Hegel would attack Kant for what he saw as this most fundamental howler: "We must be quite surprised, therefore, to read so often that one does know not what the *thing-in-itself* is; for nothing is easier to know."[61] For his part, Schopenhauer has believed he has escaped from the madhouse of the "thought-determination" problem that led to the "lunatic" Hegel, so he can find no common cause with Hegel on this, or any other point. For Schopenhauer, it is the body's activity and our self-awareness that dissolves the dualism that Kant had contrived which separates our knowledge of the experience of nature of things (the phenomena) with what nature/things are in-themselves: "thus it happens that to everyone the thing-in-itself is known immediately in so far as it appears as his own body, and only mediately in so far as it is objectified in the other objects of perception."[62]

This will have all manner of implications for why Schopenhauer's and Kant's philosophy are so radically different, in spite of Schopenhauer presenting himself as wrestling with similar problems to Kant. If, though, Schopenhauer's use of the term "perception" seems to me to be identical to what Fichte and Schelling refer to as "intellectual intuition," and while the opposition to Kant's dualism was also intrinsic to Fichte, Schelling, and Hegel, Schopenhauer is emphatic that he wants nothing to do with the post-Kantian idealists and their "intellectual-intuition" or the "Absolute."[63] Although Schelling's philosophy of nature is required as a counter-pole to the subjective idealism that comes from the "I's" activity on the world, Schopenhauer's philosophy makes the body but the object of the will, ultimately requiring that consciousness is ever driven by, and yet the epiphenomenon, of the blind drive of the will: "The action of the body is nothing but the act of will objectified, i.e., translated into perception."[64] And: "the whole body must be nothing but my will become visible, must be my will itself, in so far as this is object of perception."[65]

In the first preface to the *World as Will and Representation*, Schopenhauer had stipulated that to understand what he was doing an acquaintance with Kant was essential—indeed, as Fichte had done previously, he represents his philosophy as the completion of Kant's philosophy, growing, as he says, from it as "a parent's stem."[66] But he also informs the reader that knowledge of Plato is desirable.[67] But if what Schopenhauer does to and with Kant leaves little recognizable either from Kant's problem or the solution, his use of Plato is even more "violent." For having looked into the heart of the world to find there the aimless, "endless striving will"[68]—and hence having divined a metaphysics that in so many ways is the antithesis of the Platonic order with its demiurge looking to the ideas as models, its god who tends to small things, and its view of reason or intellect (*nous*) as the highest part of the soul and the most divine of all things, Schopenhauer uses the most Platonic of terms "the idea" as a means to help solidify a philosophy of a world in everlasting tumult and chaos. He writes:

> Those different grades of the will's objectification, expressed in innumerable individuals, exist as the unattained patterns of these, or as the eternal forms of things. Not themselves entering into time and space, the medium of individuals, they remain fixed, subject to no change, always being, never having become. The particular things, however, arise and pass away; they are always becoming and never are. Now I say that these grades of the objectification of the will are nothing but Plato's Ideas.[69]

And "by idea I understand every definite and fixed grade of the will's objectification, in so far as it is thing-in-itself and is therefore foreign to plurality."[70]

Whereas Plato's philosophy had focussed upon the luminosity of ideas so that human beings could find orientation in the world by means of their intelligence taking direction from an intelligible order, Schopenhauer has made of the idea a fixture of a philosophy in which no such order exists. There is no real good to be found in life itself—for the only real good consists in ceasing to comply with the will's drives, and hence escaping life itself. And just as "every organism represents the Idea of which it is the image or copy, only after deduction of that part of its force which is expended in overcoming the lower Ideas that strive with it for the matter,"[71] every organism represents the Idea of which it is the image or copy, only after deduction of that part of its force which is expended in overcoming the lower Ideas that strive with it for the matter. . . . Thus everywhere in nature we see contest, struggle, and the fluctuation of victory, and later on we shall recognize in this more distinctly that variance with itself essential to the will. Every grade of the will's objectification fights for the matter, the space, and the time of another. Persistent matter must constantly change the form, since, under the guidance of causality, mechanical, physical, chemical, and organic phenomena, eagerly striving to appear, snatch the matter from one another, for each wishes to reveal its own Idea.[72]

What Nietzsche would represent in terms of the Apollonian and Dionysian spirits which the Greeks had conjured and which he hoped to revive in a culture suffering from spiritual and cultural death, is vividly expressed by Schopenhauer:

Accordingly, as, by reason of that harmony and accommodation, the species in the organic, and the universal natural forces in the inorganic, continue to exist side by side and even mutually to support one another, so, on the other hand, the inner antagonism of the will, objectified through all those Ideas, shows itself in the never-ending war of extermination of the individuals of those species, and in the constant struggle of the phenomena of those natural forces with one another, as was stated above.[73]

The only comprehensible reason why Schopenhauer presents himself in any way or shape as a Platonist of sorts is that Plato offers a version of the thing-in-itself that he can use, whereas Kant makes an error by "not reckoning among these forms ["that adhere to knowledge"], before all others, that of being-object-for-a-subject," which, he says, is the first and most universal of all phenomena."[74]

On the other hand, the Platonic Idea is necessarily object, something known, a representation, and precisely, but only, in this respect is it different from the thing-in-itself. It has laid aside merely the subordinate forms of the phenomenon, all of which we include under the principle of sufficient reason; or rather it has not yet entered into them. But it has retained the first and most universal form, namely that of the representation in general, that of being object for a subject. It is the forms subordinate to this (the general expression of which is the principle of sufficient reason) which multiply the Idea in particular and fleeting individuals, whose number in respect of the Idea is a matter of complete indifference.[75]

Thus it is that Schopenhauer, having used the dualist Kant to establish a monist metaphysics, and the great defender of the primacy of reason, Plato, to argue for an essentially irrationalist world, speaks of having provided "the ground of the great agreement between Plato and Kant."[76] If that were not enough injury, the next insult he adds to Plato is to claim:

now, what kind of knowledge is it that considers what continues to exist outside and independently of all relations, but which alone is really essential to the world, the true content of its phenomena, that which is subject to no change, and is therefore known with equal truth for all time, in a word, the *Ideas* that are the immediate and adequate objectivity of the thing-in-itself, of the will? It is *art*, the work of genius. It repeats the eternal Ideas apprehended through pure contemplation, the essential and abiding element in all the phenomena of the world. According to the material in which it repeats, it is sculpture, painting, poetry, or music. Its only source is knowledge of the Ideas; its sole aim is communication of this knowledge. Whilst science, following the restless and unstable stream of the fourfold forms of reasons or grounds and consequents, is with every end it attains again and again directed farther, and can never find an ultimate goal or complete satisfaction, any more than by running we can reach the point where the clouds touch the horizon; art, on the contrary, is everywhere at its goal.[77]

Again the Platonic orientation is completely inverted. Plato had emphasized the pedagogical importance of music for cultivating good philosopher citizens, whilst at the same time warning of the social dangers of discordant music, and how it may corrupt the soul.[78] Music is valuable as part of an education only to the extent that it helps the soul develop its rational capacity, the idea that it could be a superior means for knowing, though, would have been seen by Plato as a fraught with danger to the soul.

Given, then, what Schopenhauer makes of Kant and Plato, it should not be surprising that his most important "pupil," Nietzsche, would take this central idea of the world as driven by the blind drives of the will (though Nietzsche adds the all-important caveat that it is seeking ever more power) whilst not only dispensing with Kant, and such vestiges as the thing-in-itself, and Plato, but setting them up as representatives of all that must be overcome in the greater philosophical project. Nietzsche would also depart from what could reasonably be said to be the central idea of Schopenhauer's philosophy: the idea that the only rational choice of philosophical value was to escape from the hell of the world and the subject-object representations which reproduced it. Nietzsche would thus argue that tragic as life was, it was "blessed" (a term that occurs with great frequency in *Thus Spake Zarathustra*).[79] Hence, for Nietzsche, the point was not as Schopenhauer counsels to renounce the will-to-live by adopting a position of ascetic resignation and willlessness, as saints have done, and is practiced within Buddhism, but to embrace life.

Given the virulence and frequency of Schopenhauer's attacks upon Hegel, it is worth mentioning that Hegel would have trapped Schopenhauer immediately in his own logic of using the secondary to identify the nature of the primary. For surely the subject upon which Schopenhauer insists all representation comes is intrinsic to the Absolute (Schopenhauer detested the term, but contempt does not render it invalid), and hence Schopenhauer's dream of escape from the will is just a dream. For Schopenhauer invokes an Absolute only to claim that it can be extinguished, and hence that it is not really Absolute. It is difficult to see the comeback to this position, because Schopenhauer has made the problem and its solution so Absolute, i.e., the will is defining and forming of everything, and he has done so by taking what was originally in modern philosophy, a cognitive function that served as little more than a kind of on and off switch, as the substance of all substances.

While Schopenhauer's philosophy is ultimately one that supports how one comports oneself within life, and hence one can say it is ethical in its consequences, if not in the original ground, Schopenhauer is also very much a man of the Enlightenment even if his influence will be on those who ultimately do battle with the shallow myths of the Enlightenment. Nevertheless, he holds that "the human mind, still not content with the cares, anxieties, and preoccupations laid upon it by the actual world, creates for itself an imaginary world in the shape of a thousand different superstitions," which his philosophy can help alleviate.[80] At the same time, he has no faith in any Enlightenment narrative of progress.

Schopenhauer's assumption is that a particular orientation and modality of knowledge is appropriate for all knowledge, and his philosophy mitigates against the social dimension of knowledge, the way that historical catastrophes and exigencies impress themselves upon a group, engendering a common sense of identity, collective representations, appeals and shared sentiments, and also new institutions that may better serve in future crises. For Schopenhauer history is not something people learn from that provides the opportunity for improved modalities of solidarity, but a mad story that goes on and on as the world continues in its havoc. As he writes of his own philosophy of history:

> It consists in the insight that history is untruthful not only in its arrangement, but also in its very nature, since, speaking of mere individuals and particular events, it always pretends to relate something different, whereas from beginning to end it constantly repeats only the same thing under a different name and in a different cloak. The true philosophy of history thus consists in the insight that, in spite of all these endless changes and their chaos and confusion, we yet always have before us only the same, identical, unchangeable essence, acting in the same way today as it did yesterday and always. The true philosophy of history should therefore recognize the identical in all events, of ancient as of modern times, of the East as of the West, and should see everywhere the same humanity, in spite of all difference in the special circumstances, in costume and customs. This identical element, persisting under every change, consists in the fundamental qualities of the human heart and head, many bad, few good.[81]

Although Schopenhauer's view of politics is rationalistic—a social contract—and minimalist—the state's "sole purpose is to protect individuals from one another and the whole from external foes,"[82]—ultimately he sees that no institutional bulwarks can protect us from the savagery of the will-to-life, everything life has to offer will end badly. And apart from the fact that hitherto the state has been incapable of securing peace,

> and even with its attainment, innumerable evils, absolutely essential to life, would still always keep it in suffering. Finally, even if all these evils were removed, boredom would at once occupy the place vacated by the other evils. Moreover, even the dissension and discord of individuals can never be wholly eliminated by the State, for they irritate and annoy in trifles where they are prohibited in great things. Finally, *Eris*, happily expelled from within, at last turns outwards; as the conflict of individuals, she is banished by the institution of the State, but she enters again from without as war between nations, and demands in bulk and all at once, as an accumulated debt, the bloody sacrifices that singly had been withheld from her by wise precaution. Even supposing all this were finally overcome and removed by prudence based on the experience of thousands of years, the result in the end would be the actual over-population of the whole planet, the terrible evil of which only a bold imagination can conjure up in the mind.[83]

While, on the one hand, it is possible to look at institutional and social relationships as improving in some important ways over times and at least in some places, it is difficult to deny the fact that suffering and evil have been constant components of human experience and that human beings have never devised a means to ensure a fail-safe set of institutions guaranteeing the elimination of collective acts of evil. Schopenhauer is a deeply thoughtful person addressing a perennial feature of human existence, and his philosophy is ultimately a philosophy of compassion, and love, albeit requiring "surrender of the will-to-live."[84] Further insofar as his philosophy culminates in a negative disposition toward life, Schopenhauer's solution and his view of life seem to confirm the famous adage of Fichte that "what sort of philosophy a man chooses depends upon what sort of man one is."[85] Indeed, his philosophy not only provided a metaphysical account of art and the role of genius, it also served as a kind of bridge for modern men and women as a means of understanding the traditions of resignation and renunciation, and hence especially to the East, as well as to more generally understanding a perennial human type, the saint. In its way, it also offered a philosophy of existence.

If, then, Schopenhauer's philosophy is also grounded in an absolute idea, while he sees it applying to everything, as with Kierkegaard, it is really a philosophy that addresses the self and the best kind of action the self may take for itself. By contrast, Marx did not really touch this at all. His appeal was to a world that could be. But why, though, someone would want to sacrifice themselves to this world "to come," he does not explain at all. Indeed, sacrifice itself plays no part in his thought; yet to realize the world he wants is impossible to imagine without massive sacrifice. Although it is not a rights-based philosophy, Marx's philosophy is of a piece with those liberal rights-based philosophies which ignore the duties and costs that must be undertaken for the rights to be realized. This tendency to ignore what to ancient and Christian societies is central to their very being, the sacrificial character and order of social and political life was, however, not something overlooked by Nietzsche. Like Marx, his philosophy was directed to a future condition and type of person (Marxists longed for the "new man" under socialism, Nietzsche the superman). It was inevitably social, even if much of it is pitched in terms of the individual. In this respect, as a form of idea-ism, the potential for disaster is amplified by virtue of it being not just a philosophy making a case for a set of ideas guiding our personal action in the world, but as triggers for collective action.

The central idea around which Nietzsche's thought occurred was always culture, beginning with his first book *The Birth of Tragedy*. Just as it had held up the Greeks as the greatest of all cultures, *The Birth of Tragedy* had identified the root cause of cultural degeneracy in the Socratic and Alexandrine culture of reflection and its celebration of the Dionysian roots of tragedy[86]—the "Dionysiac versus the Socratic" approach to culture sums up the book's essence.[87]

> Whereas in the case of all productive people instinct is precisely the creative-affirmative force and consciousness makes critical and warning gestures, in the case of Socrates, by contrast, instinct becomes the critic and consciousness the creator—a true monstrosity *per defectum*![88]

As his philosophy developed, so would his diagnosis of the crisis of the times, and his ideas about the type of action that was needed. In the note book which he had intended to transform into a book to be entitled *The Will to Power*, Nietzsche would put the problem thus:

> For some time now, our whole European culture has been moving as toward a catastrophe, with a tortured tension that is growing from decade to decade: restlessly, violently, headlong, like a river that wants to reach the end, that no longer reflects, that is afraid to reflect.[89]

Given the catastrophe is a collective cultural one, it is extraordinary that Nietzsche has so often been read as essentially a more philosophical version of a "self-help" guru.

The rather commonplace division of Nietzsche's works into early, middle, and late periods exaggerates the extent of discontinuity in Nietzsche's thinking. Of course philosophers may change their mind—and of course Nietzsche did change his about Wagner and Schopenhauer, for example, and the possibility of Germany itself being culturally rejuvenated (he would, as the above citation implies, become a pan-European), among other things. But the combination of a large number of central concepts derived from Schopenhauer's philosophy and his own preoccupation with spiritual and cultural degeneracy were constant throughout. The ideas of the world as driven by one source of power, the will (hence the anti-dualism), of the subject as also object, and hence of representation as being intrinsic to the organism (perspectivism), of the different individuations of the will being in constant biological conflict, hence the denial of a spiritual life that is not also biological is all Schopenhauer. But as his awareness developed about *the* problem to be solved, the differences with Schopenhauer take on greater emphasis, and it is true that the core difference comes from a fundamental choice and disposition about what they want from life: Schopenhauer wants to escape from suffering and evil and live in a world that is both more compassionate and intelligent, at least in his terms; Nietzsche wants to live in a world of great deeds, a higher culture, which he recognizes requires embracing the very tumult and conflictual drives and the "never-ending war of extermination" that Schopenhauer had sought to extinguish in himself through adopting an ascetic orientation and practices that would close down the will's drive. In the preface to *On the Genealogy of Morality*, Nietzsche states that he had "to confront my great teacher Schopenhauer," once he had arrived at the idea that the moral constraint of the energies that created great culture and that "the instincts of compassion, self-denial, self-sacrifice which Schopenhauer had for so long gilded, deified and transcendentalized," and morality itself were "the *great* danger to mankind, its most sublime temptation and seduction—temptation to what? to nothingness?"[90] (Although he refers to his reflections upon morality in *Human All Too Human* and *Daybreak,* his position is anticipated in his earlier claim that Homeric man and the Dionsyian underpin the tragic view of life). By the time he had written *On the Genealogy of Morality*, Nietzsche had come to see that his enemy was "ascetic ideals" themselves, that this was a primordial response of the will to life itself viz. "its *horror vacui; it needs an aim*, and it prefers to will *nothingness* rather than *not* will."[91] Belief in "ascetic ideals" was a response that came from a pathology of the will and it would find itself socially instantiated in the ascetic priest, although Nietzsche emphasizes that "the ascetic priest makes his appearance in almost any age; he does not belong to any race in particular; he thrives everywhere; he comes from every social class."[92] What is defining, though, is that:

> For an ascetic life is a self-contradiction: here an unparalleled *ressentiment* rules, that of an unfulfilled instinct and power-will that wants to be master, not over something in life, but over life itself and its deepest, strongest, most profound conditions; here, an attempt is made to use power to block the sources of the power; here, the green eye of spite turns on physiological growth itself, in particular the manifestation of this in beauty and joy; while satisfaction is *looked for* and found in

failure, decay, pain, misfortune, ugliness, voluntary deprivation, destruction of selfhood, self-flagellation and self-sacrifice . . . the physiological capacity to live, *decreases.*[93]

The effects of ascetic ideals and the will to power of the "ascetic priest"
could be found everywhere. It was as common to Buddhism, as to Christianity, as to Socrates and Platonism, as to Schopenhauer, as to all manner
of artists "and decadents." It could be found wherever there is some kind
of hostility to the world as such, and a preference for an "after-world" or
"other world" that did away with the struggles and power of life itself.
Above all it took on the form of a particular moral attitude to life, the
topic of his first essay in *On the Genealogy of Morality*, "Good and Evil,"
"Good and Bad," a slave morality which postulated its morality of good
and evil against the more healthy aristocratic morality which saw the
antithesis of the good as bad, i.e., unfortunate. This latter morality was
the antithesis of the kind of master morality one could find among the
pre-Socratic Greeks and other high, invariably, aristocratic cultures.

The catastrophe facing Europe, this will to nothingness that defined
the ascetic ideal, is ultimately a choice between life or death, health or
sickness, culture or nothingness, a world of the superman or the world of
the herd, depicted in *Thus Spake Zarathustra*, at its worst as "the idiotic
blinking" seeker of comfort, the "last man." Although philosophy had,
from Socrates on, generally considered the moral health of the community and the individual and attempted to provide ideas which would
improve moral character, for Nietzsche, was a particular form of the ascetic ideal that had completely triumphed in Europe, the "slave morality"
that had evolved out of the experience of enslavement of the Jews, and
had been consolidated and "universalized" by Christianity. This morality, which according to Nietzsche had been used to hunt down and extinguish the higher types, was the danger that threatened all that gave life
value; it was the normalization of sickness, which, for Nietzsche, only
showed how urgent the problem was: "The *sickly* are the greatest danger
to man: *not* the wicked, *not* the "beasts of prey."[94]

> That the sick should *not* make the healthy sick—and this would be that
> kind of mollycoddling—ought to be the chief concern on earth:—but
> for that, it is essential that the healthy should remain *separated* from the
> sick, should even be spared the sight of the sick so that they do not
> confuse themselves with the sick. Or would it be their task, perhaps, to
> be nurses and doctors? . . . But they could not be more mistaken and
> deceived about *their task*,—the higher *ought* not to abase itself as the
> tool of the lower, the pathos of distance *ought* to ensure that their tasks
> are kept separate for all eternity! Their right to be there, the priority of
> the bell with a clear ring over the discordant and cracked one, is clearly
> a thousand times greater: they alone are *guarantors* of the future, they
> alone have a *bounden duty* to man's future. What *they* can do, what *they*
> should do, is something the sick must never do: but *so that* they can do

what only *they* should, why should they still be free to play doctor, comforter and "saviour" to the sick? . . . And so we need good air! good air! At all events, well away from all madhouses and hospitals of culture! And so we need good company, *our* company![95]

In the first instance, the company that Nietzsche sought would consist of other value-creators, who shared Nietzsche's diagnosis of spiritual ill-health, and vision for a new kind of future, and new kind of human being cured from the sickness that Socrates, Plato, Christianity et al. had spread. This was all expressed in the form of what was intended to be a great work of mythic proportion, written for the "higher men" who would join Zarathustra in preparing the world for the superman. In *Beyond Good and Evil*, Nietzsche would address himself specifically to "philosophers of the future" who would join him creating a new world with new values, having, however learnt from past high cultures. Their task, as Nietzsche urges in *Beyond Good and Evil*, was:

> To teach humanity its future as its *will*, as dependent on a human will, to prepare for the great risk and wholesale attempt at breeding and cultivation and so to put an end to the gruesome rule of chance and nonsense that has passed for "history" so far (the nonsense of the "greatest number" is only its latest form): a new type of philosopher and commander will be needed for this some day, and whatever hidden, dreadful, or benevolent spirits have existed on earth will pale into insignificance beside the image of this type.[96]

While in *On the Genealogy of Morality*, he would write:

> *All* sciences must, from now on, prepare the way for the future work of the philosopher: this work being understood to mean that the philosopher has to solve the *problem of values* and that he has to decide on the *rank order of values*.[97]

This new philosopher will have to throw off all the mendacious ideas of Platonism, and Christianity with their wills to truth that end up creating *nothing* but a world which is not worth living in. Plato and Christianity have also cultivated types of people who are not even worthy of giving their own life its meaning, if they are worthy of anything more than servitude. Nietzsche's fellow value-creators need to reconsider the past, review it free from the kind of moral blinkers that lead them to morally appraise societies as if they were, at best, but steps or stages on a way to a more humane or democratic society. Rather Nietzsche urges those who would join him to understand that:

> Every enhancement so far in the type "man" has been the work of an aristocratic society—and that is how it will be, again and again, since this sort of society believes in a long ladder of rank order and value distinctions between men, and in some sense needs slavery. [98]

Likewise, "slavery" is "a condition of any higher culture, any elevation of culture."[99] The "European problem," then, as he also calls it in the same work, requires "the breeding of a new caste to rule Europe,"[100] a new aristocracy who can take advantage of the "future Europeans [who] will probably be of exceedingly garrulous, impotent and eminently employable workers who *need* masters and commanders like they need their daily bread."[101] Moreover,

> considering the fact that Europe's democratization amounts to the crea-
> tion of a type prepared for *slavery* in the most subtle sense: taking all
> this into account, the *strong* person will need, in particular and excep-
> tional cases, to get stronger and richer than he has perhaps ever been so
> far,—thanks to a lack of prejudice in his schooling, thanks to an enor-
> mous diversity in practice, art, and masks. What I'm trying to say is:
> the democratization of Europe is at the same time an involuntary exer-
> cise in the breeding of *tyrants*—understanding that word in every
> sense, including the most spiritual.[102]

The problem and solution are problems and solutions of breeding. Earlier I made the point that in Kant without our moral ideas we are mere animals. He thought this because this is the logical consequence of mechanism. Thus it was that Descartes had seen animals as soulless, and his argument that human beings had souls had to be accompanied by the idea of language being a condition and symptom of our free will. For if, as is the case with Descartes, the human soul is simply a bundle of cognitive functions, then all moral talk is just hot air, ephemera of our wild imagination. Few, if any Western philosophers, apart from the Marquis de Sade, who had combined mechanism, sexual energy, cruelty and death and destruction and ecstasy, had been so consistent in combining a completely naturalistic view of human beings with a program that was so resolutely opposed to Platonic or Christian virtues as Nietzsche (though Nietzsche was far more prudish than Sade). For Nietzsche, if the sciences of his time had confirmed that we are purely the result of natural drives, instincts and mechanisms, the rights-based narratives that Kant's moral ideas had lent such power to had no chance of retaining their philosophical defences against the more probing and fearless philosophical intellects of the sort Nietzsche hoped to gather.

In our own time where the language of rights has reached a strident moral pitch that affects all aspects of private and public life, it is evident that the grounding of freedom in moral certitude as is found, with far more sophistication in Kant and Fichte, is very much alive. Hence it is easy to overlook the forcefulness which earlier generations accepted that Nietzsche's "will to power" had completely vanquished any notion that reason itself could yield moral ideas. Yet so many in our age segue from a moral ideational world of right to the social essence of identity—another idea, but this now is socially constructed as well as ontological rather than rational—to affirm how power should be. None who follows Nietzsche at all seriously can see this as anything other than one more variant of a world of competing wills to power taking place under the moralistic fog that has spread from Plato to Christendom to Kant and beyond. Whether Nietzsche would be correct or not may be left to the reader to ponder, along with what one makes of his more general attacks upon the various egalitarian movements—democracy, socialism, feminism, etc.—that he sees as but the spawn of the Christianized will to power—and the ideas and breeding that had operated in tandem with its spread.

Again, whether rightly or wrongly, Nietzsche believed that due to the spread of Christianity and its sick ideas a "herd animal, something well-meaning, sickly, and mediocre has finally been bred: the European of today,"[103] whereas wherever there had been high culture it was due to "the 'wild animal'" not being "killed off at all; it is alive and well, it has just—become divine."[104] That "wild animal," of course, can also be identified as the "Dionysian" force of life. The problem again can be formulated in a minor variant of that presented in the *Birth of Tragedy*: "Dionysos versus the crucified," as he will put it in *Ecce Homo*.[105] In the *Anti-Christ* Nietzsche will present his values thus:

> What is good?—Everything that enhances people's feeling of power, will to power, power itself.
> What is bad?—Everything stemming from weakness.
> What is happiness?—The feeling that power is growing, that some resistance has been overcome.
> Not contentedness, but more power; not peace, but war; not virtue, but prowess (virtue in the style of the Renaissance, *virtù*, moraline-free virtue).
> The weak and the failures should perish: first principle of our love of humanity. And they should be helped to do this.
> What is more harmful than any vice?—Active pity for all failures and weakness—Christianity.

And, in what has surely to be the most terrifying passage, ever written by a philosopher, we read in the *Will to Power*:

> To gain that tremendous energy of greatness in order to shape the man of the future through breeding and, on the other hand, the annihilation of millions of failures, and not to perish of the suffering one creates, though nothing like it has ever existed! [106]

To speak of all this talk of enslavement, breeding, biology, annihilation, and the task that is required, as Walter Kaufmann among numerous others would have us believe, as metaphors for much more benign processes requires a great deal of hermeneutical dexterity, and very little capacity to think through more obvious connections that are intrinsic to Nietzsche's "ideas" and how he has construed the problem and the solution.[107]

It also illustrates how, just as in Marx, when ideas that could not possibly mean anything other than the willingness to engage in mass slaughter can fail to be understood by a class of readers who have become like the "lotus eaters" feasting on ideas, more concerned with the congruence and fit between the idea and the actuality than with what ideas do once they are released into the world as a means of shaping it, and circulate and adapt to the realities that our ideas never completely identify.

Both Marx and Nietzsche had made of their ideas means for transforming the future according to their idea of what a far better world would like. But just as Marx had not established at all that the real world with its economic conditions would conform to his interpretation of the laws of economic development, Nietzsche's solutions to our cultural ailments are not in the least compelling, even if his work bristles with astute insights into the human condition and contains all manner of astute psychological and cultural insights. Yet Marx and Nietzsche are themselves the products of a society in which the philosopher and intellectual plays a leading role in shaping the future. And they do so in a context where an ever increasingly large number of the population, through the course of their education, becomes exposed to ideas which ostensibly identify who is to blame for why the world falls short of the great idea they would incarnate.

Historically Marx's and Nietzsche's emergence occurs in the immediate vicinity of a great social and political revolt in which the class of those who broker in ideas has replaced the class who pray as offering the major means for social orientation. And of that class who broker in ideas, it is the philosopher who has generally frequently sought to be the head of this new church (it would take the followers of August Comte, a philosopher who has not impacted so well, to build a literal "church").

Insofar as Nietzsche, like Marx, was wanting the social instantiation of his ideas on a large scale, he was a founder. But the problem with any philosopher founder is that their ideas have been distilled from so much information so that they become much more clear and distinct, that is much more abstract, than the ideas of everyday speech, which have not been formed by such a sharp division between reason or the understanding and the imagination. What Nietzsche had identified as the perversion inaugurated by Socrates, namely that "instinct becomes the critic and consciousness the creator,"[108] is replicated by Nietzsche, who wants to use the results of conscious analysis to provide a solution that is intended to ensure healthy instincts.

Religious founders of the past have been conduits for the accumulation of social forces and practices embedded in a community's mythic narratives that they then add to—and/ or break from through a practice of such novelty and power that they attract others who will follow along their path and attempt to transform the world and behavior so that it conforms to the spirit of the founder. A founder is the product of multiple generations and life-practices, the culmination of a vast social unconscious, who, invariably due to some great catastrophe, finds a new way. It is true that they call for a new world, but while founders cast long shadows, the subsequent history of a faith is the real revelation of what the faith *is*; and Nietzsche's genealogical approach is itself based upon this simple truth that something is what it becomes, and it is not to be mistaken for the "essence," or "idea" we ascribe to it. Nietzsche, on the other hand, is a philosopher (and also the product of accumulated forces and an accompanying narrative disposition). But he is not a new type, whereas Moses, Buddha, Jesus, and Mohammad were most definitely new types—and this is evident in their religious differences, something that should not be occluded by the rather narrow idea of "religion." The hiving off of a "religious" view of reality, or something called religion, from the reality of everyday life is a very late socio-historical development, and is predicated on the existence of a semantic field in which people can ponder whether the gods really exist. In the ancient world, with the exception of a small handful of philosophers, the question was not do the gods exist, but which gods do you follow, pray to, perform rites to etc. Founders are not without precursors (or prophets), but what they do is new: none can be dissolved into what precedes them. They open up ages. (Calling religious founders charismatic, à la Weber, is hardly helpful: a word that can be equally useful for a strong personality, or a celebrity to someone who founds an age is not throwing much light on anything.)

Nietzsche is a philosopher. He does not *do* anything new—he writes books on philosophy. He most certainly *wants* to open up an age. He wants to be a "religious" founder, but he can only do that in fantasy. He is not Zarathustra, and Zarathustra does not exist. The idea that a religious founder did not exist only occurs to those who are outside of that body of faith that takes its orientation from the founder.

The "doing" that Nietzsche asks for is that some others join in promoting and following him in "realizing" his vision so that they can *create* values which will then in turn help found a great culture with the superman giving meaning to the earth. Nietzsche has seen what (may perhaps be) connections between cultures he believes are great examples of human achievement and their moral codes. But there is absolutely no certainty that he can cultivate a kind of moral code that will achieve a "great" culture. On the contrary, those who wish to create new values may do nothing other that perpetrate great cruelty and imbecility.

Historically, we know that narratives ("myths" in the most elemental sense of the term) develop around founders. That is the myth arises out of an event or contingency (at least believed to be true): myth is not principle in operation, but is the narrative development through the assembling of impressions that certain actions make in establishing significant meaning. Nietzsche proceeds in the opposite direction: his starting point is that truth is a "lie" when it comes to values, and hence we need to live with fictions. He sees that myth and symbol contribute to the spread of a doctrine, so he wants to discover a myth that he believed was powerful enough to consolidate his view of life as innocent and hierarchical, and an array of "symbols" to sustain it as well as "the idea" that will lead to his goal. The myth he discovered was that of eternal return.

It was a myth with an ancient pedigree, and it had been entertained by the conspiratorial socialist Louis Blanqui. Friedrich Engels also talks about it, and Nietzsche may well have initially read of it in Friedrich Lange, whom Carl Bernouilli called the "best path-finder through the labyrinth of Nietzsche's philosophical presuppositions."[109] Although Nietzsche thought it was an idea that could be scientifically defended, what appealed to Nietzsche so much about the idea of all things, great and small such as the "spider that creeps along the moonlight," or the barking dog eternally recurring,[110] was that it was, so he believed, the idea of the ultimate affirmation of life. For if true, there was never an escape: the play and innocence of life was not only endlessly occurring but endlessly returning to exactly the same constellations. There was neither beyond, nor redemption, nor escape—"All things are chained and entwined together, all things are in love."[111] The value of this truth/myth "idea" was that it would appeal to those "strong" enough to embrace it, while the "weak" would see it as a "curse:" Amongst his notes for the *Will to Power* dealing with the "Eternal Recurrence," he wrote:

> My philosophy brings the triumphant idea of which all other modes of thought will ultimately perish. It is the great cultivating idea: the races that cannot bear it stand condemned; those who find it the greatest benefit are chosen to rule.[112]

Like Marx, Nietzsche had set himself up as the great judge of who is to live and who is to die, who contributes to the redemption of the world, to use a more archaic and non-Nietzschean term. That the entire philosophy, as with Marx's, is plagued by a dialectic in which determinism and voluntarism seamlessly roll in and out of each other to produce their respective versions of reality and the purpose that provides meaning for our lives on earth. On the determinist side, the fact that both Marx and Nietzsche had not only insisted that being (social in Marx, physiological in Nietzsche) is the condition of consciousness, but had made this insight central to their own critiques of Platonism (in Nietzsche), and Hegel and idealism generally (in Marx) does not change the fact that both were spokesmen and representatives of ideas that were ostensibly drawn from flesh and blood human beings (higher men in Nietzsche: the proletariat in Marx), who they shared little in common with. That is, just as Rousseau had written a book instructing the world on child-rearing, while orphaning his own children, Marx was not a proletarian, and Nietzsche, who suffered from poor health, who had next to nothing in common with such precursors of the superman as Julius Caesar or Napoleon, was not a whit less a physiological product of the race mixture he saw as part and parcel of the modern European because he dreamed of breeding a higher type. To say this is not to take a cheap shot at either, but to highlight that in the age in which ideas play such a dominant role in providing a critique of the world as well as in providing a vision of the world they want to herald, the idea that takes precedence over the reality that it is meant to have identified is often not even confirmed by its leading exponents.

Just as Marxists now want to protect Marx from actual Marxism, the one attempt to genetically construct a new man, Nazism, is seen by many who admire Nietzsche as having nothing in common with him. And while there are key differences—Nietzsche's hostility to German race purists, anti-Semites, socialists, and nationalists, most obviously, these strike me as far less significant than the readiness to enslave and annihilate entire groups because they are seen as "sick," mere "*Untermenschen*."[113] (Another of Walter Kaufmann's false claims that has been widely accepted is that Nazi Nietzscheans such as Alfred Baeumler were unaware of, or even tried to conceal, where Nietzsche departed from National Socialism.)

It is not only the idea-ism of Nietzsche and Marx that is so historically proximate to us, but, more generally, the institutional spread and instantiation of philosophical ideas largely severed now from any more encompassing religious faith. This phenomenon has proceeded hand in hand with a new social and political order. And modern social and political orders are still so historically recent that they are very much an experiment; that is, we do not have enough knowledge to know what kind of world we have been making with the overthrow of the ancient regime. Nietzsche understood this, and jumped at the opportunity to give a greater meaning to this experiment. He saw the philosopher of the future as a maker of truth, and in so doing he found the pre-Socratics (though not all, especially not Parmenides whom he sees as a false step on the way to Plato) and the poets as a source of inspiration. For he had seen that the moral ideas of philosophers were not robust enough to withstand the onslaught of questions he directed at them. If Kant had called moral values "mere Ideas," Nietzsche understood that they could be blown away rather easily. His persistent attacks upon Plato, especially, were an attack upon what he saw as being the core weakness of philosophy, its faith in reason, and the inadequacy of that faith to establish the truth of value. For Nietzsche, "the will to truth" would only drive us further into the recognition that value is contingent, that what one values depends upon who one is, upon the cultivations that have formed one. This insight seems to me to be irrefutable. Further he also understood that insofar as truth as value is lived, its best form of expression will be aesthetic. Thus for him: "we possess *art* lest we *perish* of the truth"[114] and "art is

worth more than truth."[115] The philosopher of culture and of the superman, then was not humbled by the little that he knew, for knowing was
not as necessary as art, and the kind of art involved in making human
beings and society was mythmaking. It is symptomatic of Nietzsche's
thought—in the best and worst sense—that he could manage to provide a
one page history of what led to his philosophy.

How the "True World" Finally Became a Fable

The history of an error

1. The true world attainable for a man, who is wise, pious, virtuous—
    he lives in it, *he is it*. (Oldest form of the idea, relatively coherent,
    simple, convincing. Paraphrase of the proposition: "I, Plato, *am* the
    truth.")
2. The true world, unattainable for now, but promised to the man
    who is wise, pious, virtuous ("to the sinner who repents").
    (Progress of the idea: it gets trickier, more subtle, less comprehen-
    sible—it becomes female, it becomes Christian . . .) (Progress of the
    idea: it becomes more cunning, more insidious, more incompre-
    hensible—*it becomes a woman*, it becomes Christian . . .)
3. The true world, unattainable, unprovable, unpromisable, but the
    very thought of it a consolation, an obligation, an imperative. (Ba-
    sically the old sun but through fog and scepticism; the idea become
    elusive, pale, Nordic, Konigsbergian.
4. The true world—unattainable? At any rate, unattained. And as
    unattained also unknown. Consequently not consoling, redeem-
    ing, obligating either: how could we have obligations to something
    unknown? . . . (Gray morning. First yawn of reason. Cockcrow of
    positivism.)
5. The "true world" —an idea that is of no further use, not even as an
    obligation—now an obsolete, superfluous idea, consequently a re-
    futed idea: let's get rid of it! (Bright day; breakfast; return of bon
    sensl6 and cheerfulness; Plato blushes in shame; pandemonium of
    all free spirits.)
6. The true world is gone: which world is left? The illusory one, per-
    haps? . . . But no! we got rid of the illusory world along with the
    true one! (Noon; moment of shortest shadow; end of longest error;
    high point of humanity; INCIPIT ZARATHUSTRA. [116]

Zarathustra's entrance appears at "the end of the longest error." How
blessed must a people be to have such a genius as Nietzsche among them,
one who could make sense of all that has thwarted human achievement,
of what has made us sick, and one who knows how to prepare the way
for "the great health." But that the idea of the superman was as empty in

its details as Marx's ideas of communism suggests how desperate was an age, which had understood itself through its ideas, to believe in something. And Nietzsche himself well grasped this need to believe in a nihilistic world. The more sceptical and more traditionalist minded Chesterton, who had a profound sense of the desperateness of the age to find idols everywhere, found in the superman, a topic to be ridiculed rather than taken seriously, depicting it as a fragile feathered creature, killed by a draft at the age of fifteen in his parents's house in Croydon.[117]

What Chesterton understood is the archaic truth that preceded the modern elevation of the self as the source of its own worldmaking: our lives are ever in service to something beyond ourselves (to be fair to Nietzsche, he attempts to retain this archaic "truth" about the sacrificial character of existence in his call for "going under.") For premodern tribal and ancient imperial peoples the service was largely preordained, but when people entered into other tribes or empires, via enslavement, or marriage they may well respond to different voices or gods calling for service.

As we can see, a number of the most important philosophers of the nineteenth century moved against the metaphysical currents that led up to and included Kant and even Hegel. These philosophers were interested in how we participate in the world, and the ideas that were important related to this project of existence in the world. Of the four—Marx, Kierkegaard, Schopenhauer, and Nietzsche—two were focused upon changing the world, and those two were so sure of the ends they were pursing that they abandoned any philosophical critique altogether of what might be the problems of socialism (Marx), or a revived aristocracy (Nietzsche). Likewise, they would read out of history what would bolster the primary ideas—communism, or the superman—that gave their action purpose. History that did not conform to their end-idea was ignored as irrelevant. In their selectivity, they were continuing the Enlightenment approach to history.

In both cases it sufficed to simply focus upon who one was, as if one's being and one's idea were so firmly cemented that one did not need to dialogue more with those who did not share their purpose: they were either too weak (Nietzsche), or bourgeois dupes (Marx). In this respect, they too had also brought philosophy to an end, once they knew what kind of world they wanted and how they could (ostensibly) achieve it. With Kierkegaard and Schopenhauer, philosophy was also a means rather than something that retained a permanent value in relationship to the acquisition of knowledge; indeed, knowledge itself was not an end of any sort. The end was the act and decision of one's life. Marx, Nietzsche, and Kierkegaard (Schopenhauer would never reach such acclaim though he would be appreciated by Wittgenstein, Adorno, and authors such as Thomas Mann and Jorge Louis Borges) would all continue to exercise their influence upon philosophical movements of the twentieth century, and Marx and Nietzsche continue to do so.

Given that post-Hegelianism tends to bring philosophy to an "end" by requiring extra-philosophical commitments, it should not be surprising that there were a great many philosophers, indeed who would form a major "school" or way of doing philosophy, that remained essentially untouched by post-Hegelian philosophy because they simply were not philosophical enough.[118] What would come to be called analytic philosophy was, initially at least, a retreat from the action-based, and "irrational" philosophies of the post-Hegelians, as well as a refusal to enter into the kinds of idealisms that had arisen as a response to Kant. It would address the most fundamental of philosophical questions: What is the task of philosophy? And its answer to this was based upon a very specific idea of what philosophy was—though as specific as it was and is, identifying it precisely, as we shall see in the next chapter has proven no easy matter for a tradition that prides itself in continuing the Cartesian dictum of requiring that philosophy concern itself with ideas and problems whose answers are clear and distinct.

Its founders are generally considered (though not without some contestation) to be Frege, Russell, More, and Wittgenstein. And while analytic philosophy is defined more by a style of philosophy than by the tradition, generally the philosophers who may have something worth considering, for analytic philosophers, are Plato, more importantly Aristotle, and Descartes, Locke, Leibniz, Berkeley, Hume, Kant, Boole, Lotze, Bolzano, and Franz Brentano. But originally at least, they were not interested in the history of philosophy as such, only the arguments that philosophers brought to the "table" of a more rationally rigorous understanding of truth, and the insights they had about the nature and value of argument.

NOTES

1. Georg Lukács, *History and Class Consciousness: Studies in Marxist Dialectics* (Cambridge, MA: MIT, 1971), translated by Rodney Livingstone, 27.
2. Ibid.
3. The central criticism that Roger Scruton makes against communists and fascists is that their political vision requires the absolute removal of all opposition; whereas any kind of politics that is to be consistent with any kind of free society has to be reconciled to the existence of opposition. Which is why Scruton correctly observes: "the question of opposition is . . . the single most important issue in politics." *Fools, Frauds, and Firebrands: Thinkers of the New Left* (London: Bloomsbury, 2015), 204–5. It should not need to be said that to agree with this view of politics does not mean one is a conservative, but it is to accept that politics is a means of keeping war between different community interests at bay rather than simply getting what one's own group wills. This is precisely why the Greeks were the inventors of politics, even if they were still owners of slaves.

4. Karl Marx, *A Contribution to the Critique of Political Economy*, translated by S. W. Ryazanskaya, edited by Maurice Dobb (Moscow: Progress, 1977), 22. The idea, now somewhat commonplace among academic and cultural Marxists, that Marx's theory had little impact upon real existing communism suffers from one central flaw: the failure to think through what Marx's call for the abolition of classes and private property could only mean in practice: active seizure and inevitable response. Marx's most fateful contribution to the mass violence of communist societies would be in the call, in the *Communist Manifesto*, for "industrialized armies" for agriculture. Karl Marx and Friedrich Engels, *The Manifesto of the Communist Party*, in Karl Marx, *The Revolutions of 1848: Political Writings*, Volume 1, edited and introduced by David Fernbach (Harmondsworth: Penguin, 1973), 87. The difference between urban/ agrarian interests is one of the most ancient and elemental of political life. The creation of industrialized armies of agriculture could only ever mean one thing: collectivization, and hence the seizure of farms and the imprisonment or liquidation of those who fought to retain their property. Moreover, there could be no real socialism if socialist urban producers were beholden to non-socialist agrarian producers. In this respect, Stalin's collectivization program was fully in keeping with the logic of communism; communist opposition was not over the practice, but the pace and risks and horrors of implementation.

5. Georg Lukács, "Telos 10 (Winter 1971), 23–25.

6. *Prolegomena to a Historiosophy* of 1838, in *Selected Writings of August Ciezkowski*, edited, translated and introduced by André Leibich (Cambridge: Cambridge University Press, 1979), 73.

7. G. W. F. Hegel, *The Difference between the Fichtean and Schellingean Systems of Philosophy*, 10.

8. Ibid., 23–27.

9. Ibid.

10. Ibid., 11–12.

11. See especially *Foundations of the Entire Science of Knowledge*, in J. G. Fichte, *The Science of Knowledge with the First and Second Introductions*, 203–6.

12. Fichte's lectures "On the Life According to Reason" in *The Popular Works of Johann Gottlieb Fichte*, translated William Smith (London: Trubner, 1889), 35–68.

13. *Faith and Knowledge*, 153. Apart from the same critique being directed at Kant and Jacobi in *Faith and Knowledge*, in his Preface to the *Philosophy of Right* he makes essentially the same critique of Jacob Fries.

14. Note that Strauss refers to "theatre" numerous times in *The Life of Jesus* in his representation of how Jesus and the early Christians present themselves. Thomas Fabisak in "The Nocturnal Side of Science" in David Friedrich Strauss's *Life of Jesus Critically Examined* (Atlanta: SBL Press, 2015), 188 accurately sums up *The Life of Jesus* as a "paean to quietist bourgeois secularism and modern scientific thought." In his essay on Strauss in *Untimely Meditations*, Nietzsche would attack Strauss for being the embodiment of the *Bildungphilister* (the cultured philistine).

15. See, for example, Bruno Bauer, *The Trumpet of the Last Judgement against Hegel the Atheist and Antichrist: An Ultimatum* (Lewiston, NY: E. Mellen Press, 1989).

16. Of the numerous books on the young Hegelians, although only going up to 1841, John Edward Toews's *Hegelianism: The Path Towards Dialectical Humanism 1805–1841* (Cambridge: Cambridge University Press, 1980) remains the indispensable work on the subject.

17. He repeats the criticism in numerous places such as in his *Critique of Hegelian Philosophy*, but it goes back to 1827–1828 and would be expressed in his fragment "Zweifel" ("Doubt"). Feuerbach does not provide an adequate response to Hegel's section in the *Phenomenology of Spirit*, "Sense-Certainty: Or the 'This' and 'Meaning' (Meinen)," 58–66, not to mention the irrefutable truth that plays such a decisive role in Hegel's thought, viz. that without its predications, a subject is empty. That is, to repeat, Hegel's position is built upon the fact that anything at all that we encounter and name is "placed" within a great conceptual chain of knowledge and its underlying principles; the less this takes place, the less we know about it.

18. *The Holy Family, or Critique of Critical Criticism: Against Bruno Bauer and Company* (Moscow: Progress, 1975), 148–49.

19. Timothy D. Terrell, "The Economics of Destutt de Tracy," in Destutt de Tracy, *A Treatise on Political Economy to Which is Prefixed A Supplement to a Preceding Work on the Understanding Or, Elements of Ideology,* translated by Thomas Jefferson (Auburn, AL: The Ludwig von Mises Institute, 2009), i. As Manfred Steger says, the word initially refers to "his rationalist method of breaking complex systems into their basic components," *The Rise of the Global Imaginary: Political Ideologies from the French Revolution to the Global War on Terror* (Oxford: Oxford University Press, 2008), 11.

20. Karl Marx and Friedrich Engels, *The German Ideology* (London: Lawrence and Wishart, 1974), 47.

21. Ibid., 107.

22. To Joseph Weydemeyer Marx writes that he had proven: "(1) that the existence of classes is merely linked to particular historical phases in the development of production, (2) that class struggle necessarily leads to the *dictatorship of the proletariat,* (3) that this dictatorship itself only constitutes the transition to the abolition of all classes and to a classless society." Marx to Joseph Weydemeyer, *Marx/Engels Selected Correspondence* (Moscow: Progress, 1955), 64.

23. *Marx Engels Werke* Bd. 3, (Berlin Dietz, 1958), 13 and 38. In the *Communist Manifesto,* the terms are used interchangeably cf. *Marx Engels Werke,* Bd. 4 (Berlin: Dietz, 1959), 478, 480, 481.

24. *Capital, Volume 1,* translated by S. Moore and E. Aveling (London: Lawrence and Wishart, 1954), 19.

25. See for example *Grundrisse,* translated by Martin Nicolaus (Harmondsworth: Penguin, 1973), 100–101, and *Capital, Volume 1,* 19. Also the comments on essence and appearance in *Capital, Volume 3,* translated by C. Kerr (London: Lawrence and Wishart, 1959), 817.

26. *Capital, Volume 1,* 29.

27. In response to Hegel's insistence that he is identifying not the state as it should be but its actuality, and with that he lays down his "Here is Rhodes dance," Paulus asks: "but where is Rhodes supposed to be, where the philosopher is supposed to have his political dance—is it Germany or France, England or even Spain?" See Manfred Riedel, *Materialen zu Hegels Rechtsphilosophie,* Volume 1 (Frankfurt am Main: Suhrkamp, 1975), 63–64.

28. In Marx's case, this provides him with the advantage of showing the horror of capital's entrance into the world, while leaving unasked whether in different contexts capitalism might have other trajectories, and thus enter into some parts of world in more benign forms.

29. Milovan Djilas, *The New Class: An Analysis of the Communist System* (San Diego: Harcourt Brace Jovanovich, 1957).

30. See Jaroslaw Piekalkiewickz, and Alfred Wayne Penn, *Politics of Ideocracy* (New York: SUNY, 1995). The key to professional power requires the replication of norms, and rules—consensuses. Thus the dangers that Tocqueville recognized in democracies are compounded by the social importance of those who select, monitor, and refine the ideas that are essential for social reproduction in general. Narrative contradictions are but the expression of the contrary interests that are managed and consolidated by a power elite. Our modern revolutions are of such relatively recent occurrence, that it is easy to miss the one thing they have in common: the great transfer of political power between a traditional, i.e., premodern elite, and a modern elite in which the professional classes are essential to the running of the society (more politically important in terms of supplying authority than the unskilled workers championed by Marx). Elites, by their nature, fulfill essential social functions. But the functions required by premodern and modern societies differ significantly. Hence too, and contra Marx, the great *long-term* disputes are not between competing modern ideologies, but between an ideological view of life predicated upon the predominance of certain philosophical

ideas, and a view of life in which ideas are subordinate to more visceral narratives, traditional roles and expectations.

31. *Capital, Volume 1,* 95.

32. Ibid., 80.

33. Ibid.

34. Ibid., 604.

35. *Capital, Volume 3,* 820.

36. Unlike other modern political ideologies such as liberalism and nationalism, Marxism is unique in being named after the ideas of a particular person. This is, in part, also because those other ideologies, while having philosophical defenders are not simply, or even primarily the result of a philosophy. That is, they grow out of a collective practice and then attract philosophical support, which is why they play no large role in this book. I will mention in passing, though, that "liberalism" is also a form of "idea-ism," and to the extent that liberal economists see an open society (to use Popper's famous term) as capable of rational construction on a global scale (which, for example, is what von Mises thought was necessary for a genuine liberal order) its indifference to actual loyalties and social bonds of existing life-worlds and traditions is a recipe for social mayhem.

37. *Philosophical Crumbs or a Crumb of Philosophy by Johannes Climacus Published by S. Kierkegaard* in Søren Kierkegaard, *Repetition* and *Philosophical Crumbs,* translated by M. G. Piety, with an introduction by Edward F. Mooney and notes by Edward F. Mooney and M. G. Piety (Oxford: Oxford University Press, 2009), 89 (220).

38. *Concluding Unscientific Postscript to the Philosophical Crumbs: A Mimic, Pathetic, Dialectic Compilation An Existential Contribution* By Johannes Climacus Responsible for Publication: S. Kierkegaard translated by Alastair Hannay (Cambridge: Cambridge University Press, 2009), 29.

39. Ibid., 288.

40. Ibid., 68.

41. Ibid., 276.

42. Ibid., 277.

43. Søren Kierkegaard, *Two Ages: The Age of Revolution and the Present Age, A Literary Review,* edited and translated by Howard and Eva Hong with introduction and notes (Princeton, NJ: Princeton University Press, 1978), 78.

44. Ibid., 81.

45. Søren Kierkegaard, *The Point of View: On My Work as an Author, The Point of View for my Work as an Author, Armed Neutrality,* edited with instruction and notes by Howard and Edna Hong (Princeton, NJ: Princeton University Press, 1998), 20.

46. Thus Lukács depicts Kierkegaard as "a pure apologist of bourgeois decadence, and nothing else," *The Destruction of Reason,* translated by Peter Palmer (London: Merlin, 1980), 296. If one is defending a system of thought in which the individual must succumb to a larger objectively knowable set of social forces and relations, then Kierkegaard is indeed the class enemy.

47. Eugen Rosenstock-Huessy, *Der Atem des Geistes* (Wien: Amandus, 1990), 27. In this particular passage, he is placed in the same company as Feuerbach and Nietzsche.

48. Eugen Rosenstock-Huessy and Franz Rosenzweig, *Judaism Despite Christianity,* edited by Eugen Rosenstock-Huessy (New York: Schocken, 1971), 104.

49. Simon Podmore in *Kierkegaard and the Self Before God: Anatomy of the Abyss,* (Bloomington and Indianapolis: Indiana University Press, 2011) emphasizes the affinity between Karl Barth and Kierkegaard.

50. Søren Kierkegaard, *Fear and Trembling in Fear and Trembling and Sickness unto Death,* translated with notes by Walter Lowrie, introduction by Gordon Marino (Princeton, NJ: Princeton University Press, 2013), 110.

51. Søren Kierkegaard, *The Concept of Anxiety: A Simple Psychological Orienting Deliberation on the Dogmatic Issue of Hereditary Sin* (Princeton, NJ: Princeton University Press, 1980), edited and translated with introduction and notes by Reidar Thomte in collaboration with Albert Anderson, 155.

52. *World as Will and Representation, Volume 1*, 3.

53. Ibid., 3–4.

54. Ibid., 3.

55. Ibid., 25.

56. Ibid., 15.

57. Ibid., 27–28.

58. Ibid., 50.

59. Ibid., 19.

60. Ibid., 20.

61. G. W. F. Hegel, *The Encyclopaedia Logic (with the Zusätze): Part 1 of the Encyclopaedia of the Philosophical Sciences*, para. 44, 87. See also, the discussion of the thing-in-itself in the context of "shine" and "The Thing and its Properties," *Science of Logic*, 343, and 423–432.

62. *World as Will and Representation Volume 1*, 19.

63. "As I am completely lacking in all reason-intuition, I shall not venture to speak of the aforesaid revered identity and of the Absolute." Ibid., 26.

64. Ibid., 100.

65. Ibid., 107.

66. Ibid., 501.

67. Ibid., xv.

68. Ibid., 171.

69. Ibid., 129.

70. Ibid., 134.

71. Ibid., 146.

72. Ibid., 146–47.

73. Ibid., 161. In his retrospective "An Attempt at Self-Criticism" of *The Birth of Tragedy*, Nietzsche would regret the Schopenhauerian (and Kantian!) formulations of the book distancing himself from his former "teacher." Friedrich Nietzsche, *The Birth of Tragedy and Other Writings*, edited by Raymond Geuss and (translated) by Ronald Spies (Cambridge: Cambridge University Press, 1999), 10.

74. *World as Will and Representation, Volume 1*, 175.

75. Ibid.

76. Ibid.

77. Ibid., 184.

78. Thus are the "wailing" "mixed and 'tight'" Lydian modes to be excluded from the ideal city because "they're useless even for women who are to be decent, let alone for men," as well as the "slack" Ionian modes and other Lydian modes, which "are soft and suitable for symposia," but useless "for war-making men." Indeed, the *Republic* is as ruthless in its purging of music as it is of poetry. Of the modes, Socrates says only two should be spared and included in the guardians's education, "a violent one and a voluntary one, which will produce the finest imitation of the sounds of unfortunate and fortunate, moderate and courageous men," while "there'll be no need of many-toned or panharmonic instruments for our songs and melodies." Thus the city will be free of "craftsmen who make lutes, harps, and all the instruments that are many-stringed and play many modes," as well as "flutemakers and flutists": "the lyre and the cither are left you as useful for the city. . . . And further, for the country, a sort of pipe for the herdsmen." *The Republic of Plato*, translated with notes and interpretative essay by Allan Bloom (New York: Basic Books, 1991), 398–99.

79. For Schopenhauer, "the life of every single individual, viewed as whole and in general . . . is really a tragedy; but gone through in detail it has the character of a comedy." Ibid., 322.

80. Ibid., 322.

81. *World as Will and Representation, Volume 2*, translated by E. F. J. Payne (New York: Dover, 1969), 444.

82. Arthur Schopenhauer, *On the Basis of Morality*, translated by E. F. J. Payne (Cambridge Massachusetts: Hackett, 1995), 153. For a good account of Schopenhauer's poli-

tics and how it relates to his ethics, see Neil Jordan, "Schopenhauer's Politics: Ethics, Jurisprudence and the State," in *Better Consciousness: Schopenhauer's Philosophy of Value* (Oxford: Blackwell, 2009), edited by Alex Neill and Christopher Janaway, 171–88.

83. *World as Will and Representation*, Volume 1, 350.

84. Ibid., Vol 1, 374.

85. *Introduction to the Science of Knowledge*, in J. G. Fichte, *The Science of Knowledge with the First and Second Introductions*, 16.

86. In *Ecce Homo*, he will say of the *Birth of Tragedy*, "Everything is announced in advance in this essay: the imminent return of the Greek spirit, the need for counter-Alexanders to retie the Gordian knot of Greek culture after it had been undone *Ecce Homo* in *The Anti-Christ, Twilight of the Idols and Other Writings*, edited by Aaron Ridley and (translated by) Judith Norman (Cambridge: Cambridge University Press, 2005), 111, para. 4 of "the Birth of Tragedy." In *Twilight of the Idols*, "the Greeks are the *first cultural event* in history, 221. Though he will also see that the Greece could not be replicated, for his endeavour it is the Romans that must be followed, not because they were culturally superior to the Greeks, but because "the Greeks cannot be to us what the Romans are." *The Anti-Christ, Twilight of the Idols and Other Writings*, 224.

87. *The Birth of Tragedy and Other Writings*, 60.

88. Ibid., 66.

89. Friedrich Nietzsche, *The Will to Power*, translated with introduction by Walter Kaufmann and R. J. Hollingdale (New York: Vintage Books, 1967), para. 3, 32. Nietzsche announces in the third essay of *On the Genealogy of Morality* that he will be publishing a work entitled *The Will to Power: Attempt at a Revaluation of all Values. On the Genealogy of Morality*, edited by Keith Ansell Pearson, and translated by Carol Diethe, (Cambridge: Cambridge University Press, 2007), 103.

90. *On the Genealogy of Morality*, 34.

91. Ibid., 73.

92. Ibid., 83.

93. Ibid., 83.

94. Ibid., 85–86.

95. Ibid., 87.

96. Friedrich Nietzsche, *Beyond Good and Evil: Prelude to a Philosophy of the Future*, edited by Rolf-Peter Horstmann and (also translated by) Judith Norman (Cambridge: Cambridge University Press, 2002), 91, para 203.

97. *On the Genealogy of Morality*, 51.

98. *Beyond Good and Evil*, 151.

99. Ibid., 129.

100. Ibid., 143.

101. Ibid., 134.

102. Ibid.

103. Ibid., 57.

104. Ibid., 120.

105. *Ecce Homo* in *The Anti-Christ, Twilight of the Idols and Other Writings*, 151 (para. 9).

106. *The Will to Power*, 445–56, para 964.

107. Walter Kaufmann was an excellent translator of Nietzsche, who dominated Nietzsche studies in the English-speaking world for decades. His *Nietzsche: Philosopher, Psychologist, Antichrist* (Princeton, NJ: Princeton University Press), originally issued in 1950, was an attempt to rescue Nietzsche from what he saw as the "myth of Nietzsche" that had been propagated by the Nazis, and his sister. All of Nietzsche's "dangerous" ideas were reduced to versions that were palatable to the postwar American college student and the, then, prevailing existentialism. According to Kaufmann: Nietzsche did not really advocate the revival of master morality; when he spoke of war he was just being metaphorical; when he spoke of breeding the superman he did not mean it; he was not really praising the caste system as presented in the Book of Manu; his eugenicist and physiologist claims were not to be taken at face value, etc. Thus Kaufmann's translations are replete with footnotes "explaining" to the

reader that what they are reading is not what Nietzsche meant. Given this approach, it should be no surprise that his reading of Nietzsche has nothing in common with the earlier generation of translators and proselytizers who had translated Nietzsche's *Complete Works* in English. The project was presided over by Oscar Levy, a German Jew, whose first book was *The Revival of the Aristocracy*. While Levy was forthright about the need for a new aristocracy to save higher types from the herd, and he believed that Nietzsche's critique of Judaism and Christianity as slave religions was correct, he rightly saw that Nietzsche himself had been forthright in his rejection of a number of the planks of the Nazi platform: viz., Aryan racial purity, socialism, and racial anti-Semitism. One of the other translators of the *Complete Works*, Anthony Ludovici, believed that the "last great movement of anything like the same importance as National Socialism was the Reformation," (36) and that Hitler (in one of his most remarkable achievements (234)), attempted to drive out Socrates" influence upon German culture. Anthony M. Ludovici, "Hitler and the Third Reich," in *The English Review*, 63, 1936, 35–41, 147–53, 231–39. For the fascinating story of English Nietzscheanism and eugenics, see Dan Stone, *Breeding Superman: Race and Eugenics in Edwardian and Interwar Britain* (Liverpool: Liverpool University Press, 2002).

108. *The Birth of Tragedy*, 66.

109. Carl Bernouilli, *Franz Overbeck und Friedrich Nietzsche: Eine Freundschaft Band 1* (Jena: Eugen Diedrichs, 1908), 146. Friedrich Lange's *Geschichte der Materialismus*, was translated into English as *History of Materialism and Critique of Its Present Importance*, in 1877 and appeared in three volumes. Lange's impact upon Nietzsche has been commented upon by many, but articles by Jörg Salaquandra such as "Nietzsche und Lange" *Nietzsche-Studien*, Band 7 (1978), "Der Standpunkt des Ideals bei Lange und Nietzsche," *Studi Tedeschi*, XXII, I (1979), and George Stack's, *Lange and Nietzsche* (Berlin: Walter de Gruyter, 1983) have demonstrated how so many of his central ideas are to be found in Lange's work. These include anti-Platonism, anti-Christianity, the matter of Darwin and teleology, Boscovich's idea of "a force-point world," and what Lange would call "materio-idealism," which is in all but name Schopenhauer's position, and the materialist arguments for an eternal return. Interestingly, Stack (15) notes that Marx appears in four places in Lange's second edition. He also points out that Nietzsche had read Henry Carey's *Lehrbuch der Volkwirtschaft*, which discusses Marx.

110. *Thus Spake Zarathustra: A Book for Everyone and No One* (Harmondsworth: Penguin, 1969), translated by R. J. Hollingdale, 182.

111. Ibid., 29.

112. *Will to Power*, 544, para. 1053.

113. Given Nietzsche's differences with such core components of Nazism, it should not be surprising that there were not only Nazi Nietzscheans like Baeumler and Heinrich Härtle, but also Nazi anti-Nietzscheans such as Marti Löpelmann, Hans Goebel, and Heidegger's Nazi nemesis, Ernst Krieck. The idea that Nazi intellectuals were either worse at reading books, and interpreting philosophies, or more determined to lie about their precursors is simply silly. Modern ideologies are, to various degrees, philosophical narratives, and modern ideological crises are crises of ideas. Neither mass liquidation, nor genocide are modern phenomenon, but what is modern is that philosophers call for such mass liquidation, or, more commonly, help frame narratives in which such liquidation is implicitly justified as the oppressors reaping what they sowed. I am unaware of any historical analysis on fascist and Nazi Nietzsche reception that has treated this topic with the scholarly depth required. The best studies I have come across are Bernard Taureck, *Nietzsche und der Faschismus* (Leipzig: Reclam, 2000), and Steven Ascheim *The Nietzsche Legacy in Germany, 1880–1990* (Berkeley: University of California Press, 1992), 232–307.

114. Friedrich Nietzsche, The *Will to Power*, para. 853, 453.

115. Ibid., para. 822, 435.

116. *Twilight of the Idols*, in *The Anti-Christ, Ecce Homo, Twilight of the Idols and Other Writings*, 171.

117. Though, he adds, not as we understand "feathers." G. K. Chesteron, *Selected Essays*, introduced by John Guest (London: Collins, 1939), 128.

118. Generally, what is noticeable when analytic philosophers turned to Hegel (Paul Reading), Nietzsche (Arthur Danto, John Wilcox, Bernard Williams), or Marx (Gerry Cohen and Jon Elster), they still treated these thinkers in the analytic fashion which we discuss in detail in the next chapter. On the other hand, some philosophers as different as Alasdair MacIntyre, Bernard Williams, Stanley Cavell, and John Rawls could be placed in the analytic "camp" on the basis of how they argue, while also strongly identifying themselves with larger philosophical and historical traditions.

EIGHT

The Analytic Retreat to Reason and the Relative Splintering of the Idea

WHAT IS ANALYTIC PHILOSOPHY?

That there is or was (for it may be that is now in serious decline) such a practice as "analytic philosophy" is obvious to anyone who has encountered it. But when we seek to go more deeply into identifying its nature we not only find all manner of disputes, but also anomalies that suggest whatever it is is largely due to what Wittgenstein called a "family resemblance" rather than any one central common characteristic. Thus:

Frege is really the source of it all (Dummett); no Russell is (Monk), and Frege was never really an analytical philosopher (Capaldi).

Language is the root of it all (again Dummett and then ordinary language philosophy); well then (one of) its founder(s), Russell, who did not ascribe such significance to language, would have to be left out (Monk).[1]

Hume is a forefather (Russell); no he isn't, he commences the Copernican philosophical turn which poses insurmountable challenges to analytic philosophy (Capaldi).

Wittgenstein is a central figure in analytic philosophy and this doesn't really change with the *Investigations* (Glock); Wittgenstein became the twentieth century exemplar of the "anti-analytic philosopher" (Capaldi).

Analytic philosophy is the only real philosophy and will save us all from irrationalism (pretty well all of those who do it); no, their preoccupation with "in-house puzzles" has made them "ignorant [of] the damage their neglect is wreaking in the wider world" as they leave it to "philosophically naïve exponents of other disciplines to wreak ontological havoc" (Mulligan, Simons, and Smith—who, nevertheless, are analytic philosophers).[2]

189

Given this state of affair, I have to admire the tenacity of Mulligan et al. for their rousing final sentence of "What's Wrong with Contemporary Philosophy?" with its appeal to being "unwaveringly resolved to discover, however complex, frustrating and unlovely it may be, the truth." This kind of clamor has a desperateness about it, and depending upon what one thinks is at stake, it may be read as the philosophical equivalent of either "once more unto the breach" — to face slaughter yet again in the face of all "truth's" hostile adversaries — or "let's drink the bar dry" — because this Truth stuff is so great we need to imbibe all we can.

Let us briefly observe Hans-Johann Glock's answer/response to the question, which is also the title of his book, *What Is Analytic Philosophy?* The book is exemplary in the way in which the task of identifying analytic philosophy is conducted analytically, albeit at a breakneck pace that is not usually the analytic's favorite speed. With po-faced Buster Keaton-like burlesque, Glock sets off on an expedition, if not for *"the definitive meaning"* of analytic philosophy, at least for something that is a recognizably acceptable version of what it is. With a combination of rapid scaling of human constructions, high wire dancing around delicate distinctions, and balletic escapes from a series of potential disasters that might accompany exaggerated ontological commitments and which could kill the project before it is born, it is difficult to tell whether the slapstick of Glock's performance simply illustrates the nature of someone seriously under the influence of the analytic concoction or whether it has been staged from the outset. Anyway this is how the expedition commences:

> If analytic philosophy cannot be defined, whether for general or specific reasons, this is something that should emerge in the course of our exploration. This leaves open entirely the question of what type of definition or explanation is appropriate. One important distinction here is that between nominal definitions, which specify the linguistic meaning of words, and real definitions, which specify the essence of the things denoted by them. Some philosophers, including Wittgenstein and Quine, reject the idea of real essences. But even if this blanket repudiation of essentialism is unwarranted, there are grounds for doubting that analytic philosophy is the proper subject of a real definition.[3]

Glock then agonizes over whether he can ascribe anything to the topic, given Davidson on meaning, Kripke and Putnam on semantics and the nature of reference, and Hanfling and Jackson on natural kinds, the nominalists and realists, before throwing these concerns aside and picking up Aristotle's reliance upon the commonplace use of the term *sophia* by his contemporaries for his "systematic search for philosophy" (while also marshaling Ernst Tugendhat to anchor a "preliminary notion" to answer the "what is X"?). This gives him some confidence because it is the kind of thing ordinary language philosophers do as well as their critics such as

Quine (p. 14). Then drawing on Ryle's everyday versus technical use of language, he has a brief Mexican stand-off with Hacker, who "denies that the term 'analytic philosophy' *has* an established use," and moves on to note that: "what Grice and Strawson pointed out about the terms "analytic" and "synthetic" holds equally of the term "analytic philosophy." Although we may lack a clear and compelling explanation, "we by-and-large agree in our application of these terms" (p. 14). Having found his Archimedean point, he proceeds to list who should be included among analytic philosophers—and apart from those he has already mentioned he adds Carnap and Austin (while pointing out that Heidegger and Lacan do not fit the profile!), as well as Frege, Russell, Quine (again) and such border line cases as Bolzano, Whitehead, late Wittgenstein, Popper, and "neurophilosophers." He rounds off with the observation:

> we need to rely on a preliminary idea of what philosophers generally count as analytic, and on what grounds. For this reason, I shall be guided by the question whether suggested definitions include all generally acknowledged instances of analytic philosophers and exclude all generally acknowledged instances of non-analytic philosophers. In other words, I shall measure conceptions of analytic philosophy in the first instance against the commonly acknowledged extension of the term. In fact, even if a genuine definition of analytic philosophy were a red herring, it would be profitable to ascertain whether and to what extent the countless general claims about it actually hold. By testing these claims for their suitability as definitions, we also test them for their accuracy as generalizations.[4]

To all that I can only say: "Phew. I'm glad we got that far—right back to square one!" And I can't help but note that this is where clarity, understood a certain way, leads us. To be fair to Glock, who provides an admirable overview of what is going on in the analytic tradition, in the book's conclusion he provides an anecdote from Adam Swift, which I think is as modest but pithy a summation of analytic philosophy as can be found anywhere, and which suggests to me what a good sport and playful wit Glock intentionally brings to the table: "Asked at a party, what he actually did, an analytic philosopher replied: 'You clarify a few concepts. You make a few distinctions. It's a living.'"[5] Mulligan, Simons, and Smith essentially say the same thing when they write: "A[nalytic] P[hilosophy] is at its core a culture driven by puzzles, rather than by large-scale, systematic theoretical goals. Russell recommended stocking up on puzzles from as early as 1905."[6] While they are right about the "puzzle" component, the claim about "systematic theoretical goals" is misleading. For while this may be how it works out in practice, many analytic philosophers see the puzzle approach as theoretically contributing to a larger, and more accurate picture of the world. Thus, for example, Bernard Williams in his *Ethics and the Limits of Philosophy*, saw his own work as coming out of the analytic tradition, although the book makes the case for the need to recognize the limits of "abstract ethical theory," while acknowledging importance of social and historical knowledge. For him:

> What distinguishes analytical philosophy from other contemporary philosophy (though not from much philosophy of other times) is a certain way of going on, which involves argument, distinctions, and, so far as it remembers to try to achieve it and succeeds, moderately plain speech. As an alternative to plain speech, it distinguishes sharply between obscurity and technicality. It always rejects the first, but the second it sometimes finds a necessity.[7]

Unlike many analytic philosophers, Williams is well versed in, and takes seriously the history of philosophy, which he draws upon to make "big picture" arguments about life. It is analytic philosophers like Williams who lend support to James Conant's very similar observation that:

> What it is to be an analytic philosopher has more to do with a certain conception of how one ought to do philosophy than it does with *what* one ought to conclude on the basis of so doing it—with *the character of the activity of philosophizing* rather than with *the body of doctrine* in which it issues.[8]

Like every tradition, analytic philosophy has evolved and mutated. And in what follows I will discuss some of the important mutations that occurred in earlier phases of its development. There is a strong case that the desire for a certain kind of clarity that is best rendered by breaking philosophy down into arguments, consisting of puzzles and problems, is important to the root of the movement. And it is this feature, however varied in its exemplars, that makes it identifiable. Moreover, although, problems and puzzles regularly occur in pre-analytic philosophy, it is the weight and significance that the puzzle/problem solving aspect tends to have, and hence the accompanying weight that is ascribed to the mental/logical and semantic tools and techniques for solving those puzzles that is a distinctive feature of analytical philosophy. Further, a major way to make reality and the problems we wish to solve more clear is to cast them in more elementary, i.e., propositional forms, which are then treated as logical problems. Thus much of analytic philosophy, especially in its initial phases, was devoted to the less messy "language" of symbolic logic and set theory. The importance of this logically "analytic" approach to propositions is evident in Frege's remark that "I do not begin with concepts out of which the thought or judgment is composed, but I get to the parts of the thought through its analysis."[9] And, once more from Frege, "Only in propositions have the words really a meaning. It is enough if the proposition has a sense; it is this that confers on its parts their content."[10] Along similar lines, G. E. Moore claims in his classic essay of 1899 "The Nature of Judgment," that "A thing becomes intelligible first when it is analysed into its constituent concepts,"[11] while Russell says: "the chief thesis I have to maintain is the legitimacy of analysis."[12]

While there may be dispute about where the range of analysis should take place, the feature of analyticity, what Michael Beaney calls "decompositional analysis," is the common starting point that would, initially at least, be typical of the logical atomistic approach to the world that Wittgenstein would "perfect" in the *Tractatus*. This is not identical to, but stands in extremely close relationship to what Beaney sees as "the single most significant event in the development of analytic philosophy: the *transformative* or *explicatory* conception . . . the *rephrasing* of the sentence to be analysed, a sentence of the form 'the F is G,' where the 'F' represents the definite description, into a sentence of quite different form.'" [13] Thus Beaney considers Russell's classic example of analyzing the statement that the "the Present King of France is bald" by rendering it as "there is one and only one King of France, and whatever is King of France is bald." [14] For Beaney the key issue is that "the definite description is 'analysed away.'" [15]

This issue of rephrasing, or what Capaldi calls "subtraction," plays a key role in Capaldi's analysis of analytic philosophy, which is, in my opinion, still by far the most important sustained critique of analytic philosophy and its history and character to date. Capaldi rightly notes that "redefining" or reframing is a typical Enlightenment practice of "elimination"—which is an "explicit substitution of new ideas for old ideas" [16]—a practice that is required, and indeed apposite, for technical and mechanical problems. But if this practice is taken as tolerable for any kind of claim then "*there must be some independent criterion or set of norms in terms of which we can judge an elimination successful.*" [17] The practice is one that ultimately requires an appeal to a metaphysic that inevitably cannot be supplied unless one moves beyond any elimination which would leave any part unaccounted for. In the scientific revolution the new metaphysics was predicated around claims, which themselves became important to contesting the metaphysics being postulated, about what were secondary or epiphenomenal ideas. But, as we argued in detail above, as that paradigm becomes wrecked by the questions that emerge from Hume and Reid, this became unsustainable. [18]

As we can see the more we try to be precise about the analytical turn, the more occasion there is for disputation: a kind of confirmation of the process as well as the central problem with the process (something I will return to); for rather than getting to the end of something, arriving at the truth, analytical philosophy is a way of perpetually being on the way, a way that does not so much lead to the home of truth, but right back to the starting point, as each and every analytic philosopher lives to start again on another day. Analytical philosophy is simultaneously the kind of philosophy that assures us that there are definite signs of (technical) progress, as it is a denizen of an increasing array of puzzles that one can always come back to and investigate. It is a comforting journey—one sets out everyday with new worlds to conquer, but one always returns home comforted by the fact that the same old puzzles are still there.

From Russell through to the Vienna circle and beyond, analytical philosophy was frequently driven by a deep desire to make philosophy a science, while at the same time bringing philosophy to the point where it accepts that truth and science are of a piece. Thus Nicholas Capaldi cites Russell—"Whatever can be known can be known by means of science"; Sellars—"science is the measure of all things, of what is that it is, and of what is not that it is not"; and Dummett—"[Most American philosophers] are unanimous in regarding philosophy, with Quine, as at least cognate with the natural sciences, as part of the same general enterprise as they are." Capaldi continues that:

> If one looks at the early careers of prominent and influential analytic philosophers like Russell, Carnap, Schlick, Quine, even the early Wittgenstein, Kripke, and many others one sees an early aptitude, training, and even some accomplishments in the sciences, mathematics, and engineering. Analytic philosophers are often products of scientific training. In most cases, academic philosophy was not their first career choice. [19]

In its most fundamental assumptions or disputations analytic philosophy continually draws upon, or unwittingly repeats, or comes up against positions worked out by Plato, Aristotle, Descartes, and Hume. And there are certain common features of analytic philosophy which illustrate its own historical heritage: it is Platonic and Aristotelian in that it gathers examples into their respective classes for analysis and accepts the fundamental distinction between rational and irrational; Cartesian in the weight it gives to clarity and distinctness; Humean because it has to make do with thought experiments, though it generally regards them as if they were in some way equivalent to "real" laboratory experiments. It is also generally caught up in or defines itself against other metaphysical positions that are intrinsic to mechanism and the scientific revolution such as, and not to be exhaustive, dualism (Descartes), monism (Spinoza), panlogicism (Leibniz), empiricism (Locke and Hume), and phenomenalism (Berkeley).

Analytical philosophy is also a living and ever-changing body of practitioners, and hence it should be no surprise that its program has not remained constant. Peter Hacker in his "Analytic Philosophy: Beyond the Linguistic Turn and Back Again" has argued that the history of analytic philosophy consists of what can be broken up into five phases: 1 & 2) a commitment to realism and analysis (as opposed to idealist/Hegelian synthesis) culminating in the *Tractatus* and then continuing with the Cambridge School until repudiated by Wittgenstein; 3) the Vienna Circle's repudiation of metaphysics and restricting philosophy to "the logic of scientific truth"; 4) postwar Oxford analytic philosophy of Ryle, Austin, Hampshire, and Hart, with an emphasis upon investigating the meaning of words; anti-metaphysical; and contrary to the Vienna School is distinct science and hence not the job to improve the language of science; and what he hesitates to call a fifth phase—"the project of constructing a theory of meaning for a natural language . . . focussed largely on mind/body questions and converging on emergent cognitive science."[20] Although we will not be discussing all of these phases or the major representatives of these phases, this does provide a reasonable overview of the evolution of dominant trends within the practice.

LOGIC, LANGUAGE, AND METAPHYSICS

As much as a number of analytic philosophers may have liked to compare themselves with scientists, or have taken the practice of the sciences as central to their own inquiries, philosophical activity is based around the investigation of propositions and arguments, not experiments upon "things." Insofar, then, as analytical philosophy was looking for the kind of truth that was able to be presented as logical, yet also capable of being subject to standards of veracity that were not merely subjective, but capable of being built upon just as laws of natural science are developed, it was inevitable that language itself would become a central problem for it. Thus according to Michael Dummett, "analytic philosophy was born when the 'linguistic turn' was taken," and he sees Frege as the philosopher who decisively takes that turn.[21] Against this, though, Monk makes the point that Russell not only never thought that the philosophy of language was the foundation of all other philosophy,[22] but he despaired over its elevated philosophical role. Hence Russell's strongly supportive preface to Gellner's *Words and Things*, a polemic against ordinary language philosophy, which we discuss below.

This dispute about the role of language within analytic philosophy does indeed point to an unforeseen development that occurred when Wittgenstein went from being a philosopher who differed over fundamental aspects of logical atomism with Bertrand Russell (and his criticisms of Russell had left the latter deeply shaken about the merits of his own philosophy) to a philosopher who saw nothing salvageable in logical atomism, and hence much of the core of what seemed to be a philosophical program. Ironically, though, it was the deployment of the puzzle approach, which had worked so well for an atomistic approach to the fit between propositions about the world and mental states and logic, that had remained constant in Wittgenstein and that had been turned against what seemed to be central to the program. In pitting puzzling observations about language and the world which defied the logical atomistic approach Wittgenstein had become was the first heretic of a style of philosophy which ultimately demonstrated by its own development the impossibility of achieving anything remotely resembling the formation of a body of truth in the manner of the natural sciences.

The following claim from Frege, though, takes us back to what lends credence to Dummett's identification of "the linguistic turn" to a moment when the potential disjuncture of that turn has not become manifest, because the way language is being construed here is, as this and the citations immediately following it indicate, in such close association with logic.

> If it is a task of philosophy to break the domination of the word over the human spirit by uncovering deceptions about the relations of concepts which arise almost inevitably from common linguistic usage, and by freeing thought from that with which it is infected only by the means of linguistic expression, then my *Begriffsschrift* can become a useful tool for the philosopher, if it further developed for their purposes.[23]

And: "Work in logic is to a large extent a battle against the logical blemishes of language, though, language is, none the less, also an indispensable tool."[24] And: "the business of the logician is a continuous fight against the psychological, and, in part, against language and grammar."[25]

It is precisely this distinction between thought and language that we noted from the outset in Plato's critique of names that is being replicated here: thought, when it is logical, is greater than language. Language is a tool for thought. The tool-like nature of language, with language as a servant of thought, is one of the most persistent ones in the tradition.

In the case of what Dummett calls the "linguistic turn" it is important to distinguish between two ways of viewing language. One, which is common to Russell, Frege, and Dummett, sees language itself as a problem of the sort that requires moving beyond it into a higher kind of thinking, i.e., philosophy, that deploys logic to clean the "logical blemishes of language." The other view of language does not deny that language is an essential source of error. But it starts from the position that language is not primarily a means for denoting meaning which the mind, unencumbered by language, then could clear up by resorting to some more fundamental feature of existence, that "sense data" and "logic" can simply rectify. Rather it concedes that we still have to resort to language, however, we think. The emphasis then is upon the (unavoidable) *use* of language. Analytic philosophy reached a crossroad when the first view was challenged, "analytically," by Wittgenstein in the *Philosophical Investigations*.

As with Frege, Russell was looking for a more sophisticated, i.e., "technical vocabulary," that can get closer to the real nature of things and help free us from the griminess of words.[26] This need for a "technical vocabulary" would be bound up with the logical atomistic approach that Russell would adopt. In his 1906–1907, "The Monistic Theory of Truth,"

Russell had "pitched" the problem of truth in such a way that he saw there were two fundamental alternatives: the (wrong) one privileged "an organic unity or significant whole" over the parts. This he identified as "monistic idealism." The other (Russell's position), commenced with the truth of the parts. Monistic idealism, for Russell is then taken to mean that:

> the truth about any part of the whole must be the same as the whole truth; thus the complete truth about any part is the same as the complete truth about any other part, since each is the whole of truth.[27]

While Russell directs his arguments specifically at F. H. Bradley and Harold Joachim, as a critique of Hegelian idealism (which, is the real figure in his sights), this is simply not what Hegel is arguing.[28] Likewise, when Russell argues that the central flaw of "monistic idealism" is due to what he calls "the axiom of internal relations" ruling out "the possibility of partial truth . . . because we do not know the "whole,"[29] he is missing the point of Hegel that while each part only makes sense in a greater totality of conceptual relations, it is not the case that we cannot make claims about the parts. Rather, for Hegel, the claims do not subsist in complete isolation, so that they are absolutely finite, and thus the entities that Russell takes as in-themselves, and are pitted against each other, for example, mind and matter, yet insofar as they have a content we cannot help but notice that we are deferring to some identity in their difference. Oddly enough Russell himself was disturbed by this dualism enough to come up with his own metaphysics of "neutral monism."[30] Yet, in spite of his metaphysics, Russell insists upon the primacy of the parts, and hence a view of truth which appeals to sense data as providing confirmation of a plurality of distinct entities that form atomic facts, which we can then bring to bear against larger mistaken claims. In this respect Russell is a "Humean."

Irrespective of whether Russell's critique of Hegel is adequate, Russell saw that "the influence of language on philosophy has . . . been profound and almost unrecognized,"[31] and that what is needed—and what he supplies—is "an ideal logical language (which would of course be wholly useless for daily life)," the purpose of which is twofold:

> first, to prevent inferences from the nature of language to the nature of the world, which are fallacious because they depend upon the logical defects of language; secondly, to suggest, by inquiring what logic requires of a language which is to avoid contradiction, what sort of a structure we may reasonably suppose the world to have.[32]

Insofar, though, as philosophy is not simply devoted to logic in itself, i.e., insofar as it addresses our concerns in and about the world, Russell asks the question: "What are we to take as data in philosophy?" And answers:

science has a much greater likelihood of being true in the main than
any philosophy hitherto advanced (I do not, of course, except my own).
In science there are many matters about which people are agreed; in
philosophy there are none. Therefore, although each proposition in a
science may be false, and it is practically certain that there are some
that are false, yet we shall be wise to build our philosophy upon science, because the risk of error in philosophy is pretty sure to be greater
than in science.[33]

It would, then, be a mistake, as Monk rightly argues, to claim that, for
Russell, the primary concern was with language; any concern Russell had
with language was due with it being an impediment to thought, and as
he became disillusioned with logic and mathematics as the key to truth
(and mathematics consisting of "tautologies"),[34] his emphasis shifted to
"psychology" and "cognitive relations." As Monk says, "Logic had been
shown to be essentially symbolic, and therefore fairly trivial: what remained was to theorize –psychologistically—about symbolism."[35] That
is, what was constant about Russell was also what had been constant to
much of the British empiricist tradition: that thought was greater than
language.

But let us ask: What world we would be actually thinking about if
neither the world itself we were thinking about, nor the thinking we were
doing about the world were not language-saturated? We might notice a
feature of something by looking at it, we might smell something, hear
something, etc.—which is Russell's starting point. But once we start as-
cribing meaning to it, our process of ascription taps into a plethora of
ascriptions, which are in social circulation, and hence also developmental, insofar as language users also keep on making the language in their
encounters with each other. Language is not a substitute for sensuous
experience, except at the imaginative level, but language saturates the
choices we make concerning the meanings we ascribe to our sensations,
though meanings are not settled and hence not stable enough to provide
a kind of new "site of objectivity," a point that Wittgenstein emphasises
in the *Philosophical Investigations*. Just as our disposition and encountering
are so bound up with the why and what of our doings, language and (our
role in the) world cannot be pitted against each other as mutually exclusive except in a stark and threadbare manner to make a point about the
there-ness and that-ness of the mute world. The exception to this is precisely where Russell, Locke, etc. start from—in sensory experiences. But
the idea that if we just gather up all these experiences we would have
something that roughly corresponds to our picture of the world is the
kind of thinking that Wittgenstein broke with when he recognized that
language does not operate as if the world was a "thing" about which we
merely have a picture—though the point had already been made by Hamann, Herder, and even Hegel, who, to be sure, recognizes language as
important in world shaping, but requires its cooperation with reason as

the Absolute. Furthermore, all our semantic choices, specifications, explications feed into a greater process of concatenation of circulatory meanings that are in transformation along with us that are significant to us, and part of a way or "form of life," as Wittgenstein would call it in the *Philosophical Investigations*. Thus it is that while, for example, we see a building as simply "there," it is easy to assume that therefore language is not necessary to the building: which of course simply means we are not thinking about the way in which planning, engineering, schooling, economic organization and all the other conditions of the "building" are implicated in communication, i.e., in language. In other words, the dualism between our world and our language seems the most natural and obvious of dualisms, but it is only sustainable for the most elemental of considerations: the more we want to think about something of the world the more we need to draw upon and add to the ever growing and transforming "stock" of named knowing that can help attenuate our concern.[36] Invariably our very placements in the world implicate us in a praxeological dimension to any problem. What language is is only *revealed* in its use, not what is grasped by standing outside of it to observe it, and once it becomes a thing like any other thing, it is truncated and deformed. Whether this truncation is done through the imposition of a formal language as Frege, early Russell, young Wittgenstein, Tarski et al. attempted, or done psychologistically, is beside the point.

In sum, the difference between these two different ways of viewing language, then, is indicative of what would not only come to divide Russell and Wittgenstein's view of philosophy, but the analytic tradition itself. Nevertheless, insofar as the *Philosophical Investigations* was a collection of puzzles, it was still in the analytical vein, even if, Wittgenstein, as Monk rightly observes, and as he puts it, subjects the idea of a whole being broken down and re-assembled by its component parts, "to a withering piece of scorn."[37] Nevertheless, the importance that Wittgenstein attributed to "language games" and "forms of life" in the exploration of meaning had steered his philosophy into a more philosophical anthropological direction. Now whether the prophet and/or poet, who stand in a close relationship to each other insofar as they are deeply attentive to the great sensorium of a culture and its language and its hopes and fears, like seismographs attuned to the subterranean tremors, or the philosopher, reflecting upon us and our circumstance, is better equipped to fathom the most pressing issues of the day and best responses, is itself a philosophical question. But because the philosopher is better positioned to "ask" the question does not mean that the answer favors philosophy. Be that as it may, this does not diminish the value of the question.

In the *Philosophical Investigations*, Wittgenstein had famously answered that question "What is your aim in philosophy?," with "to shew the fly the way out of the fly-bottle."[38] Wittgenstein's "fly bottle" was the equivalent of muddles that have been made of the philosophical mind's own making, largely resulting from a failure to appreciate what the central insight upon which the *Investigations* is built (and the logical atomistic foundations of the *Tractatus* destroyed): "the speaking of language is part of an activity, or of a form of life."[39] Thus, for Wittgenstein, "philosophical problems arise when language goes on holiday."[40] Likewise, because "A philosophical problem has the form: 'I don't know my way about,'"[41] the task of philosophy is therapeutic, i.e., its purpose is to help one know one's way about, or get out of the fly bottle. Thus, as in propositions 126 and 127:

> 126. Philosophy simply puts everything before us, and neither explains nor deduces anything.—Since everything lies open to view there is nothing to explain. For what is hidden, for example, is of no interest to us. One might also give the name "philosophy" to what is possible before all new discoveries and inventions.[42]
>
> 127. The work of the philosopher consists in assembling reminders for a particular purpose.[43]

Whereas Descartes, Spinoza, Locke, etc. were wanting to replace one "form of life" with another by transforming not only the world, but also the words that had emerged due to a lack of correct understanding, Wittgenstein, focuses upon "forms of life" as containing their own rules, assumptions, inductions, and (Gellner's problem) value for the participants (which is not to say that the form of life does not have its own victors and vanquished). How one responds to a situation or a game is not, as such, philosophically dependent, as if philosophy holds the magic key to assessing value. That is another issue, but what interests Wittgenstein is the philosophical identification of the "going on." The following three sets of propositions provide both a good summing up of what Wittgenstein is doing with philosophy, as well as an outline of the new philosophical program more generally.

> 130. Our clear and simple language-games are not preparatory studies for a future regularization of language–as it were first approximations, ignoring friction and air-resistance. The language-games are rather set up as objects of comparison which are meant to throw light on the facts of our language by way not only of similarities, but also of dissimilarities.[44]
>
> 131. For we can avoid ineptness or emptiness in our assertions only by presenting the model as what it is, as an object of comparison–as, so to speak, a measuring-rod; not as a preconceived idea to which reality must correspond. (The dogmatism into which we fall so easily in doing philosophy.)[45]
>
> 133. It is not our aim to refine or complete the system of rules for the use of our words in unheard-of ways. For the clarity that we are aiming at is indeed complete clarity. But this simply means that the philosophical problems should completely disappear. The real discovery is the one that makes me capable of stopping doing philosophy when I want

to. –The one that gives philosophy peace, so that it is no longer tormented by questions which bring itself in question.–Instead, we now demonstrate a method, by examples; and the series of examples can be broken off.–Problems are solved (difficulties eliminated), not a single problem. There is not a philosophical method, though there are indeed methods, like different therapies.[46]

Against what Wittgenstein calls (in proposition 593) philosophy's "one-sided diet: one nourishes one's thinking with only one kind of example,"[47] Wittgenstein does indeed want philosophy to follow through on clarity, but ultimately the philosopher is no longer the seer or director of worldmaking, but the puzzled observer sharing the experience of puzzlement, and finding ways to break the spells of a certain kind of language game. In other words, so much of philosophical puzzlement is due to philosophers being bewitched by language in ways that perhaps the majority of language practitioners—i.e., the rest of us—aren't. "Yes," says Wittgenstein elsewhere, "philosophical problems emerge when we hand the reins to language instead of *life*").[48] All of this is pertinent to Capaldi's claim that Wittgenstein was "the major anti-analytic philosopher in the twentieth century,"[49] a statement which is true, if, as Capaldi argues, the analytical philosophical method is all of a piece with its own contribution to the Enlightenment program. And we should also highlight here that Wittgenstein's late philosophy inaugurates (as spelled out in #131) a definite break with what I have been calling idea-ism, and which Wittgenstein notes is the "dogmatism into which we fall so easily in doing philosophy," viz. deferring to "a preconceived idea to which reality must correspond." Yet, it was the case that Wittgenstein himself was indisputably analytic in his approach, as were the Wittgensteinian practitioners of ordinary language philosophy.

Most of Wittgenstein's followers tended to repeat or reapply what he was doing in a purely philosophical way, rather than go through the door leading beyond philosophy pure that he had opened. Thus, generally, ordinary language philosophy that was influenced by Wittgenstein was mostly an exercise in diminishing the returns of Wittgenstein's insights into the role and relation of language within and to a "form of life." One of the people who picked up on the philosophical anthropological side of Wittgenstein and took it further was Peter Winch in his *The Idea of a Social Science and Its Relation to Philosophy*. He followed Wittgenstein in seeing the ideas of language games and forms of life as having important implications for our understanding of human activity, hence the social sciences—and not merely treating it under the wrong "language game." He further realized that philosophy is a peculiar and particular "language game," which not only nudges against other language games involved in generalising and making claims about human practices, i.e., other reflective language games, it draws upon them and feeds into them. They share a certain reflexivity, which is not to say that certain questions inevitably take place on relatively distinct horizons and regions for their answers. That is, so much that *happens* within the social sciences comes from the questions being posed, hence they are problems within philosophy, and not resolvable simply by looking at empirical data—they are, as he put it, first and foremost conceptual problems: "It is not a question of what empirical research may show to be the case, but of what philosophical analysis reveals about *what it makes sense to say*."[50] And what it makes sense to say cannot be the exclusive prerogative of natural science, because were it so, we would inhabit a denuded world that bears no relationship to this one, apart from our obedience to physical, chemical, and biological laws. Even the technological objects of science would disappear were it not for the desire and want (covering a range of social actions from commerce to industry to advertising to distribution to the personal proclivities) of the object, which given the social and cultural impact upon desire and the kinds of objects people want, is hardly "natural." In this respect, Winch was not only developing Wittgenstein's thought, but by addressing the question of the social sciences, he had inadvertently entered into territory and disputations about the foundations and nature of the non-natural sciences that had embroiled the early generation of Wilhelm Windelband, Heinrich Rickert, and Wilhelm Dilthey. While they agreed that there existed such a realm, they could not concur on the name for what Dilthey had termed "sciences of the spirit" (*Geisteswissenschaften*),[51] Windelband "the historical sciences" (*Geschichtswissenschaften*), and Rickert "the cultural sciences" (*Kulturwissenschaften*). While, then, their disagreements were strident, particularly the disputation over whether, as Windelband claimed, the difference could be described as one between the nomothetic science dealing with general laws or idiographic sciences focused on individual acts.[52] Ultimately, and seen in retrospect, their disagreements amounted to very little in comparison to their agreements about the need to find a foundation that accounts for the kind of knowledge which we have about human supra-naturalistic happenings.[53] What they had recognized and what Winch has in common with them is the recognition that social appeals, claims, and truths cannot adequately be accounted for by a logic that looks at causality to the exclusion of meaning. But it was precisely this disjuncture that Gellner saw as the dangerous legacy of Wittgenstein in Winch (he also goes after Alasdair MacIntyre, whom he believes is guilty of the same fallacy) in his *Cause and Meaning*. Winch will clarify in his book *Ethics and Action*, where he differs from the arguments MacIntyre was raising at that time.

Gellner argued that a philosophy of social life which emphasizes meaning and the life world over more straightforward causal and rational relations inevitably opens the gates to the various spectres of cultural relativism. According to Gellner, arguments about understanding the world from the inside leaves no room for evaluation so that the sick, broken or deluded world or form of life becomes rationalized in the very depiction. That is, the emphasis upon connection between "socially available descriptions and conduct" raises the problem that either "we live in a realm of Meaning, into which no blind and extraneous necessity intrudes," or "if only some connexions are of the internal kind, then we can hardly tell *a priori* which ones and the methodological recommendations no longer follow." [54] The core concern of Gellner's (which is a reasonable concern) is that there is a danger that the emphasis upon meaning may lead a philosopher to romanticize a world and the roles within it that do not deserve to continue. As he says, the whole point of principles of selection is that they "must sit in judgment on the various practices." [55] That this position of Gellner is not intended to be as eschatological as, say, the idea-ism of Marx and Nietzsche, does not make it any less an instance of philosophical idea-ism, and a disposition which is prepared to say who must be sacrificed for a better world. Though, he puts the case, less brutally, Gellner makes the important point that merely appealing to how we live within a social or cultural milieu relativizes knowledge, which, in turn, leads to inadvertently protecting the toxic, the mad, and the bad, and thereby is an act that contributes to greater suffering. Gellner also uses the example of how relativizing the value of witchcraft which occurs in certain tribes hinders the culture from coming to grips with the fact that there is a science of medicine and real doctors far more skilled and knowledgeable in dealing with health issues. [56]

The Gellner-Winch debate tacitly taps into a tragic truth about culture, viz. modernizing and not modernizing are both destructive acts. For his part, though, what Gellner fails to address (a point which is crucial to Winch's approach) is that roles, beliefs, and "life-world" form a totality, so the problem is not simply, or even primarily open to a philosophical investigation of one "thing," but part of a network of value-practices involving social stakes and status. In other words, a practice such as witchcraft is not simply or even primarily a moral matter, but it is also a social and political one that raises all manner of questions about what would happen (and the scale of havoc and conflict that would be unleashed) were some more philosophically enlightened leader attempting to act on the judgment that has been formed out of a reasoning process in which all manner of other contingencies and social norms are ignored or invoked. To repeat, focussing upon moral reasoning and principles, as if they could be separated from the reasons of groups enmeshed in their everyday lives, may do far more damage than good. Of course, if one commits to a line of moral reasoning that eschews any kind of consequences then one may well be consistent in how one thinks about morality, but not very helpful in contributing to any kind of better world.

I should also add, contra Gellner, that Winch is not saying that one cannot raise criticisms about ways of behavior from another world, [57] but the criticism itself invariably involves a praxeological dimension that needs to be taken into account if any communication between people from different "forms of life" are to meaningfully interact and cooperate, even critically.

Insofar, though, as the investigation of ordinary language statements become a philosophical end in itself, and insofar as the practice does not push the practitioner further into the study of the anthropological dimensions of language and into considerations of what ends a people are pursuing and to what effect, Gellner's attack upon the philosophical focus upon language has a point. The weakness of the sort highlighted by Gellner is conspicuous in the response by Dummett cited (approvingly) by T. P. Uschanov's devastating critique of *Words and Things*, which is a spirited defense of the best of ordinary language philosophy:

> What *is* indeed common to almost all the philosophers Gellner attacks . . . is the view that philosophical problems mostly arise from misunderstandings of certain concepts, and are to be resolved by giving a correct account of those concepts. Gellner complains that this excludes the possibility of a philosopher's enunciating any substantive truths. I think that most Oxford philosophers would not be dogmatic on this point (thereby eliciting Gellner's accusations of evasiveness). They would not reject the possibility that philosophy could arrive at substantive truths: they would merely say that they do not see how this is to be done, and add that, while much past philosophy makes clear sense, understood as elucidation of concepts, they have not found a single convincing example of a philosophical demonstration of a substantive truth.[58]

Ordinary language philosophy, though, was only ever one phase of analytic philosophy, but it was indicative of a substantive overturning of the earlier aspiration to make philosophy a science. Equally as radical in terms of directional change was the matter of the relationship between whole and parts. As we saw earlier, Russell had been emphatic about the primacy of the part and his opposition to the idealism that deferred to the primacy of the whole. Russell had not put the issue in terms that were congruent with Kant's discussion of the whole, yet Kant's relevance strikes me as pertinent. The gathering of knowledge that emphasizes moving from part to whole, is only possible insofar as the unknown (and unknowable at least apart from the parts) whole still serves as a heuristic. Not surprisingly, the problem about whether the whole is seen as so necessary for our making sense of the parts that it must in some sense be true or real would again become a problem, and would spawn the holism of Quine, Kripke, and Davidson. For each requires our appreciation of any truth being dependent upon a prior whole or All, which cannot really be the case if we are simply invoking a heuristic.

This act of exploration culminating in an appeal to substantiation is rightly picked up by Capaldi as the reason why "analytic metaphysics is often and inevitably in its pursuit of coherence and comprehensiveness driven in the direction of Hegelianism."[59] Capaldi is well aware of the irony in this development, given how Hegelianism was originally the position against which the new program had defined itself. But, the fact that what transpired and what Russell and the pioneers of the analytical tradition desired for the philosophy only serves to show, as Capaldi puts it: "What emerges in the metaphysics of analytic philosophy is a constant and unresolved tension between what it wishes to say and what its pursuit of coherence forces it to say."[60]

One metaphysician in the analytic tradition, whose importance has been frequently acknowledged, is Aristotle.[61] As we have said on a number of occasions, the anti-Aristotelianism of most of the metaphysicians of the new science derived from the distortions they saw entering into our understanding of nature if we made nature just like us—as opposed to seeing us as just like nature. One of the central features of Aristotelianism is its fundamental refusal to follow Plato's dualist structure of world and intelligibility, and its foundational determination to see a continuity of process between the world and its intelligibility—neatly expressed by Capaldi thus: "we understand both ourselves and the world in the same way. Hence, Aristotelianism is monistic."[62] Hence also it is not surprising that the analytic philosophical founders, who were not physicists—though physicists and technicians would quickly join their ranks—but logicians would not follow Descartes et al. in their hostility to logic.

Like Aristotle and Leibniz (the only philosopher on whom Russell wrote an entire book), early on Russell believed in the intelligibility of the universe because of our own intelligibility (thus for Russell the key to Leibniz's metaphysics comes down to a small number of logical principles), the most important of which is: the world is reasonable, even if we don't understand all its reasons (and even if we human beings are rarely reasonable in our decisions and actions). Thus "the plan" is to find the rational structure of intelligibility so that the world can be brought within its fold—which it already is, but we just don't see it. Russell's job is to show us that is the case and how.

That Aristotle and Leibniz require a divine mind to lend sense to the metaphysics does not worry Russell, but it does point to the fact that while the philosophers' God was not "made" for religion, it is far from obvious why any metaphysics can provide a compelling argument that rules out intelligence as immanent in nature, and intelligible immanence as unintentional. We can concede that the universe evolves out of chance, nevertheless chance conforms to nature's law. But what is law but a sign of intelligible order? The decisive issue is not which laws, but that there are laws. I made it clear enough earlier in this book, I do not think the philosopher's God offers much to those seeking religious or existential solace, but it does seem that if one makes of the universe an intelligible process then one ends up with some kind of absolutization of the intellect that runs through the entire cosmos. Had Kant pulled off his explanation that would have indeed put an end to metaphysics of the traditional or "pre-critical" sought which is rearing its head here. But he could not do it.

Russell's breezy indifference to intelligible order—his philosophical atheism—might be typical of the analytic tradition, not to mention the lack of existential anxiety (something that is replicated in the entire demeanour of analytic philosophy). But Dummett, Elizabeth Anscombe, and Peter Geach are generally highly esteemed analytic philosophers who all thought their Catholicism eminently reasonable; while Anthony Flew had a belated deist conversion, seeing God as an intelligent designer. But now we are back with the seeming tension between reason and experience—which is why it is easy to imagine Hegel sitting arms folded with a great big smirk because his philosophy definitely solves this tension. He is being watched by Schelling, who is not impressed with such a "conceptual" victory and who wants us all to "metaphysically" dive further into the act of revealed creation.

Philosophical work is itself part of the world, and not only its continuity but its "direction" is the issue; intelligence is not confined to philosophy: philosophy needs to catch up to it, not lead it. Late Wittgenstein grasped this, and it is why respect for forms of life cannot simply be compartmentalized into the Humean Enlightened divide between the reasonable and the superstitious or merely crazy, i.e., irrational (i.e., other people—especially continentals, post-moderns and the like, who don't share the conviction about this philosophical way of doing things). That the world is also we who are making it spoils the picture that philosophy is breaking up the world into what is rationally explicable only for there to be these irrational creatures—who most analytic philosophers, if writing on the topic, are convinced are determined because we are pieces of nature and nature obeys causal laws.

This central paradox of so much analytical philosophy will not go away: we do philosophy in order to have a rational grasp of things because the nature of things is essentially rational, yet the world is out of kilter because we are not rational in how we treat things, so the things of the world—i.e., most people except analytical philosophers (and even then not all philosophers can be trusted—there are theists and other crazies getting into the analytic game) are irrational and need to brought into the fold of reason via *their* rational arguments. Although the analytic program continues, what it has yielded is not anything resembling its initial faith in combining science, logic and argument. It has proven that it is compatible with all manner of positions and preferences, and even where certain dispositions may still predominate, such as "naturalism," there is nothing about analytical philosophy that is naturalist in and of itself, and indeed some of the most highly regarded analytical philosophical work in some fields such as ethics is decidedly non-naturalistic. Yet if, we focus, as Richard Rorty does in *Philosophy and the Mirror of Nature*, on the epistemological primacy of so much of analytic philosophy and the kinds of conceptual assemblages (beginning with such elementary ostensibly "neutral" designators as "subject" and "object") and ontological elements and quandaries which drive it, then it is difficult to dispute the following claim:

> to think that to understand how to know better is to understand how to improve the activity of a quasi-visual faculty, the Mirror of Nature, and thus to think of knowledge as an assemblage of accurate representations. Then comes the idea that the way to have accurate representations is to find, within the Mirror, a special privileged class of representations so compelling that their accuracy cannot be doubted. These privileged foundations will be the foundations of knowledge, and the discipline which directs us toward them-the theory of knowledge-will be the foundation of culture. The theory of knowledge will be the search for that which compels the mind to belief as soon as it is unveiled. Philosophy as epistemology will be the search for the immutable structures within which knowledge, life, and culture must be contained-structures set by the privileged representations which it studies.[63]

But the desire analytic philosophers have for what Rorty calls "privileged representations" does not change the fact that analytic philosophy has created a philosophical environment in which the projects and the truths yielded by the projects become increasingly splintered, as philosophers identify themselves by virtue of holding a certain position that they argue for and publish on, but which they generally remain committed to in relative isolation. The method, in so far as it is a method, is a method that generates disagreement rather than agreement. And the relativism that is typically seen by analytical philosophy as the post-modern disease is far more evident in analytical philosophy, than the much more commonly shared post-modernist "absolutist" political commitment to expose "domination."

We started this chapter by noting that analytic philosophers had returned to a greater demand upon rationality than the post-Hegelians. In keeping with this, with some exceptions coming from Wittgenstein inspired quarters, analytical philosophers (though this is equally true for the "continentals" and anti-domination philosophers) generally do not link their "philosophical problems" to the institutional factors in their own practice—if relevant at all, that would be the job of some other "discipline." Yet the prestige of one's "school," one's journals of publications, one's citations and so forth are far more decisive in the "selection" of which philosophical ideas circulate and receive attention than the "truth" of an argument. In other words, analytic philosophy can readily be read in light of Nietzsche's idea of "will to power." But the idea of the "will to power" wreaks of the kind of speculative metaphysics that is generally outside of the more usual "tools" of analytic philosophers who work in such areas as philosophy of mind, theory of knowledge, ethics, etc., where each field is constituted by its own network of arguments, positions, consensuses, etc. This is not to say that this is something unique about analytical philosophy, only that it illustrates why the various forces of compartmentalization, specialization, and professionalization contribute to making the hope of analytical philosophy anything other than one more attempt, with no special privilege, to understand what is going on. A more generous way to put this is that analytical philosophers, like all of us, are very attentive to some things but not others, which is because, to put it again in Schopenhauerian and Nietzschean terms, they, like all of us, want something/the world and the way it is made and not others, and hence they focus upon and represent what (they *believe*) suits that activity.

Not surprisingly, the philosophical revolution of analytical philosophy does not spill much, if at all, outside the profession (although it may have application, as in artificial intelligence and cognitive science and such like). This is in in stark contrast to the analytic *bête noir* continental philosophy, more precisely the more overtly socially based post-Hegelian (Marxian-Nietzschean-Heideggerean) philosophies of the '68 generation. Although analytic philosophy sees itself as the heir of all that is good and true, scientific, enlightened and rational, while the "Continental" tradition, if any sense at all can be gleaned from its monstrosities, is viewed as relativistic nonsense, both are deeply dogmatic and are symptomatic of the last gasps of what deserves to die philosophically. Both also are unimaginable without the Enlightenment: though they tend to draw upon different seams of that event. Or to say it another way, if taken as whole movements or entire paradigms, both blind and fragment, distract and destroy — which is not to say that their adherents never have any valuable insights, but those insights exist because a human being, especially a very clever one is often far more capable than the narrative paradigm, the idea-ism that they are invested in.

THE ANALYTIC—CONTINENTAL DIVIDE: RESPONSES TO DIFFERENT WORLDS

In his excellent paper "Whose Fault? The Origins and Evitability of the Analytic Continental Rift," Peter Simons, asks the important question *why* did the philosophical landscape divide into the analytic and continental.[64] As he observes: "If we examine the philosophical landscape of 1899, we see a vastly different picture from today."[65] He rightly points out that philosophy was a far broader church then, and the numerous differences between Russell, William James, Brentano, Meinong, Husserl, and a host of others were not seen as indicative of a division so vast that philosophical communication between camps was simply not possible.[66]

While I weigh some of the details differently than Simons, I share his conjecture that the Great War and the respective responses to it do help us identify why Britain, France, and Germany would spawn three disparate philosophical responses. Great convulsions are invariably *faith shaping events*. And there is a serious case to consider that the entire history of philosophy may be fruitfully read, as Rosenstock-Huessy had observed in his *Das Gehemnis der Universität* (The Secret of the University), as responses to great social convulsions—especially wars and revolutions.

Thus it was that while the rudiments of analytic philosophy were not exclusively formed in Great Britain—as Simons and others rightly point out (Simons' masterly *Philosophy and Logic in Central Europe* is also pertinent), the history of analytical philosophy includes various Europeans outliers such as Bolzano, Brentano, and Lotze. The difference, say, between early Frege and Russell, on the one hand, and Husserl, on the other, does not really suggest a dividing of philosophical seas. The division comes from a convulsive event, the response to which intensifies the importance of philosophical choices and commitments. In considering the history of philosophy, it is important to distinguish between philosophical work which was indeed important to the philosophers pursuing that work, and the flash or tipping point when what was curiosity and intellectual endeavor transforms into the foundational platform for what will become a philosophical paradigm. Foundations are only ever consolidated retrospectively, because no founder can be sure that the foundation is sturdy enough to support an institution; likewise no founder knows what the institution will look like when the great vision is realized—indeed most would not recognize themselves or even their aspirations in what follows. This, of course, is Dostoevsky's point in "the Grand Inquisitor," and why academic Marxists at least completely sever the nexus between Marx and Stalin. Ultimately a founder is only a founder because he or she is recognized as such, because someone else (Plato to Socrates, Paul to Jesus, Lenin to Marx) who are part of a broader circle passionately respond and are so transformed by the labors of the founder that their energistic devotion, proselytizing, and replication of what they see as the teachings of the founders now begin to incarnate. What holds true for major movements also is relevant for moderate institutional changes such as occur with philosophy making an analytic turn. Now in this case, it is a turn along a way and not the founding of a way such as we find in Socrates, where martyrdom, as he himself warns his judges and enemies in the *Apology*, is the deed that displays the sacrificial truth and ultimate meaning of philosophy that initially propeled men into the philosophical life. (Plato's *Phaedo* [64a] also makes the point that philosophy is "preparation for death.") In the case of the Great War, it was not a philosopher's death but mass death that was ubiquitous: mass death in the name of the nation and the empire, mass death that seemed meaningless and the result of terribly bad ideas, terrible choices of faith.

Thus while the founders of the analytic movement included Germans and Austrians, the locus of its consolidation, the formation into a "school" of what could be identified as analytical philosophy was Cambridge (and later Oxford). Viewed from the comforts and old world stability and good sense of Cambridge, the gore and carnage, the sheer wastage of all those young lives on battlefields in far-away lands that simply made no sense confirmed the lunacy and madness of irrationality. The rooms and halls, and playing fields of Cambridge by contrast provided the picture of what a world of reason could be. As with all convulsions, the response very much depends upon where one is in the fallout, and what one has brought into one's situation. The war—with its daily telegrams of lost loved ones, and deformed, limbless, wounded soldiers returning home—invoked the tremendous sense of urgency that was needed to erect the bulwarks against such irrationalism. The task at hand only confirmed the basic faith in logic and science of those whose work preceded the war. Moreover, as Russell, C. E. M. Joad, and subsequently Ryle and émigrés like Popper, and Isaiah Berlin would argue German philosophers (Fichte, Hegel, and Nietzsche) all contributed to a statist irrationalism that was behind not only the First World War but the Second. Moreover, that Germany would breed Nazism out of the furnace of its defeat in the Great War only confirmed for Joad and Russell the original diagnosis of the immanent horrors that lay pulsating in the heart of German irrationalism. England and reason and common sense lined up as symmetrically as Germany, statism, national fanaticism, and cruelty.[67] Thus Russell would write to Ryle in 1965, "No one ever had Common Sense before John Locke—and no-one but Englishmen have ever had it since." And, "when I was young the British universities had been invaded by German idealism, but when the Germans invaded Belgium it was decided that German philosophy must be bad. And I came into my own, because I was against German philosophy anyhow."[68]

In contrast to the safety and calm provided by the armchairs and civilized discussions over port and sherry in the common rooms, the libraries, and hills and fields of Cambridge and Oxford, the French had the war on their soil. Being rained on by bombs and mown down by machine guns drove home the role of technology and machinery in their plight. The English derision of Descartes as a non-empirical "rationalist," repeated by the Anglophile Voltaire, was, as we have seen, a caricature; Descartes's metaphysics and theory of knowledge were an answer to a problem of method for gathering data. Above all, Descartes's philosophy was devoted to science and technical calculation, to improving life through understanding and tinkering with the great machine. And the machine had become the source of mass death. The radical wing of French intellectual life was indelibly stamped—and remains so—by its early historical Cartesian legacy and subsequent reaction. In France, World War I had spawned such desperately truthful mad ravings as exhibited by Artaud, and the search for pataphysics and surreal dream logics, as well the Sadean view of life advocated by figures such as Pierre Klossowski and Georges Bataille. They were all anti-fascist, and yet their sensibility was contiguous with fascism, others such as Tzara (French in sensibility, if not birth), Eluard and Aragon, in spite of their Dadaism/ Surrealism turned to Stalinism: the turn to one or the other was almost like a flip of the coin, as the examples of the fascists Drieu La Rochelle and Céline typified. As for Germany, let me quote Simons:

> In Germany the mood of post-war pessimism encapsulated by Spen- gler saw greatest disillusion with the scientific and technological ad- vances which were supposed to have brought victory. Neo-Kantian- ism, despite gaining a new and exceptional recruit, Ernst Cassirer . . . ceased to be the dominant form of philosophy in Germany. Husserl's cautious Cartesian foundationalism and intellectualism were out of temper with the times. His transcendentalism was shrugged off. Hus- serl had never been the only person practising "phenomenology," and the movement was a broad church. Its intellectual leader in the 1920s was Max Scheler, the heir apparent, until his early death in 1928. Schel- er emphasized feeling over intellect. Husserl's successor at Freiburg in that year was Heidegger. Probably no individual was more responsible for the schism in philosophy than Heidegger's *Sein und Zeit* (1927).[69]

To be sure, there were dozens of Austrian and German philosophical refugees, including members of the Vienna Circle and those wanting to bring the logic of science and philosophy into closer conjunction, such as Rudolf Carnap, Hans Reichenbach, Carl Hempel, Ernst Nagel, Herbert Feigl, and the neo-Kantian Ernst Cassirer, who saw a deep connection between the overwhelming wrath of the defeated and the dangerous direction in which the feelings of betrayal and injustice were going, and who were horrified by the irrationalist outpourings in their homelands. But, in the main, very different energies and forces swept up the victors of Britain, the rescued of France, and the defeated and (so they thought) betrayed of Germany. It would be Britain that would ultimately incorpo- rate and export the tone and program of philosophy to its colonies and the United States, which to be sure had had some remarkable philoso- phers in Peirce, James, and Royce and the extraordinarily popular Dewey, but the generation of fleeing émigrés brought with them their analytic concerns along with their faith in reason and science, as well as their respective pro- or anti-communist views.[70]

The pervasive attitude in analytic philosophy that led it, in the main, to ignore the post/anti-Kantian/Hegelian developments in Europe out- side the more logically driven philosophies exemplified by Bolzano, Lot- ze, and Frege was as decisive a statement about method as it was about the kinds of questions that seemed appropriate. From the other side of the channel, this most fundamental decision about the nature of philoso- phy was seen as the suffocation of philosophy. Thus Gilles Deleuze and

Felix Guattari (who for many analytical philosophers, are part bad joke and part nightmare):

> By confusing concepts with functions, logic acts as though science were already dealing with concepts or forming concepts of the first zone. But it must itself double and scientific with logical functions that are supposed to form a new class of purely logical, or second zone, concepts. A real hatred inspires logic's rivalry with, or its will to supplant, philosophy. It kills the concept twice over. However, the concept is reborn because it is not a scientific function and because it is not a logical proposition: it does not belong to a discursive system and it does not have a reference. The concept shows itself and does nothing but show itself. Concepts are really monsters that are reborn from their fragments.[71]

The logician's and analytical philosopher's desire for precision is rooted in a fundamental failure to grasp the way we make concepts, not through a simple process of correspondence or copying, or, for that matter, a careful alignment in which we test their application like an element in a lab. Rather they are part of the flux of being alive—indeterminacies and creations that emerge through our own unexpected and creative interactions.

> It is true that the concept is fuzzy or vague not because it lacks an outline but because it is vagabond, nondiscursive, moving about on a plane of immanence. It is intensional or modular not because it has conditions of reference but because it is made up of inseparable variations that pass through zones of indiscernibility and change its outline.[72]

Everything about these passages speaks to and of another, an alternative philosophical purpose and approach than that of the analytic tradition. Its emphasis upon the visionary role of the philosopher is Nietzschean. But for all its arresting insights concerning film and aesthetics, the paradigm of which it is part is, however, as we shall argue in a later chapter, as misleading and blinding in its way as that of the analytics.

Of the post-Nietzschean continentals the two, prior to the 68ers, that mattered most were Husserl and Heidegger. Had it not been for the impetus Husserl gave to Heidegger, Husserl may have even remained a member of the analytic canon: his "radical reconstruction which will satisfy the ideal of philosophy as being the universal unity of knowledge by means of a unitary and absolutely rational foundation," "*a universal science based upon absolute proof,*"[73] was no different in aspiration or rational faith from that of the founders of the analytic movement. Its consequences, however, have played out very differently.

Once a style or "habitus" becomes institutionally entrenched it is hard to change unless some other event shifts a generation. It becomes a paradigm because it has stakeholders protecting their "vision" of the world.

Unlike philosophy, literature in North American and English universities had no Russell and no set paradigm. There were grand theorists— Richards, Abrams, Frye, and Harold Bloom in North America, F. R. Leavis in Britain. But the discipline was disparate until the generation of the 1960s, another generation shattered by another war, brought their politics, their "philosophical" Marxism with them to the study of literature. Thus the aesthetic writings of Theodor Adorno, and Walter Benjamin, among others, would begin to be translated. This was still very much in embryo (Frederic Jameson's *Marxism and Form* did not appear until 1971) when the greatest seismic shift in the study of literature occurred in 1966—a conference took place at Johns Hopkins University on structuralism. Its organizers included René Girard (himself neither a structuralist nor post-structuralist, the latter which did not yet have that name), while its participants included Jacques Derrida, Roland Barthes, Jacques Lacan, Lucien Goldman, Jean Hyppolite, Georges Poulet, and Tsvetan Todorov. Whatever one thought of them philosophically, one thing was certain, this was not a group who could be accused of not being assured about the social and political role of literature and philosophy. Moreover, analytic philosophy, in the main, had also steered away from the existential and personal dimensions of philosophy which the generation raised in the 1950s and 1960s found in Sartre and Camus, both novelists and playwrights as well as philosophers, who were becoming somewhat passé to the new philosophical generation in France. In France, the shift from existentialism to structuralism was the great burning question at the time, but analytic philosophy was then as untouched by the personal as by the big moral (at this stage metaethics dominated moral philosophy), social and political questions (Rawls' *A Theory of Justice* would not appear until 1971). There was, in short, a great opportunity for those wanting to address the big philosophical questions—What to do? What to believe in? Although the impact upon public narrative by two generations brokering in ideas and influenced by social theory has impacted even upon members of philosophy departments, everyone who has taught in the humanities will have come across disappointed students who wanted to study the big questions of life's meaning only to discover that this is not what (most) analytic philosophy is about[74]—many shift over to literature, where they then quickly discover that their search for meaning is not to be found by reading Shakespeare, Milton, Blake, etc., who may not have any role at all to play in their reading program, but in the social and political readings of the books they are assigned to "critique." Very often the lack of satiation found by those hungry to explore what "it all means" in philosophy departments that are largely analytic, is catered for by the sharp and frequently morally enthusiastic politicized often (what to an undergraduate is a) dazzling social analysis of post-Marxist (continental) philosophers and literary (and film) theorists. The conflict of the faculties has basically led to a territorial divide in which continental philosophy has very much been a minority concern in most philosophy departments in the US, UK, and Australasia, while in literary departments where identity politics and "theory" loom large literary theory means how to subject a text to (depending upon the teacher's whim) the ideas of Benjamin, Deleuze, Foucault, Derrida, Kristeva, Lacan, Butler, Heidegger, Adorno, Levinas, Said, Bhabha, Žižek, Badiou, etc. This latter group has much greater social efficacy not only across the humanities than analytic philosophy, but in the cultivation of moral and political consensuses around rights and, social justice, and equality that take on administrative, legislative, and hence institutional efficacy. Although there is no shortage of analytic philosophy in ethics, the relative side-lining of analytic philosophy in comparison with literature courses drawing upon Marx, Nietzsche, Heidegger, post-structuralist philosophers et al. as has much to do with the technical nature of analytical philosophy. But in general, the so-called Continentals are read and taught under the broad ethico-political telos of anti-domination. These two different philosophical paradigms, one of which is mainly housed in literary departments, are indicative of different "arcs of concern or focus," each of which is enmeshed in a diagnostic that (like all diagnostics) are themselves questionable—thus my critique of both paradigms is essentially a critique of the accuracy of their diagnostics.

In spite of its commitment to truth and accompanying hostility to relativism, the irreducible residues of contingency and "relativism" are conspicuous features in the practice of analytic philosophy not only in the splintering of truth it generates, but in the very act of deciding to work on this rather than that problem. That is to say, even the problem, as well as the style and field to which philosophers devote their energies, depend upon what "appeals" to them. Something peaks his or her interest, touches them, while another philosopher remains unfazed by a field, and its problems. The body of ever growing problems touches the expanding mind/body of philosophers and philosophies. The truth lies in the appeal—appeal in both senses of the term, i.e., the appeal it has and the appeal that is made on its behalf. To live in this openness is only a philosophical failure, if one expects philosophy to conjure up the horse and cart for the exploration. The nihilist on discovering philosophy can't conjure them up can only be taken seriously among those who made or believed in the absurd possibility of the conjuration.

Nihilism is but the demonic Siamese-twin of absolute reason. The contemporary philosophical spirit most antithetical to analytic philosophy is not simply continental philosophy, but poststructuralism. And it was ever accused of being relativistic and nihilistic. But as it evolved it became more assured of its ethical character and rectitude. In its ethico-political embrace, and in spite of its various refusals to tolerate a totality, it carries within it a spirit of moral absolutism that is utterly totalizing.

But before discussing the nightmare of the analytics, the dreaded/ dreadful poststructuralists and other philosophies of anti-domination, we shall turn to those two other continentals, Husserl and Heidegger, who opened up a way so foreign to the analytic turn.

NOTES

1. Monk claims that the divide between analytic philosophy and phenomenology or continental philosophy is somewhat misplaced, the real divide is between analytical Wittgenstein and the rest.

2. "What's Wrong with Contemporary Philosophy?" Kevin Mulligan, Peter Simons, and Barry Smith, *Topoi*, 25. (1–2), 2006, 63–67. According to them, analytic philosophy's problem is threefold: it is "sceptical about the claim that philosophy can be a science"; continental philosophy is "never pursued in a properly theoretical way," and history of philosophy "is mostly developed on a regional rather than objective basis." On the history of philosophy, Simons' exploration of the history of the Anglo-Continental divide in his "Whose Fault? The Origins and Evitability of the Analytic Continental Rift," *International Journal of Philosophical Studies*, vol. 19, (3), 295–311, 2009, and his *Philosophy and Logic in Central Europe from Bolzano to Tarski: Selected Essays* (Dordrecht: Springer, 1992) are exemplary contributions to the history of philosophy.

3. Hans-Johann Glock, *What Is Analytic Philosophy?* (Cambridge: Cambridge University Press, 2008), 11.

4. Glock, 15.

5. Swift, A. "Politics v. Philosophy," *Prospect*, August/September 2001, 40–44.

6. "What's Wrong with Contemporary Philosophy?," 64.

7. Bernard Williams, *Ethics and the Limits of Philosophy*, with a commentary on the text by A. W. Moore and a foreword by Jonathan Lear (London: Routledge, 2005), XVI.

8. James Conant, "The Emergence of the Concept of the Analytic Tradition as a Form of Philosophical Self-Consciousness," in *Beyond the Analytic-Continental Divide Pluralist Philosophy in the Twenty-First Century*, edited by Jeffrey A. Bell, Andrew Cutrofello, and Paul M. Livingston (London: Routledge, 2017), 19–20.

9. Hans Sluga, *Gottlob Frege: The Arguments of the Philosophers* (London: Routledge, 1980), 92, Sluga's translation from *Nachgelassene Schriften*, ed. by H. Hermes et al., Hamburg, 1969, 273.

10. *Die Grundlage der Arithmetik [The Foundation of Arithmetic]*, ed. and translated by J. L. Austin (Oxford: Basil Blackwell, 1969), 71.

11. G. E. Moore, "the Nature of Judgment" in *Selected Writings*, edited by T. Baldwin (London: Routledge, 1993), 8.

12. Bertrand Russell, *The Philosophy of Logical Atomism* (London: Routledge, 1972), 15.

13. Michael Beaney, "Introduction" to *The Analytic Turn: Analysis in Early Analytic Philosophy and Phenomenology*, edited by Michael Beaney (London: Routledge, 2007), 2.

14. Ibid., 1–2.

15. Beaney, somewhat misleadingly, says "there is nothing decompositional in this type of analysis," 3. But surely Russell has used more words to *simplify* the meaning of the concept so that it can be more clearly discussed on purely logical terms, which Beaney concedes as he clarifies that "Russell's and Frege's use of transformative analysis is to make the sentence formalizable into quantitative logic."

16. Capaldi, *The Enlightenment Project in its Analytic Conversation* (Dordrecht: Springer, 1998), 2–3.

17. Ibid., 3.

18. I am not suggesting that all thinking must be metaphysical—but thinking predicated upon a totality being of a certain kind, having *an essential nature,* cannot help but be metaphysical.

19. Capaldi, *The Enlightenment Project,* 41–42.

20. Peter Hacker in his "Analytic Philosophy: Beyond the Linguistic Turn and Back Again" in Michael Beaney, *The Analytic Turn: Analysis in Early Analytic Philosophy and Phenomenology* (125–41), 126–27. In terms of the first phases a distinction also needs to be made, as Hans Sluga has argued, between the motivations of the Anglo stream in its origin and the more continental stream. See Sluga, *Frege,* Introduction and chapter 1, 1–34.

21. Michael Dummett, *Origins of Analytic Philosophy* (Oxford: Duckworth, 1993), 5.

22. See Ray Monk, "What Is Analytical Philosophy?" in *Bertrand Russell and the Origins of Analytical Philosophy,* edited and introduced by Ray Monk and Anthony Palmer (Bristol: Thoemmes, 1996), 1–22. and "Was Russell an Analytical Philosopher? *Ratio,* Vol. 9, No. 3 (December 1996), 227–42. Even Husserl along with Frege and Dummett ends up in the same camp as Russell—with Wittgenstein the lone philosophical outlier.

23. Cited and translated by Sluga, 67 from Frege's *Begriffschrift,* edited by I. Angelelli, Hildesheim, 1964, xii–xiii.

24. Cited in and translated by Sluga 64 from Frege, *Nachgelassene Schriften,* 272.

25. NS 7, Sluga 64.

26. In his 1913 manuscript the *Theory of Knowledge,* Russell says: "the word 'experience,' like most of the words expressing fundamental ideas in philosophy, has been imported into the technical vocabulary of daily life, and it retains some of the grime of its outdoor existence in spite of some scrubbing and brushing by impatient philosophers." Bertrand Russell, *Theory of Knowledge: The 1913 Manuscript,* edited by Elizabeth Eames in collaboration with Kenneth Blackwell (London: Routledge, 1984), 5.

27. "The Monistic Theory of Truth," in Bertrand Russell, *Philosophical Essays* (Longmans, Green and Co., 1910), 150–51.

28. Cf. Russell's claim of 1918 that the "logical doctrine" and "kind of metaphysics" he propounds is "atomistic" and that this is "opposed to the monistic logic of the people who more or less follow Hegel." *The Philosophy of Logical Atomism* (London: Routledge, 1972), 2.

29. Ibid., 164.

30. From 1914, Russell held a metaphysical position, which he called "neutral monism." For Russell: "the whole duality of mind and matter . . . is a mistake; there is only one kind of stuff out of which the world is made, and this stuff is called mental in one arrangement, physical in the other." See Vol. 7 of Bertrand Russell, *Collected Papers,* ed. E. R. Eames with K. Blackwell (London: Allen and Unwin, 1984). See Robert Tully, "Russell's Neutral Monism," in *Russell: The Journal of Bertrand Russell Studies,* volume 8, issue 1, 1988, 209–24. The very solution, i.e., there is "one kind of stuff," however, illustrates the problem, from a Hegelian perspective of staying with "things," and the essentially empiricist position of Russell.

31. Russell, *The Philosophy of Logical Atomism,* 135.

32. Ibid., 144.

33. Ibid.

34. Monk, "Russell and the Origins of Analytical Philosophy," 6.

35. Ibid., 8.

36. In their Wittgensteinian inspired *Word and World: Practice and the Foundation of Language* (Cambridge: Cambridge University Press, 2004), Patricia Hanna and Bernard Harrison argue against "the philosophical mainstream descending from Frege and Russell to Quine, Davidson, Dummett, McDowell, Evans, Putnam, Kripke and others," ii. The core of their argument is: "Meaning . . . is a relationship between language-elements and practices, whereas the relationship between language and reality is reconstructed as a relationship between those practices and the aspects and elements of the extralinguistic world on which they operate," 9. And: "Language cannot

transcend practice, and hence, although what we truly say about the world is in a quite unproblematic sense true of *it*, as spoken *by* it, discourse can never emancipate itself from the possibility that the devising of a new practice will enable the world to speak its nature in altogether new and unexpected forms," 13. I would like to thank Alan Tapper for drawing this work to my attention.

37. Monk, "What is Analytical Philosophy?," 12–13.

38. Ludwig Wittgenstein, *Philosophical Investigations*, translated by G. E. Anscombe (Oxford: Basil Blackwell, 1958), #309, 103.

39. Ibid., #23, 11.

40. Ibid., #38, 19.

41. Ibid., #123, 49.

42. Ibid., #126, 50.

43. Ibid., 50.

44. Ibid., 50.

45. Ibid. 51.

46. Ibid., 51.

47. Ibid., 155.

48. The Big Typescript: TS 213, German English Scholars' Edition, translated by C. Grant Luckhardt and Maximilian E. Aue (Oxford: Wiley-Blackwell, 2005), #105.

49. Nicholas Capaldi, *The Enlightenment Project*, 39.

50. Peter Winch, *The Idea of a Social Science and its Relation to Philosophy* (Atlantic Highlands, NJ: Humanities Press International, 1990), 72.

51. Dilthey's nomenclature suggests his appreciation of the Romantics (particularly Schleiermacher, but also Hegel [who makes the term *Geist* central while himself often being a major critic of romanticism]). Dilthey was eclectic and in his own way he sought to bridge the various methodological divisions that he saw as developing out of important insights into history and the human condition.

52. Wilhelm Windelband, "History and Natural Science," *Theory and Psychology*, 1998, Vol. 8 (1): 5–22. Rickert favored the term "individualizing" rather than idiographic, while Dilthey argued that any individual case occurs against a backdrop of generalities, which cannot be ignored by the student of the *Geisteswissenschaften*. Wilhelm Dilthey, "Contributions to a Study of Individuality" in Wilhelm Dilthey *Selected Works, Volume 3: Understanding the Human World*, edited and translated by Rudolf A. Makkreel and Fithjof Rodi (Princeton, NJ: Princeton University Press, 2010), 22–228. Windelband would later relent and concede the distinction was not so sharp as his earlier formulation. See the discussion on Dilthey and Windelband and Rickert in H. A. Hodges, *The Philosophy of Wilhelm Dilthey* (London: Routledge and Kegan Paul, 1952), 225–52.

53. Thus in a work which undertakes to retrieve Rickert's importance, Anton Zijderveld exclaims, after running through what is a central concept in Rickert's work: "Rickert's own conception of *Verstehen* is not really that different from Dilthey's!" *Rickert's Relevance: The Ontological and Epistemological Functions of Value* (Leiden: Brill, 2006), 264.

54. Ernst Gellner, *Cause and Meaning in the Social Sciences* (London: Routledge and Kegan Paul, 1973), 86.

55. Ibid., 79.

56. Pritchard's anthropological classic the *Witchcraft, Oracles and Magic among the Azande* figures largely in the debate, especially as it is continued by Winch in *Ethics and Action* (London: Routledge and Kegan Paul, 1972). See the chapter "Understanding a Primitive Society," 8–49.

57. In his "Introduction" to *Ethics and Action*, Winch concedes that perhaps in his essay "Understanding a Primitive Society" he may not have emphasized enough the "absurd" argument "that ways in which men live together can never be criticized," 3. Ultimately what Winch is trying to do is open up dialogue so we can better understand each other and why we do what we do.

58. Michael Dummett, "Oxford Philosophy," in *Truth and Other Enigmas* (London: Duckworth, 1978), 431–36. Even Uschanov in his defense of ordinary language philosophy can't help himself from conceding that "the most important valid criticism of OLP is that its view of ethics and moral philosophy concentrated too much on analysing certain words removed from the human context in which all oral reflection and decision making take place." T. P. Uschanov, "the strange death of ordinary language philosophy," at www.helsinki.fi/~tuschano/writings/strange/. Last sighted September 23, 2018.

59. Capaldi, *The Enlightenment Project*, 112.

60. Ibid.

61. This is also recognized by Capaldi who cites Passmore's reference, in *A Hundred Years of Philosophy*, to the "centrality of Aristotle for Oxford trained philosophers" (17 (1985) and Robert Turnbull's observation from his article of 1988, "Aristotle and Philosophy Now," (in P. H. Hare (ed.), *Doing Philosophy Historically*. 117–26); "[T]he twentieth century provides many examples of very influential Anglo-American philosophers who can properly be called Aristotelians. John Austin, Gilbert Ryle, Peter Strawson, Elizabeth Anscombe, Peter Geach, and Donald Davidson come readily to mind." Capaldi, *The Enlightenment Project*, 113, and 147, fn 15.

62. Capaldi, *The Enlightenment Project*, 113.

63. Richard Rorty, *Philosophy and the Mirror of Nature* (Princeton, NJ: Princeton University Press, 1979), 163.

64. Peter Simons, "Whose Fault? The Origins and Evitability of the Analytic Continental Rift," 295–311.

65. Ibid., 297.

66. Carnap not only attended Husserl's lectures, but Husserl left a deep and lasting impact upon him. See Guillermo E. Rosado Haddock, *The Young Carnap's Unknown Master: Husserl's Influence on Der Raum and Der logische Aufbau der Welt* (Aldershot, UK: Ashgate, 2008), vii.

67. Russell quoted in Gilbert Ryle, "John Locke," in *Collected Papers Volume 1*, edited by Gilbert Ryle (Hutchinson, 1971), 147. This reference is taken from Thomas Akehurst, *The Cultural Politics of Analytic Philosophy: Britishness and the Spectre of Europe* (London: Continuum, 2010), 1.

68. Russell, Bertrand, and Woodrow Wyatt. *Bertrand Russell Speaks His Mind* (World Publishing Company, 1960), 116 in Akehurst, 76.

69. Simons, "Whose Fault? The Origins and Evitability of the Analytic Continental Rift," 302.

70. George Reisch presents the political infighting in the context of the Cold War within the "Unity of Science Movement" of Otto Neurath, Philipp Frank, Rudolf Carnap, and Charles Morris in his *How the Cold War Transformed Philosophy of Science: To the Icy Slopes of Logic* (Cambridge: Cambridge University Press, 2005).

71. Gilles Deleuze and Felix Guattari, *What Is Philosophy?*, translated by Hugh Tomlinson and Graham Burchell (New York: Columbia University Press, 1994), 140.

72. Deleuze and Guattari, *What Is Philosophy?*, 143

73. Edmund Husserl, *The Paris Lectures*, translated and Introductory essay by Peter Koestenbaum (The Hague: Martinus Nijhof, 1975), 3 and 38.

74. For a telling anecdote on this, see Bruce Wiltshire, *Fashionable Nihilism* (New York: State University Press of New York, 2002), 1–2.

NINE

Husserl's Idea of Phenomenology and Heidegger's Being (an Idea in Spite of Itself)

HUSSERL'S ENLIGHTENED FAITH IN THE THEORETICAL DOMINATION OF THE WORLD

On the final page of David Carr's translation of yet another of Husserl's grand unfulfilled ambitions,[1] *The Crisis of the European Sciences and Transcendental Phenomenology*, we read: "Phenomenology frees us from the old objectivistic ideal of the scientific system, the theoretical form of mathematical natural science, and frees us accordingly from the idea of an ontology of the soul which could be analogous to physics."[2]

That this is the concluding idea of the work is a sad irony indeed. For from the outset, the one thing that phenomenology had, throughout Husserl's various and numerous philosophical formulations, always managed to convince those sympathetic to its procedures and aims was that it had liberated the sciences from the metaphysical straight-jacket of naturalism. In *The Crisis* Husserl finally seemed to be rising to the historical, existential, linguistic, and vitalist challenges, that in the nineteenth century were becoming increasingly prevalent in German philosophical circles. Though his attack upon the reductionist tendency in natural science also had affinities with philosophies of action and the subject of the nineteenth century. Furthermore, Husserl brought to his critique an indisputable degree of philosophical sophistication, in part because he too was deeply interested in logic itself and, more broadly the "Ideas" that would serve as the phenomenological foundations of the sciences. On the other hand, the new founding in phenomenology that Husserl had believed would make philosophy, and the sciences more rigorous and ultimately more theoretically secure and valuable, would be shaken and given a new direction by Husserl's favourite and most gifted student, Martin Heidegger. Thus it was that when, having originally received the manuscript as a birthday gift, Husserl sat down to read *Being and Time*, it slowly dawned on him that not only had Heidegger philosophically disappointed him, he had betrayed him and the entire phenomenological project.[3]

The duration and extent of Heidegger's dissatisfaction with Husserl can be gauged from a disparaging comment as early as 1919 about his ostensible mentor on "the overall dominance and primacy of the theoretical." Whereas, for Heidegger, "what is primary . . . when you live in a first-hand world (*Umwelt*), everything comes at you loaded with meaning, all over the place and all the time, everything is *enworlded*, '*world happens*.'"[4] On another occasion, Heidegger's frustration with Husserl (which he seems to have expressed privately to anyone but Husserl himself) led him at one point to say to Karl Löwith that he has just given a seminar in which he has

> publicly burned and destroyed the Ideas to such an extent that I dare say that the essential foundations for the whole (of my work) are now cleanly laid out. I am now convinced that Husserl was never a philosopher, not even for one second in his life. He becomes ever more ludicrous.[5]

The key problem facing Husserl's legacy which ultimately blunted his impact upon the succeeding generation is powerfully expressed in these dismissive remarks of Heidegger. For on the one hand, Husserl frees philosophy from the shackles of his time: the host of isms which he sees as symptomatic of the crisis of the European sciences—naturalism, historicism, relativism, and the compartmentalisms which plague the modern disconnections of science from contributing to the greater penetration into reality that is philosophy's *raison d"être*. On the other, the importance he did ascribe to a "life-world" and "environing world" was generally seen as "too little, too late."[6]

That "too little, too late" is the really telling moment of what is in many ways Husserl's finest and most important philosophical work—if not in terms of "logical" or reflexive "stringency," then certainly in terms of existential and historical urgency, *The Crisis of the European Sciences*. For the overwhelmingly disappointing feature of the *Crisis* is that what looks on the surface to be a break-out for Husserl, i.e., really getting to grips with the life-world and the crisis of the times, circles back and closes yet again with the idea that science and reason must not become the prisoner of naturalism. His ambition, though, had long been animated by a desire to "encompass all worlds and . . . the actual through the possible," and he continues:

It has to do with logic as much as it does with ethics, aesthetics and all parallel disciplines. *The Logical Investigations* offered tentative beginnings of a phenomenology of the logical, since it accomplished a first breakthrough to phenomenology generally. The scope of the phenomenological problematic extends to nature (the consciousness constituting nature and of nature as a constituted unity), a phenomenology of corporeality, of the spiritual, of social spirituality and its constituted correlate standing under the title culture, etc.[7]

It does seem that Husserl's ambitious extension of logical investigations to such a vast phenomenological enterprise, which emerges in the development of Ideas, was also spurred on by Dilthey having identified the value of his phenomenology for "finding a philosophical grounding of the human sciences," (and subsequently Husserl's reading of Rickert and Windelband).[8] For his part, Husserl's appreciation of Dilthey was always tempered by what he took as Dilthey's lack of rigor. Dilthey's very public positive appraisal of some of Husserl's writings were, on the other hand, tempered by what Bob Sandmeyer frankly, yet not inaccurately, describes as Husserl remaining "philosophically tone deaf to history."[9] How it must have hurt Husserl as he worked his way through *Being and Time*, discovering departure after departure in Heidegger's complete refabrication of the entire philosophical purpose of phenomenology (in the work dedicated to him!), and recognizing with mounting disappointment that it all but culminates in the claim that the work was a "preparatory existential-temporal analytic of *Dasein* [which] is resolved to foster the spirit of Count Yorck in the service of Dilthey's work."[10] Friedrich von Hermann simply states (and devotes a book to demonstrating) that the difference between Husserl and Heidegger comes down to a reflexive as opposed to an hermeneutical phenomenology[11]—which is true, or true while Heidegger is in the process of formulating the questions that will transcend phenomenology. The distinction also conceals the fact that for Husserl an hermeneutical phenomenology, a phenomenology in the spirit of Dilthey, is no phenomenology at all because it has dispensed with the reflexive rigor that makes philosophy what it is. Thus in his "Phenomenology and Anthropology" of 1931, Husserl addressed what he calls the "influence" of Dilthey upon the accelerating "gravitation" to "philosophical anthropology by "some of the younger generation of German philosophers." Although he does not mention Heidegger by name his reference to "a doctrine of the essence of human being's concrete worldly Dasein" makes it clear that he is seeing Heidegger at the forefront of those engaging in a "complete reversal of phenomenology's fundamental standpoint."[12]

Husserl may have been honest in his claim to Dilthey that the attack upon historicism in "Philosophy as Rigorous Science" was not an attack upon Dilthey himself. But as "Phenomenology and Anthropology" unequivocally shows the "Diltheyians" posed a far greater danger to his version of phenomenology than the naturalists. That Heidegger was thinking in regions beyond what he saw as Dilthey's inadequate appreciation of the character or power of metaphysics and anthropology, as "that interpretation of humanity which already knows, fundamentally, who man is and can, therefore never ask who he might be," while still taking historicity as intrinsic to temporality and being as Er-eignis—event, appropriation, or en-owning (to take the three most widely used translations)—ultimately blunts the power of Husserl's response to Heideggerean objections.[13] If the *Crisis*, in spite of being incomplete, is the most systematic attempt to stave off criticism from that quarter, it is difficult to dispute Heidegger's comment to William Richardson, as he reflects back upon his own philosophical continuities and turnings, that "phenomenology in Husserl's sense was elaborated into a distinctive philosophical position according to a pattern set by Descartes, even Kant, and Fichte. The historicity of thought remained completely foreign to him."[14] Quentin Lauer's accurate observation not only of the *Crisis* but the posthumously published *First Philosophy* with its "Critical History of Ideas" (written in 1925) makes essentially the same point about how Husserl's focus, even when thinking it is allowing for historical "influence," remains ever focused on the *telos* devised from the outset of Husserl's phenomenological commitment:

> Husserl may have been honest in his claim to Dilthey that the attack upon history continues to have no philosophical significance whatever, and the history of philosophy from Plato to Husserl with notable gaps records only the vicissitudes of the scientific ideal in philosophy, not the process of philosophizing.[15]

But, as we have said, Husserl was ever circling around the same problem, attempting to find the definitive formulation and demonstration that was meant to be as apodictic as the consciousness and its *a priori* that convinced Husserl where the solution to philosophy's rigorous founding was to be sought. The search and rigor in Husserl—in a manner analogous with the "rigor" of analytic philosophy—and the faith in reason and science themselves are decisive in the limits that haunt and ultimately derail the philosophy in a manner far more devastating than can be even said of Hegel's philosophy. Much like most of the analytical philosophers across the channel, there is nothing in Husserl (unlike Heidegger) to suggest that he ever had more than a superficial knowledge of Hegel. As Lauer points out there are a handful of references to Hegel in Husserl: in *Logical Investigations*, Husserl refers to Hegel denying the principle of non-contradiction, and there is also "a reference there to Hegel's desire in the *Phenomenology* to make of philosophy a foundational science,"[16] and in "Philosophy as a Rigorous Science" he observes that naturalism intensified as a reaction to Hegelianism, and that in spite of Hegel's system "pretending to absolute validity," Hegelianism spawned generations of historicists.[17] These observations by Husserl are fair enough, although they could be made by anyone who has not opened a page of Hegel. Yet Husserl in that same essay depicts his own view of philosophy's importance in the most Hegelian of ways: "Every great philosophy is not only a historical fact, but in the development of humanity's life of the spirit it has a great, even unique teleological function, that of being the highest elevation of the life experience, education and wisdom of its time."[18] But it is difficult to have confidence in Husserl's comments on Hegel when he claims that Hegel's "system lacks a critique of reason."[19] Whichever way we "cut" Hegel this is simply silly: his system is nothing other than an exploration of reason, including its critique by the understanding (the arc from Descartes through Locke to Kant). Those who pit faith and feeling against the Absolute of reason, as the condition of organization of sensory materials, of thinking and of any kind of knowing, for Hegel, comprised pretty well the entire generation of contemporaries and their modern predecessors, who were, as he made the case in detail in *Faith and Knowledge*, either helping form or under the spirit of the principle of the "Protestant" "North." This use of reason to absolutely limit reason, for Hegel, must only serve as one more spur to reason's expansive actualisation: a moment in its ceaseless dialectical drive. Moreover, it is also far from obvious that Husserl's logical investigations and the conceptual alignments he espies or designates are really more rigorous or beneficial than Hegel's, let alone—to use another of Husserl's favorite terms—more "radical."[20] That is, in spite of Husserl's indisputable contribution to philosophical taxonomy or nomenclature (to be random: phenomenology itself, the *epochē*, horizonality, regionality), as well as the new "curve" he puts on such terms as transcendental, monad, etc., from Hegel's perspective, as is evident in his reliance upon the subject/object bifurcation, Husserl is still caught up in the pre-Hegelian dualisms that defined the metaphysics of Descartes up to Kant.

That Husserl believes he commences outside of or beyond reason, only to allow in its substantiations at his own discretion, hardly weakens the Hegelian critique. For irrespective of the fact that Husserl wants to be more radical than Descartes, in his very first move he succumbs to the same temptation as Descartes and the entire lineage of post-Cartesianism. That temptation, in Hegelian terms, lies in its absolutization of a finite moment, the initial indubitable "fact" and *a priori* positing of consciousness, as opposed to commencing with the substance of what is thought as a form and content which is the thread of the active Absolute that gives consciousness the very materials it draws upon to make its classifications. Viewed from a Hegelian position, Husserl's manner of procedure is typical of reasoning which is defined and circumscribed by the primacy of the "understanding." As I have said earlier, Hegel's weakness is in the "end," but his power is disclosed in its initial insight about the beginning of any philosophical inquiry. It is a compelling insight. Husserl is con-

demned to find confirmation of the dualism through the materials generated by the finititudes of its own Absolute, and thus is imprisoned in a
dualism from the very first move he makes philosophically. If Hegel had
made the idea the Absolute that spawns consciousness, Husserl makes
consciousness the Absolute that becomes the idea. The one path does
lead to a totality in which subject, object, reason, and history are ever but
"moments"; the other is ever in search of the formulation—itself an
idea—of the character of the very "being"—consciousness—that is its
grounding.

That Husserl remained the captive not to nature, but rather to the idea
as a philosophical idea, is amply evident in the *Cartesian Meditations*,
which was but one more unfinished attempt to nail down the solution to
the problem of the nature of phenomenology. The ways already opened
by language, history, and tradition which would be taken up productive-
ly by Heidegger were closed off to Husserl by his initial decision to get an
ever clearer founding idea for philosophy than Descartes, who for him
was the philosopher who first identified the problem of philosophical
grounding.

> First, anyone who seriously intends to become a philosopher must
> "once in his life" withdraw into himself and attempt, within himself, to
> overthrow and build anew all the sciences that, up to then, he has been
> accepting. Philosophy (sic.) wisdom (*sagesse*) is the philosophizer's
> quite personal affair. It must arise as *his* wisdom, as his self-acquired
> knowledge tending toward universality, a knowledge for which he can
> answer from the beginning, and at each step, by virtue of his own
> absolute insights. If I have decided to live with this as my aim the
> decision that alone can start me on the course of a philosophical devel-
> opment I have thereby chosen to begin in absolute poverty, with an
> absolute lack of knowledge. [21]

Husserl believes he needs a doubt more radical than Descartes', not to
mention a stance far more radical than the irony of the Socratic and
subsequent classical philosophical spirits seeking to create a philosophical "space" for the dialectical interrogation of *doxa*, so that he can found
"a unitary living philosophy," [22] "aiming at the ultimate conceivable freedom from prejudice, shaping itself with actual autonomy according to
ultimate evidences it has itself produced, and therefore absolutely self-
responsible." [23] The solipsistic monadological move is meant to provide
this as it then opens up to a world of "monadological intersubjectivity,"
which is the subject matter of the fifth meditation. While Heidegger also
adopts the "radical" stance of the phenomenologist in order to attack the
enormous residual prejudice and deformities and defacements of Being,
and hence our world, flowing from the calculative telos of the predominance of the "ontic" in the play out of metaphysics, Heidegger's approach renders this monadological elevation a question in itself. For the

initial elevation is the confirmation of the very metaphysics that phenomenology is meant to encounter and appraise. The role allotted to "intentionality" and the accompanying "horizon structure" of the "modes of Ego comportment" (see e.g., §19–22 of the Second Meditation) rather than being the opening to the world to be reviewed as a totality of objects, regions and horizons, as Husserl desires, is but the ensconcement of the reflective disposition and mood that is the repository of Husserl's vast stock of the *a priori*. The privileging of this mood and disposition can easily be rendered as but another prejudice, at least in so far as it limits the world to being what is disclosed *through* the transcendental subject's "ideas" insofar as those ideas are themselves only accessible through the original mood and disposition. At the same time, the world itself as a becoming and historical reality becomes restricted to being the repository of intentionalities.[24] It is true that a vast amount of the environing world, even in its dormancy, can be "itemized" through the intentionalities of production and creation (as post-Kantian idealisms also suggest via the weight paced upon the Idea and/or consciousness). But both our original intentionalities, and, more importantly, the shimmerings and interplay of the things of the world transpiring over time and hence outside of the horizon of an earlier mode of intentionality and consciousness—a most common interplay whose importance is felicitously identified by political scientists and economists as "unintended consequences"—make any such itemization but a small part of the world we confront and engage with. It is, as Heidegger rightly saw, only through *Dasein's* engagements and projections, that whatever is there comes to bear meaning: and this is not necessarily because of *anyone's* intention, either from the past or in the present. The unintended consequences stand in the closest relationship to the matter of prejudice that Husserl wants to do battle against. Husserl seems to think that by the mere naming of "prejudice" as the "enemy," he has provided a justification for his *Meditations*. But we are far less likely to be convinced of this if we consider Burke's account of prejudice:

> as ready application in the emergency; it previously engages the mind in a steady course of wisdom and virtue, and does not leave the man hesitating in the moment of decision, skeptical, puzzled, and unresolved. Prejudice renders a man's virtue his habit; and not a series of unconnected acts. Through just prejudice, his duty becomes a part of his nature.[25]

Burke's appeal to resolve immediately conjures up Heidegger's "fundamental analysis of *Dasein*"—which is not surprising once the desire to make sense of our engagement is shifted away from the self-certainty of the rational disposition of the maker.[26] It also throws open the question of what constitutes evidence. In Burke, the entire thrust of a metaphysical representation of social existence was analogical with geometrical or axiomatic reasoning. Hence Burke predicted how the Rousseauian reasoning that had become so common among those professionals steering the French Revolution would lead to a far greater outpouring of judicially justified violence than the initial eruptions. The conflation of the social and political into the philosopher's assemblage of ideas is indeed fraught with disasters—disasters that cannot simply be dismissed as concealing a conservative disposition.

This stands in close relationship to another section from the First Meditation—"§ 5 Evidence and the idea of genuine science." As Husserl writes:

> the Cartesian idea of a science (ultimately an all-embracing science) grounded on an absolute foundation, and absolutely justified, is none other than the idea that constantly furnishes guidance in all sciences and in their striving toward universality whatever may be the situation with respect to a de facto actualization of that idea. [27]

And,

> Evidence, which in fact includes all experiencing in the usual and narrower sense, can be more or less perfect. *Perfect evidence* and its correlate, *pure and genuine truth*, are given as ideas lodged in the striving for knowledge, for fulfilment of one's meaning intention. By immersing ourselves in such a striving, we can extract those ideas from it. Truth and falsity, criticism and critical comparison with evident data, are an everyday theme, playing their incessant part even in prescientific life. For this everyday life, with its changing and relative purposes, relative evidences and truths suffice. But science looks for truths that are valid, and remain so, *once for all and for everyone*; accordingly it seeks verifications of a new kind, verifications carried through to the end. Though de facto, as science itself must ultimately see, it does not attain actualization of a system of absolute truths, but rather is obliged to modify its "truths" again and again, it nevertheless follows the idea of absolute or scientifically genuine truth; and accordingly it reconciles itself to an infinite horizon of approximations, tending toward that idea. By them, science believes, it can surpass *in infinitum* not only everyday knowing but also itself; likewise however by its aim at systematic universality of knowledge, whether that aim concern a particular closed scientific province or a presupposed all-embracing unity of whatever exists as it does if a "philosophy" is possible and in question. [28]

It is precisely Husserl's faith not only in philosophy as providing the science but in himself as the deliverer of the grounds for the scientific work—for all must begin again, otherwise we merely continue in the prejudicial labors of the pre-phenomenological scientists. Thus rigor and responsibility pertain to the existential and rational burden of philosophy, as Husserl sees it. Ultimately, this responsibility and burden is perfectly summed up by Buckley's observation that for Husserl: "philosophy is responsible for culture as whole." [29] Apart, again, from the affinities with Hegel about such a claim, it represents a highly dubious view of culture, as well as an even more questionable view of the relationship between creative and traditional practice and reflective consciousness.

Whatever semblance of sanity such a quixotic project may have comes from the way Husserl constructs Europe and the role of the sciences in it. Not surprisingly, Husserl prefers his construction of Europe to the real "things themselves" that have made Europe what it is. The Europe of the *Crisis* is little more than Enlightenment Potted History 101: Greeks hoorah! Middle Ages—loud "boo"; Renaissance yippee—the cavalry are finally here! As Eric Voegelin caustically commented about the *Crisis* in a letter to Alfred Schütz:

> In this essay Husserl develops an idea of history which in its general features . . . is Victorian. The relevant history of humankind consists of ancient Greece and the modern age dating from the Renaissance. Hellenism, Christianity, and the Middle Ages—an insignificant span of time lasting just over two thousand years—is a superfluous interlude; the Indians and the Chinese (put in quotation marks by Husserl) are slightly ridiculous curiosities found on the periphery of the flat earth, at the center of which we find, not Occidental man, but humanity per se. The human being is a rational being. "Philosophy and science would accordingly be the historical movement through which universal reason, "inborn" in humanity as such, is revealed." Humanity's entelechy emerged in Greek humanity. Following the primal establishment [*Urstiftung*] by the Greeks and the two-thousand-year interlude in which the entelechy obviously sought amusement elsewhere, the new establishment of philosophy was made by Descartes. As a result of a few imperfections, which are excellently analyzed by Husserl, Descartes's new establishment took a bad turn. Kant had a good but incomplete starting point for getting it back on the right path. We ignore German Idealism and the Romantic Movement and then come to the final establishment [*Endstiftung*] in Husserl's Transcendental Idealism.[30]

Certainly, Hegel's is also a schematic rendition of history that enables the philosopher to ignore what doesn't fit into the net. But in Hegel philosophy comes late to the scene, and its role is restricted to providing rational form for what has already occurred in actuality in the struggle for freedom that is first expressed as sensory in art, then as intuition in religion, and only finally as philosophy. By contrast the following from *The Crisis of the European Sciences*, could not be summed up better than Buckley does—but the summing up only shows the disturbing nature of the *hubris* of the project. First Husserl himself:

> there are many infinite ideas . . . which lie outside the philosophical-scientific sphere (infinite tasks, goals, confirmations, truths, "true values," "genuine goods," "absolutely valid norms"), but they owe their analogous character of infinity to the transformation of mankind through philosophy and its idealities. Scientific culture under the idea

of infinity means, then, a revolution of the whole manner in which
mankind creates culture.[31]

Now Buckley:

> Philosophy, or true science, this is the leading idea of the culture de-
> voted to the idea. This is to say that all of life can be led philosophically,
> all of life can be determined by a philosophical form of rationality.
> Philosophy is thus not merely one form of life among others, but it is
> the leading form, the model upon which every aspect of life can be
> based.[32]

Whereas Plato had outlined an ideal state as a means to help our ascen-
sion to an understanding of the idea of the good, Husserl outlines an
entire philosophical understanding of the world which thereby serves as
the *model* for the totality of our lives. This dialectical interplay of emancipative rationality and the philosophical totalization of culture that drives
Husserl's philosophizing is itself part of the greater current of modern
philosophy. For their part, the *philosophes* laid claim to being able to rationally justify the kind of world they were trying to make as well as
explaining why the world is as it was: the world as it was, though, failed
to recognize genius (especially theirs) and (their) rational principles of
justice and political obligation which could put an end to the parceling
out of privilege on the basis of brute power, superstition, and fakery.
Unlike the classical philosophies of Plato and Aristotle, though, they had
agreed upon what was primarily a materialist or naturalist view of nature—with varying degrees, as we have seen, of theological (specifically
deist) metaphysics to make sense of the whole. The banishment of the
biblical God who spoke largely in the "languages" of command, allegory,
and parable—but not the language of metaphysics, experiment, or formula—follows upon the Reformist banishment of the clergy as the legitimate mediator between humanity and the Creator. In the French revolution, and in its secular aftermath, the vacuum of mediator was filled by
the *philosophes* themselves. To this day, it is precisely this role that the
intellectuals and academicians wish to fill, thereby displacing the first
estate—those who pray—with their own role as "knowers," teachers,
spokespeople of the general will, and hence the definers of legitimacy.
That the *philosophes* inevitably reproduced the "difference" of opinions/
philosophies, which is the inevitable accompaniment of ostensible objective truth, has never been a game-breaker in the language game of philosophy. Just as the Enlightenment ranges politically from the idealistic
Thomas Paine, Thomas Jefferson, and worldly-wise Benjamin Franklin to
the mass-murdering Robespierre and the utterly psychopathic St. Just,
the philosophies ranged from the preening "know-it-allness" congenial-
ity of Voltaire, to the more morally troubling Diderot (whose *Rameau's
Nephew* Hegel found deeply disturbing, and, as Lionel Trilling put it: "the
paradigm of the modern cultural and spiritual situation")[33] to the Mar-

quis De Sade's enlightened justification of rape and carnivalesque sexualized mass murder. That is to say, there was indeed a political and philosophical consistency to the Enlightenment which encompassed the range of its diverse and contradictory ideas and behaviors—in the elevation of a class who carried forth the narrative of Enlightenment as a means to their own professionalism, increased political power, and prestige as social educators. That the march of Enlightenment in the guise of nationalism through the nineteenth and twentieth centuries eventually draws all the European empires into its flanks is the new idol that replaced the Christian God is all too rarely noticed: and it remains unnoticed by Husserl.

While the philosophers of the Enlightenment aspired to emancipate humanity from the goblins of its imagination and enable human beings to flourish in the techniques and technologies wrested from nature, and in more rational political, social, and economic systems, the fact was that the Enlightenment was pushed on by its own mythmaking prowess—equality, fraternity, liberty, and the "people" being its most conspicuously unassailable mythic archetypes. This was in large part why Romanticism, even as a reactive form of consciousness to Enlightenment which rescues myth, was the inescapable accompaniment of Enlightenment. What holds it together and where it continues in the classical tradition but intensifies it is, as Heidegger rightly observes in numerous places, the reconfiguration of entities that it systemizes. This systematization is itself based upon an unmitigated faith in the power of the intellect (and intellectual) to fill in the spiritual void that it has opened. Somewhat cynically, but not inaccurately, what we are talking about in the distinction between the pre-modern and modern Enlightened worldviews is the collision of imaginations: and above all the collision of faiths. This takes place alongside the leaping ahead of technology and instrumentalized science.

Husserl's phenomenology is one further movement in that collision; although it rests upon a faith that is too infrequently seen as *faith*. Nevertheless, a defender of Husserl, Philip Buckley does concede that the entire enterprise of phenomenology—and hence the knowledge and the purpose of the knowledge that the science hopes to provide a foundation and a methodology for—is based on faith. Thus on Husserl's *Kaizo-articles*, Buckley writes:

> The fundamental crisis which Husserl describes in these *"Kaizo-articles"* is a loss of *faith*. Renewal is thus the renewal of faith, a re-establishment or rekindling of faith. The faith which has been lost is that faith which has sustained Europe since its "foundation" or origin, that is, since the Greeks. This faith can be described in the first place as a belief in the possibility of rational existence. It is a sense that human life can be fully rational, a belief that all human activity can be guided by rationally established means. It is a belief that human beings can justify what they do, have insight into what they do, know what they do and why they do it. For Husserl, this faith also has what might be called a "moral

dimension." It is not just a belief that human life *can* be rational, that human actions *are able* to be justified, but that human life *ought* to be rational, that truly human actions *must* be justified. Thus, this faith not only proclaims that rational existence is possible, but that such an existence constitutes a goal for authentic humanity, that for human life to be truly human, it must be rational. It is also a faith in the moral sense of human culture, that is, of rationally determining values within a culture. It is thus a rational faith in morality, and a moral faith in rationality.[34]

That the Great War intensified the feeling of crisis and lack of faith is also brought out by Buckley.[35] The Great War, though as essentially the collision of European empires driven by the tumult of the emergent ambitions and conflicts of nations only brings to a head the revolutionary powers which burst asunder at this moment and have continued to do so throughout the twentieth and twenty-first centuries. Husserl remains part of the symptomology of the process. This is indeed something of an irony as his philosophy takes him to the life-world with its cruelties, blindness, deafness, dumbness: its pathogenetic and destructive idolatries, but which, nevertheless, "greets us" insofar as we are capable of an encounter with all manner of associations and relations which we are kin to. But like Hume, Husserl's real kin are—philosophers; i.e., people just like himself. His truth is in the type he is facilitating.

That Husserl's *epoché* inevitably leads back to the "life-world" and "intersubjecivity" also adds little to Nietzsche's teaching of "perpectivism," which is why unsurprisingly, and in spite of Husserl wanting to distance himself from the kind of irrationalism he finds in Nietzsche, there have been numerous authors arguing that Nietzsche and phenomenology converge.[36] But Husserl's phenomenological opening of perspective and "life-world" or "environining world," as we commenced the chapter with, breaks down in its ambition and requirement for reason, which was precisely what spawned Heidegger's frustration with "the overall dominance and primacy of the theoretical" in Husserl.

HEIDEGGER AND THE PROSPECT OF POSSIBILITY OF A TRANSFORMED SOJOURN IN THE WORLD OF HUMAN BEING

While Husserl's reaction to the phenomenological shift of emphasis to Heidegger's *Being and Time* with its focus upon *Dasein's* moods and comportment in its temporal directedness in was one of bitter disappointment at what he saw as the overthrow of his new science for a mere philosophical anthropology, the fact is that *Being and Time* was but a preliminary exploration of Heidegger's life-long philosophical problem—the problem and history of Being.[37] That a philosopher whose central topic seems so scholastic and arcane was among a handful of the most influential philosophers of the twentieth century had to do with the fact that his philosophy opens up, in the most radical of ways, the prospect of "possibility." This contiguity between the study of Being, and its history, and possibility was emphasised in a letter summing up Heidegger's life's work, written just six weeks before he died:

> To think in its own proper character—*aletheia* as such—which in the legacy from the beginning of the history of Being has remained necessary still unthought in and for this beginning; and thereby [by bringing *aletheia* into such thoughtfulness] to prepare the possibility of a transformed sojourn in the world of human being.[38]

This undertaking involved a critical reading and diagnosis of the nature, history and continual impact of metaphysics. If that reading and diagnosis had been spurred by Husserl's critique of naturalism, it was in complete antithesis to Husserl's radical Cartesianism and its more congenial reading of metaphysics generally. It was also predicated upon a continuous appeal to a poetic idyll of farmhouses, fields, pathways, forests, and rivers (recounted not only in his numerous reflection on poetry, but in the elevated status he accords the poets)[39] that offered a vision of rootedness and the simple acts of everyday life far removed from the urban machinated life that lay at the centre of Heidegger's diagnosis of the metaphysical ailments of *Dasein*. Heidegger's narratives on the history of metaphysics transport us outside of the frenzied machinations of the modern fabrications of life that is driven by the accursed "will to will," which he notes is "the highest and unconditional consciousness of the calculating self-guaranteeing of calculation,"[40] into the forest ways where we might experience certain *lightings*, *clearings*, and be open to sheer astonishment at and by the "event" or appropriation of Being, and tarry in this before being drawn back into our worlding.[41] It is a poeticized world in which "thinking in turn goes its way in the neighbourhood of poetry."[42] For Heidegger the proximity between poetry and language and the special role that poetry offer in thinking provides the placement from which he is able to enter into an alternative to metaphysical thinking in this "destitute time," so pronounced by Hölderlin, in which not only have "the gods and the god fled, but the divine radiance has become extinguished in the world's history."[43] As Heidegger put it in his "Letter on Humanism":

> in thinking Being comes to language. Language is the house of Being. In its home man dwells. Those who think and those who create with words are the guardians of this home. Their guardianship accomplishes the manifestation of Being insofar as they bring the manifestation to language and maintain it in language through their speech.[44]

He adds: "the liberation of language from grammar into a more original essential framework is reserved for thought and poetic creation."[45] Thus as he jotted down in his *Ponderings*, "[w]e must philosophize ourselves out of "philosophy,"[46] "philosophy is "merely the retuned reverberation of the great poetry."[47] Poetry had preceded metaphysics and in spite of the totalizing aspiration driving metaphysics in its cloaking, darkening, desertification of Being, for Heidegger, the contiguity between Being, language, and poetry still lives in the very questioning of thinking that is capable, as his thought is, of thinking beyond metaphysics. For Heidegger, non-metaphysical thinking of the sort he wishes his philosophy to open up can be found in its philosophical flourishing in the pre-Socratic philosophies of Parmenides, Heraclitus, and Anaximander. Our fall from the poeticization of thinking and from poeticized existence is, as Nietzsche had argued before him (but to different effect), immanent in the Platonic turn toward the idea of truth.

With Plato truth as Being's un-concealment is brought under the dominion of the idea and the ratiocination of the *logos*. For Heidegger this is the beginning of the eclipse and forgetting of the four-foldness of earth, sky, mortal, and gods. Of the fatality that Heidegger ascribes to Plato, and the end of philosophizing in the good that will be taken up by Aristotle as well as Plato, the following formulation is as taut as any to be found in Heidegger:

> The estimation of the *agathon* (the good) as the *teleutaia idea* [last idea] beyond *aletheia* [truth] as *gignoskomenon* [what is known] is the first, i.e. the authentic step that goes the furtherest toward the serial production of long-range bomber planes and the invention of radio technological news reported, with whose help the former are deployed in service of the unconditioned mechanization of the globe and humanity, equally predetermined by that step.[48]

If Plato provides "the first step" of the metaphysical history of the presiding, compartmentalisation, and ultimately systemic disclosure of the terrifying destructive potencies of beings—"the development of sciences within the field which philosophy opened up"[49]—it is through the modern metaphysical turn of *representation*, commencing with the Cartesian cogito, that underpins the more mathematized, systematized, and calculative character of modernity.[50] The metaphysics of calculativeness and machination is, for Heidegger, the unifying feature of all modern philosophy leading from Descartes through Leibniz to Nietzsche's "will to power," which is the culmination of the West's metaphysical purposefulness: the potential destruction of the earth.[51] We now live in this end-time of metaphysics, which is also the time of the end of philosophy, that is, as Heidegger formulates it "that place in which the whole of philosophy's history is gathered in its most extreme possibility,"[52] and the dominion and dominance of its calculative-ness is one in which "the essence of life is supposed to yield itself to technical production."[53] This is an abode of total desertification (*Verwüstung*) of everything. This horrific dominion of machination and desertification was, for Heidegger, as conspicuous in the bombings of the world war, as in the enormous scale of scientific planning and mass production of modern societies: a total continuum in the depiction and manufacturing of the beings that we had drawn into the world of our *Dasein*, only for it to threaten us with extinction.[54]

While Heidegger and Nietzsche differ about the meaning of metaphysics, both attempted to think outside and beyond it, and are drawn in the direction of the Greek pre-Socratics and poets. Heidegger asks directly "What task is reserved for thinking at the end of philosophy?"[55] The kind of thinking Heidegger claims for his philosophy is "preparatory rather than founding," or as he says in the "Letter on Humanism" the laying of "inconspicuous furrows in language—indeed even less conspicuous than the furrows "drawn through the field."[56] If this sounds modest enough—and after the chastening experience Heidegger had when he hoped to be the advisor to the "dark prince" Hitler, his humility was an understandable stance—that modesty is to be understood as: "awakening a readiness in man for possibility whose contour remains obscure, whose coming remains uncertain."[57]

If Heidegger could not abide Husserl's theoreticism driving out *Dasein's* "worlding," he was, nevertheless, no less attracted to the same kind of philosophical *ascesis* and the same *role* of the intellectual leader as Husserl. This aspiration would take him through his delusions of political grandeur up to the more hallowed, and politically safer peaks of the solitary thinker.[58] "Language," after all, he would proclaim, "is monologue,"[59] a position which conveniently reserves a special place at the table within the House of Being for one who can really hear it speaking.

Heidegger's aspiration was a drama of two acts. The initial act plagued him like a figure in a Greek tragedy, whose very escape route to avoid one's terrible destiny is what delivers the protagonist to it. It was built upon an act of "authentic resoluteness" and decision of the political will precisely of the sort outlined in the section "temporality and Historicality" (chapter V, Division II) of *Being and Time*. Its denouement lay in Heidegger taking on the role of Rectorship of the University of Freiburg, giving public speeches enthusiastically supporting Hitler, betraying Husserl (something Heidegger, unconvincingly, denied), denouncing some Jewish colleagues, and engaging in "leadership" squabbles with other Nazi "educators" like Ernest Krieck and the philosopher Alfred Bäumler. All this was undertaken in order to create a new direction and place for a philosophically led pedagogy, dispersed through the university, for a National Socialist regime. Only if National Socialism could be drawn away from the globally engulfing calculative forces of total destruction, i.e., only if the Nazis listened to him, he thought, could they emancipate the German people from the machinative logics of Great Britain, Russia, and the "giganticism" of the United States, and (as has been discovered more recently) the unrooted calculativeness of world Jewry.[60] The aspiration was a failure in every way: and the publications of Heidegger's *Black Notebooks* show just how tormented Heidegger was by National Socialism failing to live up to his vision for it. The first Act of Heidegger's aspiration was laid out for the post-Second World War generation, by Guido Schneeberger, in 1962, in a collections of speeches and statements from Heidegger's public Nazi years.[61] Some twenty-five years later this Act of Heidegger's drama was re-examined in light of extra incriminating material, initially in books by Victor Farias and Hugo Ott—books that subsequently laid the foundations for an academic industry devoted to the question of Heidegger and Nazism.[62]

The second "Act" of Heidegger's drama of the philosopher's aspiration is the portrayal of the persona he would maintain to the end of his life: the sage in patient and humble supplication in the temple of Being awaiting "the new god" of salvation. What previously had been political decision and will becomes the piety of thinking: the thinking that is a poetic alternative to metaphysics and its calculative ratiocination is now hived off from any politics of the present: for none is capable of living up to the deed.

Both acts reveal a man whose aspiration for greatness shrouds him in a repellent aura of self-delusion: the second one to be sure is less immediately dangerous, but it does freight his philosophy with a simple-minded arrogance that does none, least of all his followers, any good. By his own lights, Heidegger saw the first Act as bound up with the political "errancy" he was willing to enter into so as to become the philosophical saviour he aspired to be.[63]

Of Heidegger's great, even enduring, philosophical virtues two stand out, and they are closely related: the acuteness of its depiction (to use a term that he rarely does) of modern alienation and the specifically philosophical "contributions" to that alienation.[64] This is not changed by the fact that the repulsion at the machination of human life is a dominant theme of twentieth century thought, including by thinkers (to take a tiny sample) like Weber, Adorno, Marcuse (whose *One Dimensional Man* is but a leftwing application of Heidegger), Benjamin, Buber, Rosenstock-Huessy, Marcel, Ellul, many of whom have little in common with each other and, often, even less with Heidegger. Hence it is no wonder that authors who cannot stomach Heidegger's oratorical formulations, and who focus upon the relationship between those formulations and his politics are often driven to despair by how little writers on Heidegger seem to know about contemporaries of Heidegger who offered far more compelling spiritual and practical alternatives.[65]

Heidegger's most effective disciples, particularly in France,[66] would not merely echo his poeticizings, as his more merely "scholarly" disciples would do—but they would politicize/ethicize, and thereby adjust them by speaking/thinking on behalf of the different groups of the oppressed. Their appropriation of Heidegger, as we will discuss in the following chapter, was part of a broader set of poetic, philosophical, and psychological appropriations and thematics that would forge a rather motley crew in which Marx, Nietzsche, and Sade, among others, would also be marshaled. In many ways they were a French post-Nazi left-wing variant of the same radicalized youthful energies of the Nazi youth that Heidegger had mused upon (at different phases with excitement, hope and exasperated contempt) in the *Black Notebooks*.[67] Not surprisingly in placing their philosophizing and poetics into the service of "politics," in a far more consistent and protracted manner, much of what they took from Heidegger can be espied from his more rarefied peak as caught up in the same will-to-willing he was renouncing. In contrast to the Heideggerean appropriation taking place in France, in Germany the more politicized generation of the 1960s were, in the main, far too scarred by Nazism, to be able to ignore Heidegger's National Socialist past. Hence they much preferred to look for their own radical search for new possibilities to more overtly Marxist teachers like Bloch, Lukács, Marcuse, Adorno, and Benjamin. Likewise in the UK, Heidegger was a latecomer to the left—his way cleared by poststructuralism, which had to counter a much more classical orthodoxy, often including Trotsky as well as Lenin.

If Heidegger's turn against Husserl's "theroeticism" had started with such a devastating critique of his teacher, Heidegger's own philosophy, nevertheless, succumbs to the very metaphysics it seeks to overcome; in a manner confirming Spinoza's/Hegel's "negation is determination," of the sort that Hegel applies in his critique of Kant. Given Heidegger's turning of the tables on Nietzsche this might seem contrived and fatuous. But Heidegger's philosophy is thwarted by a number of fundamentals which lock the philosophy in another variant of the "principle-driven" and "representational picture" that goes back to the idea and attached itself to philosophy with Plato. That is, Heidegger's philosophical and poetic "lapidarianism," his ceaseless nuancing and crafting of words, which extended to the most primordial terminology of his questioning, including Being (*Sein*) itself—sometimes replaced by *Er-eignis*, or the crossed out Sein, or the archaic *Seyn* entrap him in the very thing—philosophy— he is ostensibly overcoming.[68] The irony is that he keeps circling Being by continuously demonstrating language's poetic prowess in overcoming philosophy, yet its inadequacy in the face of its greatest task is the mirror image of Husserl's circling of the phenomenological foundation.[69] The grave weaknesses of Heidegger all require being prefaced by a series of "in spite ofs," which do not prevent the entrapment, even if they do illustrate that, as with any genuine philosopher of importance, there is more to Heidegger than his "errancy."

In spite of: 1) the depth of Heidegger's metaphysical critique of the idea and representation; 2) his emphasis upon historicity, and his opening up the problem of human temporality that liberates us from thinking in merely causal chronological relations and about how the future, present, and past are co-active constituents of our self- and worldmaking; and 3) the turn toward the indispensable-ness of the need for philosophy not to bypass language on the way to thought: Heidegger's poetic philosophy is inadequately historical, and inadequately attuned to language.

These two inadequacies are, in large part generated, by the greatness he wishes to draw to himself on behalf of being a poetic custodian of Being, and, in spite of (to repeat) its powerful diagnostics of the dangers of metaphysics and the role played by metaphysics in our technologicization of ourselves and the world. First, as I have already said, Heidegger's critique of metaphysics is made against the idyllic backdrop whose reality is at times detectable within certain parts for certain moments of the world, and which Heidegger in his *Schwarzwald* sojourns certainly participated in, but the conditions of these dwellings is not simply the "clearings," "lightings" et al. of Being; they involve all manner of non-metaphysically founded social, economic, political, "faithed," and symbolically constituted formations which carve out their own "spaces," frequently through slaughtering and driving out inhabitants already "dwelling" there, and founding their own times. That so much of the human story is a far more savage and precarious one of tribes, empires, nations, religions, revolutionaries, wars of people caught up in their respective "logics" of survival and expansion, and "resource" accumulation, and that so much of it for so long lay outside any kind of metaphysics—so conspicuous in the grim warful history of his beloved Greeks—would be impossible to gauge from the polarization of Being and beings to which Heidegger devotes his philosophical storytelling. Heidegger frequently disparages "historiological" knowledge, but the grander story he tells is one that is but a mythic substitute—a poetic bewitchment over the very real and tumultuous processes of life, death, sacrifice, loss, rejuvenation, and replenishment of peoples.

This is not to deny that Heidegger's analysis of the metaphysical underpinnings of the "theoretical" matrices driving so many modern discourses and institutional decisions devoted to profit, science, planning, resource allocation and the technological "carving up of the world," offers salient and even brilliant insights into much of what we are doing. But insofar as this analysis completely ignores other historical processes that are intrinsic to our appeals, to our hates and loves, to us and our symbolically historically saturated "world," which rests on a far richer historically active, often incubating plethora of powers, memories, narratives, and names than Heidegger's philosophy ever discloses, his philosophy ends up replicating the central defect of metaphysics: the drawing of our existence into the more limited construction that can be "managed" by our ideas and representations.

Heidegger's "idea-istic" substitution of real history by his metaphysical history is amply illustrated by his remarks on Christianity. There has been a great deal written on Heidegger's relationship to Christianity and he has been an important source of philosophical inspiration to some theologians, most notably Rudolf Bultmann and John Macquarie. There have been arguments and discussions about whether his view of Being is essentially the same as can be found in the onto-theological scholastic arguments, or in the more apophatic writings of Meister Eckhart, that God is beyond being. But such discussion is, so to speak, playing on Heidegger's "home ground." Hence such a riposte, even if true, will ignore the question of the symbolic stock and sociological and anthropological emphases that Christianity either inherited, and reshaped, or founded and generated. Heidegger's *Black Notebooks* contain numerous musings upon Christianity; they are mainly acrimonious. For Heidegger, Christians were "seducers of the age,"[70] who wear the "mask for the assertion of a now brittle global domination."[71] "Christianity," he notes, "is the most extreme dehumanisation of man and the de-divinisation of his God."[72] Not only did he detect a deep affinity between Christianity and democracy (which he equated with anarchy)[73] and the spiritual "flattening" of the world,[74] but the Christian Churches were "the great slave holders for great fascism."[75] At one point, and in defiance of any historical facts, he even goes so far as to say: "the modern system of the total dictator arose from Jewish-Christian monotheism."[76] For Heidegger Christianity is in its origins, development and legacy essentially metaphysical. Thus, for him: "the premise of Christianity is the positing of man as a rational animal, whose endurance and salvation is in 'metaphysics.'"[77] "Christianity is metaphysics, which makes of Christian faith a science."[78] As these and many other such musings indicate, Heidegger basically accepts and repeats Nietzsche's equation of Christianity and Platonism. To be sure, Heidegger's own theological training meant that he had least acquainted himself with Catholic, especially scholastic, philosophers. But what is so problematic is his readiness to take the more philosophical and theological narratives of the Church as not only emblematic of the "thing itself" (at the same time we might recall Heidegger denying that any Christian thinking has any real merit as thinking),[79] but as hegemonic rather than as a particular cluster of institutionalized narratives in a far greater, more sprawling enterprise that was never philosophically, let alone metaphysically, driven. The following from "Metaphysics as History of Being" is typical of this flaw of treating Christianity as a metaphysical enterprise:

> Being which has changed to *actualitas* gives to beings as a whole that fundamental characteristic which the representational thinking of the biblical-Christian faith in creation can take over in order to secure metaphysical justification for itself. Conversely, through the dominance of the Christian-ecclesiastical.[80]

That Heidegger can so blithely equate scholastic philosophy with the kind of thinking that is displayed in the Bible itself is indicative of a thinking that pulls all into its own "representations," which, as here, are fundamental misrepresentations. Biblical thinking does not compartmentalize the world and ourselves in a manner commensurate with the Greeks; the Jewish Bible, and hence too the Christian Old Testament, valorizes neither poets, nor philosophers, let alone does it provide orientation in a way that can, with any accuracy, be designated as metaphysical, which is not to deny that subsequent theologians may then treat the more figurative narratives as metaphysical material. Metaphysics inevitably transfigures figurative "language" into conceptual "language." But the Bible is not a story of types or kinds, nor of essences, but it relates contingent events and encounters of the sort that are bound up with a people's relationship to their creator. The people and their God are each revealed over time—as Rosenstock-Huessy in his paean to the "course" of Jewish "lived experiences" (*Ereignisse*) writes: "A people to be created, and the God who will create them, reveal each other mutually. The secret of the people is the secret of God; the omnipotence of God creates people for as long as they obey God more than other men."[81] That story is one that covers multiple generations, trials, achievements and losses. Its focus shifts from the smallest to the grandest, from the hovel and tent to the empire, from the origin to the end of times. Likewise the assortment of its characters, the gamut of its gestures and the diversity of its moods endow it with the same kind of creaturely strengths and weaknesses, hopes and despairs as its creaturely composers. It is polychronic, polyphonic, polygeneric. It is simply—the book. No subsequent book, no matter how much better composed or crafted encompasses the range and combination of contributing voices covering such a vast temporal expanse. It is vaster than any epic in its scope, and more *packed* with interconnected dramas that any drama, which is why it has had such cultural fecundity. Yes it was retrospectively assembled—on multiple occasions to diverse ends: but the discernible lines of continuity of peoples and promise testify to the scale and scope of a work that is nothing less than "people making." The fact that its presence is not limited to being a "thing in itself" but that it plays such a significant role in rite and ritual adds yet another layer of potency to its formative armoury. Only the Koran and hadith have had even remotely comparable impact, and the Koran and hadith, though collected over a protracted time, lack the poly-dimensional features (it is mono-vocal and mono-temporal—at least in its presentation) that are intrinsic to the Bible. Ultimately, though, and for the reader for whom the Bible is simply a "no go/no care zone," the case, though different in scale, but not completely in kind, for a thoughtfulness that is non-metaphysical can be found in drama and dramatic literature where character, encounter, "plot" as the configuration of characters and deeds drawn into a temporal enclave *matter* or (to use a noun as a verb) *"event."* Heidegger's literary choice—poetry, and for that matter, non-epic and, with the occasional exception, non-dramatic poetry—is but one further symptom of the underlying orientation of his thinking: it is literally a thinking without *character*. It passes too much over to the very metaphysics that it seeks to counter.[82]

Those who take their orientation from biblical (as opposed to scholastic) thought do not supplicate themselves before the authorities of the three towering "P's" of Greek thinking—Poetry, Philosophy, Politics. Moreover, the almost total eclipse of Christianity in Western Europe and other parts of the developed world has gone hand in hand with the triumph of the active and reactive powers motivating Heidegger's thinking: the seemingly unstoppable expansion of the totalizing calculative economic and technological machinations; and the reactions of the philosophical (normative/ethical), aesthetic (which as Rosenzweig so brilliantly foresaw is not so much spiritual rejuvenation, but a drug-like distraction from the day to day realities and the routine machinations of daily life), and the political (with infinitely proliferating measures of ambition, control and command).

Heidegger's philosophy, much as Husserl's, much as Descartes's, ultimately rejects tradition as a wave of potencies to be attuned to in favor of the philosopher's decision to "start again." Being conscious of the pulsing currents of a tradition does not automatically provide guidance at any moment of how to act or think about something, but it has incomparable value in its vast stock of names, its massive itinerary of imprints of events, its associative potentials available to the imagination and the understanding.

To be sure, a massive convulsion such as that of the Great War illustrates the enormous collision of forces from traditions vying for survival, or competing for territory as well as alternative futures in a world where zero-sum games between alternative "life-ways" is not altogether unavoidable—and the past is always full of multiple traditions. But this only highlights how important it is to get the diagnosis correct. The vast complex array of forces that constitute modernity, and the challenges confronting modern peoples makes diagnostics the difference between perishing or survival. And the willingness that people have to rush into the armies of the diagnostician prophets like Nietzsche (it is Christianity that is to blame so we should revive paganism and create a superman), Marx (it is capitalism that is to blame so we should be communists, even though we have no idea exactly what that would be), and Heidegger (it is the preoccupation with beings that is to blame so we should thank/think Being) is an alarming indictment of how willing people are to feast off so little, how successful philosophers have been in recruiting on behalf of their ideas and idols, and how desperate people are ready to believe in something or someone in the age of the shadow of God's death. The kind of thinking that looks deep into language and history by its nature is incapable of providing such neat solutions. For the ideas that circulate in language itself are far more porous than those that are designed—to be sure design may be good, but if it is at the expense of all past wisdom and experience it becomes suicidal. Saying this about tradition does not change the fact that we must ever negotiate future and past, and we are ever in the situation of only partial attunement to either. The great and destructive temptation is to seek for a new ideational assemblage, a new philosophy, rather than more humbly dialogically engage with those we encounter as we patiently work through the meanings for the future and from the past in our present: all of which can never be completely unveiled. There are, in other words, simply too many hidden powers to be held in one philosophy: "there are more thing in heavens and earth Horatio, than are dreamt of in your philosophy."

To conclude this account of what Rosenstock-Huessy once mischievously called "Philosophy Secunda"—philosophies which are but the individual derivations by philosophers musing on the far greater stock of social and historical communal experiences—let us turn to the philosophies that now hold so much sway, the philosophies I will encapsulate under the rubric of the anti-domination philosophies.[83] Much "anti-domination" philosophy may be grouped under the banner of poststructuralism, though until that fateful day in Baltimore in 1966, at the aforementioned conference on structuralism, when the young Jacques Derrida delivered his brilliant critique of structuralism, "Structure, Sign and Play," it seemed that the new future of philosophy would be a structuralist one. But, to be fair to those he embarrassed, while Derrida made his philosophical entrance with one hell of a bang, the differences were relatively minor to what they shared. Thus Deleuze, whom I take for the most brilliant of the philosophical poststructuralist, in 1967 still designated the philosophical direction of his time as structuralism: and along with himself he refers to Jacobson, Levi-Strauss, Lacan, Foucault, Dumezil, Althusser, Barthes, Sollers, and even Lewis Carroll.[84] What concerns me, though, is not the nomenclature—for not all the family members I wish to briefly discuss conform either to the rubric of poststructuralist or structuralist. And yet there is a discernible spirit which cannot remain nameless if we are to engage with it, and for all their intellectual wizardry and status they have achieved, they were still just a group of enthusiastic idolaters of the idea, albeit now the most dominant within the "ideas-broking class," who occupy the place formerly occupied by those who pray.

NOTES

1. Herbert Spiegelberg's comment about Husserl is especially pertinent: "While it is true that Husserl is the founder [of phenomenology] and remains the central figure in the Movement, he is also its most radical representative, and that not only in the sense that he tried to go to the roots, and that he kept digging deeper and deeper, often undermining his own earlier results; he was always the most extreme member of his

Movement and hence became increasingly the loneliest of all." Herbert Spiegelberg, *The Phenomenological Movement: A Historical Introduction: Volume 1* (the Hague: Martinus Nijhof, 1965), XVIII.

2. Edmund Husserl, *The Crisis of European Sciences and Transcendental Phenomenology*, translated by David Carr (Evanston, IL: Northwestern University Press, 1970), 265.

3. Thus, for example, he writes to Alexander Pfänder on January 6, 1931. "I arrived at the distressing conclusion that philosophically I have nothing to do with this Heideggerian profundity, with this brilliant unscientific genius; that Heidegger's criticism, both open and veiled, is based upon a gross misunderstanding; that he may be involved in the formation of a philosophical system of the kind which I have always considered it my life's work to make forever impossible." *Edmund Husserl Psychological and Transcendental Phenomenology and The Confrontation with Heidegger (1927–1931)*, translated and edited by Thomas Sheehan and Richard Palmer (Dordrecht: Kluwer, 1997), 482. The collection of marginal comments, in Sheehan and Palmer, on Husserl's copies of *Being and Time* and *Kant and the Problem of Metaphysics* as well as the accompanying essays on them is invaluable. Dorion Cairns informs us that Husserl told his student Eugen Fink that Heidegger simply did not understand the phenomenological reduction. Dorion Cairns, *Conversations with Husserl and Fink* (The Hague: Martinus Nijhof, 1976), Conversation XXVII, 43. Given Heidegger's talent and the length of time the two men spent in each other's philosophical company, this comment cannot but rebound badly on Husserl's own psychological capacities.

4. The translations from Heidegger's *Gesammtausgabe*, 56/57, 89 are by Thomas Sheehan in his "General Introduction Husserl and Heidegger: The Making and Unmaking of a Relationship," in *Edmund Husserl Psychological and Transcendental Phenomenology and The Confrontation with Heidegger (1927–1931)*, 18–19.

5. The translation is from Theodore Kisiel, in Sheehan Ibid., 21. Heidegger's ambition, pride, betrayal, political choices, and his self-serving comments and concealments about his past are of Shakespearean proportions. Of his opportunism, Rosenstock-Huessy relates the story of Elfriede Heidegger saying to a visitor, who while waiting for an audience with the great man noticed the piles of Nazi and Bolshevik books sitting on his desk, that they were waiting to see which group "has the greater chance of winning power" in order to see which political direction they should take. Eugen Rosenstock-Huessy, *Im Kreuz der Wirklichkeit*, Band 2, 52. While interminable amounts have been written on Heidegger's Nazism and with the discovery of the anti-Semitic "musings" in the *Black Note Books* the saga repeats itself with even more intensity, there is a more interesting question, about the relationship between ideas, and character and the world being made. But such a question requires thinking of ideas in terms of how they impact upon people and what people do with and because of them. The kind of thinking that asks either after the rational, or ideological coherence of ideas or their meaning operating *over*, or *apart* from what they *do to* and *in the hands* of people is invariably "idea-ist." Literature had traditionally considered the idea and the person, who acts in accordance with certain ideas, as part of a coherent "whole," i.e., character. Characters are invariably contradictory, sometimes deliberately (they may be hypocrites), sometimes through their own lack of self-knowledge, but also simply because our response to the powers of life are not rationally determined.

6. Cf. Phillip Buckley's neat summary of Husserl—that he had "to do battle with the various forms of thought that have misconceived, and continue to misconceive, misrepresent, or forget human subjectivity in all its wonder," R. Philip Buckley, *Husserl, Heidegger and the Crisis of Philosophical Responsibility* (Dordrecht: Springer, 1992), 3.

7. Edmund Husserl to Eduard Spranger, ca. November 1, 1918 in Bob Sandmeyer, *Husserl's Constitutive Phenomenology: Its Problems and Promise* (New York: Routledge, 2009), 65.

8. See the discussion of the letter to Dietrich Mahnke in Sandmeyer, 66.

9. Dilthey even held a seminar on Husserl's *Logical Investigations*. See all of chapter 2 of Sandmeyer, also Herbert Spiegelberg, *The Phenomenological Movement: A Historical Introduction: Volume 1*, 122–24. Spiegelberg cites a note from Dilthey, written after

"Philosophy as a Rigorous Science had appeared" in which he identifies Husserl as the "most extreme case" of the "Brentano School" of "psychological scholastics" who want to build up life from abstract "entities," Spiegelberg, 123.

10. *Being and Time*, translated by John Macquarie and Edward Robinson (Oxford: Blackwell, 1963), 404 (marginal page number).

11. Friedrich Wilhelm von Hermann, *Hermeneutics and Reflection: Heidegger and Husserl on the Concept of Phenomenology*, translated by Kenneth Maly (Toronto: University of Toronto Press, 2013).

12. Sheehan and Palmer, *Edmund Husserl Psychological and Transcendental Phenomenology and The Confrontation with Heidegger (1927–1931)*, 485.

13. Appendix 10 to "Philosophy in the Age of the World Picture" in Martin Heidegger, *Off the Beaten Track*, translated and edited by Julian Young and Kenneth Haynes (Cambridge: Cambridge University Press, 2002), 82. And from the same essay: "that Dilthey disavowed metaphysics—that, at bottom, he no longer understood its question and stood helpless before metaphysical logic—is the inner consequence of the anthropological character of his fundamental position." Ibid., 75. Richard Palmer recounts a meeting with Heidegger when as a young student, following a seminar with Gadamer and Heidegger, he had tried to make conversation with the latter by commenting on how proud Heidegger must be of his student, Gadamer—to which Heidegger replied: "Do you know his *wirkungsgeschichtliches Bewusstsein?*," only to add, pejoratively, "straight out of Dilthey!" And when the stunned Palmer inquired further with "what do you think of philosophy today?," Heidegger's blunt reply was: "Going to the dogs!" see Richard E. Palmer, *The Gadamer Reader: A Bouquet of His Later Writings* (Evanston, IL: Northwestern University Press, 2007), 323.

14. Martin Heidegger, Preface "to William Richardson, *Heidegger: Through Phenomenology to Thought* (New York: Fordham University Press, 2003 [4th edition]), xiv.

15. Quentin Lauer, *Essays in Hegelian Dialectic* (New York: Fordham University Press, 1977), 41.

16. Lauer, *Essays*, 42. But see the entire chapter "Phenomenology: Hegel and Husserl," 39–60.

17. "Philosophy as Rigorous Science" in *Phenomenology and the Crisis of Philosophy*, translated by Quentin Lauer (New York: Harper and Row, 1965), 76–77.

18. Ibid., 130.

19. Ibid., 77.

20. Quentin Lauer is one of the few philosophers to write substantial works on both Husserl and Hegel. He concludes his chapter comparing them thus: "Perhaps what we should ask of Hegel is that he takes more methodological pains to show where he is going and how he gets there, while asking of Husserl to show us that he is going anywhere at all, and that it is worthwhile going there." Quentin Lauer, *Essays in Hegelian Dialectic* (New York: Fordham University Press, 1977), 59–60, but see the entire chapter "Phenomenology: Hegel and Husserl," 39–60. I am more inclined to think the question to Husserl better posed than the request of Hegel, and that few works are as steeped in methodological pain as Hegel's *Science of Logic*.

21. Edmund Husserl, *Cartesian Meditations; An Introduction to Phenomenology*, translated by Dorion Cairns (The Hague: Martinus Nijhoff, 1960), 2.

22. Ibid., 5.

23. Ibid., 6.

24. Cf. Transcendental "phenomenology uses intentionality to interrogate the sources of that world's meaning and validity for us, the sources that comprise the true meaning of its being. That is precisely the way and the only way, to gain access to all conceivable problems about the world, and beyond them, to the transcendentally disclosed problems of being, not just the old problems raised to the level of their transcendental sense." "Phenomenology and Anthropology" in Sheehan and Palmer, 498. Note the regularity with which Husserl appeals to "intentionality" on the margins of *Being and Time* by way of a justification of his position viz-a-viz Heidegger. Sheehan and Palmer, 263–423.

25. Edmund Burke, *Reflections on the Revolution in France* (Oxford: Oxford University Press, 1999), 87.

26. Stephen K. White, in his *Edmund Burke: Modernity, Politics and Aesthetics* (Lanham, MD: Rowman and Littlefield, 2002), also picks up on affinities between Burke and Heidegger.

27. *Cartesian Meditations*, 11.

28. Ibid., 12.

29. Ibid.

30. "Letter to Alfred Schütz," September 20, 1943. *A Friendship that Lasted a Lifetime: The Corrrespondence Between Alfred Schütz and Eric Voegelin*. Translated by William Petropulos, edited by Gerhard Wagner and Gilbert Weiss (Columbia: University of Missouri Press, 2011), 31.

31. Edmund Husserl, *Philosophy and the Crisis of the European Sciences, The Crisis of European Sciences and Transcendental Phenomenology*, 279.

32. *Op. Cit.* Buckley, 32.

33. Lionel Trilling, *Sincerity and Authenticity* (Cambridge, MA: Harvard University Press, 1972), 27. Though I don't agree with Trilling that Hegel has misread Diderot, 33ff. On the contrary, Diderot is a pivotal player in the Enlightenment. Diderot does accentuate aspects of the Enlightenment (its dark energistic and exotic side) which is also an important part of romanticism. As in so many things, where the average "understanding" presents stark contraries such as Enlightenment and Romanticism, Hegel grasped the inner unity that made any opposition possible, and thus how they share so much more than is usually acknowledged. For Hegel, *Rameau's Nephew* is an important symptom of the one-sided abstract consciousness of Enlightenment. This is brought out for him perfectly in *Rameau's Nephew* with its mockery of tradition and religion. "Wit runs the whole gamut of the serious and the silly! The trivial and the profound, the lofty and the infamous, with complete lack of taste and shame (see Diderot's *Nephew of Rameau*)" *Phenomenology of Spirit*, translated by A. V. Miller, para. 522. And "Enlightenment thinks that it will win its way to men's minds without a painful struggle, and by a simple infection. One fine day the false idols of religion will simply lie flat on the floor before it." para. 545.

34. *Op.Cit.* Buckley, 69.

35. Ibid., Buckley, 70.

36. E.g., *Nietzsche and Phenomenology: Power, Life, Subjectivity*, edited by Élodie Boublil and Christine Daigle (Bloomington: Indiana University Press, 2013)—but see especially Rudolf Boehm's "Husserl and Nietzsche," *Nietzsche and Phenomenology*, edited Andrea Rehberg (Newcastle on Tyne: Cambridge Scholars Press, 2011), Lars Torjussen, "Is Nietzsche a Phenomenologist—Towards a Nietzschean Phenomenology of the Body," in *Analecta Husserliana CIII*, edited by A-T Tymieniecka, 2009, 179–89, Keith Ansell Pearson, "Incorporation and Individuation: On Nietzsche's Use of Phenomenology for Life," *Journal of the British Society for Phenomenology*, vol. 38, no. 1, January 2007, 61–88. Pearson rightly notes insofar as Nietzsche is a naturalist "it is necessary to note, [his] is not the naturalism that is subject to Husserl's criticism, which is a physicalism and objectivism that Nietzsche too would not be content with."

37. Thus, in *Ponderings*, for example, Heidegger notes that "*Being and Time* is a very imperfect attempt to enter into the temporality of *Dasein* in order to ask the question of being for the first time since Parmenides," *Ponderings II-VI, Black Notebooks 1931–1938*, translated by Richard Rojcewicz (Bloomington: Indiana University Press, 2016), 8 (9), and "there is no other option except to write this book [*Being and Time*] and only this book again and again," 24 (55). I would venture that in terms of depicting his own philosophical standpoint as opposed to the metaphysics he is critiquing, "Time and Being," brief as it is, is a perfectly crafted essay that provides an astonishingly pithy outline of his "problematic." Heidegger's relentless "hammerings" upon philosophical and poetic language to wrest from it what he sees as requiring to be thought in an "age of world civilization imprinted by technology," itself an intensification of the "forgottenness of Being" at the heart of Western metaphysics, has created a massive

industry of interpretation which vehemently disputes even the question he asks. Thus out of exasperation one lifelong Heidegger scholar, Thomas Sheehan, has called for a new paradigm of interpretation. According to Thomas Sheehan, "*Sein* was not his final topic," 9. For Sheehan the issue for Heidegger the central problem is "meaning." *Making Sense of Heidegger: A Paradigm Shift* (Lanham, MD: Rowman and Littlefield, 2014). Sheehan's shift of emphasis to the hermeneutical is largely due to Sheehan's frustration with "*Heideggergegacker*" (Heidegger cackling) of Heidegger scholars and the desire to "translate" the spirit of Heidegger. Having attended classes with Heideggeran teachers (Friedrich Wilhelm von Hermann, Werner Marx and Ute Guizzoni) at the University of Freiburg in the mid-1980s I am sympathetic to Sheehan's frustration, but Capobianco's first chapter of *Engaging Heidegger* (Toronto: University of Toronto Press, 2010), shows why, in spite of the book's many virtues, Sheehan takes a step too far. See the next footnote.

38. Cited in Richard Capobianco, *Engaging Heidegger*, 32. To quote from the same letter to the Heidegger colloquium: "the question with which I greet you is the only question that, even up to the present hour, I seek to inquire into ever more inquiringly. One knows this question under the title "the question of Being," Capobianco, 31. For another excellent but critical engagement with Sheehan's reading see Richard Polt, "Meaning, Excess and Event," *Gatherings: The Heidegger Circle Annual*, 1, (2011): 26–53. Cf. Also on possibility: "the impossible is the highest possibility of man: grace or destiny." Martin Heidegger, *Überlegungen, XII-XV, (Schwarze Hefte 1939–1941), Gesamtausgabe, IV Abteilung: Hinweise und Aufzeichnungen Band. 96* (Frankfurt am Main: Vittorio Klostermann, 2014), my translation, 273 (37).

39. To take just a small sample of writings/ lectures, *Hölderlin's Hymn "the Ishter," Elucidations of Hölderlin's Poetry, Hölderlin's Hymne "Andenken," Hölderlin's Hymn "Germania" and "the Rhine,"* "Language in the Poem," "The Thinker as Poet," "What is the Poet For?" (also translated as "Why Poets?"), "Poetically Man Dwells." These and other writings of Heidegger illustrate his appeal to the constant presence of an Other by means of whose "lighting" (if I may borrow from Heidegger), one can see more clearly the nature of metaphysics and its "worlding."

40. "Overcoming Metaphysics" in Martin Heidegger, *The End of Philosophy*, translated by Joan Stambaugh (New York: Harper and Row, 1973), 100.

41. Capobianco has done some excellent detective work in tracking Heidegger's ultimate dissatisfaction with the word "lighting" and his eventual preference for "clearing." See his *Engaging Heidegger*, 87–103.

42. Martin Heidegger, *On the Way to Language*, translated by Peter Hertz (New York: Harper and Row, 1971), 68.

43. "What Are Poets for?" in *Poetry, Language, Thought*, translated by Albert Hofstadter (New York: Harper and Row, 1971), 89.

44. "Letter on Humanism," in Martin Heidegger, *Basic Writings: Nine Key Essays, plus "Introduction to Being and Time,"* edited, translated and introduced by David Farrell Krell (London: Routledge and Kegan Paul, 1978), 217.

45. Ibid., 218.

46. *Ponderings, II-IV*, 16 (512).

47. *Ponderings, II-IV*, 18 (56). Also see "the Thinker as Poet" in *Poetry, Language, Thought*.

48. Quoted in Peter Trawny, *Heidegger and the Myth of the Jewish World Conspiracy*, translated by Andrew J. Mitchell (Chicago: University of Chicago Press, 2015), 75, from Martin Heidegger *Gesamtausgabe, Band 67: Metaphysik und Nihilsmus*, (Frankfurt am Main: Vittorio Klostermannn, 1999), 164. I have latinized the Greek. For Heidegger, as indeed for anyone who identifies what is so radical in the Socratic-Platonic turn, all metaphysical differences between Plato and Aristotle, including Aristotle's critique of Plato's ontology and his subsequent doctrine of the immanence of form in substance, are relatively inconsequential in comparison to what they share. The following from "Metaphysics as History of Being" succinctly formulates the Aristotelian dependency upon the Platonic idea: "Aristotle was able to think *ousia* as *energeia* only

in opposition to *ousia* as idea, so that he also keeps *eidos* as subordinate presence in the essential constitution of the presencing of what is present," in Martin Heidegger, *The End of Philosophy*, 10.

49. "The End of Philosophy and the Task of Thinking," in *On Time and Being*, translated by Joan Stambaugh, (New York: Harper and Row, 1972), 57.

50. To pick one of hundreds of formulations about what is going on: "What is happening? The destruction of the earth–the reciprocal waylaying of peoples along with a bustling about that lacks a direction and a goal." *Ponderings II-VI*, 230 (3). The Nietzschean element in Heidegger's diagnosis "the 'last human being' is raging through Europe," *Ponderings II-VI*, 175 (102).

51. This thematic is repeated so often throughout Heidegger's work that any specific reference is more or less arbitrary. But to someone just coming to Heidegger's critique of metaphysics two places to start would be "Plato's Doctrine of Truth" and "Philosophy in the Age of the World Picture."

52. *On Time and Being*, 57.

53. "What Is Poetry For?" in *Poetry, Language, Thought*, 110.

54. See especially Martin Heidegger, *Überlegungen, XII-XV (Schwarze Hefte 1939–1941), Gesamtausgabe*, 260 (14), where he speaks of "planetarianism (*Planetarismus*)" as "the last step of the machination of the essence of the power for destruction of the indestructible on the way to desertification." Cf. also the claim about planetarianism that it corresponds to idiotism, in the Greek sense of *idion*, the "private person" who finds himself in the "mass order" (*Massenordnung*), 265 (22).

55. *On Time and Being*, 55.

56. *Basic Writings: Nine Key Essays, plus "Introduction to Being and Time*, 242.

57. *On Time and Being*, 60.

58. *Poetry, Language, Thought*, 114.

59. *On the Way to Language*, 134.

60. The publication of the *Schwarze Hefte* (Black Notebooks) has not only reignited the debate about the extent of Heidegger's National Socialism and what it means for his philosophy but among its thirteen hundred pages, it contains some five pages on the Jews. There is no doubt that while Heidegger stuck to his guns in his opposition to Nazi race theory (just another calculative ratiocination and metaphysical deception), in very typically National Socialist fashion, he saw Jewish internationalism as pernicious and the German people as a victim of Jewish machination. According to Heidegger, the Jews invented race theory, but attack the Germans for wanting to live by the same theory; and the Jews are cunning in that other peoples die in wars that Jewish global machination has contributed to/caused. For a good discussion of the matter, see Ingo Farin, "The Black Notebooks in their Historical and Political Context," *Reading Heidegger's Black-Notebooks* (Cambridge, MA: MIT, 2016) edited by Ingo Farin and Jeff Malpas, 289–322. Peter Trawny's *Heidegger and the Myth of the Jewish World Conspiracy* contains translations of the relevant passages. Also see Martin Heidegger, *Anmerkungen I-V (Schwarze Hefte 1942–1948). Gesamtausgabe, Band 97* (Frankfurt am Main: Klostermann, 2015), 20.

61. Guido Schneeberger, *Nachlese zu Heidegger* (Bern: Suhr, 1962).

62. Victor Farias, *Heidegger and Nazism* (Philadelphia: Temple University Press, 1991), and Hugo Ott, *Martin Heidegger: A Political Life* (New York: Basic Books, 1993) both added biographical details which reignited the question of how Nazi Heidegger really was. Thomas Sheehan's "Heidegger and the Nazis," *New York Review of Books*, June 16, 1988, provided an excellent summation of what was new in Farias. Heidegger's enduring animosity to liberal democracy is central to Richard Wolin, *The Politics of Being: The Political Thought of Martin Heidegger* (New York: Columbia University Press, 1990), and his edited collection *The Heidegger Controversy* (Cambridge, MA: MIT Press, 1993). Emmanuel Faye has attempted, very unconvincingly in my view, to discredit every idea Heidegger had as being tainted by his Nazism, *Heidegger: The Introduction of Nazism into Philosophy in Light of the Unpublished Seminars of 1933–1935* (New Haven: Yale University Press, 2011). For a critique of Faye, see Sheehan's "Em-

manuel Faye: The Introduction of Fraud into Philosophy?" in *Philosophy Today*, Volume 59, Issue 3 (Summer 2015).

63. Expressed in the self-serving self-exculpatory formulation: "He who thinks greatly must err greatly," "The Thinker as Poet" in *Poetry, Language, Thought*, 9.

64. Christopher Rickey's *Revolutionary Saints Heidegger, National Socialism and Antinomian Politics* (University Park, PA: University of Pennsylvania Press, 2002) puts it bluntly, but not inaccurately: "Heidegger's aim was to heal the alienation inherent in modernity," 4.

65. Cf. Joseph Agassi's concluding remarks on Buber, Niehbuhr, and George Jacob Holyoake on the cooperative movement, Gustav Landauer's communitarianism, and Einar Thorsrud and his colleagues of the Tavistock group of the movement for the reform of the quality of working life, in his thorough but exasperated review of Rickey in "Heidegger Made Simple (and Offensive)," *Philosophy of the Social Sciences*, Vol. 34 No. 3, September 2004, 423–31. Nevertheless, few other original philosophers (Hegel aside) have provided anything approximating the breadth and depth of Heidegger's readings of the history of philosophy. Were I to have mentioned at every step where I concur or diverge from Heidegger on this or that philosopher, this book would have been still-born at a few thousand pages. On the other hand, Heidegger's deliberations are primarily informed by the direction of his own philosophical path and the choices (the resolve leading to the initial questioning) that dictate that direction. Hence if one sees the path itself as well as some of the initial choices as, at the very least, questionable, then as much as one may applaud and learn from Heidegger's often spell-binding writings on the Pre-Socratics, Plato, Aristotle, Duns Scotus, Descartes, Leibniz, Kant, Hegel, Schelling, and Nietzsche, one who is less inclined to take Heidegger as his guide on them will inevitably be drawn to various other features of these philosophies than Heidegger is. Nevertheless, anyone familiar with Heidegger's writings on the history of philosophy will see that this book is broadly sympathetic to many of the dangers he identifies in key metaphysical moments in the history of philosophy and its entrance into social life. It is also broadly in agreement with Heidegger's belief that a better way of philosophizing must think beyond and outside of philosophy.

66. A number of works discuss the enormous scope of this influence which extends far beyond the more obvious Heideggereans among existentialists and poststructuralists. See Dominque Janicaud, *Heidegger in France* (Bloomington: Indiana University Press, 2015), Tom Rockmore, *Heidegger and French Philosophy: Humanism, Anti-Humanism and Being* (London: Routledge, 1995), and Ethan Kleinberg, *Generation Existential: Heidegger's Philosophy in France, 1927–1961* (Ithaca: Cornell University Press, 2005). Gary Gutting provides a brief comparative analyses of Heidegger, Deleuze, Foucault, and Derrida showing some overlaps and differences in *Thinking the Impossible: French Philosophy Since 1960* (Oxford: Oxford University Press, 2013), 50–56.

67. See *Ponderings, II-IV*, 44 (153), 85 (29), 86 (34), 91 (54). 91 (56), 112 (97).

68. On another matter, it is difficult not to see Heidegger's attempts to represent Being as unbeholden to a metaphysics of presence as moving in terrain already pioneered by Schelling's Absolute, with each time, as Jason Wirth puts it, "alive, an inhaling and exhaling, contracting and expanding, systolic and diastolic force." Jason Wirth, "Translator's Introduction" to *The Ages of the World*, xix. See also Tyler Tritten, *Beyond Presence: The Late F. W. J. Schelling's Criticism of Metaphysics* (Berlin: De Gruyter, 2012), which juxtaposes Schelling with Heidegger and Derrida on metaphysics.

69. Cf. Heidegger's note on *Being and Time*, "there is no other option except to write this book and only this book again and again," *Ponderings II–VI*, 24 (55).

70. *Ponderings, II–IV*, 241 (37).

71. *Ponderings, II–IV*, 380 (180).

72. *Heidegger Gesammtausgabe IV Abteilungen*, 158 (110).

73. *Anmerkungen*, V. 461 (50).

74. *Anmerkungen* V, 459 (57).

75. *Anmerkungen*, III, 247 (43.

76. *Anmerkungen*, V, 438 (10).

77. *Überlegungen XII*, 11 (5).

78. *Anmerkungen II*, 205 (147).

79. "There is no Christian thinking that could be a thinking. *Anmerkungen, II*, 199 (138).

80. *The End of Philosophy*, 14.

81. *Im Kreuz der Wirklickeit*, Band 2, 227.

82. Heidegger's most notable references to tragedy occur in his discussions of Sophoclean tragedy in the 1935 lecture course, An Introduction to Metaphysics, and the lectures on Hölderlin's "Der Ishter." Both discussions confirm the essential point I am making. Cf. also the remark by Véronique M. Fóti in "Heidegger, Hölderlin, and Sophoclean Tragedy" that "Heidegger divorces it [the *Antigone*] from ethical engagement and human action, that is, from the entire praxis component of the vita activa, in favor of his focus on technē and poiēsis," in *Heidegger Toward the Turn* (Albany, NY: SUNY, 1999), edited by James Risser, 180.

83. Thus he writes "we have a *Philosophia prima* of society itself taken as a whole, and a *Philosophia secunda* of individual philosophers in their own thoughts, which we must carefully distinguish." Eugen Rosenstock-Huessy, *In the Cross of Reality: Volume 1, The Hegemony of Spaces*, 91. The mischief lies in Rosenstock-Huessy taking what since Aristotle is commonly the name for metaphysics and applying it to the thought of society as a whole.

84. Gilles Deleuze, "How Do We Recognize Structuralism," in *Desert Islands and Other Texts 1953–1974*, edited by David Lapoujade and translated by Michael Taomina (Los Angeles: Semiotex(e), 2004), 170–92.

TEN

The Chosen Path of the Idea-isms of the 1960s

Anti-domination, Limitless Freedom, and the Politics and Ethics of the Impossible

The difference between the dominant ideas and "values" in the Western world that were taught and published by academics and university publishing houses in the humanities and the arts in higher education in the 1950s and today is a cipher of the transformation of the appeals and motivating spirits that has taken place in that time. The most conspicuous feature of the change is the demarcation of human knowledge along the lines of identity, or group membership, and the kinds of oppression experienced (or in the case of groups such as whites, men, capitalists the oppression created) by members of the identified group. The characteristic defining identity may vary—usually along the lines of class, race, gender, ethnicity, sexuality, and religion. In the 1960s, due to the huge influence of Weber and Marx, class was a common enough variable in sociology and disciplines which drew upon its categories, but the humanities largely gravitated around a core vagary: "humanity."

This appeal to the "human as such" had come under attack by Heidegger and it would form a core component of French structuralist and poststructuralist thought (to loosely deploy this not unproblematic term) of the 1950s, 1960s, and 1970s. In his excellent work *Modern French Philosophy*, a book that originally appeared in 1979, Vincent Descombes quotes the anti-Cartesian and anti-humanist French Heideggerean Jean Beaufret's prescient remark from 1947 that: "So long as philosophy maintains the interiority of being the subject, in whatever form, at the root of its own certainties, it is condemned to organize only the invasion of the world by a haemorrhaging of subjectivity."[1] In France in the 1960s the subject along with cogito-based philosophizing from Descartes through to Sartre, whose popularity had given way to social, psychological, political, and literary analyses by a new generation of stars: Lévi-Strauss, Lacan, Barthes, Kristeva, Derrida, Althusser, Foucault, and Deleuze, among others. While Deleuze was the one of the few to still hold Sartre in esteem, he nevertheless summed up the anti-existential mood in *Difference and Repetition*, when he said the attack upon any philosophy of the subject was "manifestly in the air": "Man did not survive God, nor did the identity of the subject survive that of substance."[2] That too had been the conclusion of *The Order of Things*, the book that established Michel Foucault as a major Parisian intellectual—and if, as many hold, Paris is the center of the intellectual world we might say it is the work that made him one of the most important thinkers in the world. On the final page of that work Foucault wrote what are among the most famous lines of poststructuralism: "man is an invention of recent date. And one perhaps nearing its end," adding ominously, "Man, would be erased, like a face drawn in sand at the edge of the sea."[3] For Foucault the conclusion supports the argument that "the historical analysis of scientific discourse should, in the last resort, be subject, not to a theory of the knowing subject, but rather to a theory of discursive practice."[4] Elsewhere he writes, in a pithy formulation of what is essentially the core thesis of his critique of classical representation running through *The Order of Things*, that the subject "is a place of rest, certainty, reconciliation, a place of tranquillized sleep,"[5] a way of warding off the "researches of psychoanalysis, linguistics, and ethnology [that] have decentred the subject in relation to the laws of his desire, the forms of his language, the rules of his action, or the games of his mythical or fabulous discourse."[6]

Whether rightly or wrongly, critics of the developments that were taking place in the disciplines mentioned by Foucault would complain that it was precisely rigor that was lacking in these authors. Foucault's appeal to the scientific rigor of the analyses he was supporting was a typical, albeit briefly held, motif of authors brandishing the latest discoveries or consensuses from semiotics, structuralist linguistics, and psychoanalyses. Any appeal to a transcendent or transcendental (these two radically distinctive Kantian terms would typically be mixed up) subject was seen as a subversion of the scienticity which would enable a mapping of social operations and praxes.[7] The importance of Louis Althusser's writings on Marx (most notably *For Marx* and *Reading Capital*) lay in its association of Marx with the more "sophisticated" theoretical discoveries in literature, and psychoanalysis, and Foucault's sociological analyses taking place in Paris. Althusser himself would ostensibly mediate Marx through Lacan.[8] His major theoretical "discovery" lay in dividing Marx into a pre-scientific humanist writer of such works as the *1844 Manuscripts*, which Marxists elsewhere had been eagerly absorbing, and one of the greatest scientists of all times, who could take his place alongside Newton and Einstein. Marx's great discovery, according to Althusser, was that we are not subjects, but the bearers of structures. These structures at different "moments" take on positions of relative determinative dominance. Thus Althusser had an answer to why the economy was not always the determining instance, an understandable position if one considers that with the relative strength of Western capitalist economies in the 1950s and 1960s, some other *modus operandi* other than the economic collapse of capitalism was needed by those advocating for its overthrow.[9] Althusser's Marxism was, as Rancière, one of his former students has noted, a context in which the chief problems and solutions were all the conjurings of the intelligentsia.[10]

What would also become an increasingly common complaint by critics of Heidegger, would, at least until the 1980s, also become the predominant criticism made of the anti-humanist structuralist and "poststructuralist" analyses of Althusser, Foucault, Derrida, Kristeva, and numerous others: these theories and strategies, so it was argued, ultimately deprived humanity of any agency, and hence any moral or ethical responsibility. The complaints must have hit their mark. For over the next couple of decades a great shift would take place among the generation of philosophers who blazed like comets against the Parisian skies of the 1960s away from what critics identified as its Nietzschean and Heideggerean nihilism toward ethics. Foucault, for example, in *The Order of Things*, like a seer returning from the dark essence of the world, had decreed: "For modern thought no morality is possible."[11] The same Foucault would say in an interview shortly before he died, and somewhat astonishingly, to anyone who had noted his earlier contempt for moralists but been otherwise unaware of the trajectory of his development, that "In fact what interests me is much more morals than politics, or in any case, politics as an ethics."[12] In his *Archaeology of Knowledge*, Foucault had already informed his readers that his writings were "a "labyrinth," adding pointedly: "Do not ask who I am and do not ask me to remain the same: leave it to our bureaucrats and our police to see that our papers are in order. At least spare us their morality when we write."[13] Given this stance one could fairly register surprise at Foucault (still smarting from Derrida's critique of his ostensible misreading of Descartes, in *The History of Madness*)[14] expressing to John Searle his irritation at Derrida's "obscurantism of terrorism."[15] But by the time Foucault had "outed himself" as an ethicist, he had refashioned himself, along the lines of the ancients, as a parrhēsiastic having the courage to tell the truth to power, as he, and others in his community, turned their attention to "caring for the self."[16] If Foucault had allowed back a view of the subject that could be subject to ethical investigation for the purposes of its own betterment (a kind of intellectually upmarket self-help), Foucault's ground-breaking significance—and hence enthusiastic reception—rested upon his analysis of the subject as subjected. As he put it in "Two Lectures": "subjects are gradually, progressively, really and materially constituted through a multiplicity of organisms, forces, energies, materials, desires, thoughts etc. We should try to grasp subjection in its material instance as a constitution of subjects."[17] The large scale of his influence upon teachers and students in the humanities would be due to the subjections he explored or touched upon in the institutions of the prison, the school, the hospital and clinic, and the confessional. Foucault would map, as he said of his work on prisons (and with some variation of terms one can see this applies equally to all "the manifold forms of domination that can be exercised within society"),[18] "the local, regional, material institutions, which are concerned with torture or imprisonment, and to place these in the climate-at once institutional and physical, regulated and violent-of the effective apparatuses of punishment."[19] The "project" was to identify the modalities and techniques of domination, all the better to expose both their latent nature and ubiquitous brutality. Thus he writes:

> I then wanted to show not only how right is, in a general way, the instrument of this domination which scarcely needs saying—but also to show the extent to which, and the forms in which, right (not simply the laws but the whole complex of apparatuses, institutions and regulations responsible for their application) transmits and puts in motion relations that are not relations of sovereignty, but of domination.[20]

Although Foucault would eventually become one of the most frequently cited voices of social critique, his works, at least until his later "ethical" works, belong to a much greater body of social criticism, in which each author undertook to subject some particular feature of social and political domination, or some aspect of thinking that contributed more generally to social and political domination, to criticism. In France these social critics were broadly united against "the system," though, in their relationships with each other, they often behaved more like members of a squabbling family than a group committed to a common core of radical social and political principles. They would include: Gilles Deleuze and Felix Guattari, with their critiques of Oedipus and the family, their "celebration" of "difference," the nomad, and "lines of flight;" Jacques Derrida, with his textual, deconstructionist depiction of the endless "movement of *supplementarity*," and the "play of the disruption of presence,"[21] and his overall critique of stable meaning and totalization (which extended to Foucault's concept of the *epistēmē*),[22] and his invocation of the empowerment of the marginal; Julia Kristeva, working between structuralist linguistics, semiotics, and psychoanalytics; Jean François Lyotard, with his critique of "grand narratives" and "peregrinations" of the *diffe-*

rend that exposes the disempowerment flowing from the invocation of rules and criteria favoring dominant narratives; Louis Althusser's account of repressive state apparatuses and their interpellations; Jacques Lacan (an older and, in some ways, a much more politically suspicious and conservative figure, but an important source of inspiration for many of the 68ers) in his attempt for his "patients" to find a way to live in their *jouissance* and embrace "the impossibility of the Real," in spite of social demands by the Big Other and the cruel and "insatiable" "parasitical" "character of this moral conscience"[23]; Alain Badiou, whose deployment of set theory, mathematics, and ontology amounts to the invocation "to want what conservatives decree to be impossible";[24] Jean Baudrillard, with his hi-tech Kafkaesque vision of a world of endless simulacra; and, Emmanuel Levinas, whose insistence upon the primacy of the ethical, with its emphasis upon alterity, was belatedly received with widespread enthusiasm, as it was becoming ever more evident that what had so often, at least in France been cast in the form of antinomian revolt, was increasingly being accepted as an ethical, and not merely political stance. Insofar as the reception and reputations of all these philosophers (leaving aside Levinas as a special case) would be inflected through the social revolt in France that found its flashpoint in May 1968, Julian Bourg in his aptly named *From Revolution to Ethics: May 1968 and Contemporary French Thought* rightly observes that "the language of ethics was almost entirely absent among the actors of the May events (of 1968),"[25] and "One of the most important aspects of May 1968 was its manifestation of an antinomian revolt against norms."[26] Equally as arresting as the ethical turnabout in Foucault was Derrida's transformation from the staunch Heideggerean critic of Levinas—laid out in "Violence and Metaphysics: An Essay on the Thought of Emmanuel Levinas"—to a Levinasian. The great shift, though, had every bit as much to do with the change in reception, and in the manner and range of expectations of a generation who now found themselves appointed to academic and other professional positions rather than marching, writing on walls, building make-shift barricades, occupying buildings, and lighting fires. They had, in short, along with a number of other philosophers—"grown up."

Though one antinomian feature that remained within this transition and which was also a strong line of demarcation between the poststructuralists and the analytic tradition had to do with the respective styles of "speech." The importance in France of figures such as Mallarmé, Artaud, and Bataille stood in the closest relationship to the hermeneutical suspicion toward the clarity and distinctiveness of ideas that Descartes had called for, and which was seen as standing in the closest relationship to the fixed stabilities of subject and object that poststructuralist thought was critiquing or "deconstructing." But speech that is at the very "limit" of comprehension is not necessarily meaningless, nor lacking in truth capacity. However, one must "work" at it, parse it in an altogether different manner than what is required for clearer kinds of enunciation. Thus it was not only the energistic convulsions of writers upsetting more stable totalities but as much the linguistic tumult that would figure so decisively in the poststructuralist orientation to the world and self. But even this could be interpreted, and was seen as such, as an ethical elevation, as it was in Levinas' ethics, which was far more sibylline than the more elaborately and tightly argued proceduralist, axiomatic, and linguistic based analyses and investigations of cases or models of (meta-)ethical philosophy that were developing in the UK and USA.

Although different in its sources from the French critics of totalisation and domination, and, originally at least, operating outside of any mutual influence upon each other, the critique of "the rationality of domination,"[27] as Max Horkheimer and Theodor Adorno formulate it, would also be central to the work of German authors, a number of whom would become refugees from fascist Germany. Perhaps the most brilliant and influential was Walter Benjamin, who imagines "the Angel of History" blown by the storms of paradise "irresistibly into the future to which his back is turned, while the debris [of progress] before him grows toward the sky. What we call progress is this storm."[28] Benjamin infuses Marxism with a Jewish messianic potentiality. The historical materialist, like himself, he writes:

> approaches a historical object only where it confronts him as a monad. In this structure he recognizes the sign of a messianic arrest of happening, or (to put it differently) a revolutionary chance in the fight for the oppressed past. He takes cognizance of it in order to blast a specific era out of the homogeneous course of history; thus, he blasts a specific life out of the era, a specific work out of the lifework.[29]

The voices of the silenced and the crushed return to haunt the living on the day of revolutionary judgment. His friend, a leading member of the Frankfurt School, Theodor Adorno, would also consider himself a historical materialist. Like Benjamin, he also adopted the redemptive perspective of a messianic time, a utopia, as a means for assessing just how badly damaged we had become through our processes and instrumentalities of domination. In a famous passage he writes: "the only philosophy which can be responsibly practised in the face of despair is the attempt to contemplate all things as they would present themselves from the standpoint of redemption."[30] Like Georg Lukács who would also be an important theorist for young German Marxists of the 1960s, Ernst Bloch was generally far too close to the Stalinist line. Nevertheless, his *Spirit of Utopia* and three volume magnum opus, *The Principle of Hope* also picked up on the religious and utopian heritage informing Marxism. Other members of the Frankfurt School and critical theorists such as Herbert Marcuse, who like many of the French theorists would supplement Marxism with Freud, depicted the spiritless-ness of an age lacking in real solidarity and communality, while critiquing the oppressive present from the perspective of the emancipated intellectual, who had seen through the instruments and powers of domination. For his part Jürgen Habermas (whom Horkheimer saw as too doctrinaire in his Marxism, and thus threatening the legacy of critical theory that Adorno and himself had built up) would address the communicative distortions and illegitimacies of power flowing of domination.[31] As with the French, the critics of domination in Germany were frequently embroiled in their own quarrels.

Not surprisingly, then, the spats over philosophical accentuations and nuances that differentiated critical theorists from poststructuralists, deconstructionists, and postmodernists could easily occlude the very large common ground they shared. Jürgen Habermas (more Kantian than Nietzschean) in *The Philosophical Discourses of Modernity*, for example, would be highly critical of the lack of normative elements in Foucault and Derrida, reminiscent of Georges Bataille, a major source of inspiration for their generation. Foucault and Derrida were somewhat stunned by the critique. But in post-World War II Germany a left-winger such as Habermas had been privy to an entirely different "reception-history" of the Nazi-tainted Nietzsche and Heidegger than the French anti-Cartesians. In the earlier part of the twentieth century, the amalgam of "irrationalisms" that gave birth to Dadaism, surrealism, situationism, and writers such as Sade, Mallarmé, Lautréamont, Saussure, (Lacanized) Freud, Artaud, Bataille, and Blanchot in France and which were part of the "shock tactics" against bourgeois rationality was also drawn upon to counter fascism.[32] But in Germany Nazism was typically critiqued because of its irrationality—thus the diagnosis in Lukács's *The Destruction of Reason*, or Thomas Mann's allegory about fascism in *Mario and the Magician*. Richard Wolin, a US admirer of critical theory, and a critic of Heidegger and post-Heideggerean thought, is informed by that same hermeneutical trajectory. In Great Britain, Peter Dews' *Logics of Disintegration: Post-structuralist Thought and the Claims of Critical Theory* also argued along these lines. For Dews, poststructuralism succumbed to the disintegrative tendencies which drove its own form of critique, while the superiority of critical theory was due to its "commitment to that coherence of thought which alone ensures its emancipatory power."[33] In the larger scheme of opposition to domination, and in spite of it rendering excellent accounts of the thinkers it discusses, this is, to put it bluntly, complete tosh, implying, as Marx and subsequently Leninists and Stalinists would, that the efficacy of social and political critique must conform to a specific ("materialist") metaphysics and the rectitude of its interpretation. Apart, perhaps, from the squabbles over whether a university philosophy or literary studies department committee might appoint a Habermasian or a Derridean, such claims as Dews's has little to do with political decisions as such, and is symptomatic of the conflation of political action with a "theory" of action that is required to demonstrate the doctrinal purity of one's "idea-ist" faith.

Habermas would eventually make up with Derrida—though, by this stage, both had become "elder statesmen" of the European Union vision. And Derrida would, by way of Levinas, invoke a "weak messianism," not unrelated to Benjamin, and a normative position that seemed to be lifted straight out of Habermas's theory of communicative action, and, which, if probed a little, is burdened with the same problems that make Habermas's thinking so "idea-ist." This is obvious in the following:

> When I speak to you, I am telling you that I promise to tell you some-thing, to tell you the truth. Even if I lie, the condition of my lie is that I promise to tell you the truth. So the promise is not just one speech act among others; every speech act is fundamentally a promise. This uni-versal structure of the promise, of the expectation for the future, for the coming, and the fact that this expectation of the coming has to do with justice–that is what I call the messianic structure. This messianic struc-ture is not limited to what one calls messianisms, that is, Jewish, Chris-tian, or Islamic messianism, to these determinate figures and forms of the Messiah. As soon as you reduce the messianic structure to messian-ism, then you are reducing the universality and this has important political consequences. Then you are accrediting one tradition among others and a notion of an elected people, of a given literal language, a given fundamentalism. That is why I think that the difference, however subtle it may appear, between the messianic and messianism is very important. On the side of messianicity there is faith, no doubt. There is no society without faith, without trust in the other. Even if I abuse this, if I lie or if I commit perjury, if I am violent because of this faith, even on the economic level, there is no society without this faith, this mini-mal act of faith. What one calls credit in capitalism, in economics, has to do with faith, and the economists know that. But this faith is not and should not be reduced or defined by religion as such.[34]

Derrida's "kiss and make up" with Habermas was largely able to take place because Derrida's later writings are far more restrained in their celebration of jouissance than were his earlier writings: age had chas-tened him, and the bad boy had become a model of chivalry.

In literary studies, especially, a slew of younger academics in the US and UK were happy to abandon their own literary traditions to embrace Parisian and German "theories" which would make their reading and teaching of literature take on greater social and political "relevance."[35] But in the UK, more steeped as it was in the less aesthetically developed and more empirical philosophical traditions, the typical reaction to the French style of Derrida, Lacan, et al. was and is akin to what Gerard Manley Hopkins is reported to have said of Robert Browning: "with the air and spirit of a man bouncing up from table with his mouth full of bread and cheese and saying that he meant to stand no blasted nonsense,"[36] or "Victor Meldrew-like" cries of "I can't believe it!" French philosophy from the 1960s was/is mere *"meta-merde,"* as Roger Scruton labels the French '68 philosophers.[37] The British Marxist historian E. P. Thompson's ire at Althusserian anti-empiricist Marxism was an early symptom of the divide of the channel. But as the reception of the French theoretical "style" grew in literary departments, as well as in the visual arts and film studies spreading into politics and even philosophy, and as publishers increasingly fell over themselves to publish anything with "postmodernism" in the title, reactions appeared such as Scruton's mentioned above, Raymond Tallis' *Not Saussure* and *Theorrhoea and After* M. J. Devaney's *"Since at Least Plato . . ." and Other Postmodernist Myths*, and Francis Wheen's *How Mumbo-Jumbo Conquered the World*, or (the eloquently argued case for old fashioned reasonableness) Rainer Friedrich's two part essay, "The Enlightenment: Gone Mad: The Dismal Discourse of Postmodernism's Grand Narrative." [38] Reading critiques of poststructuralism, though, is generally like watching someone trying to nail smoke to the wall. For we are witnessing fundamentally different contingent appeals, and ways of conversing. Having said that, the critique of Alan Sokal and Jean Bricmont, which critically dissects numerous examples taken from physics, set theory, mathematics, topology, etc. used by Lacan, Baudrillard, Deleuze and Guatarri, Kristeva, and Virilio shows how sloppy French (or continental) philosophers could be around more stringent materials. Sokal and Bricmont insisted that politically they were of the left, and clearly think that the preposterous "bull-shitting" in logic and the sciences by the "bull-shitters" does not help the cause, even though they are cautious in identifying what it is precisely they are attacking in these thinkers—they realize that being a "bull-shitter" in some ways does not make one a "bull-shitter" in everything. Needless to say, their criticisms had little impact upon the appeal of these writers: unsurprisingly poststructuralists are a far rarer breed in the disciplines of physics and logic than they are in film or literature.[39] Nevertheless, when faced with the interminable number of examples that Sokal and Bricmont make their case with, it is perfectly understandable why someone reading it thinks it all *"métamerde."*

The widespread nature of that kind of response by those more embedded in the Anglo-American philosophical tradition was exhibited by the (in)famous letter to the *Times* (May 9, 1992) by philosophers as illustrious as Quine, Barry Smith, and David Armstrong protesting the award of an honorary doctorate being conferred on Jacques Derrida, who, they said, offered "little more than semi-intelligible attacks upon the values of reason, truth, and scholarship."[40] Derrida was all too aware of the irony in their criticism, complaining, reasonably enough, that these "critics" say his work "defies comprehension" when they are denouncing its excessive influence," and end up saying that "they themselves have very well understood that there is nothing to understand in my work except the false and the trivial?"[41] Apart from the continental philosophical influences of Hegel, Nietzsche, Husserl, and Heidegger, the French "monsters" of "un-reason" have been spawned by an entirely different set of philosophical and literary/aesthetic/linguistic elements, authorities, and appeals (few of which mean much at all to those in the Anglo-analytic tradition). Not surprisingly, then, it has taken a long time for analytic philosophers to begin to see what is genuinely philosophical and interesting within the "*métamerde.*"

The British tradition had generally been far more cautious in its social critique, though, as in the US, sociological studies and political discussions of social inequality were typical enough, even if Marxism was a rarer plant in the general population than social democracy, and where it did exist was largely consigned to universities. The kind of Marxism that did take academic root in the United Kingdom, which included the likes of the economist Maurice Dobb and geneticist J. S. Haldane, bore little resemblance to the surrealist and Dadaist Marxism of Breton, Aragon, Eduard, Tzara, Bataille et al. in France—it was far more in tune with the sober "science" of economics and the anti-utopianism that Marx had identified in the *Communist Manifesto* and which Engels followed up on in *Socialism: Utopianism and Scientific*.

Nevertheless, a younger generation of Marxists were open to a version of Marxism that extended beyond the classical capitalist vs proletariat dynamic to a broader picture of domination that also extended into culture. These included: the art critic and novelist John Berger; the literary critic and novelist Raymond Williams; his student Terry Eagleton (who to be sure was influenced by Benjamin and for a while sympathetic to poststructuralism before thinking better of it); the founding editor of the *New Left Review*, Stuart Hall, whose *Marxism and the Interpretation of Culture* would be a pivotal work in drawing Marxism into the superstructural accentuations of cultural studies; the historian Perry Anderson; as well as other prominent Marxists such as Robin Blackburn, Alex Callincos, Tariq Ali, and, before crossing over to what looked like pretty standard new-agism, Roy Bhaskar.[42]

As the examples of the British Marxists and figures like Lukács and Bloch illustrate, neither critical theory nor French poststructuralist thought created the paradigm of "anti-domination." But rather there were a slew of anti-domination narratives, not only drawn from (selective rendering and combinations of) Marx, Lenin, Trotsky, Mao, and Gramsci, as in the UK, but also the liberal rights tradition, as evident in the USA by the likes of John Rawls and the legal theorist Ronald Dworkin. Rawls and Dworkin were just as much philosophizing on behalf of a radically just and fair society free from domination as the Marxists or the poststructuralists or critical theorists (even though they were usually cast in a more conservative light by Marxists). Rawls, in particular, was possibly *the* major figure in reigniting the entire discipline of political theory, which to be sure with some notable exceptions such as Hanna Arendt, Leo Strauss, Sheldon Wolin, and Eric Voegelin in the US, and Michael Oakeshott and Isaiah Berlin in the UK, was very marginal within the discipline of political science.

Due to Rawls the study of distributive justice became a minor academic industry. But if Rawls's contribution to political theory was an important moment in redefining a discipline, the fact was that his work was but one more piece in the pluralistic democratic intellectual tradition that had even dominated such behavioral studies of politics as those conducted by Robert Dahl, and the entire discipline of sociology which had risen to such prominence in the United States by the 1950s. As John Cuddihy, picking up on the works of Talcott Parsons and Robert Bellah, has argued, in his sadly neglected study *No Offence: Civil Religion and Protestant Taste*,[43] the sociological advocacy of social pluralism as a means of political mediation between different communities was an academic symptom of the successful entrenchment in the United States of Unitarian Calvinism. Indeed, although French theory and philosophy provided a generation of young PhD students and early career academics in the United States with a heavily stylized, "highbrow" and novel approach to literature and culture more generally, which would make their work not only "relevant" but even hegemonic within the humanities, the fact was that the plurality of different community identities was already an existing reality, as was the awareness of and concern about inequality.[44] Much like the British invasion in popular music, the French theoretical invasion in the United States could be seen as a kind of homecoming—pluralism coming back in a reinvented flashier version. And if the Parsonians, Rawls, and Dworkin did not have the appeal of the Parisians in impacting upon identity or cultural and literary studies, the fact was that their work was part of a broader political transformation that required redefining the value and nature of "merit" for the allocation of office-holding— highly conspicuous in the affirmative action admissions programmes to medical and legal schools and such like. More broadly, changes to legislation to advance minority "rights" and opportunities (even if in *A Thousand Plateaus* Deleuze and Guattari had announced that "Ours is becoming the age of minorities")[45] owed little to French theory, but were one more indicator of the predominance and circulation of the spirit of opposition to "domination." Ultimately it was the paradigm of anti-domination itself, which helped create a platform for the French philosophies of structuralism, poststructuralism, deconstruction, postmodernism, and whatever one may wish to call Levinasian ethics in the United States. Not surprisingly, also, as French intellectuals from the period became stars in the United States, they would tend to loosen their more Parisian 68er anarchic poses and adopt the much more commonplace bargaining "chips" and appeals in the universities in the USA of rights and legalities.[46]

As different as the conditions of "domination" were between regions and cultures, what overshadowed the realities of youth in North America and Europe was the historic reality and "knowledge" of the tremendous catastrophe of the world wars. To be sure, outside of those fighting in Vietnam, or those who were teenagers in Germany's last days of war, this generation was generally too young to have made the sacrifice unto death. But the catastrophe of the Second World War had touched all insofar as it sowed the seeds for a general narrative breakdown among the generation coming of age in the 1960s. Most importantly, this was not only a phenomenon among the losers, but also among the victors.[47] For all around this generation in its growing up were stories and images of war and death camps, of the Nazi horror that has supposedly outdone all horrors.

Marx had famously spoken of capital coming into the world dripping blood from every pore. But mass bloodletting did not start in Great Britain with capitalism. Jefferson had famously stated that the tree of liberty needed nourishment from time to time by the blood of patriots. For blood, not innocence, was the loam not only of the new nations, but, as the Bible wisely identified by making the murderous Cain the founder of the city, of all settlement, ancient as well as modern. Likewise, bloodletting seems to have even been the norm rather than the exception in tribal societies.[48] If bloodshed has generally been more typical of human experience than what the post-Second World War generation thought, the fact remained that they themselves were the products of faith in the goodness of people and peace as a natural condition. Hence they were charged with ensuring we could be restored to our natural condition, and all this required was ensuring that the various poisonous "fascisms" that had been incubating in the West be cut out.

Even leaping back to before the Second World War as well as its immediate aftermath, no matter how abstract, and poorly or bullishly thought through, it was generally the political left who forced the victors to confront the dark and bloody truths that were their own history. People furious at the extent of human suffering wrote, spoke, taught, made films—and above all smashed through the narrative fabrications that had served as mythic totems of good conscience. Who could not have a bad conscience?—provided, of course, one had been "cultivated" in such a way as to believe in the moral goodness and providence of one's nation's foundations. The aftermath of the Second World War, with its spread of mass education, was an age where the overwhelming questions were: what has happened? why did it happen? who is really to blame? The nineteenth century secular eschatologists, Marx and Nietzsche, had a new relevance for a generation who had lost all faith in a certain kind of innocence and faith in the moral purity of past founders of modern liberal and democratic political institutions. The new innocence and new purity would be projected onto the future and placed upon the shoulders of the young and innocent—too young to have blood on their hands, and determined not to do so. This was above all a revolution of "new" ideas and the new ideas inevitably were defined in relationship to a rotten past, which would ultimately come to mean everything. And all had their own rotten past whose features were all too evident in their present.

In the United States, that past was the extent and horror of slavery and the ongoing segregationist and denial of rights to blacks, the destruction wrought upon Native Americans through disease, the extermination of bison, forced removal from traditional land, broken treaties, and wars. Then, there had been the explosion of the atom bomb, when the war was all but over. Thus it was that the Vietnam War could be read as one more symptom of all that was wrong with the United States.

The history across the Atlantic was different in the details, but its past burdens and reasons for guilt no less onerous. As in the USA, there was a great gulf between the generation who fought in the Second World War, and the generation of those who were children or born during or just after it. When a child of the immediate post-World War Two generation entered primary school in the UK, the British Empire, though largely over, was still taught as a sign of Britain's greatness. Maps hung on classroom walls proudly displaying the extent of the Commonwealth at its height, in pink. When those same children entered university, they learned that the empire was not a testimony to the greatness of a civilization but a monument of shame.

French guilt was of a particular variety. For whereas the Germans knew that most of their parents and relatives had been butchers or silent accomplices to the holocaust, the French had largely concealed the speed and scale of their capitulation, but the degree of their complicity in not only fighting alongside Germany after that capitulation, but in the willingness of so many to hand over Jews to the Gestapo. All of this shame was barely papered over by the myth of the scale of the resistance.

It is hard to know for certain where genuine guilt and trauma about the past ended and the moral inexperience and idealism of youth began—but they flowed effortlessly into each other. But the fact remains that the politicization of the generation of young French, German, North Americans, British, Australians, and others cannot be separated from the common appeal to, and deployment of shame against myths and symbols that once were the very lifeblood of communal solidarity. This sense of shame as well as the desire to create a new world free from all this horror eventually found a great variety of applications, thus fueling feminism, black liberation, indigenous rights and/or separatists's activism, environmentalism, gay liberation, anti-colonialism, the campaign against nuclear arms, and (in the US and Australia) demonstrations against the Vietnam War. All these movements took place with various degrees of theoretical sophistication and nuance. They were also occurring as new attitudes to pleasures, especially sexuality (the invention of a pill blasting away what was seen as the prudery and prejudice of two millennia of Christian neurosis), appearance and style generally had radically transformed youth. What had been sexually shocking for their parents quickly became as much the norm as what had once been artistically and visually shocking. Perhaps most conspicuous of all was the music which blew down the old walls of social encrustation. At its most socially powerful, music would lyrically, sonically, and melodically synoptically formulate "ideas" that would be theoretically developed, with far greater prolixity in entire fields of study. Does Judith Butler add anything more than "words" and "theory" to Velvet Underground's playing with transgression or Ray Davies "Lola" with its girls being boys and boys being girls in the mixed-up world? Likewise, "I am woman" may have been a commercially opportune "hit" that was sonically bland and lyrically trite, but it summed up the spirit of Gloria Steinem, Germaine Greer, Betty Friedan, and so many others in three words.

In sum, and in different ways artists, movements, philosophers, and young people were all saying a great No to the world they were heirs to. They were also saying Yes to the antonym of domination—emancipation. What exactly "emancipation" meant would vary from very precise demands such as to stop the war in Vietnam or end segregation and laws of racial discrimination in parts of the United States to the far vaguer and more abstract demands to "overthrow the system." More generally, though, it became a matter of listening to the voices of, and securing more power for the "minorities"—who were all construed in some way as the subjugated and marginalized. Behind this vision—which is still the most prevalent way of forming ideas in the humanities in the United States, United Kingdom, Australasia, and to a lesser, though, not insignificant extent in Western Europe—was the idea that disadvantage was *de facto* injustice, that misery was caused by someone gaining something: men gained from women, straights from gays, whites from blacks. There was also, in most cases, an acceptance of the assumption that derived from social contract theory (which Rawls would attempt to theoretically justify) that equality was both a natural and achievable condition. Where it did not exist it was because some injustice had occurred. Thus, for example, women earned less because men oppressed them was but an extension of the idea that men and women should or might have been equal had it not been for males wanting to enslave all women. The complexities of gender, mores, interests, historicity could be easily cut through by the domination principle or model. From within the perspective, the answer to whose advantage the family existed was all too obvious—and in the academy only a malfeasant could quibble: it existed to institute the oppression of women. There was evidence to support this. Indeed, pre-feminists historical accounts took for granted that war and plunder and sexual enslavement were what warriors did, and that warriors were the walls of civilizations (unashamedly depicted in the stand-off between Achilles and Agamemnon in that foundational poem of the Greeks *The Iliad*). Men were physically stronger and wanted sex—women, on the other hand, were more vulnerable and sought a protector. But it was also undeniable that pagan tribes and empires had little in common with the post-Calvinist and bourgeois mores consolidated by the professional classes spearheading the French and Russian revolutions that provide the cultural loam for ideas appealing to freedom and equality, the abolition of the family, and religion. Nevertheless, historians writing prior to the anti-domination model of social life also indicate that the family provided a degree of mutual benefit, and it involved different kinds of sacrifice from its social members. Men of sufficient age and strength had to be prepared to sacrifice their lives to protect their women and their children, women had to preserve the hearth. There were no men and women as such, there were the women and men of specific locations and traditions in constant potential conflict with other men and women. The slave would be a benefit to women as well as to men; just as enslavement could befall the vanquished whether one was a man or a woman. In the premodern world, the reciprocity of social roles was intrinsically allied with the different obligations according to age, gender, and class.

In sum, the anti-domination model enabled women (and minorities) to read the past in order to illumine the dark thickets of human record and memory, to bring into the light the scale and extent of oppression in order to bring about its end. The dyadic "idea" of "domination/anti-domination" was the light of empowerment for those who had ostensibly suffered injustice through lack of power. It was not just rights that were needed, but power, just as it was not simply the lack of rights, but the social construction of the entire system was one in which power was domination.

The great luminosity of the idea of "domination/ anti-domination," however, also meant that other questions, and other aspects of history were generally occluded, downplayed, ignored. To raise this, though, was easily taken as a confirmation that the person asking such a question was merely being complicit with those who benefited from injustice. Thus, the injustice and the suffering was too great to require too much nuancing. In this respect, like every paradigm, the idea served to wall-off questions as well as preserve the acquired knowledge and within the narratives of the citadel of expertise. And as with every paradigm, the question is: How sound are the joins, and structural features which support the large body of knowledge? What questions threaten to bring about the collapse of an entire body of knowledge, and hence also threatens the professional credibility of those who operate under the unassailable authority of the idea? The paradigm also serves as a cipher of a particular kind of self, a self that is not at all universal (and anti-universalism was a recurrent feature of many wings of anti-domination philosophy). For the idea emerges at a particular moment, and it services, and is serviced by, a particular interest—in the case of feminism the interest of a new class of professional women. This class of women did what all wielders of ideas for social transformation do: they read the world through the prism of their interest. They went looking for themselves in history and found they were not there. They found, with a few notable exceptions, women who lived the kinds of lives they did not want to live. That most men were living precarious and wretched lives was not the issue for them. Why should it be? That was not in their interest, any more than it was in the interest of any other group pushing for power to share its power. Feminist theory would examine the anthropological and onto-logical assumptions of past and present knowledge so that reason itself, it was argued, had previously been man writ large.[49] And, again, much evidence could be found to support this claim.

Seen retrospectively, then, it is obvious why Benjamin's history of the repressed, Habermas' theory of communicative action, Adorno's attack upon identity in *Negative Dialectic*, as well as the French theorists with their different kinds of difference, or cultural studies would be so theoret-ically appealing—and why the differences between the authors and "movements," when considered in light of the larger picture of human society, amounted to an idealization of the identities that were to be emancipated, and a representation of the past as a story of a privileged few overpowering the greater majority of human kind. And, to repeat, there was plenty of evidence to support this view. Though, one did have to largely ignore the same fact that Marx had also downplayed: that group conflict in the struggle for survival, territory, and resources (in-cluding "man power") had traditionally been largely horizontal and not just, or even primarily, vertical, and that societies are essentially "protec-tion" operations, at best, or, at worst, "rackets," in which some sacrifice their lives (and earn spoils from this) so that others can survive, though they must pay the protectors. But it was also true, as the French and Russian revolutions had driven home, that authorities who lived off their past sacrificial responsibilities, and who were seen as no longer playing any such role, but were living off the sacrifice of others, had no real future. Further, the industrialization and professionalization of urban life had created a world of potential material abundance, as well as ambition, and a desire for opportunities and power on an heretofore unprecedent-ed scale. That is, the anti-domination/domination dyadic idea became a dominant idea at a time when the opportunities to enjoy the advantages of socioeconomic powers were so abundant, and among other things, the traditional roles and expectations were seen by many as an impediment to those advantages. The language of power was largely cast in the kind of geometrical and axiomatic terms that Burke had discerned in Rous-seau, and one major reason it could be invoked so regularly was that the ideas of justice, equality, opportunity, seemed to be so readily applicable to the kind of world people were living in. I add one caveat, that is still relevant: in the West.

However, before the politicization of the different "minority voices" with their singularized identity-demands were settled was the broader and more generalized cry of youth simply for freedom. In his reflections on May 1968 in Nantes and Paris, Michel de Certeau would sum up the demands and street cries with the observation that "today it is imprisoned speech that was freed." [50] The speech that had been "set free" was the speech of freedom itself, freedom not to be part of a world gone so wrong. It was a romanticist, ultimately a "child's" view of freedom as absolute, an uncompromising all or nothing that could just be plucked from the air if one willed it so and fought against *the system*, which was rotten to the core. The placards and graffiti of 1968 serve as perfect ciphers of the spirits of the time: "Be realistic: Demand the Impossible"; "the barricade blocks the street but opens the way"; "No replastering, the structure is rotten"; "those who make revolutions by halves do but dig themselves a grave"; "We will claim nothing, we will ask for nothing. We will take, we will occupy"; "In a society that has abolished all adventures, the only adventure left is to abolish society"; "All that is sacred—there is the enemy"; "We are all German Jews." [51]

The sense of victimhood in the last example is a particularly telling cipher of what is both sensitivity to the world's suffering, and a parody of the very suffering that the students claimed to represent but, especially in France, where there was no conscription, did not actually bear. It was this sense of the intolerableness, the total injustice of the world as the students saw it that found its outlet in the tones of total defiance and romantic yearning. Although Paris was gripped by strikes, and although there were barricades and Molotov cocktails, smashed windows, burnt cars, police using truncheons, students throwing stones, this was never a civil war, which had almost always (albeit sometimes belatedly) been the *sine qua non* of revolutionary regime change. An election was called to resolve the situation and although there were subsequent demonstrations, everything appeared to go back to normal. But this did not mean, as Alexander Kojéve is reported to have said that "since there had been no bloodshed nothing had happened." [52] The totality of the act of defiance had erupted, but the very nature of what it was that was being attacked—"All that is sacred"—meant that it would take time to break down the wider faith that had built up over time in the institutions and loyalties that this segment of this generation did not share.

Another piece of graffiti put it remarkably succinctly: "Building a revolution is also breaking all the inner chains." This was precisely what the students could and eventually did do, though the one thing they could not radically change was the most resilient of material conditions: the economy itself. This was an obstacle that was to be bypassed in much the same way by Benjamin and German/American critical theorists and British exponents of cultural studies, that is, by dwelling primarily upon what could be "captured" culturally: the superstructure. The radical students of 1968 spoke interminably about how bad society was, and how there was something better, but there was no clue as to how to create the material conditions for social reproduction: the best on offer was Marxism *redux*, but more commonly it was just assumed that anything had to be better. As the horrors of Pol Pot would illustrate, as the other large scale horror that had taken place approximately a decade earlier in China, with the Great Leap Forward, had also shown: political revolt and social collapse can make for a world infinitely more cruel and bloody than that engendered through the structural inequities of modern commercial industrial Western societies.

Speech is, indeed, an important component of social and political coordination, but the workers who briefly tied in their lot with the students quickly saw that these interests, in the longer term, did not coincide. The students were the privileged for whom powerful positions would eventually be allocated, and until then, their parents would foot the bill. This "taking for granted" of the economy and other institutions which had been paid with sacrificial blood of earlier generations was as typical of the philosophies of the period as the student movement.

According to Levinas, "the 1968 Revolt in Paris was a revolt of sadness,"[53] a sadness that he believed came out of the realization of the failure of communism to deliver salvation. This is akin to a child's sadness upon discovering that there is no Santa Claus. Serious theoretical criticisms of why communism could not work had been mounting up since the nineteenth century with such works as Eugen Böhm-Bawerk's *Karl Marx and the Close of His System*. As we also argued earlier in the discussion of Marx, in large scale societies there is also the need for a market with its information gathering methods and processes which may be far more efficiently and swiftly generated in economic action and hence not simply subjected to centralized computation and guess work. There is also the need for a state, and for lawyers, and interest groups will invariably seek to have legislators serve their interests. To think these matters mere quibbles is intellectually derelict, but what matters such dereliction when it is the "impossible" one is striving for?

The students shared Marx's social vision of calling upon negations— to repeat a point we made earlier: there would be no alienation, and no poverty, because there was no money, law, state, religion, family, property, nor division of labor. Processes and events which took eons to establish in order to better survive the perils and fragility of group survival are, from this way of thinking, mere "social constructions," "ideas" that can be easily represented on the blackboard in a classroom, and just as easily wiped away. Those who teach these ideas, though, do not actually have to survive without money, state, law, or property or production occurring through a division of labor (religion and family are different insofar as one can opt out them). In this respect the ideas of 1968 were a more "sexed-up" version of the neo-Hegelian ideas of the 1840s.

"Underneath the stones—the beach!" was another 68 slogan/placard, a distant echo of Montaigne's essay "On Cannibalism" held up only to be put to the sword by Shakespeare in the *Tempest*, as the good natured, but incessantly optimistic babbler, Gonzalo engages with the two mocking cutthroats Antonio and Sebastian, who would immediately murder Gonzalo, and enslave all they could, if his dream of being king on the isle were realized:

Gonzalo: Had I plantation of this isle, my lord,—

Antonio: He'ld sow't with nettle-seed.

Sebastian: Or docks, or mallows.

Gonzalo: And were the king on't, what would I do?

Sebastian: 'Scape being drunk for want of wine.

Gonzalo: I' the commonwealth I would by contraries

Execute all things; for no kind of traffic

Would I admit; no name of magistrate;

Letters should not be known; riches, poverty,

And use of service, none; contract, succession,

Bourn, bound of land, tilth, vineyard, none;

No use of metal, corn, or wine, or oil;

No occupation; all men idle, all;

And women too, but innocent and pure;

No sovereignty;—

Sebastian: Yet he would be king on't.

Antonio: The latter end of his commonwealth forgets the beginning.

Gonzalo: All things in common nature should produce

Without sweat or endeavour: treason, felony,

Sword, pike, knife, gun, or need of any engine,

Would I not have; but nature should bring forth,

Of its own kind, all foison, all abundance,

To feed my innocent people.

Sebastian: No marrying 'mong his subjects?

Antonio: None, man; all idle: whores and knaves.

Gonzalo: I would with such perfection govern, sir,

To excel the golden age.[54]

That such a large number of intellectuals demonstrated as much knowledge about the ways of the world as Gonzalo and chose to ignore the
rudiments of economic analyses, far preferring Bataille's anthropological
frenzied accounts of potlatch, excess and blood sacrifice and magical invocations of a non-capitalist future (all of which are undoubtedly more
thrilling than any economic formulae) might well illustrate a kind of
political commitment and a desire that the world be a certain way that it
had never been before. But this hardly makes it anything other than one
more idea, whose substance (what actually occurs once there is an attempt to implement a society without property—civil war, bureaucracy,
total statism, etc.) is the dark abyss and antithesis of what the idea
"should" be.

Communism was a blank check promising and requiring the ultimate
of human beings so that they could partake, to quote Marx himself, in a
society run by the principle "from each according to his ability to each
according to his needs." The idea that human beings are infinitely giving
and neighborly is but an intensified version of Pelagian faith in the goodness of the human essence, which is to say it is a theological idea that
requires not seeing what humans have collectively always consistently
done: screw-up, or to put it in the theological parlance of Pelagius' critic,
Augustine, fall into "original sin."

But the Marxism of the 68ers was the Marxism that had not actually
gone through the birth pangs and trials of incarnation. The philosophical
ideals of this generation would undergo transformation as the tension
between the impossible of "total freedom" that was reached for and the
humdrum of social reproduction veered inexorably, dragging all along
its vector, to the actual.

One French intellectual who explored the importance of the demand
for "total freedom," in the context of its results, was Albert Camus.[55] He
was dead by the time of the revolts of 1968. He was also largely unloved

by the philosophers and writers whose philosophies and political stances would ride the wave and seek to lead the way of the '68ers. Echoes of his voice, however, were belatedly present in the critiques of Marxism aired by the "new philosophers" of the 1970s. But them aside, the fact that in 1949 Camus had written *The Rebel*, which had provided a devastating critique of totality and teleological views of history which renders Lyotard's attack on grand narratives superfluous was simply ignored. *The Rebel* was Camus' diagnosis of the intellectual currents that had created a century reveling in political murder.[56] At the core of his diagnosis was the search for a freedom and justice so total that they amounted to what he called "metaphysical rebellion." For Camus:

> Metaphysical rebellion is the movement by which man protests against his condition and against the whole of creation. It is metaphysical because it contests the ends of man and of creation. The slave protests against the condition in which he finds himself within his state of slavery; the metaphysical rebel protests against the condition in which he finds himself as a man. The rebel slave affirms that there is something in him that will not tolerate the manner in which his master treats him; the metaphysical rebel declares that he is frustrated by the universe. For both of them, it is not only a question of pure and simple negation. In both cases, in fact, we find a value judgment in the name of which the rebel refuses to approve the condition in which he finds himself.[57]

Camus had also identified the Marquis de Sade as the thinker who first expressed this point of view:

> Historically speaking, the first coherent offensive is that of Sade, who musters into one vast war machine the arguments of the freethinkers up to Father Meslier and Voltaire. His negation is also, of course, the most extreme. From rebellion Sade can only deduce an absolute negative. Twenty-seven years in prison do not, in fact, produce a very conciliatory form of intelligence. Such a long period of confinement produces either weaklings or killers and sometimes a combination of both. If the mind is strong enough to construct in a prison cell a moral philosophy that is not one of submission, it will generally be one of domination. Every ethic based on solitude implies the exercise of power. In this respect Sade is the archetype, for in so far as society treated him atrociously, he responded in an atrocious manner. The writer, despite a few happy phrases and the thoughtless praises of our contemporaries, is secondary. He is admired today, with so much ingenuity, for reasons which have nothing to do with literature.
>
> He is exalted as the philosopher in chains and the first theoretician of absolute rebellion. He might well have been. In prison, dreams have no limits and reality is no curb. Intelligence in chains loses in lucidity what it gains in intensity. The only logic known to Sade was the logic of his feelings. He did not create a philosophy, but pursued a monstrous dream of revenge. Only the dream turned out to be prophetic. His desperate demand for freedom led Sade into the kingdom of servitude;

his inordinate thirst for a form of life he could never attain was as-
suaged in the successive frenzies of a dream of universal destruction.
In this way, at least, Sade is our contemporary.[58]

And:

Sade, in reality, obeys no other law than that of inexhaustible desire.
But to desire without limit is the equivalent of being desired without
limit. License to destroy supposes that you yourself can be destroyed.
Therefore you must struggle and dominate. The law of this world is
nothing but the law of force; its driving force, the will to power.[59]

This linkage, identified by Camus, between Sade's absolute rebellion and
Nietzsche's will to power was precisely the kind of alliance, which would
also include Marx, that was taking hold in the French intellectual imagination even in the late 1940s. Georges Bataille had put the case for Sade's
importance and revolutionary credentials in his "The Use Value of D. A.
F. de Sade—Open Letter to My Current Comrades," where he wrote:

During the revolutionary phase, the current phase that will only end
with the world triumph of socialism, only the social Revolution can
serve as an outlet for collective impulses, and no other activity can be
envisaged in practice.

But the postrevolutionary phase implies the necessity of a division
between the economic political organization of society on one hand,
and on the other, an antireligious and asocial organization having as its
goal orgiastic participation in different forms of destruction. In other
words, the collective satisfaction of needs that correspond to the necessity of provoking the violent excitation that results from the expulsion
of heterogenous elements.

Such an organization can have no other conception of morality than
the one scandalously affirmed for the first time by the Marquis de
Sade.[60]

Bataille's search for the limit experience, a vital reason for existence as
much a defiance as a celebration against the utilitarian and mechanistic
world, marshals the shocking carnivalesque grand theatres where *jouissance* is cruelty, rape (frequently of children), torture, mass murder.
Whereas there have been countless examples of murdering Sadists fuel-
ling their imaginations with the divine marquis, Bataille and the literary
and philosophical circles stress the "writerly" imaginative play behind
the boundlessness and excess. Thus, for example Blanchot, writes of
Sade:

He is nothing more than a writer, and he depicts life raised to the level
of a passion, a passion which has become cruelty and madness. He
turns the most bizarre, most hidden, the most unreasonable kind of
feeling into a universal affirmation, the reality of a public statement
which is consigned to history to become a legitimate explanation of a
man's general condition. He is, finally, negation itself: his *oeuvre* is

nothing but the work of negation, his experience the action of furious negation, driven to blood, denying other people, denying God, denying nature and . . . , revelling in itself as absolute sovereignty.[61]

In an intellectual landscape that has so lost its moral bearing that it finds Sade's apologetics for libertine murders mere "writing," in a world in which anything and everything is demanded, and in a group whose chief currency and source of status and economic agency is their "learning" and their "words," it is not surprising that this group would set itself up as ethical instructors. They were to the more intellectually well-bred what the self-help books would be to the new-agers, and what the vision and mission statements were to the managerialists: symptoms of the kinds of ideas that were forming an "idea-ocratic" world, a world in which more sacrificial, visceral, and tragic features of reality were being blasted away with words which were realizing the "impossible."

THE STRUGGLE OF IDEAS BETWEEN ANTI-DOMINATION PHILOSOPHIES AND UBIQUITOUS FASCISM—ANTI-TOTALIZATION

In many ways Hegel, as an apologist of all that he blessed as rational— state, family, law, ethical life, history, etc.—with his implacable rejection and refutation of any concepts that derived from nothing more substantial than the beyond (*Jenseits*) of the soul's own abstract longing was the antithesis of Marx and Sade. Indeed he was perceived as an intolerable reactionary to the generation of the 1840s who found neither dwelling nor reconciliation with the institutions that constituted their reality. But Hegel, after being forced into a period of protracted slumber, was revived. And to the generation of philosophers working in France in the 1930s and 1940s, he along with Husserl and Heidegger had become a decisive figure in the shaping of French thought by the middle of the twentieth century. Aside from the writings of Jean Wahl's book on the unhappy consciousness in Hegel (1929) and Jean Hyppolite's *Genesis and Structure of Hegel's Phenomenology* (1947), it was Alexander Kojéve's lectures on Hegel, attended by everybody who was anybody, and recorded for posterity by the novelist and poet Raymond Queneau, that captured the spirit of French philosophy from the 1940s until Hegel's suffered philosophical regicide at the hands of a number of the leading lights of the 68ers. Kojéve's Hegel had foretold the "end of history." In Kojéve's account Hegel's historical rationality drew its primary sustenance from the battle between master and slave for recognition—and when that battle ceased basically there was little left worth living for. Humanity would bore itself to death under the empty yet enormous weight of its own triumph. This Hegel bore only passing resemblances to the "old boy" (as Marx would fondly refer to him in reminiscences with Engels) who had dispensed with the idea of making the *Phenomenology* the introduction to his system; the account of the master-slave dialectic then appeared in the *Encyclopedia* as a necessary, but only partial, moment in the development of Absolute Spirit.

In his discussion of Hegel in France, Vincent Descombes makes three particularly pertinent points. The first was that Kojéve's Hegel provided "a *terrorist conception of history*" —that is to say he was a revolutionary Hegel along the lines that we also can find in Marcuse, and Žižek.[62] Second, "[i]n 1945 . . . all that was modern [in French philosophy] sprang from Hegel," while, thirdly, "[i]n 1968 all that was modern—that is Marx, Freud etc. as before—was hostile to Hegel." Thus the 68er anti-Hegelian philosophy, as the neo-Hegelian reaction had been, was very much a generational reaction to a spirit that was abandoned as not being sufficiently revolutionary, even though, ironically, the French Hegel had generally played a far more rebellious role in inciting the mind-set of French intellectuals than he had in Germany.[63] But the idea that one had to accept a totality, even one as dynamic as Hegel's, in which history mattered as a rationalizing power more than the desires to create a new future, was hard for a generation who had no faith in their immediate past. And in the case of the French the fact was that the intellectual capitulation to Nazism was on the same grand scale as the rest of the nation: when it came to action, the overwhelming majority of intellectuals under Nazism (Camus and a few others were notable exceptions) had not acted, as Sartre's philosophy had incessantly preached, heroically and freely, but, as with Sartre himself, with the more routine complicity of keeping one's head bowed in bad faith.

In their complicity, the French who had supped off Hegel's conception of freedom but done nothing to actualize the great irrational threats to it, had been weak and deluded. No wonder Gilles Deleuze and Guattari and Foucault, in particular, despised Hegel's legacy—by dubiously making Hegel responsible for acquiescence with fascism. Althusser, contrary to Marx's own Hegelian allegiances, attempted to strike out all vestiges of Hegel in Marx, and his allegiance with poststructuralism was part of a generational anti-Hegelianism. The other figure who could be marshaled into the anti-Hegelian and anti-dialectical camp was Nietzsche (who had also been the subject of books by Bataille and Klossowski). As Deleuze wrote in *Nietzsche and Philosophy*, "modern philosophy has largely lived off Nietzsche."[64] As for Schopenhauer, again Deleuze provided the essential reason why he was not of much use to the 68ers: he, like Kant, remains too close to existing values, and thus was not radical enough.[65]

After fascism, though, Nietzsche's revival (which took almost two generations after the Second World War in Germany, but was incorporated by French philosophers in the 1960s in France) dispensed with the eugenicist and physiological emphases that the Nazis had enthused over.

Poststructuralists, on the other hand, simply matched Nietzschean energistics with Marxian political objectives; in a manner not altogether dissimilar from Georges Sorel's Nietzschean/Marxian/populist hybrid, albeit without Sorel's openness to fascism.

But it was not only the physiologics that poststructuralist Nietzscheans dispensed with: the philosophy was immediately severed from the socio-cultural and ultimately political ends which Nietzsche unashamedly advances: his ends were anti-democratic, anti-feminist, anti-socialist, and anti-anarchist—all these modern movements were, for him, the modern fruits of the Christian tree which he wished to tear out root and branch. If one compares Nietzsche's pagan revivalism with that of Deleuze and Guattari's, it is immediately conspicuous that they have no interest whatever in Nietzsche's great loves—higher culture, an aristocratic revival, the superman unrestrained by good and evil. In their naturalistic vitalism, Deleuze's and Guattari's celebrate the sheer bodily flow of the swarming schizzos, as if they were no different from a swarm of ants or herd creatures searching for new territory. In *Anti-Oedipus*, the great obstacle to social frenzy and freedom, is no longer the "herd" and the blinking idiots of mass democratic society, the "last men," but the psychiatrist, who, in their hands, and somewhat bizarrely (given what a minor profession it is),[66] has become the warder of bourgeois conformity and hence the guardian of social misery, and society's lack of vitality. This reconfiguring of Nietzsche to make him less aristocratic and his philosophy far more marketable to "the herd," found its apotheosis years later in Derrida, who transformed Nietzsche into a lovable teddy-bear fully consistent with the Disneyland "primitive" and other liberal/"progressive" safe and certain "goods," by claiming (without a shred of textual support) that not only was Nietzsche "not an enemy of democracy in general," but that he (just like Levinas and Derrida himself) was a member of the secularized messianic community appealing "to a democracy to come."[67] In the 1960s the spearhead of this "democracy to come," whose theoretical preparation had managed to synthesize Sade, Marx, Nietzsche, Bataille, Artauld et al., was a new revolutionary type: the criminal and delinquent, the transgressor, up to and including the mad, and even the pedophile.[68] One of the many virtues of Bourg's *From Revolution to Ethics* is that he brings back into view the extent to which the Sadean emancipation of sexual energies including rape and pedophilia was seriously discussed—eventually giving way to the feminist moral backlash.[69] This openness to pedophilic narratives of pleasure would come back to haunt the German Green Party in 2013, with earlier public remarks by its Euro-Green representative "Danny the Red" Cohn-Bendit claiming that earlier televised and written remarks about his easiness with child eroticism, which extended to children playing with his penis, had been misconstrued.[70] Of the leading transgressive philosophical voices from the 1960s, Foucault sailed most dangerously to the edge of these troublesome waters. As Bourg rightly says of Foucault: "It is by no means an exaggeration to claim that child sexuality lay at the very origins of his history of sexuality project."[71] Again Foucault, along with Deleuze and Guattari, was very much at the theoretical head of the various social movements acting on behalf of the incarcerated "refuse" of a society of unparalleled complexity in terms of the social mediations it was undertaking to keep order. Foucault had no idea that eventually the sexual revolution would create a backlash in which the safeguarding of students from sexual predators, in roles of pedagogical and spiritual authority, or the unwanted advances of celebrities and politicians (extending from inappropriate comments, to nudity and masturbation, to rape) would lead to the imprisonment of sexual offenders from acts done as far back as thirty or forty years. That this "blowback" in which state forces for safeguarding an "age of innocence" and punishing violators of that "innocence" have been so heavily mobilized has taken place in one of the most publicly sexualized cultures that has ever existed is as much an example of how much that occurred in the 1960s turned into its opposite, as it is of how societies (and individuals) incarnate contradictions.

All social order requires role recruitment and techniques of discipline and normalization so that social reproduction can take place, but when the entire society is seen as lacking any legitimacy as was the case, for a number of students and intellectuals, in the halcyon days of '68, society itself is seen as nothing but a big prison, a panopticon (Agamben will take Foucault's idea a step further by making society a death camp). In his retrospective assessments, Foucault would downplay his own role in fueling narratives calling for the abolition of prisons and asylums, casting his works in much more sober critical tones. But this was rather disingenuous. The early reception of Foucault's work was inseparable from the role it played in rallying what was essentially a sad motley crew consisting of social cast-offs and what Marx had termed the *Lumpen* proletariat was not lost on the more orthodox Marxists of the time. But, viewed sociologically, it suited the new aspiring "will-to-power" of the philosophically and tertiary educated who were able to be the spokespeople of these groups of the oppressed. The irony of this truth could not have been more contradictory (and slapstick) when family therapists, teachers, and social workers, in the late 1980s and early 1990s began to incorporate Foucault into their therapy, teaching, and social work curriculum. Naturally, the philosophers (not to mention their readers) living relatively bourgeois lives quickly tired of such reprobates who could not be relied upon to deliver the great transgressive emancipation and serve as adequate "role models."[72] As people have always done—they found a way to live with their contradictions—hence the feminist and gay studies lecturer enthusing their students in the morning about the politics of sexual transgression and who then sit on the sexual harassment board after lunch. Such a contradiction illustrates a key problem with the analytic philosophers who mistakenly think their job is to demonstrate a contra-diction as a means of refuting its author's truth claim, whereas the more helpful task is to designate how the contradictions subsist.

From a Hegelian position this Sadian confabulation was symptomatic of a torn social fabric, in which the ostensible bearers of reason were no longer, as Hegel had hoped, the healers of the ills and wounds of a society, but the wielders of weapons against the society that had brought them into being. But whereas Hegel has a profound sense of the tragic—and sought for the social reconciliation of diremptive forces, radical French philosophy from Bataille to Sartre to the '68ers reveled in sheer transformative activity of their own will. With no resistances from reality to temper their ideas of the possible, they dispensed with "man," the "subject," the "author," and the "original" to do away with every other surrogate of God. All that remained was their *jouissance*, libido, and exu-berant certainties about a world of total emancipation free from suffering and domination. Even Derrida could not help himself from commenting upon the hyperbole of the eschatological one-up-man-ship.[73]

There was one reality, though, that had been the real incubus of the West and which was the great impediment to *jouissance* and freedom: fascism. The Enlightenment story of progress had failed to grasp that what was in fact developing was what had created the death camps, and the Holocaust. Fascism was the latent and incubating essence of domina-tion: its pillars were economic (capitalism) and social (the family). This was the central rationale in Deleuze and Guattari's *Anti-Oedipus*. Indeed, although Foucault disliked much about the book,[74] his introduction suc-ceeds perfectly in identifying the preoccupation of the time—fascist dom-ination—and hence why the book was such a timely event.

> Last but not least, the major enemy, the strategic adversary is fascism (whereas Anti-Oedipus opposition to the others is more of a tactical engagement). And not only historical fascism, the fascism of Hitler and Mussolini–which was able to mobilize and use the desire of the masses so effectively–but also the fascism in us all, in our heads and in our everyday behavior, the fascism that causes us to love power, to desire the very thing that dominates and exploits us. I would say that Anti-Oedipus (may its authors forgive me) is a book of ethics, the first book of ethics to be written in France in quite a long time (perhaps that explains why its success was not limited to a particular "readership": being anti-oedipal has become a life style, a way of thinking and liv-ing). How does one keep from being fascist, even (especially) when one believes oneself to be a revolutionary militant? How do we rid our speech and our acts, our hearts and our pleasures, of fascism? How do we ferret out the fascism that is ingrained in our behavior? The Chris-tian moralists sought out the traces of the flesh lodged deep within the soul. Deleuze and Guattari, for their part, pursue the slightest traces of fascism in the body. Paying a modest tribute to Saint Francis de Sales,

276 *Chapter 10*

one might say that Anti-Oedipus is an Introduction to the Non-Fascist Life.[75]

Almost twenty years later in *Spectres of Marx* Derrida would identify those ghosts which haunted his sense of justice, politics and ethics: viz. "victims of wars, political or other kinds of violence, nationalist, racist, colonialist, sexist, or other kinds of exterminations, victims of the oppressions of capitalist imperialism or any of the forms of totalitarianism."[76] To be sure, the word fascism has been substituted with the phrase "any of the forms of totalitarianism," which runs in conjunction with "imperialist capitalism." But the meaning of fascism has been expanded so that it is essentially synonymous with domination itself rather than a specific modality of political organization. (That such nomenclature is meaningless when it comes to the kinds of marauding conquerors of the premodern age which broke out with such frequency and ferocity, is but one telling problem of how a group tended to see all of reality through its own historical immediacies.)

Insofar as post-Holocaust emancipatory narratives of anti-domination have tended to seek social empowerment through the extension of rights and legality, the program remained broadly within the parameters of liberal and democratic possibility, albeit with some voices such as Hardt and Negri, Žižek, and Badiou still calling for a Marxist revolution. Further, to the extent that any identity group seeks solidarity primarily on the basis of a singular contingent of identity the empowering group narrative is contrary to more traditional bulwarks of communality. This point was a central one in the communitarian critiques of liberalism (frequently directed at Rawlsian and Dworkin style of liberalism) advanced by Charles Taylor, Alasdair MacIntyre, Michael Sandel, and others. I think it fair to say that their invocation was not conservative, and they generally slid over the traditional importance of reciprocity of relationships that were once typical of all societies and still persist in non-Western societies. Indeed this difference takes on not only geopolitical dimensions, but it is a significant source of domestic discontent with immigrants into Western countries who are frightened by the breakdown of traditional families and the respective roles of its members, as well as the rise of single parents, publicly and widespread sexualized manners, as well as the various symptoms of alienation and atomization such as drug and alcohol dependency (now largely perceived as medical problems when the dependency makes someone unable to function), and depression. Thick communities have given way to what John Cuddihy, who traces the matter back to the peculiar social and political trajectory of Unitarian Calvinism took in the United States, to "thin communities."

Traditional communities are thick—they require everyday sacrifices to be reproduced, and they are not driven by such singular or dual modern "abstract ends" as freedom and equality. In spite of changes to our language which makes it meaningful for someone to speak of the black community, the indigenous community, the women's community, the gay etc., these names are spread thinly—as is the solidarity between the members grouped together under these "labels." The labels are indeed totalisations and a means of acquiring a degree of empowerment in an environment where power is not evenly distributed. This is also why the various dominated "thin communities" can easily be wrapped up in some broader more generic term of oppression and its capitalist source. Thus Antonio Negri and Michael Hardt in *Empire* dissolve the world into the "multitude" and capital. People are simply a "mass," raw quanta whose traditions, cultures, life-ways, decisions, hopes and past are all railroaded into the Manichean cosmic psycho/political drama that goes back to Marx. That of the countless civil wars that have gone on previously and are going on today have, outside of Jacobinism and Marxism, never (or rarely—take one's pick) been mounted under the banners of masses versus capitalists is of no matter to Negri and Hardt.

Power is never evenly generated nor distributed. Indeed the idea that it could be applicable to large groups is an abstraction lacking any referent from the past or present. Freedom itself, as Giordano Bruno put is so well, always results in bondage: rights remain meaningless unless somewhere the sacrifice can be made to grant them. Likewise, equality is an arithmetical term, and the invocation of an arithmetical term in the face of social discontents can at best be a "loose appeal" to a specifically egregious form of domination, rather than an appeal to a precise instantiation. What will or can be instantiated is a specific practice, which may be interpreted as, and indeed may well be "unfair."

Leaving aside Bataille's Sadean examples of the erotics of sacrifice, sacrifice which has a ubiquitous anthropological and sociological presence has largely been omitted from the narratives of emancipation, or, if present, interpreted as the dominator sacrificing their power to the dominated. It is telling that in his writings on bio-politics, which are generally far more sophisticated explorations of power than his earlier works, Foucault omits a central feature of sovereignty that Hobbes constructs "axiomatically" rather than historically: this is the "trade-off" for protection that is at the basis of even the most elementary political formations.[77] "States" and their "sovereigns" commence much like gangsters take over neighborhoods: but to maintain the operation, they offer protection from other groups who won't be content with extracting a surplus but will in, all likelihood, either extract more, or enslave or exterminate them in order to seize the entirety of their territory. Reciprocity—to be sure, not in equal degree or manner—is required from the start, and that will often require that able bodied men be required, when needed, to lay down their lives in war, that is to be sacrificed to their community and the lineage of ancestral and divine spirits or "god/s" that provide their orientation. That in ancient societies the "king" is originally a divine manifestation or divinely appointed and required to be a warrior is not simply a symbol of sovereign power, but an essential condition of power as a mysterious and cosmic (godly) force, whose presence must be capable of enactment and display. That tyranny frequently occurs is not in dispute—for this is not an ideal condition. Nevertheless, the tyranny of state is as much a social catastrophe as the tyrannical father who sexually molests his children, thus violating one of the most archaic kinship codes of the tribe: the former is as much an invitation for subjects to solicit an external sovereign power to free them or to take their chances at tyrannicide as the latter is an invitation to patricide.

Due to the success, in the Western world, of the social revolutions of the 1960s binaries of domination are now repeated in the media, and even churches and courts, and taught in schools and universities, where they are sifted and honed by academicians in ways reminiscent of priestly inspections, disputations, and pronouncements upon doctrine.

At the very foundation of modern political theory, the actual historical emergence, accrual and dispersal of power were mythically reconceived by the social contract theorists, primarily Hobbes, Locke, and Rousseau, whose writings, in different ways, took their bearings from the abstract ideas of equality and freedom laying the foundation for what C. B. Macpherson identified as "bourgeois" narratives of "possessive individualism."[78] Both sets of "rights" (those pertaining to liberty and those pertaining to equality) helped transform social convulsions and breakdowns into revolutions. Although the Marxian tradition would challenge the notions of rights as being a bourgeois invention, and in so far as the French philosophers of emancipation of the 1960s, in particular, originally followed Marx in this respect, the social revolts of the 1960s were all predicated upon a pre-existing set of appeals and narratives rooted in modern commercial societies: even though it was now an identity collective demanding its rights. In and of itself this is not at all "bad," but in so far as the sacrificial and the reciprocal conditions of human sociality are occluded in the narrative, this "story" contains a significant degree of failure of understanding of how the world came to be the way it is and why it is the way it is. To the extent that the French Revolution (drawing significantly upon the American Revolution which indeed drew upon the English Revolution) would not only lay down the "idea" of the nation and its members, it would also be the "model" and/or operative principle that would be replicated in the national revolutions that swept across Europe, and then in the anti-colonial nationalist movements in the twentieth century. In sum what took fire in 1789 is the great event whose fallout not only led to the extinction of the European empires (though one might plausibly construe this as a convergence into *one* European empire), but the French revolution also stands behind the social revolts of the 1960s, a point, not usually noted, but also underscored by de Certeau, who wrote: "Last May, speech was taken the way, in 1789, the Bastille was taken. . . . From the taking of the Bastille to the taking of the Sorbonne, between these two symbols, an essential difference characterizes the event of May 13, 1968."[79]

Of all the French philosophers of the 1960s, there is a strong case to be made that the two who remained most steeped in metaphysics, and thus most resistant to (though not untouched by) Heidegger's broader critique of metaphysics are the one time-sparring partners, Deleuze and Badiou. In spite of their different ontologies, both have reflected upon the most elemental tools of the philosopher's trade "concepts" and "ideas" in a way that draws out the idea-ism of the age of anti-domination. For Deleuze,

> Plato said that Ideas must be contemplated, but first of all he had to create the concept of Idea. What would be the value of a philosopher of whom one could say, "He has created no concepts; he has not created his own concepts"? We can at least see what philosophy is not: it is not contemplation, reflection, or communication. This is the case even though it may sometimes believe it is one or other of these, as a result of the capacity of every discipline to produce its own illusions and to hide behind its own peculiar smokescreen. It is not contemplation, for contemplations are things themselves as seen in the creation of their specific concepts. It is not reflection, because no one needs philosophy to reflect on anything. It is thought that philosophy is being given a great deal by being turned into the art of reflection, but actually it loses everything. . . . Philosophy does not contemplate, reflect, or communicate, although it must create concepts for these actions or passions.[80]

Deleuze has essentially restated the Nietzschean idea of the philosopher: as the creator of ideas of values to impose upon the world. The underpinning forces of creation, which in Nietzsche were physiological forces of will to power have in Deleuze, not surprisingly, been dropped in favor of the more generic collective fluxes and flows of habituation and flight. Philosophy creates ideas to orientate further action, and for Deleuze, and in keeping with the general thrust of the anti-domination philosophies, that action is primarily conceived as political. The problem of the idea as a philosophical "construction" as opposed to its more common-sensical coinage as an insight is in its focal demands and occlusions. And that is no less the case with Deleuze than it was with Plato.

We have emphasized throughout that while model-building or the accumulation of information and knowledge through the deployment of an overarching operational principle or "idea" is indeed an invaluable deployment of the imagination and our reasoning, when the idea dictates the permissible elements to be included within "the All" blinding us to other features and aspects of reality demanding response then it poses a danger to us by limiting features of life that we may need to be cognizant of.

The collapsing of the personal, the social, and the political into each other to be marshaled into identity narratives of emancipation, was one example of the danger of this kind of idea-ism. In the case of what has been understood by politics as a kind of ethics, it is actually a breach with one of the very things that politics, in its Greek and Roman forms, was meant to solve the brokering of established and significantly different interests. Plato, among the ancients, gave the political such a different emphasis that interests had to be folded into a greater ideal of unity, preferably (but so unlike as to be impossible) in a philosophically ruled state, but more likely and possible in a society with philosophically crafted laws. When the "ideal" was transferred to the will of communal subjects, as with Rousseau, the idea of politics as "interest brokering" was sacrificed altogether upon the altar of the "general will." Deleuze was far more anarchic than Rousseau, but I don't think it unfair to say that he, like the other anti-domination philosophers, has contributed to a kind of politicized narrative control of the instantiation of the ethical. The ethical being as that Rousseauian metaphysician, Kant, put it: "a mere idea of Reason," but with the rider that "reason" now is a much more unstable affair that can simply be seen as a totalizing instantiation of an identity, which is then nothing else but a "will to power." The irony is that this means that the establishment of one's narrative authority becomes no less bound to legitimacy of a kind that previously issued from the sovereign. It is just that the sovereign has changed so that the dominated, or more precisely those who speak and adjudicate on behalf of the dominated, are now sovereign because of the ethical authority that flows from their position in the new "sacred" "ideational" order. That this is a recipe for endless conflict should be obvious because substance, norm, and authority all jostle for space within the "ideas" that are bound up with institutional authority and power.

Badiou both complements Deleuze, and even more accurately identifies the importance of the idea-ism which inevitably accompanies anti-domination philosophies. Badiou emphasizes the importance of event and encounter as decisive sources of "truth procedures," as he also privileges four "generic procedures: love (I suspect it is his lingering affection for Lacan that makes him add "whether it exists"), art, science, and politics. These, he says, bring to light "the truth of the collective's being."[81] Having recognized and written on the importance of Christianity, which, as with Nietzsche, Jacob Taubes, and Giorgo Agamben, among others, seems to have next to nothing to do with Christ, but is all about St. Paul, he nevertheless only finds in (the Christian) religion a nonphilosophical truth—which only makes even more bizarre how he can ascribe to love, politics and art, and science, but not religion, a philosophical role.[82] In spite of Badiou's proclivity for mathematics, set theory, and logic, Badiou's notion of the idea is really an ethical one that reinforces and is reinforced by his maxim "keep going."[83] Badiou, completely unconvincingly in my view, believes he has successfully managed to redefine "idealism" as "dialectical materialism." The following conclusion unequivocally indicates that the "idea" and its adequacy provides the ultimate appeal, not only for him, but for all who like him want to hold onto the last wisp of a "Big Other" to justify their faith in the ideals of '68.

CONCLUSION. WHAT IS IT TO LIVE?

Statement 58. To live supposes that an evental trace is given.

Statement 59. To live supposes some incorporation into the evental present.

Statement 60. To live supposes that a body is suited to holding some points.

Statement 61. To live supposes that a body suited to holding some points is the bearer of some faithful subjective formalism.

Statement 62. To live supposes that some fidelity engenders the present of an eternal truth.

Statement 63. For the materialist dialectic, "to live" and "to live for an Idea" are one and the same thing.

Statement 64. The maxim of democratic materialism, "live without Idea," is incoherent.

Statement 65. Several times in its life, and for several types of Ideas, every human animal is granted the possibility of living.

Statement 66. Since it is indeed possible, commencing or recommencing to live for an Idea is the only imperative.[84]

Living for an idea means, to borrow and adapt Deleuze's term, living in a "fold." The extent of the idea-ism of the emancipative philosophies is less conspicuous in the philosophical pronouncement on the idea just cited by Deleuze and Badiou, but in the "folding" that has been so widely undertaken: the folding of the public and private, of the personal, the social and the political, and the towering authority given to such marks of enfolding identity which remain core ethical appeals of the "masses" (in its Marxian fold) or the "people" (the fold of 1789). The real politics behind all this is—who has the authority to undertake the fold? And what political action do they undertake to do this? The question of whether the world that the "folders" help make through their appeals, and ideas is not itself merely, or necessarily even political, but philosophical. The question also remains—who is sacrificed to whom, and for what? The philosophies of anti-domination ultimately create an alignment between the identities it emancipates and the narratives it builds to further that emancipative process. But it is only dogma that can assure anyone that this kind of idea-ism is not another exercise in social occlusiveness. Even if one concedes that certain goods flowed from anti-domination philosophies taking on a position of social dominance, such a concession must neverthe-less be based upon an appeal. There is no compelling ground, just a conversation referring to a comparative array of possibilities, instantia-tions, and (to use Rosenstock-Huessy's helpful terms) prejectives and trajectives. But it is precisely this lack of any obvious rational legitimacy to the politically and morally charged terms which identify victim and oppressor as well as the narratives that now find themselves flourishing within various economic and institutional sites of social reproduction that make their enforcement all the more necessary. The less "there" there is, the more those who live off the existence of the "there" devote their energy and time to attacking those who do not accept the authorita-tive power of their narratives. Ironically, it was Foucault who first made so much of this phenomenon: but if we concede that power is as power does then a "will to power" is neither more nor less than a "will to power."

In a less nihilistic mood, we add that by making politics and philoso-phy (not to mention other cultural components of conversations) too interdependent, the danger is that the authority (the end of politics) sul-lies the range of ideas that facilitate better conversations that may open up better ways of seeing and being in the world. If on occasion I invoke traditional and conservative insights against the more outlandish ideas it is not because I think the past must always trump the future. Such terms as conservative or radical are at best political shorthand in the context of a particular dispute. To label oneself as one or the other, though, is to surrender to thoughtlessness. Not all our past is worth jettisoning, not all worth preserving: the future brings great gifts *and* monsters. But the will-ful destruction of all past institutions as being but the means of oppres-sion, the unmitigated faith in the world to come being of our own making (as opposed to unknown benign contingencies—the most traditionally powerful—and providential—argument requires an appeal to God's grace) and then the persecution of those who do not see things this way— this is the idea-ist gallows-making of the future that continues the ideo-logical destruction that dominated so much of the twentieth century, and which is the "culmination" of the dark side of the "ideo-cratic" world set in train by modern philosophy. As it turns out, the paradox of the '68 fusion of Marx and Nietzsche is that in the preparation for a Marxian-like society free from the domination of capital, the ruling class, and other forms of domination, a new higher type, an elite, has emerged. It has positioned itself by a transfer/seizure of professional power. It controls the narratives of social value and turns those who are either to be re-educated or simply made to comply with the new order into the "under-men and women," the enemies of progress who are on the wrong side of history. The '68 generation has "bred" these new "higher men and wom-en" who are the value creators of the future. The question is: what future?

In contrast to the idea-ism which has replaced uncritical domination, with critical domination, there are other more open ways to think, and philosophy, albeit it in a more humble mode, has also contributed to those ways. This will be the topic of a future book, in which Vico, Hamann, Herder, Rosenzweig and Rosenstock-Huessy feature as important contributors to a philosophy more suited to the human condition than the idea-ist philosophies we have studied here. It is also a pathway to a potentially more convivial world insofar as it may help facilitate a more open dialogical culture, even if it cannot promise the "impossible," or "total emancipation."

NOTES

1. It comes from (to use the English title) Beaufret's "Introduction to the Philosophy of Existence," Vincent Descombes, *Modern French Philosophy* (Cambridge; Cambridge University Press, 1980), 76. The anti-humanist theme would also be central to Luc Ferry and Alain Renaut's *French Philosophy of the Sixties: An Essay on Anti-Humanism*, translated by Mary Cattini (Amherst: University of Massachusetts Press, 1990).

2. Gilles Deleuze, *Difference and Repetition*, xvii.

3. Michel Foucault, *The Order of Things: An Archaeology of the Human Sciences* (London: Tavistock, 1970), 386.

4. Ibid., xiv.

5. Michel Foucault, *The Archaeology of Knowledge*, translated by A. M. Sheridan Smith (London: Tavistock, 1972), 14. It is astonishing that a view that is no different from Hume, and indeed which is intrinsic to any logically thought through mechanised science view of the self was touted with so much bravado.

6. *The Archaeology of Knowledge*, 13.

7. If I may remind the reader not overly familiar with Kant, for Kant the "transcendental" subject is a formal operation of consciousness facilitating understanding of an object, while the "transcendent" subject of the "soul" emanates from reason's dialectical overplay in which a formal operation is rationally, and hence illegitimately, postulated as substance. In the main the attack upon stable taxonomies and terms, of which *The Order of Things* is a paradigmatic period piece, is tackling the problem of essences. Even though their anti-humanism is Heideggerean enough, Deleuze's and Guattari's epistemological insistence upon a "plane of immanence" is but one of many variants of what is essentially a Spinozian metaphysics.

8. The correspondence between Althusser and Lacan tells the story: Althusser wants to show how deeply his reading of Marx is indebted to Lacan, as he goes into some detail about the purpose of his undertaking. By contrast, although he is flattered, Lacan replies briefly, and politely, saying "sweet nothings" about Althusser's use of his work, while not engaging with the subject matter in any serious way. http://nosubject.com/index.php?title=Correspondence_with_Jacques_Lacan_%281963_-_1969%29 last viewed 9 July 2016. After Lacan had been barred by the *Société Française de Psychoanalyse (SFP)* from training students, Althusser was among those who came to his rescue getting him to lecture at *Ecole Normale Supérieure*.

9. As André Glucksmann in his savagely funny review of Althusser sums it up: Althusser's emancipatory reading of "ideological over-determination" meant that the economy mattered in the last instance, but only in the last instance—which put less "theoretically" means the economy matters except when it doesn't. André Glucksmann, "A Ventriloquist Structuralism," *New Left Review*, 1/72, March-April 1972.

10. Cf. Jacques Rancière, *Althusser's Lessons* (London: Bloomsbury, 2011).

11. *The Order of Things*, 328.

12. Michel Foucault, "Politics and Ethics: An Interview" in *The Foucault Reader*, edited by Paul Rabinow (New York: Pantheon, 1984), 375. Amy Allan in her entry on "Politics" in *The Cambridge Foucault Lexicon*, edited by Leonard Lawler and John Naler (Cambridge: Cambridge University Press, 2014) registers this remark as "astonishing," entry 62, 364.

13. *Archaeology of Knowledge*, 17. As in Foucault and what follows, the moral and the ethical are interchangeable, and do not conform to the kind of division Hegel raises against Kant in his distinction (which does not occur in Kant) between *Sittlichkeit* (the lived ethos of a community) and *Moralität* (a subjective principle for evaluating the moral worth of an intention.)

14. Although the dispute is over a few pages of Foucault's text and a passage from Descartes" *Meditations*, Derrida argues in "Cogito and the History of Madness" that Foucault misreads the significance of Descartes" Cogito, and that this misreading redounds upon the entire project of the *History of Madness: Writing and Difference*, translated by Allan Bass (London: Routledge and Kegan Paul, 1978). As Derrida puts it, Foucault's error is in thinking he could write a history of madness in which madness itself speaks, and he draws haphazardly upon Descartes (why does he take pride of place in this history?, asks Derrida) as embodying a reason that differentiates itself from madness, when, in fact—and here the point is one which enables Derrida to illustrate more about his own philosophy than what concerns Descartes or Foucault—Descartes's incursion into the idea of madness, in a strategic "moment" of hyperbolic doubt, establishes "a structure of deferral," a "regulated relationship between that which exceeds and the exceeded totality: the *différance* of the absolute excess," *Writing and Difference*, 62. For Foucault's reply, see Appendix 3 in *History of Madness*, translated by Jonahtan Murphy and Jean Khalfa, with a foreword by Ian Hacking (London: Routledge, 2006), 575–90.

15. As Searle recounts, Foucault said: "He writes so obscurely you can't tell what he's saying, that's the obscurantism part, and then when you criticize him, he can always say, "You didn't understand me; you're an idiot." That's the terrorism part." See "Reality Principles: An Interview with John Searle" in http://reason.com/archives/2000/02/01/reality-principles-an-interview, last viewed August 27, 2016.

16. Michel Foucault, *The Courage of the Truth, (The Government of self and others II Lectures at the Collége de France, 1983–1984*, edited by Frédérick Gross and translated by Graham Burchell (London: Palgrave Macmillan, 2011).

17. Michel Foucault, "Two Lectures" in *Power/Knowledge: Selected Interviews and Other Writings 1972–1977*, edited by Colin Gordon (Brighton, Sussex: Harvester Press, 1980), 97.

18. Ibid., 96.

19. Ibid., 97.

20. Ibid., 95–96.

21. Jacques Derrida, "Structure, Sign and Play" in *Writing and Difference*, 289 and 292.

22. As he writes in "Structure, Sign and Play": "it is necessary to forego scientific or philosophical discourse, to renounce the *epistēmē* which absolutely requires, which is the absolute requirement that we go back to the source, to the centre, to the founding basis, to the principle, and so on," *Writing and Difference*, 286.

23. Jacques Lacan, *The Ethics of Psychoanalysis: 1959–1960: The Seminar of Jacques Lacan Book VII*, edited by Jacques-Alain Miller, translated with notes by Dennis Porter (New York: W.W. Norton, 1992), 89. Lacan's famous riposte to the '68ers: "As revolutionaries, you are hysterics who demand a new master. You will get one," is as caustic and accurate a summation as anything Tocqueville might have conjured up when sensing the surges of underlying despotism that only become radicalized as democracy itself becomes radicalized. But in spite of this, Lacan also fully understood that the convulsions of '68 were a kind of social release and cry against very real social traumas and discontents. I hold out the hope that, on his deathbed, Žižek may suddenly turn into a true Lacanian, and say that all his paeans to Robespierre, Lenin, Stalin et al.

were just a therapeutic prank designed to expose the folly of the faith in the political Big Other, and that he never believed a word of it. This is not to deny that Žižek's (and many Marxist) criticisms of the undertow of large scale commercial societies are to a large part true: the problem is knowing what to do.

24. Alain Badiou, *Ethics: An Essay on the Understanding of Evil*, translated by Hallward (London: Verso, 2002), 38–39.

25. As Julian Bourg rightly notes: *From Revolution to Ethics: May 1968 and Contemporary French Thought* (Montreal: McGill-Queen's University Press, 2007), 6. Another typical indication of the shift can be seen in the change that takes place in Franco Rella's *The Myth of the Other: Lacan, Foucault, Deleuze, Bataille*, translated by Nelson Moe (Washington, DC: Maisonneuve Press, 1994). In his Preface to the North American edition of that work, Rella notes that it was originally written "in the second half of the 1970's in Italy," was "characterized by a widespread conflictuality which seemed in many ways to have repudiated reason and thus presented itself as an absolute negation incapable of ethically positing itself within the context of existing social antagonism," 5. He adds that in the second part of the book, devoted to Georges Bataille, he has added "a concept of beauty, "which is not aesthetic, but theoretical, and political," 9.

26. Bourg's book focusses upon the more sociologically oriented driven French philosophers of the '60s, and thus he leaves aside the more obvious case of Derrida. Nevertheless, *From Revolution to Ethics* is a meticulous examination of the themes and concerns of the French philosophies which flowed into and grew out of the May strikes and student revolt 1968. It provides a perspicuous account of the problems the '68ers got into regarding the topics of pedophilia and unrestrained male sexuality, the latter of which would be combated, and ultimately defeated by feminist voices. What is also of great value in Bourg's account is the importance he allocates to the "new philosophers"—which included Bernard Henri-Lévy, André Glucksmann, Claude Lefort (the only one more widely read outside of France), Pascal Bruckner, Jean-Marie Benoist, Christian Jambet, and Guy Ladreau. Common to them all was their anti-Nietzschean retrieval of the importance of human rights and ethics, and a greater degree of caution and suspicion about what could be achieved through politics, and their critiques of Marx. In part they were shaken out of their youthful political Marxist certitudes by the horror stories coming from Solzhenitsyn's *Gulag Archipelago*. Although the "new philosophes" were largely dismissed by the '68ers, with the noticeable exception of Foucault, their impact in France was significant. One indication of their failure to be absorbed in the Anglo-American academic world of social and literary theory and critique is that while the Holocaust is commonly identified as the evil event disclosing the true end and essence of the fascisms latent in the West, the gulags are rarely mentioned. A notable exception is ironically the Leninist Žižek—see, e.g., *Revolution at the Gates: A Selection of Writings from February to October 1917, V.I. Lenin* (London: Verso, 2002), footnote 129, 329–30.

27. Max Horkheimer and Theodor Adorno, *Dialectic of Enlightenment* (New York: Herder and Herder, 1969), 121.

28. Walter Benjamin, "On the Concept of History," in *Selected Writings, Volume 4, 1938–1940*, translated by Edward Jephcott and others, edited by Howard Eiland and Michael Jennings (Cambridge, MA: Belknap, 2006), 392: IX.

29. "Benjamin, On the Concept of History," 396.

30. Theodor Adorno, *Minima Moralia: Reflections on A Damaged Life*, translated by E. Jephcott (London: Verso, 1974), 247.

31. See the letter from Horkheimer to Adorno September 27, 1958 included as an appendix in Detlev Claussen, *Adorno: One Last Genius*, translated by Rodney Livingston (Cambridge, MA: Belknap, 2010), 254–362.

32. Blanchot, Artaud, and Bataille have all been "accused of veering" into fascist waters. Walter Benjamin's interactions with the College of Sociology, with its icon of a headless man and its pact of human sacrifice, led him to comment that the College possessed "a prefascist aesthetics." On Bataille and also Benjamin's claim, see Benja-

min Noys, *Georges Bataille: A Critical Introduction* (London: Pluto, 2000). Noys quotes Bataille's friend, and author of a ground-breaking exposé of Stalin's USSR, Boris Souvarine who states that Bataille not only would have been a fascist but a collaborator as well had he "the courage of his convictions," 43. On Artaud, see Naomi Greene, "All the Great Myths Are Dark": Artaud and Fascism," in Gene Plunka (ed.), *Antoin Artaud and The Modern Theatre* (Toronto: Associated University Press, 1994), 102–16. On Blanchot, see chapter 12, "Pour Sainte-Beuve: Maurice Blanchot, 10 March 1942," in Jeffrey Mehlman, *Genealogies of the Text: Literature, Psychoanalysis and Politics in Modern France* (Cambridge: Cambridge University Press, 1995), 174–94. To be sure, the friendships, passions, and aspirations in France in the 1930s and during its occupation often made the choices extreme, and the extreme choices attractive. Mehlman also includes a chapter on the De Man case and his collaborationist fascist writings for the Belgian paper *Le Soir* that had been uncovered by an American PhD student, see 113–30. The De Man case, along with the revival of Heidegger's Nazi past, was a major philosophical talking point in 1987, and the writings of Victor Farias and Hugo Ott on Heidegger would have an enormously negative impact upon Derrida's public reputation. In "Like the Sound of the Sea Deep within a Shell: Paul de Man's War" in *Critical Inquiry*, 14, Spring 1988, 590–652. Derrida responded to De Man's critics (whose criticisms, he rightly understood, by virtue of his friendship and theoretical affinities with De Man, also deflected onto him) by accusing them of reproducing "the exterminating gesture which one accuses de Man of not having armed himself against sooner," 651. The apology for De Man, to put it mildly, did him little credit. For a fuller discussion see Jon Wiener, "The Responsibilities of Friendship: Jacques Derrida on Paul de Man's Collaboration," *Critical Inquiry* 15(4): 797–803, 1989. I think these events were decisive in Derrida's ethical refashioning, a point also brought out in David Mikics, *Who was Jacques Derrida? An Intellectual Biography* (New Haven: Yale University Press, 2009).

33. Peter Dews, *Logics of Disintegration: Post-structuralist Thought and the Claims of Critical Theory* (London: Verso, 1987), 242.

34. Jacques Derrida and John Caputo, *Deconstruction in a Nutshell: A Conversation with Jacques Derrida* (New York: Fordham University Press, 1992), 23. For the actual encounter with Habermas which also "cashes in" on Habermas' theory of communicative action and presents Derrida at his most Kantian, see Giovanna Borradori, *Philosophy in a Time of Terror: Dialogues with Jürgen Habermas and Jacques Derrida* (Chicago: University of Chicago Press, 2003). The following is typical: In the "Foreigner Question," part of his dialogue with Habermas, Derrida writes: "Just as any utterance implies a performative promising to address itself to someone else as such ('I am speaking to you, and I promise you the truth'), just as any speech act promises the truth (even and especially if I am lying)—well, anyway, I can always lie, of course (and who could swear or prove that Kant himself never lied?), but that will signify quite simply that therefore I'm not speaking to someone else, end of story" (67). This problem with this is that speech is not only used to "reveal," but also to veil. This matter of veiling (a very Derridean thematic) and speech is one reason why speech is both decisive for the mechanisms of inclusion and exclusion required for solidarity and war. On veiling, see Eugen Rosenstock-Huessy's "The University of Logic, Language, and Literature," in *Speech and Reality*, (Eugene, OR: Wipf and Stock, 2013), 67–97. *Of Hospitality: Anne Dufourmantelle Invites Jacques Derrida to respond*, translated by Rachel Bowlby, (Stanford: Stanford University Press, 2000). Derrida himself had written on the veil—see especially his engagement with Hélène Cixous in *Veils*, translated by Geoffrey Bennington (Stanford: Stanford University Press, 2001). But Derrida's account of veiling is very much in the mold of his writings of différance, and the Heideggerean veiling of Being, and hence his preoccupation with the difficulties of definitive interpretation and meaning of a text, rather than the kind of veiling commonly deployed in indigenous societies or esoteric societies that is a deliberate means of "keeping out" in order to "weigh up" the maturity and character-worthiness of one about to receive knowledge.

35. The story of the reception of "poststructuralist" reception in the United States, and the "re-crafting" of these philosophies for the American market, the market which would be of fundamental importance for the reputations of Derrida, Foucault, and Deleuze and Guattari, Baudrillard, and others, particularly in literature departments, has been very well told by François Cusset in *French Theory: How Foucault, Derrida, Deleuze and Co. Transformed the Intellectual Life of the United States*, translated by Jeff Fort (Minneapolis: University of Minnesota Press, 2008).

36. It was Raymond Tallis in a typically hilariously caustic review, in his *Aping Mankind*, of John Gray, who drew my attention to Hopkins's apposite phrase.

37. Victor Meldrew is the central character of the British comedy *One Foot in the Grave*.

38. Raymond Tallis, *Not Saussure* (London: Macmillan 1988), and *Theorrhoea and After* (London: Macmillan, 1999), and M. J. Devaney's *"Since at Least Plato . . ." and Other Postmodernist Myths* (London: Macmillan, 1997), and Francis Wheen, *How Mumbo-Jumbo Conquered the World* (London: Fourth Estate, 2004). Rainer Friedrich's lengthy two part "essay" which appeared in *Arion: A Journal of the Humanities and Classics*, volumes: 19 No. 3, 31–78 (2012) and Vol. 20, No. 1 (Spring/Summer 2012), 67–112. While Wheen's book is definitely a contender for any Victor Meldrew award that might be out there, with its rants against postmodernism alongside eye-popping ire directed at Margaret Thatcher and Ronald Reagan and pretty well anything else that springs to his mind as causing the downfall of civilization. Knowing that the world is mad does not only not amount to very much at all (and when was it ever not mad?), but the problem is people do not all see the madness, let alone its causes, in the same way. The ranter might well believe his intelligence has found what Lacan calls his Big Other, or more popularly Santa Claus—in Wheen's case it is the "Enlightenment." The mere appeal to the "Enlightenment" as a kind of knock-down argument about anything is simply silly. Like all events it was multifaceted in all manner of ways: it spawned Robespierre, Saint-Just and the Terror, modern nationalism as indeed the Great War and its aftermath as much as a "culture" of rational legitimacy. Answers to human problems invariably contain the seeds of later problems, and this was no less the case with the Enlightenment as with the Reformation or the adoption of Christianity as the official religion within the Roman Empire. Someone's mumbo is always someone else's jumbo. So it is of little consequence that something is mad if people find something that attracts them to the madness. In the case of many of the French philosophers of '68, madness had its own appeal. That, as I mentioned previously, made sense in a culture in which Cartesianism was seen as complicit in the "rational" horror of the First and Second World Wars. The criticism of Tallis and Devaney are far more serious and definitely expose some of the more silly claims that appear in Derrida (Tallis) and literary theorists passing themselves off, usually poorly, as metaphysicians, but the appeals by Tallis and Devaney to some version of realism ultimately misses the larger woods of hermeneutics, phenomenology, and other philosophical innovations for the trees of specific overblown statements. For his part, Tallis is knowledgeable and even sympathetic to Heidegger and Wittgenstein, and he concedes that "truth is essentially a public matter" (*Not Saussure*, 249) and emergent (250), so it is somewhat perplexing that his criticisms are so contrary throughout the book to the more "discursive" aspects of communication that Derrida untangles. In *Theorrhoea* he also appeals to art's utopian role in future-making, which again places him far closer to his "enemies" than so much of the text indicates.

39. Alan Sokal and Jean Bricmont, *Fashionable Nonsense: Postmodern Intellectuals" Abuse of Science* (New York: Picador, 1998).

40. It is reproduced in Jacques Derrida, *Points: Interview, 1974–1994*, edited by Elizabeth Weber, translated by Peggy Kamuf and others (Stanford: Stanford University Press, 1995), 420–21.

41. Ibid., 404.

42. However, the cultural turn in Marxism did open a door for Benjamin, whose works began being translated for the *New Left Review* in 1968, and critical theory and poststructuralism.

43. John Cuddihy, *No Offence: Civil Religion and Protestant Taste* (New York: Seabury Press, 1978).

44. I agree completely with Stuart Sim's entry on "Difference" in *The Lyotard Dictionary* that "if there is one thing that sums up poststructuralism as a movement, it is the strength of its members" commitment to difference." *The Lyotard Dictionary*, edited by Stuart Sim (Edinburgh: Edinburgh University Press, 2011), 49. It is also the celebration of difference that becomes the core of the radical liberal assault upon conservativism in North America. But of course, and in spite of the endless celebration of "difference," the real question is what sort of difference is being talked about. We can go back to Plato who made difference along with identity a fundamental characteristic of any idea and see that in and of itself this difference is meaningless. Deleuze wanted to make the different have an ontological basis so that identity as an all-enveloping/totalizing characteristic is kept at bay, thereby ensuring that what he sees as the rigidity of arboreal logic is also warded off. But this nominalist insistence is only another metaphysical seduction away from the elementary and sensible question: different in what way and to what extent? The Nazi guard is different from the radical '68er and wants to protect the different identity of the Aryans from being "infected" by Jewish alterity. If we invoke a human identity above either Aryan and Jewish difference where do we get it from? Levinas has an answer—I think it a rhapsodic answer, and far from compelling—but it is not the kind of answer that is consistent with the general celebration of difference in itself. If we eschew metaphysics then neither difference nor identity have any compelling call upon our thinking—it depends what we are wanting to do. In the case of poststructuralism one already must buy into the dyad of oppressor and oppressed to see difference as a subordinate of identity. So if someone has a very different basis for thinking about society—one in which, for example, men are not automatically the oppressors of women, which was once the norm in Western societies, and is still the norm in Asia, the Middle East, and Africa—is that difference to be subsumed under the totality of the radical liberal narrative? Is, then, radical liberalism not just another grand narrative, and Lyotard but one more master thinker within that narrative? The '68 game is not hard to play once the rules are evident—and if the game can be played to completely contrary ends than the kind of world the '68ers were building, then we may ask, whether the "solution" is but a deferral of larger problems incubating within the paradigm?

45. *A Thousand Plateaus: Capitalism and Schizophrenia*, translated by Brian Massumi (Minneapolis: University of Minneapolis Press, 1987), 469.

46. Ben Golder's *Foucault and the Politics of Rights* (Stanford: Stanford University Press, 2015) addresses the matter of rights in Foucault's late work while arguing that Foucault is, nevertheless, consistent with his earlier writings, and hence has not gone over to the dark side of "liberalism." Even if correct, Golder's book is an interesting example of faith in narrative and doctrinal purity. I don't think Foucault really cared that much about consistency. His writings on neo-liberalism—*The Birth of Biopolitics: Lectures at the Collège de France 1978–1979*, edited by Michael Senellart, translated by Graham Burchell (New York: Palgrave Macmillan, 2008)—showed (a) that he decided to learn something about economics and (b) that he has come to realize what he shared with liberalism, which I think can hardly be surprising given that the lifestyle whose community he most identified with flourished better than anywhere in neo-liberal USA. From Derrida, let me just cite his late work *Rogues*, where he invokes what would become his standard ethico-political appeal—"the democracy to come": "the expression of 'democracy to come' does indeed translate or call for a militant and interminable political critique. A weapon aimed at the enemies of democracy, it protests against all naïveté and every political abuse, every rhetoric that would present as a present or existing democracy, as a de facto democracy, what remains inadequate to the democratic demand, whether nearby or far away, at home or somewhere else in

the world, anywhere that a discourse on human rights and on democracy remains little more than an obscene alibi so long as it tolerates the terrible plight of so many millions of human beings suffering from malnutrition, disease, and humiliation, grossly deprived not only of bread and water but of equality or freedom, dispossessed of the rights of all, of everyone, of anyone." Jacques Derrida, *Rogues: Two Essays on Reason*, translated by Pascale-Anne Brault and Michael Naas (Stanford: Stanford University Press, 2005), 86.

47. It is no accident that a vast literature on social trauma was spawned on the basis of the wounds and traumas of the post-Holocaust generation. Likewise, I think Lacan's importance to the '68ers in France did not lie in his sharing their politics, which he thought somewhat childish, but in his sympathy for what they were "going through" and his offering a kind of existential hope. This is why in spite of all the charges laid at Lacan's door, from his womanizing, crossing of patient-therapist lines to excursions into bad algebra, put with verve and wit and typical good sense by Raymond Tallis in his review of Elizabeth Roudinesco's *Jacques Lacan*, I think Lacan a much more compassionate and thoughtful figure than his critics, including Tallis, concede. "The Shrink from Hell: Jacques Lacan" in *Times Higher Education*, October 31, 1997—https://www.timeshighereducation.com/books/the-shrink-from-hell/159376. article last viewed August 17, 2016. The charge of charlatanism is frequently thrown at Lacan. Aside from the fact that much of his writing is very interesting, the entire point of his work cannot simply be equated with that of a philosopher's. As a therapist he is much more interested in changing the behavior of people who find themselves psychically "locked up." Elizabeth Roudinesco puts her case for the virtues of Lacan in a work, neatly titled *Lacan: In Spite of Everything*, translated by Gregory Elliot (London: Verso, 2014).

48. See Lawrence Kelley, *War before Civilization: The Myth of the Peaceful Savage* (Oxford: Oxford University Press, 1996).

49. E.g. Genevieve Lloyd, *The Man of Reason: Male and Female in Western Philosophy* (London: Routledge, 1993).

50. Michel de Certeau, *The Capture of Speech and Other Political Writings*, translated by Tom Conley, (Minneapolis: University of Minnesota Press, 1997), 11.

51. "Bureau of Public Secrets: May 1968 Graffiti," last viewed June 2016.

52. Vincent Descombes, *Modern French Philosophy*, 13.

53. *Face to Face with Levinas*, edited by Richard Cohen (New York: State University of New York Press, 1986), 33.

54. William Shakespeare, *The Tempest*, Act 2 Scene 1. http://shakespeare.mit.edu/tempest/full.html last viewed January 26, 2019.

55. In 1967 Foucault in the less conciliatory and less humble phase of his career, accused Camus of "soft humanism" which, he adds, is "the little whore of all the thought, culture, morality and politics of the last twenty years." It was, he said, "used in 1948 to justify Stalinism and the hegemony of Christian democracy." The blithe equation of Stalinism with Christian democracy (corrupt as it was) and Camus hardly gives one confidence in Foucault as a political analyst. "Who Are You Professor Foucault? (1967)," Michel Foucault, *Religion and Culture*, selected and edited by Jeremy Carrette (Routledge: New York, 1999), 99.

56. *The Rebel* was the final straw between Camus and Sartre, as well as de Beauvoir who refused to speak to him. Sartre's "attack dog," François Jeanson, wrote a Marxist diatribe attacking Camus for his false consciousness. Even Bernard-Henri Lévy, in his *Sartre: Philosopher of the Twentieth Century*, generally detested by the French left for extending his anti-totalitarianism to anti-Marxism, defends Sartre against Camus. The specious nature of the argument and the ideological summersaults performed by Lévy are conspicuous in the very name of the chapter: "Why we are, all the same, right to be wrong with Sartre, than right with Camus." Lévy's take on Camus strikes me as a pathetic attempt to ingratiate himself into the more radical intelligentsia by conforming to a Levinasian view of the ethical. As Lévy tells the story, Sartre's late ethical turn was a Levinasian one, mediated by the former Maoist turned religious Jew and Zion-

ist, Benny Levi, who would visit Sartre after already seeing Levinas earlier in the day brimming with enthusiasm for this ethical vision which seemed congenial to Sartre. Camus's rebel, unlike the metaphysical rebels he criticizes (and Levinas is a typical metaphysical rebel in Camus' terms), does not have any grand ethical schemas with which to ease the burden of their tragic moral and political choices—murder is still murder, death is still death, and justice is always stained and tarnished by the blood it is fought for. The sheer humanity of Camus's narrative, its commitment to discussing social and political suffering on a scale in which we do not mistake our cause or our acts of emancipation for that of the gods is precisely what excludes him from the flashier philosophers whose utopianism opens on to a vista in which history is a cosmic drama that cannot help but be at the expense of mundane suffering and the more mundane gestures of decency and humanity.

57. *The Rebel*, translated by Anthony Bower (Harmondsworth: Penguin, 1971), 26.

58. *The Rebel*, 32–33.

59. *The Rebel*, 37.

60. *Georges Bataille: Visions of Excess: Selected Writings, 1927–1939*, translated by Allan Stoekl, with Carl Lovitt and Donald Leslie (Minneapolis: University of Minnesota Press, 1985), 101. Heterogeneity will, of course, be one of Bataille's many contributions to poststructuralism. See, especially, Derrida's "From Restricted to General Economy: A Hegelian without Reserve" in *Writing and Difference*. One of the more interesting critiques of postmodernism from the left is Guido Preparata's *Bataille, Foucault, and the Postmodern Corruption of Political Dissent* (New York: Palgrave, 2007). It also contains a chapter on Sade's importance. Preparata's work is often brilliant, but its own political-economic invocations of Thorsten Veblen will only appeal to those who are attracted to the kind of techno-managerial social vision of Veblen.

61. Maurice Blanchot, "Literature and the Right to Death," in *The Station Hill: Blanchot Reader Fiction and Literary Essays*, translated by Lydia Davis, Paul Auster, and Robert Lamberton (Barrytown: Station Hill, 1999), 378. Alongside Bataille, Blanchot, and Klossowski (whose work on Sade is mentioned by Camus), Sade had already also been embraced by de Beauvoir, Jean Paulham, and, after Camus's death, by Roland Barthes, Deleuze, and Foucault—though, later Foucault will turn against the more militarized machinations of Sade's grand murderously sexual theatrics, not, though, on the more mundane moral grounds of the content, but on the grounds that the view of life is of the mechanistic sort that Foucault's idea of freedom is intended to counter.

62. Descombes, *Modern French Philosophy*, 14.

63. Gary Gutting sets up his account of French philosophies since the 1960s by first describing the institutional context of French philosophy, then providing a chapter on "The Hegelian Challenge." *Thinking the Impossible*, 24–49.

64. Gilles Deleuze, *Nietzsche and Philosophy*, translated by Hugh Tomlinson (London: Continuum, 1986), 1.

65. Gilles Deleuze, "Against Pessimism and Against Schopenhauer," in *Nietzsche and Philosophy*, 77–78.

66. Lacan and his influence were clearly the object of their critique. But Lacan held no candle for the family, and his work identified how damaging family life could be. But in this respect, he was as in so many others, and as he himself regularly acknowledged, merely reiterating Freud.

67. Jacques Derrida, *Negotiations: Interventions and Interviews, 1971–2001*, edited, translated, and introduction by Elizabeth Rottenberg (Stanford: Stanford University Press, 2002), 234–35.

68. Genet would become, as Sartre christened him in his book of 1952, *Saint-Genet, an actor and a martyr*. In *Glas*, a work which is a textual exhibition of deconstruction's triggerings of textual associations and discovery of unstable heterogeneities, Derrida provides "torn" commentaries stuffed with marginal insights and lengthy quotes of Hegel and Genet side by side, asking as he does, with the obvious allusion to the hypocrisy of Hegel's "pious" rendition of the "spirit" of family life and his own fathering of a bastard: "is there a place for bastardy in ontotheology or in the Hegelian

family?"—adding later, in tones reminiscent of Deleuze's and Guattari's critique of Hegel and the family, that "the family is both a part and whole of the system." *Glas,* translated by John Leavey and Richard Rand (Lincoln: University of Nebraska Press, 1986), 6 and 20. Alongside *The Birth of the Clinic: The History of Madness* and *Discipline and Punish,* Foucault would also be involved in a joint publication of a dossier and collection of essays on Pierre Rivière, a young man who had killed his mother, sister, and brother. The final essay by Alexandre Fontana would conclude: "Rivière seems always to have done a little more and little too much: in his 'senseless' child's game when he cut off the heads of cabbages, in his deluded emotional investments in universal history, in the construction of his machines, above all his crimes. It was by doing a little more, by doing too much, that he could exchange the alienating labor of reason for the liberated work of desire. Perhaps this—who knows?—was his inherent motive, which because of the flaw in their knowledge, the doctors could not see nor the lawyers hear." *I, Pierre Rivière having slaughtered my mother, my sister, and my brother . . . : A Case of parricide in the 19th Century,* edited by Michel Foucault (Harmondsworth: Penguin, 1975), 288.

69. See Part 3 of *From Revolution to Ethics,* "'Your Sexual revolution is not Ours'" French Feminist Moralism and the Limits of 'Desire.'"

70. www.dw.com/en/pedophilia-accusations-haunt-green-politician/a-16791213 last viewed August 23, 2016.

71. *From Revolution to Ethics,* 213 and ff.

72. The term "role model" had been coined by the sociologist Robert Merton and through the 1970s was increasingly coming into prominence in the development of "progressive" approaches to education. Robert K. Merton, *Social Theory and Social Structure* (New York: Free Press, 1969), 357.

73. Jacques Derrida, "Of an Apocalyptic Tone Recently Adopted in Philosophy," *Semeia* 23 (1982), 80.

74. Jacques Donzelot has said that Foucault told him this several times. See François Dosse, *Gilles Deleuze and Félix Guattari: Intersecting Lives,* translated by Deborah Glassman (New York: Columbia University Press, 2011), 316.

75. Michel Foucault, "Introduction" to Giles Deleuze and Felix Guattari, *Anti-Oedipus: Capitalism and Schizophrenia,* translated by Robert Urley, Mark Seem, and Helen Lane (Minneapolis: University of Minnesota Press, 1983), xlii.

76. Jacques Derrida, *Spectres of Marx: The State of the Debt, the Work of Mourning and the New International,* translated by Peggy Kamuf (London: Routledge, 1994), xviii.

77. The following is indicative of how Foucault completely displaces Hobbes' problem with his own: "We should not . . . be asking subjects how, why, and by what right they can agree to be subjugated, but showing how actual relations of subjugation manufacture subjects. Our second task should be to reveal relations of domination, and to allow them to assert themselves in their multiplicity, their differences, their specificity, or their reversibility; we should not be looking for a sort of sovereignty from which powers spring, but showing how the various operations of domination support one another, relate to one another, at how they converge and reinforce one another in some cases, and strive to annul one another in other cases." *Society Must Be Defended: Lectures at the Collège de France,* edited by Mauro Bertani and Alexandre Fontana (Picador: New York, 1997), 45. For the critique of Hobbes, 89–99. For a more complex and convincing account of how medieval social developments and conditions spawned a plurality of legal domains, which in turn provided the bases for pluralistic politics, see Harold Berman, *Law and Revolution: The Formation of the Western Legal Tradition* (Cambridge, MA: Harvard University Press, 1983).

78. C. B. Macpherson, *The Political Theory of Possessive Individualism: From Hobbes to Locke* (Oxford: Clarendon, 1962).

79. Michel de Certeau, *The Capture of Speech and Other Political Writings,* 11.

80. Gilles Deleuze and Felix Guattari, *What Is Philosophy?,* 6.

81. Alain Badiou, *Being and Event,* translated by Oliver Feltham (New York: Continuum, 2005), 16–17.

82. See Adam Miller, "An Interview with Alain Badiou: "Universal Truth and Question of Religion," *Journal of Philosophy and Scripture*, Volume 3, Issue 1, Fall 2005, 38–42, especially 40.

83. *Ethics: An Essay on the Understanding of Evil*, 52. I cannot refrain from commenting that Badiou has nothing of philosophical significance to contribute to the understanding of "evil" that is not already in Marx.

84. Alain Badiou, *Logic of Worlds: Being and Event 2*, translated by Alberto Toscano (London: Continuum, 2009), 578.

Conclusion

Plato's philosophical attempt to investigate the idea of the "good" was the noble but failed attempt to assemble contingencies in a rational manner which would enable the philosopher to distinguish good from bad, higher from lesser, and then find some way to make these ideas constitutionally active. It was a matter of persuasion—and timing. But timing is also contingent-dependent: lived time, as is evident in the ages and epochs we designate as part of our historical memory, is not mechanical time, and lived time is contingently formed. Further, although participants in a dialogue may well concur and provide reasons for why they value certain contingencies and ideals, the history of philosophy is the living demonstration of what it can't do: provide definitive, i.e., unassailable touchstones, the "eternal standards" of evaluation, or the measures for ensuring that human reason is capable of providing irrefutable arguments for any contingencies to which we value in order to live well.

To say of this that truth is thus relative is to oversimplify, just as it overly simplifies to say the truth is absolute. We have the capacity to view "things" and events in very different ways because "things" and events have multitudinous aspects to them, just as we are multitudinous. Yet strong collective consensuses, involving their various triggers and appeals, do play an important role in the historicity of each philosophy.[1] This is not necessarily a bad thing, it is just the way "things are." The value of the interplay between paradigms and networks, with their shared points of view and common concerns, very much depends upon the social "health" of the state of affairs under which philosophers are operating, that is upon the nourishing capacity of institutions and their relative stability within which philosophical dialogue is occurring. This is hard for philosophers to bear because the expanse of the mind so easily seems to soar beyond such mere social and historical bricks and mortar. But such "confines," if taken seriously, actually help philosophy fulfill a far more valuable role than fleeing the world and taking on the position of a divine eye—both these tendencies have contributed to philosophy doing a great deal of social damage. And the extent to which these tendencies are socially replicated in all manner of other narratives, indicates that philosophy itself all too easily becomes a major source of social ill, folly, and division.

Philosophy as a capacity to reflect upon the adequacy of ideas, and the relative health of institutions, has a particular task to play in facilitating social reproduction or rupture. But for it to play that role well, its questions have to be well targeted, and the adequacy of the targeting is inevitably bound up with the knowledge it brings to bear in its consideration. Of course, one way around that problem is to eschew historicity and sociality and deal in principles and axioms. Such an approach, though, is fraught with danger, for only through knowledge of ourselves and our world are we able to have any idea at all about the impact of principles. Aristotle's insistence upon the value of the comparative method remains an invaluable bulwark against so many idea-ist moves which simply brush aside the worlds that people live in, as if a world were merely a composite of no greater density nor durability than the insubstantial idea that the "clever person" can bring to bear to solve the world's problems.

The "way of ideas" is invariably "rationalist," which is not to be confused with the eighteenth century polemical deployment of the term by the equally misclassified "empiricists." For it matters little whether the original source of the chain of reasoning can be said to originate in the mind itself or whether it is based upon a contingency. Rationalism occurs when the guiding "idea" and value behind the reasoning process we have embarked upon "dictates" the "truths" we find acceptable, irrespective of what other questions and embarkations and points of view present themselves with respect to the "guiding ideas." Rationalism is not only the elaborate buildup of abstractions into a truth that seems palpable, but the genesis of "knowledge-claims" which serve as guard dogs in service to their lord of the idea holding authoritative truth status. Michael Oakeshott rightly detected how particularly prone political thinking is to rationalism; and in the main the field of ethics is rationalist.[2] Any thinking that can be classified as a kind of "ism" tends to be rationalist, including Marxism and poststructuralism, but also Lockean or Kantian liberalism.

Rationalism is ultimately the elaborate explication of a rationale. And insofar as the development of "meaning" is more web-like than "brick-like" it is all too understandable why rationalism is a perennial philosophical temptation. Moreover, to the extent that the human sciences are so often implicated within and dependent upon philosophical ideas the rationalist temptation is a persistent one within the human and social sciences. Anti-domination thinking is now the most ubiquitous form of rationalism.

Throughout this book I have argued that the idea becomes tyrannical when it becomes a sovereign principle or model of such rigidity that it is not responsive to ideas that require transformation and expansion of the concepts and other ideas that it can operate with in a comparative relationship. Ideas which have value have to be sufficiently open and porous that they are not means for the occlusion of experience but means of orientation that are adaptable and mobile enough that they grow along with our encounters, and the fresh questions that arise in response to our circumstances. Hence the close relationship between names and ideas that we have signaled from the outset has to be maintained if our ideas are to remain helpful. That is—we recognize that when speak of knowledge we are deferring to the growing and ever-changing stock of names, and our ideas are ultimately operating in such close relationship with the web of our named experiences and the concordances and contestations that emerge in our responses to our circumstances. An idea cannot be purely maintained with social circulation unless it is subject to strict operations restricting its development. In some activities such strictures may be advantageous because of the field of forces and operations we wish to scrutinise—this is especially so in technical areas where our techniques and their material are sufficiently paired that anything extraneous would be a distraction or even a problem. But in our life-world any such strictures are more than likely to bring far more burdens than benefits.

The great Platonic decision to take the idea as eternal and unchanging is the antithesis of what human beings most need—which is not to deny that understanding some aspects of our being are by their nature more dependent upon ideas and concepts that require very little if any change. The questions we put to our circumstances inevitably vary and some will be directed at more general conditions such as often emerge in ethical discussions about basic human goods or rights. Only the adequacy of the question will enable us to asses the adequacy of the ideas we find acceptable or even compelling; ideas are ultimately answers—which we agree upon, and suffice for knowledge until revisited with greater probing. The attempt to make our ideas fit an ideational matrix *a priori* (to put this in a manner that is more Hegelian in nomenclature than Kant-like) is fraught with problems—as Kant's philosophy showed in one way—the construction was insufficiently developmental—and Hegel's in another—the construction was ostensibly universal, but too susceptible to contingencies, most notably his own knowledge. That this would have the affect, by way of a reaction, of elevating the subject's action to the extent that one's subjectivity, or perspectivalism, or class consciousness sufficed to dictate to the world how it should be is one of the lasting acts of intellectual hubris of idea-ism that is very much continued in the anti-domination philosophies which is doing so much institutional and social damage today through a kind of essentialism in which substantive contingencies are but material for those prescribing how they *should* be. If the analytic tradition at least is innocent of this kind of hubris it, nevertheless, also suffers from an approach to our "problem solving" that not only leaves things too piecemeal, but subject to a constant splintering in which questioning becomes an exercise in itself. The price paid is its tendency toward irrelevance. However, this is not to say that there is never any yield in this process, only that recognition of the "yield" in not something that is patently obvious via the process itself. Such recognition requires a philosophical sensibility which is not overly separable from the kind of wholeness of the person that Herder (and Goethe) appealed to in his philosophical anthropology, with its developmental and polyepistemic approach, which I discuss at greater length in a book I am now working on. Such an approach does factor in our life-world in a way that Husserl aspired to incorporate within philosophy, but ultimately left insufficiently developed because of his preoccupation with first principles; thus like Descartes his preoccupation with foundational certitude misses the fact that the developmental nature of intelligence redounds upon the way we pitch the more preliminary questions that opened up the participative pathway of philosophy as a worldmaking process, and appraise the kinds of answers we find acceptable or compelling. It is not that questions concerning truth or value cannot be posed, but the kinds of answers that are worthy of serious consideration cannot fly in the face of the experiences, knowledge, and concerns that have built up over time, and which are too important to become simplified through modern myths of idea-ism or more outright ideology. In this respect much of Heidegger's critique of Husserl, but metaphysics more generally, and his factoring in of time and being, overlaps in its focus with the kind of thinking which informs the criticisms we raise of certain moves and tendencies with modern philosophy. But to replace history for a history of metaphysics, and discount philosophical anthropology because one is convinced that an anthropological horizon is predetermined by the underlying metaphysics is to succumb to the idea-ism, and a metaphysical presence, one has supposedly moved away from by entering into poetry—which as we argued in Heidegger is limited to a specific form of poetry, and hence to the kind of vista that is appropriately disclosed through that form. The more hermeneutic kind of thinking which we defer to in numerous places throughout, which Vico, Hamann, and Herder also brought to the attention of philosophy, and which is invaluable for any philosophy operating in conjunction with the human sciences is largely missing in all the modern current of philosophy which I have identified as idea-ist.

This book is an attempt to help rectify this omission. The importance of such a task is not purely one of philosophical precision, but rather insofar as the "way of ideas" is now so institutionally instantiated—to the extent that modern political life generally, and not just the Soviet Union (as Martin Malia had argued) is "ideo-cratic," the fate of philosophy and the fate of our world have to an important extent become inseparable.[3] Philosophies which attempt to impose conformity become tools in making a world of suffocating uniformity. The idolatry of the idea is the step that leads to the tyranny of idea-ism, and the tyranny of idea-ism is the tyranny of ideological thinking as such. Ideology then requires the suppression and extermination of thoughts that would be free from the idea-ist stricture, and then those who persist in thinking them.

NOTES

1. The importance of philosophical networking and the socio-historical role it has played in philosophy is a core theme of Randall Collins's monumental work *The Sociology of Philosophies: A Global Theory of Intellectual Change* (Cambridge, MA: Harvard University Press, 1998).

2. Michael Oakeshott, *Rationalism in Politics and Other Essays* (London: Methuen, 1962).

3. Martin Malia, *The Soviet Tragedy: A History of Socialism in Russian, 1917–1991* (New York: Free Press, 1994), 137.

Bibliography

Adorno, Theodor. *Minima Moralia: Reflections on A Damaged Life*. Translated by E. Jephcott. London: Verso. 1974.

Agassi, Joseph. "Heidegger Made Simple (and Offensive)." *Philosophy of the Social Sciences*, Vol. 34, No. 3, September 423–31. 2004.

Akehurst, Thomas. *The Cultural Politics of Analytic Philosophy: Britishness and the Spectre of Europe*. London: Continuum. 2010.

Allan, Amy. "Politics." *The Cambridge Foucault Lexicon*. Edited by Leonard Lawler and John Naler. Cambridge: Cambridge University Press. 2014.

Althusser, Louis. Correspondence with Jacques Lacan (1963–1969).http://nosubject. com/index.php?title=Correspondence_with_Jacques_Lacan_%281963_-_1969%29

Ascheim, Steven, *The Nietzsche Legacy in Germany, 1880–1990*. Berkeley: University of California Press. 1992.

Augustine. *Confessions and Enchiridion*. Translated by Albert Outler. Grand Rapids, MI: Christian Ethereal Library. 1955.

Augustine. *On Christian Doctrine* in *The Works of Augustine Vol. IX*. Translated by Marcus Dodds. Edinburgh: T and T. Clark. 1892.

Badiou, Alain. *Ethics: An Essay on the Understanding of Evil*. Translated by Hallward. London: Verso. 2002.

Badiou, Alain. *Being and Event*. Translated by Oliver Feltham. New York: Continuum. 2005.

Badiou, Alain. *Logic of Worlds: Being and Event 2*. Translated by Alberto Toscano. London: Continuum. 2009.

Barr James, *The Semantics of Biblical Language*. Oxford: Oxford University Press. 1961.

Bataille, Georges. *Georges Bataille: Visions of Excess: Selected Writings, 1927–1939*. Translated by Allan Stoekl, with Carl Lovitt and Donald Leslie. Minneapolis: University of Minnesota Press. 1985.

Bauer, Bruno. *The Trumpet of the Last Judgement against Hegel the Atheist and Antichrist. An Ultimatum*. Lewiston, NY: E. Mellen Press. 1989.

Beaney Michael. "Introduction" to *The Analytic Turn: Analysis in Early Analytic Philosophy and Phenomenology*. Edited by Michael Beaney. London: Routledge. 2007.

Beattie, James. *An Essay on the Nature and Immutability of Truth*. Edinburgh: Denham and Dick. 1805.

Beiser, Frederick. *The Fate of Reason: German Philosophy from Kant to Fichte*. Cambridge, MA: Harvard University Press. 1987.

Bell, "Martin. "Hume on Causation," *The Cambridge Companion to Hume*. Edited by David Norton and Jacqueline Taylor. Cambridge: Cambridge University Press. 2009.

Benjamin, Walter. "*Selected Writings, Volume 4, 1938–1940*. Translated by Edward Jephcott and others. Edited by Howard Eiland and Michael Jennings. Cambridge, MA: Belknap. 2006.

Berkeley, George. *Principles of Human Knowledge in Principles of Human Knowledge and Three Dialogues*. Edited, introduction and notes by Howard Robinson. Oxford: Oxford University Press. 1710.

Berman, Harold. *Law and Revolution: The Formation of the Western Legal Tradition*. Cambridge, MA: Harvard University Press. 1983.

Bernouilli, Carl. *Franz Overbeck und Friedrich Nietzsche: Eine Freundschaft, Band 1*. Jena: Eugen Diedrichs. 1908.

Blanchot, Maurice. *The Station Hill: Blanchot Reader Fiction and Literary Essays.* Translated by Lydia Davis, Paul Auster, and Robert Lamberton. Barrytown: Station Hill. 1999.

Boehm, Rudolf. "Husserl and Nietzsche." *Nietzsche and Phenomenology.* Edited Andrea Rehberg. Newcastle on Tyne: Cambridge Scholars Press. 2011.

Boman, Thorleif. *Hebrew Thought Compared with Greek.* London: SCM Press. 1960.

Borradori, Giovanna. *Philosophy in a Time of Terror: Dialogues with Jürgen Habermas and Jacques Derrida.* Chicago: University of Chicago Press. 2003.

Boublil, Élodie, and Christine Daigle (eds.) *Nietzsche and Phenomenology: Power, Life, Subjectivity.* Bloomington: Indiana University Press. 2013.

Bourg, Julian. *From Revolution to Ethics: May 1968 and Contemporary French Thought.* Montreal: McGill-Queen's University Press. 2007.

Bowie, Andrew. *Schelling and European Philosophy: An Introduction.* London: Routledge. 1993.

Boyle, Deborah. *Descartes on Innate Ideas.* London: Continuum. 2009.

Buber, Martin. *I and Thou.* Translated by Walter Kaufman. New York: Simon and Schuster. 1970.

Brito, Emilio. "L"anthropologie chrétienne de Schelling," *Revue théologique de Louvain* 18. 3–29. 1987.

Buckle, Stephen. *Hume's Enlightenment Tract: The Unity and Purpose of An Enquiry Concerning Human Understanding.* Oxford: Oxford University Press. 2001.

Buckley, R. Philip. *Husserl, Heidegger and the Crisis of Philosophical Responsibility.* Dordrecht: Springer. 1992.

"Bureau of Public Secrets: May 1968 Graffiti. "http://www.bopsecrets.org/CF/graffiti. htm

Burke, Edmund. *Reflections on the Revolution in France.* Oxford: Oxford University Press. 1999.

Camus, Albert. *The Rebel.* Translated by Anthony Bower. Harmondsworth: Penguin. 1971.

Capobianco, Richard. *Engaging Heidegger.* Toronto: University of Toronto Press. 2010.

Cairns, Dorion. *Conversations with Husserl and Fink.* The Hague: Martinus Nijhof. 1976.

Capaldi, Nicholas. *The Enlightenment Project in the Analytic Conversation.* Dordrecht: Springer. 1998.

Cassirer, Ernst. *Das Erkenntnisproblem in der Philosophie und Wissenschaft der neueren Zeit. Zweiter Band.* Berlin: Bruno Cassirer. 1922.

Cassirer, Ernst. *Substance and Function.* Chicago: Open Court. 1923.

Caton, Hiram. *The Origin of Subjectivity: An Essay on Descartes.* New Haven: Yale University Press. 1973.

Certeau, Michel de. *The Capture of Speech and Other Political Writings.* Translated by Tom Conley. Minneapolis: University of Minnesota Press. 1997.

Chesteron, G. K. *Selected Essays.* Introduced by John Guest. London: Collins. 1939.

Cixous, Hélène, and Jacques Derrida. *Veils.* Translated by Geoffrey Bennington. Stanford: Stanford University Press. 2001.

Ciezkowski, August. *Prolegomena to a Historiosophy* of 1838, in *Selected Writings of August Ciezkowski.* Edited, translated and introduced by André Leibich. Cambridge: Cambridge University Press. 1979.

Claussen, Detlev. *Adorno: One Last Genius.* Translated by Rodney Livingston. Cambridge, MA: Belknap. 2010.

Cohen, Richard. (ed.) *Face to Face with Levinas.* New York: State University of New York Press. 1986.

Collins, Randall. *The Sociology of Philosophies: A Global Theory of Intellectual Change.* Cambridge MA: Harvard University Press. 1998.

Conant, James. "The Emergence of the Concept of the Analytic Tradition as a Form of Philosophical Self-Consciousness." *Beyond the Analytic-Continental Divide Pluralist Philosophy in the Twenty-First Century.* Edited by Jeffrey A. Bell, Andrew Cutrofello, and Paul M. Livingston. London: Routledge. 2017.

Cuddihy, John. *No Offence: Civil Religion and Protestant Taste*. New York: Seabury Press. 1978.

Cusset, François. *French Theory: How Foucault, Derrida, Deleuze and Co. Transformed the Intellectual Life of the United States*. Translated by Jeff Fort. Minneapolis: University of Minnesota Press. 2008.

Dahlstrom, Daniel. "Scheler's Critique of Heidegger's Fundamental Ontology" in *Max Scheler's Acting Persons: New Perspectives*. Edited by Stephen Schneck. Amsterdam: Rodopi. 2002.

Danford, John. *Hume and the Problem of Reason: Recovering the Human Sciences*. New Haven: Yale University Press. 1990.

Day, Jerry. *Voegelin, Schelling and the Philosophy of Existence*. Columbia, MO: University of Missouri Press. 2003.

Gilles Deleuze, *Nietzsche and Philosophy*. Translated by Hugh Tomlinosn. London: Continuum. 1986.

Deleuze, Gilles. *The Fold: Leibniz and the Baroque*. Translated by Tom Conley. London: Athlone. 1993.

Deleuze, Gilles. *Difference and Repetition*. Translated by Paul Patton. London: Continuum. 2004.

Deleuze, Gilles. *Desert Islands and Other Texts 1953–1974*. Edited by David Lapoujade and translated by Michael Taomina. Los Angeles: Semiotex(e). 2004.

Deleuze, Giles and Felix Guattari. *Anti-Oedipus: Capitalism and Schizophrenia*. Translated by Robert Urley, Mark Seem, and Helen Lane. Minneapolis: University of Minnesota Press. 1983.

Deleuze, Gilles and Felix Guattari. *A Thousand Plateaus: Capitalism and Schizophrenia*, translated by Brian Massumi. Minneapolis: University of Minneapolis Press. 1987.

Deleuze, Gilles and Felix Guattari. *What Is Philosophy?* Translated by Hugh Tomlinson and Graham Burchell. New York: Columbia University Press. 1994.

Derrida, Jacques. *Writing and Difference*. Translated by Allan Bass. London: Routledge and Kegan Paul. 1978.

Derrida, Jacques. "Of an Apocalyptic Tone Recently Adopted in Philosophy." *Semeia* 23. 1982.

Derrida, Jacques. "Like the Sound of the Sea Deep within a Shell: Paul de Man's War." *Critical Inquiry*, 14, Spring 590–652. 1988.

Derrida, Jacques, and John Caputo. *Deconstruction in a Nutshell: A Conversation with Jacques Derrida*. New York: Fordham University Press. 1992.

Derrida, Jacques. *Spectres of Marx: The State of the Debt, the Work of Mourning and the New International*. Translated by Peggy Kamuf. London: Routledge. 1994.

Derrida, Jacques. *Points: Interview, 1974–1994*. Edited by Elizabeth Weber. Translated by Peggy Kamuf and others. Stanford: Stanford University Press. 1995.

Derrida, Jacques and Anne Dufourmantelle. *Of Hospitality: Anne Dufourmantelle Invites Jacques Derrida to Respond*. Translated by Rachel Bowlby. Stanford: Stanford University Press. 2000.

Derrida, Jacques. *Negotiations: Interventions and Interviews, 1971–2001*. Edited, translated, and introduction by Elizabeth Rottenberg. Stanford: Stanford University Press. 2002.

Derrida, Jacques. *Rogues: Two Essays on Reason*. Translated by Pascale-Anne Brault and Michael Naas. Stanford: Stanford University Press. 2005.

Descartes, René. *Meditations, Objections and Replies*. Translated by Roger Ariew and Donald Cress. Indianapolis: Hackett. 2006.

Descartes, René. *The Principles of Philosophy*. Translated by V. and R. Miller. Dordrecht: Reidel. 1983.

Descartes, René. *The Philosophical Writings of Descartes, Volume 1*. Translated by John Cottingham, Robert Stoothoff, and Dugald Murdoch. Cambridge: Cambridge University Press. 1985.

Descombes, Vincent. *Modern French Philosophy*. Cambridge; Cambridge University Press. 1980.

de Tracy, Destutt. *A Treatise on Political Economy to which is prefixed A Supplement to a Preceding work on the Understanding Or, Elements of Ideology.* Translated by Thomas Jefferson. Auburn, AL: The Ludwig von Mises Institute. 2009.

Devaney, M.J. *"Since at Least Plato . . ." and Other Postmodernist Myths.* Palgrave: Mac-Millan. 1997.

Dews, Peter. *Logics of Disintegration: Post-structuralist Thought and the Claims of Critical Theory.* London: Verso. 1987.

Dilthey, Wilhelm, *Selected Works Volume 3; Understanding the Human World.* Edited and translated by Rudolf A. Makkreel and Fithjof Rodi. Princeton, NJ: Princeton University Press. 2010.

Djilas, Milovan. *The New Class: An Analysis of the Communist System.* San Diego: Harcourt Brace Jovanovich. 1957.

Dosse, François. *Gilles Deleuze and Félix Guattari: Intersecting Lives.* Translated by Deborah Glassman. New York: Columbia University Press. 2011.

Dummett, Michael. "Oxford Philosophy." *Truth and Other Enigmas.* London: Duckworth. 1978.

Dummett, Michael. *Origins of Analytic Philosophy.* Oxford: Duckworth. 1993.

Esposito, Joseph. *Schelling's Idealism and the Philosophy of Nature.* Lewisburg: Bucknell University Press. 1977.

Fabisak, Thomas. *David Friedrich Strauss's Life of Jesus Critically Examined.* Atlanta: SBL Press. 2015.

Fabro, Cornelio. *God in Exile: Modern Atheism: A Study in the Internal Dynamic of Modern Atheism from Its Roots in the Cartesian Cogito to the Present Day.* Translated by Arthur Gibson. Westminster, MD: Newman Press, 1964.

Farias, Victor. *Heidegger and Nazism.* Philadelphia: Temple University Press. 1991.

Farin, Ingo. "The Black Notebooks in Their Historical and Political Context." *Reading Heidegger's Black-Notebooks.* Edited by Ingo Farin and Jeff Malpas. Cambridge, MA: MIT, 2016. 289–322.

Faurot, J.H. "Reid's Answer to Joseph Priestley," *Journal of the History of Ideas,* Vol. 39, No. 2 (April–June). 285–292. 1978.

Faye, Emmanuel. *Heidegger: The Introduction of Nazism into Philosophy in Light of the Unpublished Seminars of 1933–1935.* New Haven: Yale University Press. 2011.

Ferry, Luc and Alain Renaut. *French Philosophy of the Sixties: An Essay on Anti-Humanism.* Translated by Mary Cattini. Amherst: University of Massachusetts Press. 1990.

Fichte. J. G. *The Popular Works of Johann Gottlieb Fichte.* Translated William Smith. London: Trubner. 1889.

Fichte, J. G. "First Introduction to the Science of Knowledge" in *The Science of Knowledge with the First and Second Introductions.* Translated by Peter Heath and John Lachs. Cambridge: Cambridge University Press. 1982.

Fichte, J. G. "Concerning the Concept of the *Wissenshaftslehre,* or, of So-called "Philosophy," in *Fichte: Early Philosophical Writings.* Translated by Daniel Breazeale. Ithaca: Cornell University Press. 1988.

M. Fóti, Véronique. "Heidegger, Hölderlin, and Sophoclean Tragedy," in *Heidegger Toward the Turn: Essays on the Work of the 1930s.* Edited by James Risser. Albany, NY: SUNY. 1999.

Foucault, Michel. *The Order of Things: An Archaeology of the Human Sciences.* London: Tavistock. 1970.

Foucault, Michel. *The Archaeology of Knowledge.* Translated by A. M. Sheridan Smith. London: Tavistock. 1972.

Foucault, Michel. *"I, Pierre Rivière having slaughtered my mother, my sister, and my brother . . . : A Case of parricide in the 19th Century.* Edited by Michel Foucault. Harmondsworth: Penguin. 1975.

Foucault, Michel. *Power/Knowledge: Selected Interviews and Other Writings 1972–1977.* Edited by Colin Gordon. Brighton, Sussex: Harvester Press. 1980.

Foucault, Michel. *The Foucault Reader.* Edited by Paul Rabinow. New York: Pantheon. 1984.

Foucault, Michel. *Society Must Be Defended: Lectures at the Collège de France.* Edited by Mauro Bertani and Alessandro Fontana. Picador: New York. 1997.

Foucault, Michel. *Religion and Culture.* Selected and edited by Jeremy Carrette. Routledge: New York. 1999.

Foucault, Michel. *History of Madness.* Translated by Jonathan Murphy and Jean Khalfa, with foreword by Ian Hacking. London: Routledge. 2006.

Foucault, Michel. *The Birth of Biopolitics: Lectures at the Collège de France 1978–1979.* Edited by Michael Senellart. Translated by Graham Burchell. New York: Palgrave MacMillan. 2008.

Foucault, Michel. *The Courage of the Truth: The Government of self and others II Lectures at the Collège de France, 1983–1984.* Edited by Frédérick Gross and translated by Graham Burchell. London: Palgrave Macmillan. 2011.

Frege, Gottlob. *Die Grundlage der Arithmetik [The Foundation of Arithmetic].* Edited and translated by J. L. Austin. Oxford: Basil Blackwell. 1969.

Friedländer, Paul. *Plato, Volume 1: An Introduction.* Translated by Hans Meyerhoff. London: Routledge and Kegan Paul. 1958.

Friedrich, Rainer. "The Enlightenment: Gone Mad: The Dismal Discourse of Postmodernism's Grand Narrative." *Arion: A Journal of the Humanities and Classics,* volumes: 19 No. 3, 31–78. 2012, and Vol. 20, No. 1 (Spring/Summer 2012), 67–112. 2012.

Freund, Elsa. *Franz Rosenzweig's Philosophy of Existence: An Analysis of the State of Redemption.* Dordrecht: Springer. 1979.

Gellner, Ernst. *Cause and Meaning in the Social Sciences.* London: Routledge and Kegan Paul. 1973.

Glock, Hans-Johann. *What Is Analytic Philosophy?* Cambridge: Cambridge University Press. 2008.

Glucksmann, André. "A Ventriloquist Structuralism." *New Left Review,* 1/72, March-April. 1972.

Golder, Ben. *Foucault and the Politics of Rights.* Stanford: Stanford University Press. 2015.

Grant, Ian Hamilton. *Philosophies of Nature After Schelling.* London: Continuum. 2006.

Greene, Naomi. "All the Great Myths Are Dark": Artaud and Fascism." *Antoin Artaud and The Modern Theatre.* Edited by Gene Plunka. Toronto: Associated University Press. 1994.

Gutting, Gary. *Thinking the Impossible: French Philosophy Since 1960.* Oxford: Oxford University Press. 2013.

Guyer, Paul. "Locke's Philosophy of Language," in *The Cambridge Companion to Locke.* Edited by Vere Chappell. Cambridge: Cambridge University Press. 1994.

Hacker, Peter. "Analytic Philosophy: Beyond the Linguistic Turn and Back Again." *The Analytic Turn: Analysis in Early Analytic Philosophy and Phenomenology.* Edited by Michael Beaney. London: Routledge. 2007.

Haddock, Guillermo E. RosadoI. *The Young Carnap's Unknown Master: Husserl's Influence on Der Raum and Der logische Aufbau der Welt.* Aldershot, UK: Ashgate. 2008.

Hanna, Patricia and Bernard Harrison. *Word and World: Practice and the Foundation of Language.* Cambridge: Cambridge University Press. 2004.

Hatfield, Gary. "Descartes's Physiology and Its Relation to Psychology" in *The Cambridge Companion to Descartes.* Edited by John Cottingham. Cambridge: Cambridge University Press. 1992.

Hedley, Douglas and Sarah Hutton (eds). *Platonism at the Origins of Modernity: Studies on Platonism and Early Modern Philosophy.* Dordrecht: Springer. 2010.

Heidegger, Martin. *Being and Time.* Translated by John Macquarie and Edward Robinson. Oxford: Blackwell. 1963.

Heidegger, Martin. *What Is A Thing?* Translated by W. B. Barton, Jr. and Vera Deutsch with an analysis by Eugene T. Gendlin. South Bend, IN: Gateway. 1967.

Heidegger, Martin. *On the Way to Language,* translated by Peter Hertz. New York: Harper and Row. 1971.

Heidegger, Martin. *Poetry, Language, Thought.* Translated by Albert Hofstadter. New York: Harper and Row. 1971.

Heidegger, Martin. *Basic Writings: Nine Key Essays, plus "Introduction to Being and Time."* Edited, translated and introduced by David Farrell Krell. London: Routledge and Kegan Paul. 1978.

Heidegger, Martin. *Off the Beaten Track.* Translated and edited by Julian Young and Kenneth Haynes. Cambridge: Cambridge University Press. 2002.

Heidegger, Martin. *The End of Philosophy.* Translated by Joan Stambaugh. New York: Harper and Row. 1973.

Heidegger, Martin. *Gesamtausgabe, Band 67: Metaphysik und Nihilsmus.* Frankfurt am Main: Vittorio Klostermannn. 1999.

Heidegger, Martin. *Überlegungen, XII–XV, (Schwarze Hefte 1939–1941), Gesamtausgabe, IV Abteilung: Hinweise und Aufzeichnungen Band. 96.* Herausgegeben von Peter Trawny. Frankfurt am Main: Vittorio Klostermann. 2014.

Heidegger, Martin. *Anmerkungen I–V (Schwarze Hefte 1942–1948). Gesamtausgabe, Band 97.* Frankfurt am Main: Klostermann. 2015.

Heidegger, Martin. *Ponderings II-VI, Black Notebooks 1931–1938.* Translated by Richard Rojcewicz. Bloomington: Indiana University Press. 2016.

Hegel, G. W. F. *The Science of Logic.* Translated and edited by George di Giovanni. Cambridge: Cambridge University Press. 2010.

Hegel, G. W. F. *Vorlesungen über die Geschichte der Philosophie, III, Werke, Bd. 20.* Herausgegeben von Eva Moldenhauer und Karl Markus Michel. Frankfurt am Main: Suhrkamp. 1971.

Hegel, G. W. F. *Hegel's Philosophy of Nature.* Translated, edited, and introduced by M. J. Petry. London: Allen and Unwin. 1968.

Hegel, G. W. F. *Phenomenology of Spirit.* Translated by A. V. Miller, with analysis of the text and foreword by J. N. Findlay. Oxford: Oxford University Press. 1977.

Hegel, G. W. F. *Lectures on the History of Philosophy Volume 3: The Lectures of 1825–1826.* Edited by R. F. Brown, translated R. F. Brown and J. M Stewart with the assistance of H. R. S. Harris. Berkeley: University of California Press. 1990.

Hegel, G. W. F. *The Encyclopaedia Logic (with the Zusätze): Part 1 of the Encyclopaedia of the Philosophical Sciences.* Translated with introduction and notes by T. F. Geraets, W. Suchting, and H. S. Harris. Indianapolis: Hackett, 1991.

Hegel, G. W. F. *Faith and Knowledge.* Translated by Walter Cerf and H. S. Harris. New York: SUNY. 1988.

Hegel, G. W. F. *Hegel: The Difference Between the Fichtean and Schellingian System.* Translated by Jean Paul Surber. Atascadero, CA: Ridgeview. 1978.

Herder, Johann Gottfried. *Schriften zu Literatur und Philosophie, 1792–1800.* Edited by Hans Dietrich Irmscher. Frankfurt am Maine: Deutscher Klassiker Verlag. 1998.

Hermann, Friedrich Wilhelm von. *Hermeneutics and Reflection: Heidegger and Husserl on the Concept of Phenomenology.* Translated by Kenneth Maly. Toronto: University of Toronto Press. 2013.

Hodges, H. A. *The Philosophy of Wilhelm Dilthey.* London: Routledge and Kegan Paul. 1952.

Horkheimer, Max and Theodor Adorno. *Dialectic of Enlightenment.* New York: Herder and Herder. 1969.

Hudson, Wayne. "Aporeitic Schelling." Wayne Hudson, Douglas Moggach, and Marcelo Stamm. *Rethinking German Idealism.* Aurora, CO: Noesis. 2016.

Hühn, Lore, "A Philosophical Dialogue between Heidegger and Schelling." *Comparative and Continental Philosophy.* 6:1, 16–34. 2014.

Hume, David. *Letters of David Hume to William Strahan.* Edited by G. Birkbeck Hill. Oxford: Clarendon. 1888.

Hume, David. *Hume's A Treatise on Human Nature.* Edited by L. A. Selby-Bigge. Oxford: Clarendon Press. 1888.

Hume, David. *Hume's Enquiries Concerning the Human Understanding and Concerning the Principles of Morals.* Edited by L. A. Selby-Bigge. Oxford: Clarendon Press. 1888.

Hume, David. "The Skeptic" in *The Philosophical Works of David Hume, Volume 3.* Edinburgh: Adam Black and William and Charles Taite. 1826.

Hume, David. *The Letters of David Hume.* Edited by J. Y. T. Greig. Oxford: Clarendon Press. 1932.

Husserl, Edmund. *Philosophy and the Crisis of the European Sciences: The Crisis of European Sciences and Transcendental Phenomenology.* Translated by David Carr. Evanston, IL: Northwestern University Press. 1970.

Husserl, Edmund. *The Paris Lectures.* Translated and Introductory essay by Peter Koestenbaum. Martinus Nijhof: The Hague. 1975.

Husserl, Edmund. *Edmund Husserl Psychological and Transcendental Phenomenology and the Confrontation with Heidegger (1927–1931).* Translated and edited by Thomas Sheehan and Richard Palmer. Dordrecht: Kluwer. 1997.

Husserl, Edmund. *Phenomenology and the Crisis of Philosophy.* Translated by Quentin Lauer. New York: Harper and Row. 1965.

Husserl, Edmund. *Cartesian Meditations: An Introduction to Phenomenology.* Translated by Dorion Cairns. The Hague: Martinus Nijhoff. 1960.

James, David. *Fichte's Social and Political Philosophy: Prosperity and Virtue.* Cambridge: Cambridge University Press.

Janicaud, Dominque. *Heidegger in France.* Bloomington: Indiana University Press. 2015.

Jolley, Nicholas. *The Light of the Soul: Theories of Ideas in Leibniz, Malebranche and Descartes.* Oxford: Oxford University Press. 1990.

Jordan, Neil. "Schopenhauer's Politics: Ethics, Jurisprudence and the State." *Better Consciousness: Schopenhauer's Philosophy of Value.* Oxford: Blackwell. Edited by Alex Neill and Christopher Janaway. 171–188. 2009.

Kant, Immanuel. *Critique of Pure Reason.* Translated by Norman Kemp Smith. New York: St. Martin's Press. 1929.

Kant, Immanuel. *Prolegomena to Any Future Metaphysics That Will Be Able to Present Itself as Science.* Translated and edited by P. Gray-Lucas. Manchester: Manchester University Press. 1953.

Kant, Immanuel. *Gesammelte Schriften: Akademieausgabe. Band 12.* Herausgegeben von Otto Schöndörffer. Berlin: Walter de Gruyter. 1922.

Kaufmann, Walter. *Nietzsche: Philosopher, Psychologist, Antichrist.* Princeton, NJ: Princeton University Press. 1950.

Kelley, Lawrence. *War before Civilization: The Myth of the Peaceful Savage.* Oxford: Oxford University Press. 1996.

Kierkegaard, Søren. *Two Ages: The Age of Revolution and the Present Age, A Literary Review.* Edited and translated by Howard and Eva Hong with introduction and notes. Princeton, NJ: Princeton University Press. 1978.

Kierkegaard, Søren. *The Concept of Anxiety: A Simple Psychological Orienting Deliberation on the Dogmatic Issue of Hereditary Sin.* Princeton, NJ: Princeton University Press. 1980.

Kierkegaard, Søren. *The Concept of Irony with Continual Reference to Socrates Together with Notes of Schelling's Berlin Lectures.* Edited and translated with introduction and notes by Howard Hong and Edna Hong. Princeton, NJ: Princeton University Press. 1989.

Kierkegaard, Søren. *The Point of View: On My Work as an Author, The Point of View for My Work as an Author, Armed Neutrality.* Edited with instruction and notes by Howard and Edna Hong. Princeton, NJ: Princeton University Press. 1998.

Kierkegaard, Søren. *Repetition and Philosophical Crumbs.* Translated by M. G. Piety. Introduction by Edward F. Mooney and notes by Edward F. Mooney and M. G. Piety. Oxford: Oxford University Press. 2009.

Kierkegaard, Søren. *Concluding Unscientific Postscript to the Philosophical Crumbs: A Mimic, Pathetic, Dialectic Compilation An Existential Contribution By Johannes Climacus Responsible for Publication: S. Kierkegaar*d. Translated by Alastair Hannay. Cambridge: Cambridge University Press. 2009.

Kierkegaard, Søren. *Fear and Trembling in Fear and Trembling and Sickness Unto Death.* Translated with notes by Walter Lowrie. Introduction by Gordon Marino. Princeton, NJ: Princeton University Press. 2013.

Kivy, Peter. *The Seventh Sense: Frances Hutcheson and Eighteenth Century British Aesthetics.* Oxford: Clarendon. 2003.

Kleinberg, Ethan. *Generation Existential: Heidegger's Philosophy in France, 1927–1961.* Ithaca: Cornell University Press. 2005.

Kroner, Richard. *Von Kant Bis Hegel.* Tübingen: H. Laupp. 1921.

Kuehn, Manfred. *Scottish Common Sense in Germany, 1768–1800: A Contribution to the History of Critical Philosophy.* Kingston and Montreal: McGill-Queen's University Press. 1987.

Lacan, Jacques. *The Ethics of Psychoanalysis: 1959–1960: The Seminar of Jacques Lacan Book VII.* Edited by Jacques-Alain Miller. Translated with notes by Dennis Porter. New York: W.W. Norton. 1992.

Lauer, Quentin. *Essays in Hegelian Dialectic.* New York: Fordham University Press. 1977.

Laughland, John. *Schelling Versus Hegel: From German Idealism to Christian Metaphysics.* Aldershot: Ashgate. 2007.

Lawrenz, Jürgen. "Leibniz's *Kehre*: From Ultradeterminism to the Philosophy of Freedom." *The European Legacy* 23:5. 479–89. 2018.

Leibniz, G. W. *Discourse on Metaphysics* in *Discourse on Metaphysics, Correspondence with Arnauld and Monadology.* Introduction by Paul Janet, translated George Montgomery. Chicago: Open Court. 1902.

Leibniz, Gottfried Wilhelm. *Philosophical Papers and Letters.* Translated and edited by Leroy E. Loemker. Dordrecht: Kluwer. 1989.

Leibniz, G. W. "Pacidius to Philalethes: A First Philosophy of Motion," in *The Labyrinth of the Continuum: Writings on the Continuum Principle, 1672–1686.* New Haven: Yale University Press. 2001.

Lévy, Bernard-Henri. *Sartre: Philosopher of the Twentieth Century.* London: Polity. 2003.

Locke, John. *Locke's Essays: An Essay Concerning the Human Understanding, and A Treatise on the Conduct of the Understanding.* Philadelphia: Troutman and Hayes. 1850.

Locke, John. "An Examination of P. Malebranche's Opinion of Seeing All Things in God," in *The Works of John Locke, Volume II,* with a preliminary essay and notes by J. St. John. London: Bell and Daldy. 1872.

Ludovici, Anthony M. "Hitler and the Third Reich." *The English Review 63*, 35–41, 147–53, 231–39. 1936.

Lukács, Georg. *History and Class Consciousness: Studies in Marxist Dialectics.* Translated by Rodney Livingstone. Cambridge, MA: MIT Press. 1971.

Lukács, Georg. "Moses Hess and the Problems of the Idealist Dialectic (1926)." *Telos 10*, Winter. 1971.

Lukács, Georg. *The Destruction of Reason.* Translated by Peter Palmer. London: Merlin, 1980.

Lloyd, Genevieve. *The Man of Reason: Male and Female in Western Philosophy.* London: Routledge. 1993.

Macpherson, C. B. *The Political Theory of Possessive Individualism: From Hobbes to Locke.* Oxford: Clarendon. 1962.

Malebranche, Nicolas. *Dialogues on Metaphysics and Religion.* Translated by Jonathan Bennett. http://www.earlymoderntexts.com/pdfs/malebranche1688.pdf.

Malebranche, Nicolas. *The Search After Truth.* Edited by Thomas M. Lennon and Paul J. Oscamp. Cambridge: Cambridge University Press. 1997.

Malia, Martin. *The Soviet Tragedy: A History of Socialism in Russian, 1917–1991.* New York: Free Press, 1994.

Marková, Ivana. *The Dialogical Mind: Common Sense and Ethics.* Cambridge: Cambridge University Press. 2016.

Marx, Karl. *Capital, Volume 1.* Translated by S. Moore and E. Aveling. London: Lawrence and Wishart. 1954.

Marx, Karl, and Friedrich Engels. *Marx/Engels Selected Correspondence*. Moscow: Progress. 1955.

Marx, Karl and Friedrich Engels. *Marx Engels Werke* Bd. 3. Berlin Dietz. 1958.

Marx, Karl. *Capital, Volume 3*. Translated by C. Kerr. London: Lawrence and Wishart. 1959.

Marx, Karl and Friedrich Engels. *Marx Engels Werke, Band 4*. Berlin: Dietz. 1959.

Marx, Karl, and Friedrich Engels. *The Revolutions of 1848: Political Writings, Volume 1*. Edited and introduced by David Fernbach. Harmondsworth: Penguin. 1973.

Marx, Karl *Grundrisse*. Translated by Martin Nicolaus. Harmondsworth: Penguin. 1973.

Marx, Karl, and Friedrich Engels. *The German Ideology*. London: Lawrence and Wishart. 1974.

Marx, Karl and Friedrich Engels. *Collected Works, Volume 3*. London: Lawrence and Wishart. 1975.

Marx, Karl. *Early Writings*. Introduced by Lucio Colletti. Translated by Rodney Livingstone and Gregor Benton. Harmondsworth: Penguin. 1975.

Marx, Karl. *The Holy Family, or Critique of Critical Criticism: Against Bruno Bauer and Company*. Moscow: Progress. 1975.

Marx, Karl. *A Contribution to the Critique of Political Economy*. Translated by S. W. Ryazanskaya. Edited by Maurice Dobb. Moscow: Progress. 1977.

Mehlman, Jeffrey. *Genealogies of the Text: Literature, Psychoanalysis and Politics in Modern France*. Cambridge: Cambridge University Press. 1995.

Mercer, Christia. *Leibniz Metaphysics: Its Origins and Development*. Cambridge: Cambridge University Press. 2004.

Merton, Robert K. *Social Theory and Social Structure*. New York: Free Press. 1968 .

Mijuskovic, Ben. "Hume and Shaftesbury on the Self." *The Philosophical Quarterly* 21. (85). 324–36. 1971.

Mikics, David. *Who was Jacques Derrida? An Intellectual Biography*. New Haven: Yale University Press. 2009.

Miller, Adam. "An Interview with Alain Badiou: Universal Truth and Question of Religion." *Journal of Philosophy and Scripture*. Volume 3, Issue 1, Fall 38–42. 2005.

Monk, Ray. "What Is Analytical Philosophy?" *Bertrand Russell and the Origins of Analytical Philosophy*. Edited and introduced by Ray Monk and Anthony Palmer. Bristol: Thoemmes, 1996.

Monk, Ray. "Was Russell an Analytical Philosopher?" *Ratio*, Vol. 9, No. 3. December. 227–42. 1996.

Moore, G. E. *Selected Writings*. Edited by T. Baldwin. London: Routledge. 1993.

More, Henry. *An Antidote Against Atheism: An Appeal to the Naturall Faculties of Man, whether there be not a God*. Cambridge: William Morden. 1655.

Mulligan, Kevin, Peter Simons, and Barry Smith. "What's Wrong with Contemporary Philosophy?," *Topoi* 25. (1–2). 2006.

Nassar, Dalia. *The Romantic Absolute: Being and Knowing in Early German Romantic Philosophy, 1795–1804*. Chicago: University of Chicago Press. 2014.

Nietzsche, Friedrich. *The Will to Power*. Translated with introduction by Walter Kaufmann and R. J. Hollingdale. New York: Vintage Books. 1967.

Thus Spake Zarathustra: A Book for Everyone and No One. Translated by R. J. Hollingdale. Harmondsworth: Penguin. 1969.

Nietzsche, Friedrich. *The Birth of Tragedy and Other Writings*. Edited by Raymond Geuss and (translated) by Ronald Spies. Cambridge: Cambridge University Press. 1999.

Nietzsche, Friedrich. *Beyond Good and Evil: Prelude to a Philosophy of the Future*. Edited by Rolf-Peter Horstmann and (also translated by) Judith Norman. Cambridge: Cambridge University Press. 2002.

Nietzsche, Friedrich. *On the Genealogy of Morality*. Edited by Keith Ansell Pearson and translated by Carol Diethe. Cambridge: Cambridge University Press, 2007.

Nietzsche, Friedrich. *The Anti-Christ, Twilight of the Idols and Other Writings.* Edited by Aaron Ridley and translated by Judith Norman. Cambridge: Cambridge University Press. 2005.

Norton, David. "An Introduction to Hume's Thought" in *Cambridge Companion to Hume.* Edited by David Norton and Jacqueline Taylor. Cambridge: Cambridge University Press. 2009.

Nove, Alec. *Economics of Feasible Socialism.* London: Routledge. 1983.

Noys, Benjamin. *Georges Bataille: A Critical Introduction.* London: Pluto. 2000.

Oakeshott, Michael. *Rationalism in Politics and Other Essays.* London: Methuen. 1962.

Ong, Walter J. *The Presence of the Word: Some Prolegomena for Cultural and Religious History.* Minneapolis: University of Minnesota Press. 1967.

Ott, Hugo. *Martin Heidegger: A Political Life.* New York: Basic Books. 1993.

Owen, David. *Hume's Reason.* Oxford: Oxford University Press. 2002.

Palmer, Richard E. *The Gadamer Reader: A Bouquet of His Later Writings.* Evanston, IL: Northwestern University Press. 2007.

Pascal, Blaise. *Pensées.* Translated by A. J. Krailsheimer. Harmondsworth: Penguin. 1966.

Pearson, Keith Ansell. "Incorporation and Individuation: On Nietzsche's Use of Phenomenology for Life." *Journal of the British Society for Phenomenology* Vol. 38, no. 1, January. 61–88. 2007.

Piekalkiewickz, Jaroslaw, and Alfred Wayne Penn. *Politics of Ideocracy.* New York: SUNY, 1995.

Plato. *Cratylus, Parmenides, Greater Hippias, Lesser Hippias* Translated by Harold Fowler. London: William Heinemann, 1926.

Plato. *Phaedo.* Translated by Hugh Tredennick in *The Collected Dialogues of Plato Including the Letters.* Edited by Edith Hamilton and Huntington Cairns. Princeton, NJ: Princeton University Press. 1962.

Plato. *Symposium.* Translated by Michael Joyce in *The Collected Dialogues of Plato Including the Letters.*

Plato. *Theaetetus and Sophist.* Translated Harold N. Fowler. London: William Heinemann Ltd. 1928.

Plato. *Timaeus, Critias, Cleitophon, Menexenus, Epistles.* Translated R. G. Bury. London: William Heinemann. 1929.

Plato. *The Republic of Plato.* Translated with notes and interpretative essay by Allan Bloom. New York: Basic Books. 1991.

Pocock, J. G. A. *Political Thought and History: Essays on Theory and Method.* Cambridge: Cambridge University Press. 2009.

Podmore, Simon. *Kierkegaard and the Self Before God: Anatomy of the Abyss.* Bloomington and Indianapolis: Indiana University Press. 2011.

Priestley, J. B. *An Examination of Dr. Reid's Inquiry into the Human Mind, Dr. Beattie's Essay on the Nature and Immutability of Truth, and Dr. Oswald's Appeal to Common Sense in Behalf of Religion.* London: J. Johnson. 1775.

Polt, Richard. "Meaning, Excess and Event." *Gatherings: The Heidegger Circle Annual,* 1, 26–53. 2011.

Preparata, Guido. *Bataille, Foucault, and the Postmodern Corruption of Political Dissent.* New York: Palgrave. 2007.

Rancière, Jacques. *Althusser's Lessons.* London: Bloomsbury. 2011.

Rella, Franco. *The Myth of the Other: Lacan, Foucault, Deleuze, Bataille.* Translated by Nelson Moe. Washington, DC: Maisonneuve Press. 1994.

Reid, Thomas. *The Work of Thomas Reid with an account of His Life and Writings by Dugald Stewart, Volume 2.* Charlestown: Samuel Etheridge. 1814.

Reid, Thomas. *The Work of Thomas Reid with an account of His Life and Writings by Dugald Stewart, Volume 3.* Charlestown: Samuel Etheridge. 1815.

Riedel, Manfred. *Materialen zu Hegels Rechtsphilosophie, Band 1.* Frankfurt am Main: Suhrkamp. 1975.

Reisch, George. *How the Cold War Transformed Philosophy of Science: To the Icy Slopes of Logic*. Cambridge: Cambridge University Press. 2005.

Rosenstock-Huessy, Eugen. *Der Atem des Geistes*. Wien: Amandus. 1990.

Rosenstock-Huessy, Eugen. *I am an Impure Thinker*. Foreword by W. H. Auden. Norwich, VT: Argo. 2001).

Rosenstock-Huessy, Eugen. *Speech and Reality*. Eugene, OR: Wipf and Stock. 2013.

Richardson, William. *Heidegger: Through Phenomenology to Thought*. New York: Fordham University Press. 2003.

Rickey, Christopher. *Revolutionary Saints Heidegger, National Socialism and Antinomian Politics*. University Park, PA: University of Pennsylvania Press. 2002.

Rockmore, Tom. *Heidegger and French Philosophy: Humanism, Anti-Humanism and Being*. London: Routledge. 1995.

Rorty, Richard. *Philosophy and the Mirror of Nature*. Princeton, NJ: Princeton University Press. 1979.

Rosenstock-Huessy, Eugen. *Im Kreuz der Wirklichkeit: Eine nach-goethische Soziologie*, 3 vols. Mit einem Vorwort von Irene Scherer und einem Nachwort von Michael Gormann-Thelen, new edition of *Die Soziologie* by Michael Gormann-Thelen, Ruth Mautner, and Lise van der Molen. Tübingen: Talheimer. 2009.

Rosenstock-Huessy, Eugen. *Out of Revolution: Autobiography of Western Man*. Introduction by Harold Berman. Oxford, Providence: Berg, 1953.

Rosenstock-Huessy, Eugen. *In the Cross of Reality: Volume 1, The Hegemony of Spaces*. Translated by Jürgen Lawrenz, and edited by Wayne Cristaudo and Frances Huessy. London: Routledge. 2017.

Rosenstock-Huessy, Eugen and Franz Rosenzweig. *Judaism Despite Christianity*. Edited by Eugen Rosenstock-Huessy. New York: Schocken, 1971.

Rosenzweig, Franz. *Hegel und der Staat, Zweiter Band, Weltepochen (1806–1831)*. München: R. Oldenbourg, 1920.

Rosenzweig, Franz *The Star of Redemption*. Translated by Barbara Galli. Madison: University of Wisconsin Press. 2005.

Roudinesco, Elizabeth. *Lacan: In Spite of Everything*. Translated by Gregory Elliot. London: Verso. 2014.

Russell, Bertrand. *The Philosophy of Logical Atomism*. London: Routledge, 1972.

Russell, Bertrand. *Theory of Knowledge: The 1913 Manuscript*. Edited by Elizabeth Eames in collaboration with Kenneth Blackwell. London: Routledge. 1984.

Russell, Bertrand. *Collected Papers, Volume 7*. Edited by E. R. Eames with K. Blackwell. London: Allen and Unwin. 1984.

Russell, Bertrand. "The Monistic Theory of Truth." *Philosophical Essays*. London: Longmans, Green, and co. 1910.

Russell, Paul. "Hume on Religion" in *The Stanford Encyclopedia of Philosophy*. Edited by Edward N. Zalta. http://plato.stanford.edu/archives/ win2014/entries/hume-religion/. 2014.

Ryle, Gilbert. "John Locke." *Collected Papers Volume 1*. Edited by Gilbert Ryle. Hutchinson, 1971.

Salaquandra, Jörg. "Nietzsche und Lange." *Nietzsche-Studien*. Band 7. 1978.

Salaquandra, Jörg. "Der Standpunkt des Ideals bei Lange und Nietzsche." *Studi Tedeschi*, XXII, I. 1979.

Sandmeyer, Bob. *Husserl's Constitutive Phenomenology: Its Problems and Promise*. New York: Routledge. 2009.

Scheler, Max. "Ordo Amoris" in *Selected Philosophical Essays*. Translated by David Lachterman. Evanston, IL: Northwestern University Press. 1973.

Schneeberger, Guido. *Nachlese zu Heidegger*. Bern: Suhr, 1962.

Schelling, F. W. J. *Philosophie der Offenbarung 1841/1842*. Herausgegeben von Manfred Frank. Frankfurt Am Main: Suhrkamp. 1977.

Schelling, F. W. J. "W. J. Schelling: Further Presentations from the System of Philosophy." *The Philosophical Forum*. Volume XXXII, No. 4, Winter. 2001.

Schelling, F. W. J. *Ideas for a Philosophy of Nature as Introduction to the Study of This Science 1797 Second Edition 1803*. Translated by Errol Harris and Peter Heath with an introduction by Robert Stern. Cambridge: Cambridge University Press. 1988.

Schelling, F. W. J. *The Abyss of Freed/ Ages of the World: An Essay by Slavoj Žižek with the text of Schelling's Die Weltalter (second draft, 1813)* in English translation by Judith Norman. Ann Arbor: University of Michigan Press. 2004.

Schelling, F. W. J. *Grundlegung der Positiven Philosophie: Münchener Vorlesung WS 1832/ 33 und SS 1833*. Herausgegeben von Horst Fuhrmans. Turin: Bottega D"Erasmo. 1972.

Schelling, F. W. J. *Bruno or On the Natural and the Divine Principle of Things*, 1802, edited and translated with an introduction by Michael Vater. Albany, NY: SUNY. 1984.

Schelling, F. W. J. *First Outline of a System of the Philosophy of Nature*. Translated and with an introduction and notes by Keith Peterson. Albany, NY: SUNY. 2004.

Schelling, F. W. J. *Das Tagebuch 1848: Rationale Philosophie und demokratische Revolution*. Herausgegeben von Hans Jörg Sandkühler, Martin Schraven, and Alexander von Pechmann. Hamburg: Felix Meiner. 1990.

Schelling, F. W. J. *The Unconditional in Human Knowledge: Four Early Essays (1794–1796)*. Translation and commentary by Fritz Marti. Lewisburg: Bucknell University Press. 1980.

Schelling, F. W.J. *The Grounding of Positive Philosophy: The Berlin Lectures/* Translated with introduction by Bruce Matthews. Albany, NY: SUNY. 2007.

Schelling, F. W. J. *Statement on the True Relationship of the Philosophy of Nature to the Revised Fichtean Doctrine: An Elucidation of the Former*. Translated with an introduction and notes by Dale E. Snow. Albany, NY: SUNY. 2018.

Schelling, F. W. J. *The Ages of the World (Fragment from the handwritten remains Third Version c 1815)*. Translated with an Introduction by Jason Wirth. Albany, NY: SUNY. 2000.

Schelling, F. W. J. *System of Transcendental Idealism (1800)*. Translated by Peter Heath, introduction by Michael Vater. Charlottesville: University of Virginia. 1978.

Schelling, F. W. J. *The Philosophy of Art*. Edited, translated and introduced by Douglas W. Stott, Foreword by David Simpson. Minneapolis: University of Minnesota Press. 1989.

Sheehan, Thomas. "Heidegger and the Nazis." *New York Review of Books*. June 16. 1988.

Sheehan, Thomas. "*Making Sense of Heidegger: A Paradigm Shift*. Lanham, MD: Rowman and Littlefield, 2014.

Sheehan, Thomas. "Emmanuel Faye: The Introduction of Fraud into Philosophy?" *Philosophy Today*, Volume 59, Issue 3, Summer. 2015.

Simons, Peter. "Whose Fault? The Origins and Evitability of the Analytic Continental Rift." *International Journal of Philosophical Studies*, vol. 19, (3), 295–311. 2009.

Simons, Peter. *Philosophy and Logic in Central Europe from Bolzano to Tarski: Selected Essays*. Dordrecht: Springer. 1992.

Schmiljum, André. *Zwischen Modernität und Konservatismus: Eine Untersuchung zum Begriff der Antipolitik bei F.W.J. Schelling (1775–1854)*. Doctorate presented to the Humboldt-Universität, Berlin. 2014.

Schopenhauer, Arthur. *The World as Will and Representation, Volume 1*. Translated by E. F. J. Payne. New York: Dover. 1969.

Schopenhauer, Arthur. *World as Will and Representation, Volume 2*. Translated by E. F. J. Payne. New York: Dover. 1969.

Schopenhauer, Arthur. *On the Basis of Morality*. Translated by E. F. J. Payne. Cambridge Massachusetts: Hackett. 1995.

Schraven, Martin. "Schelling und die Revolution von 1848." *Philosophie und Literatur im Vormärz: der Streit um die Romantik (1820–1854)*. Herausgegeben von Walter Jaeschke. Hamburg: Felix Meiner. 1995.

Scruton, Roger. *Fools, Frauds, and Firebrands: Thinkers of the New Left*. London: Bloomsbury. 2015.

Earle, John. "Reality Principles: An Interview with John Searle." http://reason.com/archives/2000/02/01/reality-principles-an-interview.

Scott, H.G. and R. Liddell. *A Lexicon Abridged from Liddell and Scott's Greek-English Lexicon*. Oxford: Clarendon Press. 1977.

Shakespeare, William. *The Tempest*.http://shakespeare.mit.edu/tempest/full.html

Stuart, Sim. (ed.) *The Lyotard Dictionary*. Edinburgh: Edinburgh University Press. 2011.

Sluga, Hans. *Gottlob Frege: The Arguments of the Philosophers*. London: Routledge. 1980.

Snell, Bruno. *The Discovery of the Mind: The Greek Origins of European Thought*. Translated T. G. Rosenmeyer. Oxford, Basil Blackwell. 1953.

Snow, Dale E. *Schelling and the End of Idealism*. Albany, NY: SUNY. 1996.

Sokal, Alan and Jean Bricmont. *Fashionable Nonsense: Postmodern Intellectuals's Abuse of Science*. New York: Picador. 1998.

Spiegelberg, Herbert. *The Phenomenological Movement: A Historical Introduction: Volume 1*. The Hague: Martinus Nijhof. 1965.

Spinoza, Benedict. *Works. Volume 2: On the Improvement of the Understanding, the Ethics Correspondence*. Translated by R. H. M. Elwes. New York: Dover. 1955.

Stack, George. *Lange and Nietzsche*. Berlin: Walter de Gruyter. 1983.

Steger, Manfred. *The Rise of the Global Imaginary: Political Ideologies from the French Revolution to the Global War on Terror*. Oxford: Oxford University Press. 2008.

Stone, Dan. *Breeding Superman: Race and Eugenics in Edwardian and Interwar Britain*. Liverpool: Liverpool University Press. 2002.

Tallis, Raymond. *Not Saussure: A Critique of Post-Saussurean Literary Theory*. New York: Palgrave Macmillan. 1988.

Tallis, Raymond. *Theorrhoea and After*. New York: Palgrave Macmillan. 1999.

Tallis, Raymond. "The Shrink from Hell: Jacques Lacan" in *Times Higher Education*, October 31, 1997. https://www.timeshighereducation.com/books/the-shrink-from-hell/159376.article.

Taubes, Jacob. Letter to Rosenstock-Huessy 21.7.1953 in the Rosenstock-Huessy Archives in the Rauner Special Collections Library, Dartmouth College.

Taureck, Bernard. *Nietzsche und der Faschismus*. Leipzig: Reclam. 2000.

Tillich, Paul. "Schelling und die Anfänge des existentialistischen Protestes." *Zeitschrift für Philosophische Forschung*. 9 (2): 197–208. 1955.

Toews, John Edward. *Hegelianism: The Path Towards Dialectical Humanism 1805–1841*. Cambridge: Cambridge University Press. 1980.

Torjussen, Lars. "Is Nietzsche a Phenomenologist—Towards a Nietzschean Phenomenology of the Body." *Analecta Husserliana CIII*. Edited by A-T Tymieniecka. 179–89. 2009.

Townsend, Dabney. *Hume's Aesthetic Theory: Taste and Sentiment*. London: Routledge. 2001.

Trawny, Peter. *Heidegger and the Myth of the Jewish world Conspiracy*. Translated by Andrew J. Mitchell. Chicago: University of Chicago Press. 2015.

Tritten, Tyler. *Beyond Presence: The Late F. W. J. Schelling's Criticism of Metaphysics*. Berlin: De Gruyter. 2012.

Trilling, Lionel. *Sincerity and Authenticity*. Cambridge, MA: Harvard University Press. 1972.

Tully, Robert. "Russell's Neutral Monism." *Russell: The Journal of Bertrand Russell Studies*. Volume 8, issue 1, 209–24. 1988.

Uschanov T. P. "The Strange Death of Ordinary Language Philosophy," at www.helsinki.fi/~tuschano/writings/strange/.

Vater, Michael. "Friedrich Schelling." *The History of Western Philosophy of Religion, Volume 4*. Edited by Graham Oppy and Nick Trakakis. New York: Oxford University Press. 61–79. 2009.

Versényi, Laszlo. *Man's Measure: A Study of the Greek Image of Man from Homer*. Albany, State University of New York Press. 1974.

Vico, Giambattista. *The Autobiography of Giambattista Vico*. Translated by Max Fisch and Thomas Bergin. Ithaca: Cornell University Press. 1944.

Voegelin, Eric. *Order and History, Volume 2: The World of the Polis*. Baton Rouge: Louisiana State University. 1957.

Voegelin, Eric. *Order and History*, Volume 3. *Plato and Aristotle*. Baton Rouge: Louisiana State University. 1957.

Voegelin, Eric and Alfred Schütz. *A Friendship that Lasted a Lifetime: The Corrrespondence between Alfred Schütz and Eric Voegelin*. Translated by William Petropulos. Edited by Gerhard Wagner and Gilbert Weiss. Columbia: University of Missouri Press, 2011.

Weber, Max. *Economy and Society: An Outline of Interpretative Sociology*. Edited by Guenther Roth and Claus Wittich, translated Edward Fischoff et al. Berkeley: University of California Press. 1979.

Wheen, Francis. *How Mumbo-Jumbo Conquered the World*. London: Fourth Estate. 2004.

White, Stephen K. *Edmund Burke: Modernity, Politics and Aesthetics*. Lanham, MD: Rowman and Littlefield. 2002.

Wiener, Jon. "The Responsibilities of Friendship: Jacques Derrida on Paul de Man's Collaboration." *Critical Inquiry* 15(4): 797–803. 1989.

Williams, Bernard. *Ethics and the Limits of Philosophy*. With a commentary on the text by A. W. Moore and a foreword by Jonathan Lear. London: Routledge. 2005.

Wilson, John Elbert. *Schelling und Nietzsche. Zur Auslegung der frühen Werke Friedrich Nietzsches*. Berlin: De Gruyter. 1996.

Winch, Peter. *The Idea of a Social Science and its Relation to Philosophy*. Atlantic Highlands, NJ: Humanities Press International. 1990.

Winch, Peter. *Ethics and Action*. London: Routledge and Kegan Paul. 1972.

Wiltshire, Bruce. *Fashionable Nihilism*. New York: State University Press of New York. 2002.

Windelband, Wilhelm. "History and Natural Science." *Theory and Psychology*. Vol. 8 (1): 5–22. 1998.

Wittgenstein, Ludwig. *Philosophical Investigations*. Translated by G. E. Anscombe. Oxford: Basil Blackwell. 1958.

Wittgenstein, Ludwig. "The Big Typescript: TS 213, German English Scholars" edition. Translated by C. Grant Luckhardt and Maximilian E. Aue. Oxford: Wiley-Blackwell. 2005.

Wolin, Richard. *The Politics of Being: The Political Thought of Martin Heidegger*. New York: Columbia University Press. 1990.

Wolin, Richard (ed.) *The Heidegger Controversy*. Cambridge, MA: MIT Press. 1993.

Wood, Paul B. "Thomas Reid's Critique of Joseph Priestly: Context and Chronology." *Man and Nature*, 4, 29–45. 1985.

Wood, Paul (ed.) *Thomas Reid on the Animate Creation: Papers Relating to the Life Sciences*. Edinburgh: Edinburgh University Press. 1995.

Zijderveld, Anton. *Rickert's Relevance: The Ontological and Epistemological Functions of Value*. Leiden: Brill. 2006.

Žižek, Slavoj. *Revolution at the Gates: A Selection of Writings from February to October 1917, V.I. Lenin*. London: Verso. 2002.

Index

Absolute: Fichte and, 112; Hegel and, 4, 96–97, 100, 101, 103–105, 110, 113, 115, 141, 143, 144; Husserl and, 222, 223–224, 224; Kierkegaard and, 158, 159; Schelling and, 110, 112, 114, 117–118, 119, 121, 123, 125, 133, 135; Schopenhauer and, 165–166

Addresses to the German Nation (Fichte), 109

Adorno, Theodor, 213, 254, 264

aesthetics, 221; Kant and, 91, 92, 93, 114; Leibniz and, 66; Nietzsche and, 177, 212; Rosenzweig and, 239

Ages of the World (Schelling), 129, 133

Althusser, Louis, 252–253, 272; Glucksmann and, 283n9; Lacan and, 283n8; on Marx, 250–251

analytic philosophy, 180, 187n118, 258; applications of, 208; Aristotle and, 205; Beaney and, 193, 215n15; Capaldi on, 189, 193, 194, 201, 204–205, 218n61; Catholicism and, 206; characteristics of, 189; contradiction and, 274–275; Dummett and, 189, 194, 195, 196, 204; Enlightenment and, 208; essentialism and, 190; founders of, 210; Frege and, 189, 191, 192, 196; Glock and, 190–191; Heidegger and, 212; historical heritage of, 194; Hume and, 189, 194; Husserl and, 212, 222; language and, 190–191, 195–196, 198–199, 200, 201, 204; logic and, 195, 196, 197, 198; metaphysics and, 197, 204–206, 207; monistic idealism and, 196–197; Monk and, 189, 195, 198, 215n1; neurophilosophers and, 191; phases of, 194–195; philosophers of, 191; philosophy departments and, 213–214; post-Hegelians and, 207, 208; poststructuralism and, 214, 253; precision and, 212; progress and, 193–194; puzzles and, 191, 192, 193–194, 195; Quine and, 190, 190–191, 194; rationality and, 206, 207; relativism and, 207, 214; rephrasing in, 193; Rorty and, 206–207; science and, 194, 195, 198, 204; Simons and, 208–209, 215n2; See also Russell, Bertrand; Wittgenstein, Ludwig

"Analytic Philosophy" (Hacker), 194

analytic/synthetic method, 42

Anderson, Perry, 258

Anti-Christ (Nietzsche), 173

anti-domination, 214, 215, 276, 282; Badiou and, 280; emancipation and, 281; French philosophies and, 259; injustice and, 263; liberal rights and, 258; power and, 264; women and, 263

An Antidote Against Atheism (More), 41

anti-Hegelianism: poststructuralism and, 272; Schelling and, 111; 68er revolt and, 272

anti-humanism, 251, 283n1

Anti-Oedipus (Deleuze and Guattari), 275

Apology (Plato), 22, 209

a priori principles, 295; Hegel and, 102; Hume and, 85, 225; Husserl and, 219, 223, 225; Kant and, 85, 88, 90, 98–99, 103, 105, 118, 120, 161–162

Archaeology of Knowledge (Foucault), 251

Aristotle, 21, 190, 194; analytic philosophy and, 205; categories for, 86; on causality, 28; contemplative life for, 30; Descartes and, 80; God

314 *Index*

and, 102–103; mechanistic physics and, 50–51; method and, 44, 69, 294; Plato and, 244n48; Reid and, 80; Schelling and, 119–120, 120

Arnauld, Antoine, 62, 66

artisans: model and, 20–21; Plato, Socrates and, 16–17

ascetic ideals: Nietzsche and, 169, 169–170; Schopenhauer and, 169

Augustine, of Hippo, 29; Descartes and, 41–42; free will and, 29; love and, 29–30

Austin, J. L., 191

Bacon, Francis, 38

Badiou, Alain, 253, 279, 281; anti-domination and, 280; Christianity and, 280; idealism and, 280–281

Bataille, Georges, 285n32; on Sade, 270

Baudrillard, Jean, 253

Bauer, Bruno, 146

Bayle, Pierre, 73

Beaney, Michael, 193, 215n15

Beattie, James, 72

Beaufret, Jean, 249–250

Being: Heidegger and, 230–232, 235, 236, 236–237, 239, 246n68; Parmenides and, 18; Sartre on, 49

Being and Time (Heidegger), 219, 221, 230, 233, 243n37

Bell, Martin, 69

Benjamin, Walter, 254, 264, 265; as historical materialist, 254

Berger, John, 258

Berkeley, George, 50, 66n1, 194; *esse est percipi* and, 55; Hume and, 75; Locke and, 55; metaphysics of, 56; nature and, 51–52

Bernouilli, Carl, 176

Beyond Good and Evil (Nietzsche), 171

Bible, 27, 72–73, 237, 239; insight of lived experience and, 28

The Birth of Tragedy (Nietzsche), 168, 173

Black Notebooks (Heidegger), 233–234, 235, 237, 241n5, 245n60

Blanchot, Maurice, 270

Blanqui, Louis, 176

Bloch, Ernst, 254, 258

bloodletting, 260

Böhm-Bawerk, Eugen, 266

Bolzano, Bernard, 191, 209

Boman, Thorleif, 14

Bourg, Julian: on Foucault, 273–274; *From Revolution to Ethics* by, 253, 273; on 68er revolt (May 1968), 285n26

Bradley, F.H., 197

breeding, 173, 177, 185n107, 272

Bricmont, Jean, 257

Brito, Emilio, 134

Brown, R.F., 106n17

Browning, Robert, 256

Bruno, Giordano, 277

Buber, Martin, 5, 6

Buckley, Philip, 227, 228; on faith, 229–230; Husserl and, 226, 229–230; phenomenology and, 229

Bultmann, Rudolf, 237

Burke, Edmund, 264; evidence and, 225; on prejudice, 225

Calvinism, 259, 276

Cambridge Platonists, 23, 43, 44; Descartes and, 106n4; Leibniz and, 87

Camus, Albert, 213; Foucault and, 289n55; on metaphysical rebellion, 269; *The Rebel* by, 268–270; Sade and, 269–270; Sartre and, 289n56; total freedom and, 268–269

Capaldi, Nicholas, 189, 201, 218n61; Hegelianism and, 204–205; on science, 194; on subtraction, 193

Capital (Marx), 150, 151, 155

capitalism and, 149, 151, 153, 239, 260

Carnap, Rudolf, 191

Carr, David, 219

Cartesian Meditations (Husserl), 224, 225

Cartesian system, 57, 180, 194, 210–211

Cassirer, Ernst, 48, 52n1

causality: Aristotle on, 28; Hume and, 85–86; Schopenhauer and, 161

de Certeau, Michel, 278

Chesterton, G. K., 179

Christianity, 14, 30, 287n38; Badiou and, 280; democracy and, 237; Hegel and, 129–130; Heidegger and,

About the Author

Wayne Cristaudo is Professor of Political Science at Charles Darwin University, NT Australia. He is the author and editor of twenty books, and numerous journal articles. He is also co-editor of the journal *European Legacy: Towards New Paradigms*. His books include *The Metaphysics of Science and Freedom*, *This Great Beast: Progress and the Modern State* (with Bob Catley), *Great Literary Texts of Western Civilization* (with Peter Poiana), *Power, Love and Evil: Contribution to a Philosophy of the Damaged*, *Religion, Redemption, and Revolution: The New Speech Thinking of Franz Rosenzweig and Eugen Rosenstock-Huessy*, *A Philosophical History of Love*, and *Baudelaire Contra Benjamin: A Critique of Politicized Aesthetics and Cultural Marxism*, (with Beibei Guan).

CPSIA information can be obtained
at www.ICGtesting.com
Printed in the USA
LVHW091740070220
646229LV00006B/81

9 781793 602350